John Heneage Jesse

London

Its Celebrated Characters and Remarkable Places

John Heneage Jesse
London
Its Celebrated Characters and Remarkable Places
ISBN/EAN: 9783743392625
Manufactured in Europe, USA, Canada, Australia, Japa
Cover: Foto ©ninafisch / pixelio.de

Manufactured and distributed by brebook publishing software (www.brebook.com)

John Heneage Jesse

London

LONDON:

ITS CELEBRATED CHARACTERS

AND

REMARKABLE PLACES.

BY

J. HENEAGE JESSE,

AUTHOR OF "MEMOIRS OF KING GEORGE THE THIRD," "MEMOIRS OF THE
COURT OF ENGLAND UNDER THE STUARTS," ETC.

IN THREE VOLUMES.
VOL. I.

LONDON:
RICHARD BENTLEY, NEW BURLINGTON STREET,
Publisher in Ordinary to Her Majesty.
1871.

[All Rights Reserved.]

PREFACE.

THIS work is an amalgamation of two separate publications, the one entitled "Literary and Historical Memorials of London," published in 1847, and the other entitled "London and its Celebrities," published in 1850, the latter being in fact a sequel to the former. The first-named publication contained no preface: to the second the following introductory remarks were appended:—

"It appears to the Author that some apology is required for the publication of these volumes. When he first contemplated writing a work on 'London,' it occurred to him that to persons whose avocations, whether of business or pleasure, led them to traverse the thoroughfares of the Great Metropolis, a work might not be unacceptable, which should point out such sites and edifices as have been rendered classical either by the romantic or literary associations of past times. It was a subject which had always afforded pleasure to the Author, and he was sanguine enough to hope that he might be enabled to impart some pleasure to others.

"Other literary occupations, however, interfered to engage the leisure hours of the Author, and in the mean time, after he had collected many of his materials, Mr. Knight commenced and completed the periodical publication of his interesting work on 'London.' Had the plan of Mr. Knight's work corresponded with that of the Author, he would unquestionably have relinquished his task. But as such was not the case; and, moreover, as he was thus supplied with many valuable additional facts—which the Author gladly takes this opportunity of acknowledging—it had the contrary effect of encouraging him to resume his original project.

"But the Author subsequently found that he had other difficulties to contend against. This Second Series of his work was already in the hands of his publisher, when there appeared successively the 'Town,' by Mr. Leigh Hunt,—and Mr. Peter Cunningham's 'Handbook,'—the latter the most valuable work on 'London' which has appeared since the time of Stow. It is therefore with considerable and unaffected diffidence that the Author submits to the public this Second Series of his work; for certainly had he been aware of the formidable literary rivalship which he was likely to encounter, he would on no account have entered the lists.

"In a work like the present, where there occur minute facts and dates at almost every page, there must almost necessarily be many errors; and for these the Author can only throw himself on the consideration and indulgence of the reader.

"LONDON, AUGUST, 1850."

Since the publication of these respective volumes many, changes have taken place in the more venerable and interesting quarters of London. To the regret of the antiquary, and to the discomfiture of the chronicler, old churches and ancient graveyards have been supplanted by modern buildings; the names of streets have been altered, and the numbering of houses, in which celebrated men have from time to time resided, have been subjected to similar change. To adapt this work, therefore, to the London of the present day, has been a primary purpose with the Author; besides which, by the compression of redundant matter, and by the introduction of new and interesting facts, he is in hopes of having rendered these volumes more deserving the favour of his readers. A considerable portion, in fact, of his work may be said to have been re-written.

J. H. J.

CONTENTS OF VOL. I.

PAGE

PICCADILLY.

Traditions of Hyde Park Corner.—Sir Thomas Wyatt.—Charles the Second and the Duke of York.—Sir Samuel Morland.—Winstanley.—Pope.—Lord Lanesborough.—Apsley House.—The "Pillars of Hercules."—Origin of the name Piccadilly.—Eminent Persons who have lived in the Neighbourhood ... 1

THE GREEN PARK AND HYDE PARK.

The Green Park.—Duel between the Earl of Bath and Lord Hervey.—Hyde Park in the Reigns of Henry the Eighth, Queen Elizabeth, Queen Anne, Cromwell, and Charles the Second.—Famous Duel between Lord Mohun and the Duke of Hamilton.—M'Lean and Belchier the Highwaymen 20

MAY FAIR, GROSVENOR, PORTMAN, CAVENDISH, AND HANOVER SQUARES.

May Fair.—May Fair Chapel.—Singular Marriages.—Curzon Street.—South Audley Street.—Grosvenor Square.—Portman Square.—Cavendish Square.—Hanover Square.—Bond Street.—Berkeley Square 33

ST. JAMES'S STREET.

St. James's Street.—Colonel Blood.—Clubs.—Cocoa-Tree Tavern.—Thatched House.—Death of Gibbon.—Byron... 59

THE NEIGHBOURHOOD OF ST. JAMES'S STREET.

Bennett Street.—Arlington Street.—Park Place.—St. James's Place. — Cleveland Row. — King Street. — Almack's. — Little Ryder Street.—Bury Street 71

ST. JAMES'S SQUARE.

St. James's Square.—Duke of Hamilton.—Frederick Prince of Wales.—Johnson and Savage.—Jermyn Street.—Lord St. Albans.—Sir Walter Scott 79

PALL MALL.

Former State of Pall Mall.—Sir Thomas Wyatt.—Murder of Thynne.—Charles the Second's Mistresses.—Beau Fielding's Strange Adventure.—Schomberg House.—Star and Garter.—Duke of Buckingham's Residence.—Carlton House 89

ST. JAMES'S PALACE.

Site of St. James's Palace.—Erected by Henry the Eighth.—The Residence of Queen Mary, Henry Prince of Wales, Charles the First, Mary de Medicis, Charles the Second, James the Second, William the Third, George the First, George the Second, and Daughter 111

ST. JAMES'S PARK.

Original Enclosure.—Charles going to Execution.—Cromwell.—Skating.—Game of Pall Mall.—Charles the Second.—Queen Anne.—Marlborough House.—The Mall.—Spring Gardens.—Buckingham House 131

KING STREET, WESTMINSTER.—ST. MARGARET'S CHURCH.

Westminster, King Street.—Residence of Spenser, Carew, Lord Dorset, Cromwell.—Great Plague.—Mrs. Oldfield.—Downing Street. — Gardiner's Lane. — Cannon Row. — St. Margaret's Church.—The Sanctuary 156

WESTMINSTER.

The Sanctuary.—Persons who took Refuge there.—The Gatehouse.—Its History.—Tothill Street.—The Streets of Old Westminster.—Westminster School.—Remarkable Persons educated there 177

OLD PALACE OF WESTMINSTER.

Its Early Regal Builders and Tenants.—Edward the Second and Gaveston.—Death Scene of Henry the Fourth.—Henry the Eighth the Last Resident.—Court of Requests.—Painted Chamber.—Gunpowder Plot.—St. Stephen's Chapel.—Old and New Palace Yard 193

WESTMINSTER HALL.

Its Erector.—The Hall for the Coronation and Banquetings of the English Kings.—Extraordinary Scenes and Remarkable Trials which have occurred there from the Time of William Rufus till the Present Day 226

WESTMINSTER ABBEY.

Early Places of Worship on its Site.—Erection of the Present Edifice.—Scenes and Ceremonies in it.—Poets' Corner.—Chapels of St. Edmund, St. Nicholas, St. Paul, Edward the Confessor, Islip, Henry the Seventh.—Cloisters.—Jerusalem Chamber.—Chapter House 273

THE HAYMARKET, LEICESTER SQUARE, AND ST. MARTIN'S-IN-THE-FIELDS.

Haymarket.—Haymarket Theatre.—Suffolk House.—Leicester Square.—Anecdote of Goldsmith.—St. Martin's Church, Churchyard, and Lane.—Soho Square.—Wardour, and Oxford Streets.—Rathbone Place 310

COVENT GARDEN.

Covent Garden Market.—"Old Hummums."—St. Paul's, Covent Garden.—Russell Street and its Coffee Houses.—Bow, James, King, Rose, Bedford, and Henrietta Streets.—Maiden Lane.—Southampton and Tavistock Streets 333

CONTENTS.

PAGE

DRURY LANE AND CONTIGUOUS STREETS.

Drury Lane. — Drury House. — Wych Street. — Drury Lane Theatre.—Long Acre.—Phœnix Alley.—Queen Street.—Lincoln's Inn Fields.—Portugal Street.—Duke Street.—St. Giles's Church and Churchyard 362

CHARING CROSS AND WHITEHALL.

Statue of Charles the First.—Execution of] General Harrison and Hugh Peters.—Anecdotes of Lord Rochester and Richard Savage.—Old Royal Mews.—Cockspur and Warwick Streets. —Scotland Yard.—Attempt to assassinate Lord Herbert.—Sir John Denham.—Wallingford House.—Dukes of Buckingham. —Admiralty 396

LONDON:

ITS CELEBRATED CHARACTERS

AND

REMARKABLE PLACES.

PICCADILLY.

TRADITIONS OF HYDE PARK CORNER.—SIR THOMAS WYATT.—CHARLES THE SECOND AND THE DUKE OF YORK.—SIR SAMUEL MORLAND.—WINSTANLEY.—POPE.—LORD LANESBOROUGH.—APSLEY HOUSE.—THE "PILLARS OF HERCULES."—ORIGIN OF THE NAME PICCADILLY.—EMINENT PERSONS WHO HAVE LIVED IN THE NEIGHBOURHOOD.

HYDE Park Corner, the chief western approach to London, is a not inappropriate place from which to commence our antiquarian rambles. The spot itself is singularly interesting. It was here that Sir Thomas Wyatt "planted his ordnance" in his famous attempt on London in 1554; and here also, on the site of Hamilton Place, on the threatened approach of Charles the First and his army in 1642, the citizens of London hastily threw up a large fort and four bastions, in which zealous work they were enthusiastically aided by their wives and daughters.

> "From ladies down to oyster-wenches,
> Laboured like pioneers in trenches;
> Fell to their pickaxes and tools,
> And helped the men to dig like moles."—*Hudibras*.

It was at Hyde Park Corner that Charles the Second delivered his well-known happy retort upon his brother, the Duke of York. Charles, who was as fond of walking as his brother was of riding, was one day crossing the road between Constitution Hill and Hyde Park, accompanied by the Duke of Leeds and Lord Cromarty, when he was met by the Duke of York, who had been hunting on Hounslow Heath, and who was returning in his coach, attended by an escort of the royal Horse Guards. The Duke immediately alighted and, after having paid his respects to the King, expressed his uneasiness at the danger which his majesty ran in walking in public so inadequately attended. "No kind of danger," said the merry monarch, "for I am sure that no man in England will take away my life to make you king."* Hamilton Place derives its name from James Hamilton, ranger of the park in the reign of Charles the Second, and brother of La Belle Hamilton of De Grammont's Memoirs. No. 1, overlooking Piccadilly, was the town residence of Lord Chancellor Eldon, and No. 4, at the time of the battle of Waterloo, the residence of the late Duke of Wellington.

Close to Hyde Park Corner the well-known mechanist, Sir Samuel Morland, appears to have had a residence; a letter of his addressed to the high-minded and ingenious philosopher, John Evelyn, being dated from his "hut near Hyde Park Gate." Here also, in the reign of Queen Anne, another ingenious mechanist, Winstanley, had a "water theatre," whither, we are told, the town was accustomed to flock of an evening to witness his hydraulic experiments. Steele mentions him in one of his papers in the "Tatler," and Evelyn has thought him not unworthy of praise.

It was "by Hyde Park Corner" that many of the schoolboy days of Pope were passed. Here the poet forgot the

---
* Dr. King's "Anecdotes of my Own Time." Dr. King tells us that Lord Cromarty frequently related this story to his friends.

"little" which he had learnt from his Roman Catholic preceptor, Bannister, and from here he used to pay his pleasant visits to the playhouse; here he composed his juvenile play borrowed from "Ogilby's Iliad," in which his master's gardener personated Ajax, the other performers being the poet's schoolfellows.

On the site of St. George's Hospital stood the country residence of Theophilus, first Lord Lanesborough, celebrated by Pope, as—

"Sober Lanesborough dancing with the gout."

Here he died on the 11th of March, 1723. So paramount is said to have been his lordship's passion for dancing, that when Queen Anne lost her consort, Prince George of Denmark, he seriously advised her to dispel her grief by applying herself to his favourite exercise.

Apsley House, which stands on the site of the old Ranger's Lodge, was built about the year 1784, by Lord Chancellor Apsley, afterwards second Earl of Bathurst. Previously to its becoming the residence of the late Duke of Wellington it had been occupied by his gifted brother, the Marquis Wellesley. Almost adjoining, and to the east of Apsley House, formerly stood a noted inn, the "Pillars of Hercules," memorable as the place where Squire Western took up his abode when, bursting with vengeance against Tom Jones, he came to London in search of Sophia. About the middle of the last century the "Pillars of Hercules" was much frequented by country gentlemen from the West of England, which was probably the reason that Fielding made Squire Western take up his quarters there.

The space between the "Pillars of Hercules" and Hamilton Place was formerly occupied by a row of mean houses one of which was a public-house called the "Triumphant

Chariot." This was in all probability the "petty tavern" to which the unfortunate Richard Savage was conducted by Sir Richard Steele, on the occasion of their being closeted together for a whole day composing a hurried pamphlet, which they had to sell for two guineas before they could pay for their dinner.*

Piccadilly has been sometimes supposed to derive its name from the fashionable ruffs for the neck, called pickadels, which were introduced in the reign of James the First. Barnaby Rich, in his "Honestie of this Age," speaks of the "body-makers that do swarm through all parts, both of London and about London;" and again he writes— "He that some forty or fifty years sithens should have asked after Pickadilly, I wonder who could have understood him; or could have told what a Pickadilly had been, either fish or flesh." "Piccardil," writes Gifford, "is simply a diminutive of *picca*, a spear-head, and was given to this article of foppery from a fancied resemblance of its stiffened plaits to the bristled points of those weapons." In Ben Jonson's "Devil is an Ass," in Beaumont and Fletcher's "Pilgrim," and in Drayton's satirical poem "The Moon Calf," will be found more than one allusion to the fashionable "pickadel" or "pickadilly." It must be remarked, however, that the date of the earliest of these productions is 1616; whereas there is evidence to prove that the word "Pickadilla" was in common use as far back as 1596; our authority being Gerarde's "Herbal," where the "small wild buglosse," or ox-tongue, is spoken of as growing upon the banks of the dry ditches "about Pickadilla."

In the reign of Queen Elizabeth, as appears by Aggas's "Plan of London," the present line of Piccadilly, extending from the Haymarket to Hyde Park Corner, was a mere road

* Johnson's "Life of Savage."

running through an open country, called "the Waye to Redingc." Originally Piccadilly existed as a street no further westward than Sackville Street; that portion of it between Sackville Street and Albemarle Street having been named Portugal Street, in compliment to Catherine of Portugal, Queen of Charles the Second. Thus in the "New View of London," published in 1708, we find Piccadilly defined as "a very considerable and public street between Coventry Street and Portugal Street." Gradually, however, the name of Piccadilly was given to the whole length of the thoroughfare.

Although Piccadilly is comparatively of modern date, there is much to interest us in a stroll from Hyde Park Corner to its termination at the west end of Coventry Street. The houses numbered 138 and 139, close to Park Lane, were formerly one mansion, occupied by the celebrated William Duke of Queensberry, familiarly known as "Old Q." In his old àge it was his custom, in sunny weather, to seat himself in his balcony, with a parasol over his head, watching every attractive female figure, and ogling every pretty face that passed by. There are many, perhaps, who can call to recollection the flight of steps descending from the first floor into the street, which, in his latter days, were constructed for the especial use and convenience of the Duke.

At No. 139, then 13 Piccadilly Terrace, Lord Byron resided shortly after his marriage. Here occurred his memorable separation from Lady Byron, and here he appears to have been living when he composed "Parisina" and the "Siege of Corinth."

The first street of any particular interest diverging from Piccadilly, is Half Moon Street, which was built in 1730, and derives its name from the Half Moon public-house which stood at the corner. Here, on the 15th of March,

1797, died the charming comic actress, Mrs. Pope. After having performed at Drury Lane for forty years, she retired from the stage into private life with an unblemished character and an easy fortune. She is said to have borne a strong resemblance to the beautiful Lady Sarah Lennox, the goddess of George the Third's early idolatry. Many years after the beauty of both ladies had been on the decline, the King happened to attend the performances at Drury Lane when Mrs. Pope was acting. The recollection of his youthful love came back to his mind, and in a moment of melancholy abstraction he is said to have observed to the Queen—"*She is like Lady Sarah still.*"

In 1768, we find Boswell lodging in Half Moon Street, and entertaining Dr. Johnson as his guest. At No. 1 also, the corner house on the east side overlooking Piccadilly, resided, at the close of life, Madame D'Arblay, the celebrated authoress of "Evelina" and "Cecilia."

Passing on, we come to Clarges Street, built in 1717–18, and so called from its being the site of Clarges House, the residence of Sir Walter Clarges, nephew of Anne Clarges, wife of the celebrated George Monk, Duke of Albemarle. In this street lived at one period the great Admiral Earl St. Vincent; and here, in 1803, Charles James Fox was residing. Here also, on the 19th of February, 1806, died, in extreme old age, the well-known Mrs. Elizabeth Carter; at No. 11, between the years 1804 and 1806, Lord Nelson's Lady Hamilton resided, and at No. 12 lived the great actor, Edmund Kean, from 1816 to 1824. So late as the year 1761, a turnpike stood at the Piccadilly end of this street.

At the left-hand corner of Bolton Street stood old Bath House, formerly the residence of William Pulteney, Earl of Bath, the formidable antagonist of Sir Robert Walpole. At the opposite corner stood Watier's Club; and from the neighbouring house, No. 80, Piccadilly, afterwards occupied by the Duke of St. Albans, Sir Francis Burdett was taken to the Tower in 1810.

> "The lady she sat and she played on the lute,
> And she sung, 'Will you come to the bower?'
> The serjeant-at-arms had stood hitherto mute,
> And now he advanced, like an impudent brute,
> And said, 'Will you come to the Tower?'"

In Bolton Street resided, from 1710 to 1724, the celebrated hero, Charles Mordaunt, Earl of Peterborough.

No. 1, Stratton Street, the large mansion at the corner of Piccadilly, was the residence of the wealthy widow, Mrs. Coutts, formerly Miss Mellon, the actress, and afterwards Duchess of St. Albans.

We are glad to be able to point out in the next street the site of the London residence of the great poet, Pope. He lived at one time at No. 9, Berkeley Street, close to his friend Lord Burlington; and it was here, possibly, in 1715, on the eve of his departure to his quiet retreat at Twickenham, that he composed his "Farewell to London."

> "Luxurious lobster-nights, farewell,
> For sober studious days,
> And Burlington's delicious meal,
> For salads, tarts, and peas."

We are assured that in the lease of the house the name of "Mr. Alexander Pope" occurs as a former tenant. From the poet it passed into the hands of General Bulkeley, who died about the year 1815, at an extreme old age. A late occupant of the house well remembered that whenever the General visited it, after it had ceased to be his own, it was his invariable habit to observe, with an air of respectful interest, "*This is the house Mr. Alexander Pope lived in!*"

It was to his house in Berkeley Street that Mr. Chaworth

was carried after he received his death-wound in his memorable duel with Lord Byron in Pall Mall.

In the days of Charles the Second, when Piccadilly was almost open country, the space on the north side, between Clarges Street and the Albany, was occupied by three large villas, each surrounded by spacious pleasure-grounds, built respectively by Lord Berkeley of Stratton, by the great Lord Clarendon, and the well-known and wealthy poet, Sir John Denham. Opposite, on the site of Arlington Street, stood Goring House, the residence of the notorious statesman, Henry Bennet, Earl of Arlington.

Let us first speak of Berkeley House, which stood nearly on the site of the present Devonshire House. It was built by John Lord Berkeley of Stratton, about the year 1665, on a property called Hay Hill Farm; from which Hay Street, Hill Street, Farm Street, and Hay Hill have derived their names, as have Berkeley Street, Berkeley Square, and Stratton Street, from his lordship's titles. Evelyn writes, "On the 25th September, 1672, I dined at Lord John Berkeley's. It was in his new house, or rather palace, for I am sure it stood him in near £30,000. It is very well built, and has many noble rooms, but they are not very convenient, consisting but of one *corps de logis*: they are all rooms of state, without closets. The staircase is of cedar; the furniture is princely; the kitchen and stables are ill placed, and the corridor worse, having no report to the wings they join to. For the rest, the fore-court is noble; so are the stables, and, above all, the gardens, which are incomparable by reason of the inequality of the ground, and a pretty *piscina*. The holly hedges on the terrace I advised the planting of." The "noble gardens," as Evelyn styles them, must have been of great size, extending over the ground now occupied by Lansdowne House and Berkeley Square. When, in 1684, a part of them were let for building purposes, we find Evelyn recording his deep regret at the sacrilege offered to the "sweet place;" while at the same time he inveighs against "the mad intemperance of the age," in increasing the city, which he says is far out of proportion to the nation, and which in his time had been enlarged nearly ten-fold. What would Evelyn say to London as it *now* stands!

Berkeley House, it may be remarked, was the residence of the Cavendish family at least as early as the reign of William the Third. Here we find the venerable Christian, widow of William the second Earl, maintaining a splendid hospitality; Waller and Denham being among her accustomed guests. Here, in 1697, we find William the Third dining with William the first Duke, and here both the first and second Dukes, and the "beautiful Duchess," breathed their last.

In 1692, when Queen Anne, then Princess of Denmark, was on bad terms with her brother-in-law, King William, she took up her abode at Berkeley House, where she continued to reside till the death of her sister, Queen Mary, in 1694, when King William allowed her apartments in St. James's Palace. In 1733, when the original mansion was burnt down, the present unsightly structure was erected by William, third Duke of Devonshire, after a design by Kent. It was shortly after its completion that Sir Robert Walpole, happening to call upon the Duke at his new mansion, and not finding him at home, left the following epigram on his table—

"Ut dominus domus est; non extra fulta columnis
Marmoreis splendet; quod tenet, intus habet."

The third Duke died here in 1755. Except during the brief period when the beautiful Georgiana Duchess of Devonshire held her court within its walls, and when Fox, Burke, Wyndham, Fitzpatrick, and Sheridan did homage at her feet, little interest attaches to the present edifice. Clarendon House stood between Berkeley Street and Bond Street, looking down St. James's Street upon St. James's Palace. Its gardens appear to have adjoined those of Berkeley House, and to have extended as far east as the present Burlington Arcade. Clarendon House, the delight and pride of the great Earl of Clarendon, is said by Burnet to have cost £50,000 ; a vast sum if we consider the relative value of money in the days of Charles the Second and at the present time. Clarendon's enemies called it Dunkirk House, asserting that it had been built with money he had received as a bribe from the French government for permitting the sale of Dunkirk. "After dinner," writes Evelyn on the 15th of October, 1664, "my Lord Chancellor and his lady carried me in their coach to see their new palace building at the upper end of St. James's Street, and to project the garden." Pepys also writes on the 31st of January, 1665-6 : "To my Lord Chancellor's new house, which he is building, only to view it, hearing so much from Mr. Evelyn of it; and indeed it is the finest pile I ever did see in my life, and will be a glorious house." Evelyn speaks of Clarendon House as possessing many architectural defects, adding however, that, on the whole, it stood most gracefully, and was a stately and magnificent pile.

In Evelyn's Diary for the 27th of August, 1667, a few days after the disgrace of the great Chancellor, we find an interesting passage connected with Clarendon House. "I visited the Lord Chancellor," he writes, "to whom his Majesty had sent for the seals a few days before. I found him in his bed-chamber very sad. The Parliament had accused him, and he had enemies at Court, especially the buffoons and ladies of pleasure, because he thwarted some of them and stood in their way. I could name some of the chief." Again Evelyn writes on the 9th of December: "To visit the late Lord Chancellor. I found him in his garden at his new-built palace, sitting in his gout wheel-chair, and seeing the gates setting up towards the north and the fields. He looked and spake very disconsolately. Next morning I heard he was gone." Three years afterwards we find Clarendon House the residence of the great Duke of Ormond.

Not long after the death of the Chancellor in December, 1674, Clarendon House was sold by his son and successor to Christopher Monk, second and last Duke of Albemarle, for £26,000. Subsequently the Duke parted with it for about £35,000, when it was immediately levelled to the ground, and the present Dover Street, Albemarle Street, Old Bond Street, and Grafton Street erected on the site of its beautiful gardens. Evelyn witnessed with great pain "the sad demolition of that costly and sumptuous palace of the late Lord Chancellor, where he had often been so cheerful with him, and sometimes so sad. On the 19th of June, 1683, he writes: "I returned to town in a coach with the Earl of Clarendon. When passing by the glorious palace his father built but a few years before, which they were now demolishing, being sold to certain undertakers, I turned my head the contrary way till the coach was gone past it, lest I might minister occasion of speaking of it, which must needs have grieved him that in so short a time their pomp was fallen."

The site of Burlington House was at one time occupied by a mansion built, in the reign of Charles the Second, by the celebrated poet Sir John Denham. The mansion recently demolished to make room for the present public buildings was designed and erected by Richard Boyle, third Earl of

Burlington, the architect also of the Duke of Devonshire's palladian villa at Chiswick, and, in conjunction with the Earl of Pembroke, of Marble Hill, near Twickenham.

"Who plants like Bathurst, and who builds like Boyle?"

Of Burlington House Horace Walpole writes: "I had not only never seen it, but never heard of it, at least with any attention, when, soon after my return from Italy, I was invited to a ball at Burlington House. As I passed under the gate by night it could not strike me. At daybreak, looking out of the windows to see the sun rise, I was surprised with the vision of the colonnade that fronted me. It seemed one of those edifices in fairy tales, that are raised by genii in the night-time." Pope, who was a constant visitor at Burlington House, has celebrated "Burlington's delicious meal" in lines which we have already quoted. Gay, too, tells us that he always entered Burlington House with "cleaner shoes."

———. "'Burlington's fair palace still remains,
Beauty within—without, proportion reigns;
There Handel strikes the strings, the melting strain
Transports the soul, and thrills through every vein;
There oft I enter—but with cleaner shoes,
For Burlington's beloved by every muse." GAY: *Trivia*.

Here Handel lived for three years a cherished guest. Here also resided for some years William, third Duke of Portland, twice Prime Minister in the reign of George the Third.

Dover Street derives its name from having been built on the property of Henry Jermyn, Baron Dover—the "invincible Jermyn" of De Grammont's Memoirs—whose house stood on the east side of the street. On the east side—on the site of the "fair gardens" which he had formerly laid out for his illustrious friend, Lord Chancellor Clarendon—

lived the amiable and high-minded philosopher, John Evelyn. Another accomplished person who resided in this street—on the west side, the second house from Piccadilly—was the witty and popular Dr. Arbuthnot, beloved by Swift, Pope, Gay, and every man of genius who lived in the Augustan age of England. At this time the principal object of attraction in Dover Street was the sumptuous mansion of the frolic and eccentric Philip Duke of Wharton—

"Wharton, the scorn and wonder of our days."

In Dover Street, also, lived and died the celebrated Lord Treasurer, Harley Earl of Oxford.

Albemarle Street, originally called Albemarle Buildings, derives its name from Christopher, second Duke of Albemarle, who succeeded the Earls of Clarendon in the possession of Clarendon House. Till very recently the "Duke of Albemarle" public-house was still to be seen in Dover Street.

It was in Albemarle Street, at the house of Lord Grantham, that George the Second, when Prince of Wales, kept his court after his memorable quarrel with his father in 1717. "The Prince and Princess," writes Sir Gustavus Hume, on the 24th of December, to the Earl of Marchmont, "after having been both very ill, are now perfectly recovered; they are still at my Lord Grantham's, in Albemarle Street, where they saw company last Sunday for the first time. I am told his Highness's levee was very slender, not above three or four noblemen, and they such as have not appeared at St. James's for a long time. All such as are admitted to the King's court are under strict orders not to go at any time to the prince or princess's, more particularly all of us that have the honour to be immediately in his Majesty's service."*

In Albemarle Street, on the west side, a few doors from

* Marchmont Papers.

Piccadilly, resided at one time Charles James Fox. In this street also, in 1785, died Richard Glover, the author of "Leonidas;" and here, in 1814, at Grillon's Hotel (No. 7), on the east side, Louis the Eighteenth, when driven from France, took up his temporary abode.

Another celebrated name associated with Albemarle Street is that of Lord Rodney, who came to reside here after his great naval victory in 1781. "Lord Powys's house in Albemarle Street," writes his biographer, "had been taken for his residence, where he arrived amidst the greetings of thousands of his countrymen; the women strewing his path, as he descended from his carriage, with flowers." Here, too, he was waited upon by the ex-patriot, John Wilkes, who, as chamberlain of the City of London, came to present him with its freedom in a gold box.

Hereafter Albemarle Street will be interesting to the lovers of literary history, from its containing the residence (No. 50) of the late Mr. Murray, the

"Lintot and Tonson of his day,"

at whose "four o'clock" meetings and hospitable table have assembled so many persons of talent of the present century. It was while pacing up and down Albemarle Street, as Mr. Murray informed the author, that Lord Byron composed the greater part of the "Corsair."

On the site of the Albany stood the house and gardens of the celebrated minister Charles Spencer, Earl of Sunderland, who died in 1722. The present building in the centre, designed by Sir William Chambers, was sold by Lord Holland, in 1770, to the first Lord Melbourne, who subsequently exchanged it with the Duke of York for his mansion in Whitehall, now Dover House. Having been deserted by his Royal Highness, chambers were erected on the gardens—into which also the house was converted—which received the name of Albany Chambers, from the Duke's second title of Duke of Albany.

Many eminent persons have resided in the Albany. In 1807, George Canning occupied the apartments No. 5A; and, in 1811, M. G. Lewis the rooms No. 1K. When, in 1814, Caroline Princess of Wales carried into execution a wild design of attending a masquerade *incognita*, it was at Monk Lewis's chambers that she and Lady Charlotte Campbell, her lady in waiting, put on their masquerade dresses. In 1814, Lord Byron was residing at No. 2A, in the Albany, and it was during his residence here that "Lara" was published, and apparently composed. In his journal of the 28th of March, he writes: "This night I got into my new apartments, rented of Lord Althorpe on the lease of seven years. Spacious, and room for my books and sabres. *In the house*, too, another advantage. The last few days, or whole week, have been very abstemious, regular in exercise, and yet very unwell." And, again he writes, on the 10th of the following month: "I do not know that I am happiest when alone; but this I am sure of, that I never am long in the society even of *her* I love without a yearning for the company of my lamp, and my utterly confused and tumbled-over library. I have not stirred out of these rooms four days past; but I have sparred for exercise (windows open) with Jackson an hour daily to attenuate and keep up the ethereal part of me." Jackson himself resided and taught boxing at one time at No. 2, Albany Court Yard.

The rooms occupied by Lord Byron in the Albany were afterwards tenanted by Lord Lytton. At No. 1E Lord Macaulay wrote his "History of England," and at No. 1B, in 1862, was residing the late General Lord Clyde.

Nearly opposite to the Albany is St. James's Church, built

by Sir Christopher Wren towards the close of the reign of Charles the Second. Besides the general beauty and elegance of its interior, its exquisite font and the beautiful carved foliage over the altar—both of them the work of Grinling Gibbons—would of themselves render it worthy of a visit. Here were christened the fourth and famous Earl of Chesterfield and the great Earl of Chatham. Here lie buried Charles Cotton, the congenial friend of Izaak Walton; Dr. Sydenham, the physician; the eminent painters, James Huysman, the elder and younger Vandervelde, Michael Dahl, and George Henry Harlowe; Henry Sydney, afterwards Earl of Romney, the "handsome Sydney" of De Grammont's Memoirs; Dr. Arbuthnot, the friend of Pope and Swift; Mark Akenside, the author of the "Pleasures of Imagination," and James Dodsley, the once well-known publisher in Pall Mall. In a vault under the communion table lies interred the old Duke of Queensberry, memorable for his wealth and his libertinism; and on a pillar close by may be seen a tablet to the memory of Mary Granville, Mrs. Delany, the friend of Swift in her youth, and afterwards the venerable favourite of George the Third and Queen Charlotte.

Few persons have passed through the Jermyn Street entrance to St. James's churchyard without noticing a small stone in the wall of the tower to the memory of Tom D'Urfey, the poet, on whose shoulders Charles the Second used familiarly to lean, humming gay tunes in concert with his favourite. The inscription is sufficiently brief: "Tom D'Urfey, dyed Feb. ye 26th, 1723." On the west side of the parsonage-house was formerly to be seen a flat stone to the memory of the inimitable Gilray: "In memory of Mr. James Gilray, the caricaturist, who departed this life 1st of June, 1815, aged 58 years."

Of the past rectors of St. James's parish, three—Doctors Tenison, Wake, and Secker—became Archbishops of Canterbury. Another eminent rector of St. James's was the learned Dr. Samuel Clarke, who was presented to the living by Queen Anne.

The fine organ in St. James's Church was intended by James the Second for his Roman Catholic Oratory at Whitehall, but on his abdication was presented to this parish by his daughter Queen Mary.

Piccadilly Hall, a fashionable place of amusement in the reign of Charles the First, stood, in the midst of what were then gardens and fields, at the north-east corner of the Haymarket. Besides its Gaming House—Shaver's Hall, as it was usually called—it had its Bowling Greens, of which Suckling the poet was a constant frequenter, and its Tennis Court, the walls of which are still standing on the south side of James's Street, Haymarket. "Since Spring Gardens was put down," writes Garrard to the Earl of Strafford, in June, 1635, "we have, by a servant of the Lord Chamberlain's, a new Spring Gardens erected in the fields beyond the Meuse, where is built a fair house, and two bowling-greens, made to entertain gamesters and bowlers, at an excessive rate, for I believe it hath cost him about £4000, a dear undertaking for a gentleman-barber. My Lord Chamberlain much frequents this place, where they bowl great matches."

Again, Lord Clarendon, then Mr. Hyde, speaks of himself (1641) as "going to a place called Piccadilly, which was a fair place for entertainment and gaming, and handsome gravel-walks with shade, and where were an upper and lower bowling-green, whither very many of the nobility and gentry of the best quality resorted both for exercise and conversation."

Not far to the north-west of the Haymarket lies Golden

Square; originally, according to Pennant, called Gelding Square, from the sign of a public-house which formerly stood in the neighbourhood. This, however, is unquestionably a mistake. The name was originally Golding Square, as appears by the "New View of London" published in 1708, where it is distinctly stated to derive its name from one Golding, by whom it was built.

One would like to be able to point out the house in Golden Square which was once the residence of the celebrated Henry St. John, Lord Bolingbroke. Here it was that he entertained for the last time at dinner his former colleague and friend Harley Earl of Oxford, when, among other guests, were present the Duke of Shrewsbury, Earl Powlett, and Hyde Earl of Rochester. Here, a few months afterwards, we find him entertaining the great Duke of Marlborough as his guest;* here he was residing when the death of Queen Anne effected so extraordinary a revolution in his fortune, and hence, apparently, he departed by stealth, in the dress of a servant, on the night of his memorable escape to the Continent.

In Golden Square lived the beautiful singer Anastasia Robinson, whose beauty and virtue captivated the heart of the celebrated and eccentric Charles Mordaunt, Earl of Peterborough, who privately married her towards the close of his long life.

> "When Anastasia's voice commands the strain,
> The melting warble thrills through every vein;
> Thought stands suspended, silence pleased attends
> While in her notes the heavenly choir descends."
> GAY: *Epistle to William Pulteney.*

Their marriage, in whatever year it may have taken place, was not acknowledged till 1735; yet, as many as twelve

* Coake's "Life of Lord Bolingbroke."

years previously to its announcement, we find Lord Peterborough horse-whipping a foreign singer, Senescino, at a rehearsal, for some offence which he had given her.* It was not, indeed, till he had become broken down by disease, and till harassed by her repeated refusals to live under the same roof with him unless he acknowledged her as his wife, that he consented to divulge their secret, which he did in a very characteristic manner. One evening at the rooms at Bath, a servant, according to orders which he had previously received, shouted out in a distinct and audible voice, "*Lady Peterborough's carriage waits;*" the result, we are told, being that every lady of rank and fashion immediately rose and offered their congratulation to the new Countess. From Dr. Burney we learn that the Earl had already divulged the fact of his marriage to his nearest relations, whom he had appointed to meet him at the apartment of his nephew by marriage, Mr. Poyntz, in the great gateway of St. James's Palace, looking up St. James's Street. Lady Peterborough, on being presented to them, fainted away. Mr. Poyntz was preceptor to Prince William, afterwards the Culloden Duke of Cumberland.†

It is in Golden Square that Smollett makes Matthew Bramble and his sister take up their residence with Humphry Clinker and Winifred Jenkins. Here also, "at the centre house" of the Square, Mrs. Cibber, the actress, resided in 1746.

To the north of Golden Square is Great Marlborough Street. Here Lord Mohun was residing at the time he fought his fatal duel with the Duke of Hamilton; here, at No. 49, on the south side, Mrs. Siddons lived for several years; and here, in 1788, died the Rev. John Logan, the poet.

---

* Lady M. W. Montagu's Letters. † Burney's "History of Music."

THE GREEN PARK, AND HYDE PARK.

THE GREEN PARK.—DUEL BETWEEN THE EARL OF BATH AND LORD HERVEY.—HYDE PARK IN THE REIGNS OF HENRY THE EIGHTH, QUEEN ELIZABETH, QUEEN ANNE, CROMWELL, AND CHARLES THE SECOND.—FAMOUS DUEL BETWEEN LORD MOHUN AND THE DUKE OF HAMILTON.—M'LEAN AND BELCHIER THE HIGHWAYMEN.

PREVIOUSLY to the reign of Charles the Second, the Green Park, or Upper St. James's Park, as it was sometimes called, consisted of meadows. With the exception of its having been the scene of a remarkable duel between the celebrated minister Pulteney, afterwards Earl of Bath, and the scarcely less celebrated John, Lord Hervey, in 1730, the Green Park possesses few features of interest. "On Monday," writes Thomas Pelham to Lord Waldegrave, "between three and four o'clock in the afternoon, they met in *the Upper St. James's Park, behind Arlington Street*, with their two seconds, who were Mr. Fox and Sir J. Rushout. The two combatants were each of them slightly wounded, but Mr. Pulteney had once so much the advantage of Lord Hervey, that he would infallibly have run my Lord through the body if his foot had not slipped, and then the seconds took an occasion to part them; upon which Mr. Pulteney embraced Lord Hervey, and expressed a great deal of concern at the accident of their quarrel, promising, at the same time, that he would never personally attack him again, either with his mouth or his pen. Lord Hervey made him a bow, without giving him any sort of answer, and, to use the common expression, thus they parted." It is somewhat singular that Lady Hervey, the beautiful and celebrated Mary Lepel, should have afterwards built and resided in a house immediately overlooking the spot where her husband had so narrow an escape from the sword of Lord Bath.

Hyde Park in the time of Henry the Eighth formed part of a manor belonging to the abbot and monks of Westminster. In a survey of church lands taken in the twenty-sixth year of the reign of that monarch, it is styled Manerium de Hyde, and is valued at xiiij*l*. Although there is reason to believe that it was formed into a park while still in possession of the monks of Westminster, we possess no proof of its having been enclosed till the reign of Edward the Sixth, when one George Roper was appointed keeper, with a salary of sixpence a day!

Previously to the reign of Queen Anne, Hyde Park was of much larger extent than it is at the present time. In 1705, it was curtailed of thirty acres, to enlarge the gardens of Kensington Palace; and again, in 1730, Queen Caroline, the consort of George the Second, appropriated as many as three hundred acres more to the same purpose.

The Hyde Park of three centuries since had apparently no feature whatever in common with the Hyde Park of our own time. For instance, in the reign of Queen Elizabeth we read of its "herbage, pannage, and browze-wood for deer," and of its solitary "lodge and mansion in the Park." Again, at a much later period we find mention made of a piece of waste ground called "the Moor," the "Tyburn meadow," and a "parcel of meadow ground enclosed for the deer." As early, indeed, as the days of the Commonwealth, it had become a place of fashionable resort; but, even then, as we learn from De Grammont, the ground was a mere uncultivated waste, diversified by occasional ponds, "browzing-grounds," and thick woods; the favourite resort of the wealthy, the idle, and the gay being the famous circular drive, or "Ring," situated near the centre of the Park. Previously to the reign of George the Second, there was a string of pools, or ponds, from the Bayswater Gate—a name derived from "Bayard's watering"—to the present western termination of the Serpentine. These ponds were connected by Queen Caroline, to whom we are indebted for the present large sheet of water.

Hyde Park, in the days of Charles the First, was famous for its races, at one of which the King is said to have been ill advised enough to put an affront upon the notorious Henry Marten, which the latter would seem to have bitterly and deeply resented. "Martyn," writes Aubrey, "was a great lover of pretty girls, to whom he was so liberal that he spent the greatest part of his estate. King Charles the First had complaint against him for his wenching; it happened that Henry was in Hyde Park one time when his Majesty was there, going to see a race. The King espied him, and said aloud—'Let that ugly rascal be gone out of the Park, that w——master, or else I will not see the sport.' So Henry went away patiently, but *manebat altâ mente repostum*: that sarcasm raised the whole county of Berks against him." How little could Charles have imagined that the "ugly rascal" whom he thus rebuked was destined to sign his death-warrant!

Under the rule of the Puritans, the May meetings, the merry sports, and festive rejoicings, which had previously taken place in Hyde Park, were declared to be iniquitous and abominable, and accordingly, in 1652, the Parliament ordered the manor to be sold to the highest bidder. The purchasers were Richard Wilcox, Esq., of Kensington; John

Tracy, of London, merchant; and Anthony Deane, Esq., of St. Martin-in-the-Fields; the latter gentleman appears to have become the proprietor of that part of the park in which our ancestors were accustomed, either in their equipages or on horseback, to take the air. "I went," writes Evelyn, on the 11th of April, 1653, "to take the air in Hyde Park, where every coach was made to pay a shilling, and horse sixpence, by the sordid fellow who has purchased it of the state, as they are called." For some years after the Restoration, the park continued to be let in farms, nor was it till 1670 that it was entirely enclosed and re-stocked with deer. In the days of the Commonwealth, we find the timber alone in Hyde Park valued at £5,099 19s. 6d. The deer were valued at £765 6s. 2d.

If one of the objects of the Parliament in selling Hyde Park, was to prevent its being the scene of popular festivities, the result was certainly not what had been anticipated. For instance, under date the 1st of May, 1654, we read: "This day was more observed by people going a-maying than for diverse years past, and indeed much sin committed by wicked meetings with fiddlers, drunkenness, ribaldry, and the like. Great resort came to Hyde Park, many hundreds of rich coaches and gallants in attire, but most shameful powdered hair; men painted and spotted women. Some men played with a silver ball, and some took other recreation."* Again, the "Moderate Intelligencer," dated the same day, gives a like account of the sports in Hyde Park: "This day there was a hurling of a great ball by fifty Cornish gentlemen on one side, and fifty on the other; one party played in red caps, and the other in white. There was present his Highness the Lord Protector, many of his

* Several Proceedings of State Affairs, 27th April to 4th May, 1654.

Privy Council, and diverse eminent gentlemen, to whose view was presented great agility of body, and most neat and exquisite wrestling, at every meeting of one with the other, which was ordered with such dexterity, that it was to shew more the strength, vigour, and nimbleness of their bodies, than to endanger their persons. The ball they played withal was silver, and designed for that party which did win the goal."

When at the close of life Cromwell was suffering under a painful disorder, his physicians recommended him to take as much exercise as possible, and consequently we find him frequently either driving or riding in Hyde Park. At this period it was not unusual for him to mount his own coach-box, and to drive his six horses, surrounded by a regiment of guards, on one of which occasions an accident occurred that nearly cost him his life. "The Duke of Holstein," writes Ludlow, "made him a present of a set of grey Friesland coach-horses, with which, taking the air in the park, attended only with his secretary, Thurloe, and a guard of janizaries, he would needs take the place of the coachman, not doubting but the three pair of horses he was about to drive would prove as tame as the three nations which were ridden by him; and therefore, not content with their ordinary pace, he lashed them very furiously ; but they, unaccustomed to such a rough driver, ran away in a rage, and stopped not till they had thrown him out of the box, with which fall his pistol fired in his pocket, though without any hurt to himself, by which he might have been instructed how dangerous it was to meddle with those things wherein he had no experience." Heath, who repeats the story in his "Flagellam," also places the scene in Hyde Park. "The generous horses," he writes, "no sooner heard the lash of the whip, but away they ran, with Thurloe sitting trembling inside, for fear of his own neck, over hill and dale, and at last threw down the unexpert governor from the box into the traces." In his fall, it seems, the Protector's legs got so entangled in the harness, that for several seconds he remained suspended from the pole of the carriage. Thurloe, in great trepidation, threw himself from the door of the vehicle, and escaped with some slight bruises. Heath elsewhere likens Cromwell and Thurloe, as they figured on this occasion, to Mephistophiles and Dr. Faustus. "Cromwell," he says, "like Phaeton, fell from his chariot."* Many pasquinades were of course written on the subject, of one of which the concluding verse is not without merit,—

> " Every day and hour has shewn us his power,
> And now he has shewn us his art;
> His first reproach was a fall from a coach,
> And his next will be from a cart."

It was at Hyde Park Gate—the hinges of which they filed off in order to secure their escape—that the notable conspirators, Syndercombe and Cecil, more than once lay in wait, in hopes of finding an opportunity to assassinate the great Protector in one of his rides in the park.

In the pages of Pepys and Evelyn are some interesting notices of the gay scene presented by Hyde Park in the reign of Charles the Second. "I am sorry," writes the former, on the 30th of April, 1661, "that I am not at London, to be at Hyde Park to-morrow morning among the great gallants and ladies, which will be very fine." Evelyn, who was more fortunate, thus notices the lively scene: "May 1st, I went to Hyde Park to take the air, where was his Majesty and an innumerable appearance of gallants and rich coaches, being now at a time of universal festivity and

* "Chronicles of the Civil War."

joy." The following year we find Pepys figuring among the gay equestrians in the park. "1662, December 18th, in St. James's Park Mr. Coventry's people had a horse ready for me, so fine a one that I was almost afraid to get upon him; but I did, and found myself more feared than hurt, and followed the Duke and some of his people to Hyde Park." Again Pepys writes on the 8th of April, 1663: "After dinner to the Hyde Park; at the Park was the King, and in another coach my Lady Castlemaine, they greeting one another at every turn."

In Colley Cibber's "Apology for his Life," there is a passage referring to Hyde Park which throws a curious light on the manners of the time. Speaking of Kynaston, the actor, he says, "he was at that time so beautiful a youth, that the ladies of quality prided themselves in taking him with them in their coaches to Hyde Park in his theatrical habit after the play, which in those days they might have sufficient time to do, because plays were then used to begin at four o'clock, the hour that people of the same rank are now going to dinner."

Of a military review in Hyde Park in the reign of Charles the Second, at which Evelyn was present, he writes: "In July, 1664, I saw his Majesty's guards, being of horse and foot four thousand, led by the general the Duke of Albemarle in extraordinary equipage and gallantry, consisting of gentlemen of quality and veteran soldiers, excellently clad, marched, and ordered, drawn up in battalia before their Majesties in Hyde Park, where the old Earl of Cleveland trailed a pike, and led the right-hand file commanded by the Viscount Wentworth, his son, a worthy spectacle and example, being both of them old and valiant soldiers. This was to shew the French Ambassador, Monsieur Comminges, there being a great assembly of coaches,

&c., in the Park." The gossiping Pepys was also present in Hyde Park on this occasion. "It was a goodly sight," he writes, "to see so many fine horses and officers, and the King, Duke, and others, come by on horseback, and the two Queens in the Queen-mother's coach; my Lady Castlemaine not being there. And after long being there, I alighted, and walked to the place where the King, Duke, &c., did stand, to see the horse and foot march by and discharge their guns, to shew a French Marquis, for whom this muster was caused, the goodness of our firemen, which, indeed, was very good, though not without a slip now and then, and one broadside close to our coach, as we were going out of the park, even to the nearness to be ready to burn our hairs. Yet methought all these gay men are not the soldiers that must do the King's business, it being such as these that lost the old King all he had, and were beat by the most ordinary fellows that could be."

In reference to the mere *fashionable* history of Hyde Park, a few words remain to be said respecting the departed "Ring," of which, by-the-way, some of the trees which formerly surrounded it still survive. For instance, we read in Evelyn of a " coach-race in Hyde Park ;" or, in Pepys, of a " fine foot-race, *three times round the park*, between an Irishman and Crow, once my Lord Claypole's footman:" it was evidently "the Ring" which was the scene of their contests. " Hyde Park," writes Pennant, " was in the last century, and the early part of the present, celebrated by all our dramatic poets for its large space railed off in form of a circle, round which the *beau monde* drove in their carriages; and, in their rotation, exchanged, as they passed, smiles and nods, compliments or smart repartees."

Pope writes in his Essay on "The Characters of Women,"—

"Ah! friend! to dazzle let the vain design;
To raise the thought, and touch the heart, be thine;
That charm shall grow, while what fatigues *the Ring*,
Flaunts and goes down, an unregarded thing."

And again, to Martha Blount,—

"She glares in balls, front-boxes, and *the Ring*,
A vain, unquiet, glittering, wretched thing."

Between the Ring and the Serpentine was fought, on the 15th of November, 1712, the celebrated and sanguinary duel between Charles Lord Mohun, and James, fourth Duke of Hamilton. High and angry words having passed between them, Lord Mohun rose, and the following day sent his friend, General Macartney, to the Duke, challenging him to a sword duel in Hyde Park. Lord Mohun came attended by General Macartney, and the Duke by Colonel Hamilton. On the ground, the Duke happening to taunt Macartney with being the cause of the duel, the latter expressed his readiness to join in the conflict, to which the Duke, pointing to Colonel Hamilton, observed,—"There is my friend; he will take his share in my dance." Both principals and seconds then drew their swords and engaged at the same moment. Mohun and the Duke each received a fatal wound, the former dying on the spot, and the other immediately afterwards.

"This morning at eight," writes Swift to Stella on the day of the duel, "my man brought me word that Duke Hamilton had fought with Lord Mohun and killed him, and was brought home wounded. I immediately sent him to the Duke's house, in St. James's Square; but the porter could hardly answer for tears, and a great rabble was about the house. In short, they fought at seven this morning. The dog Mohun was killed on the spot; and, while the Duke was over him, Mohun shortened his sword, and stabbed him in the shoulder to the heart. The Duke was helped towards the Cake House, by the Ring in Hyde Park, where they fought, and died on the grass before he could reach the house, and was brought home in his coach by eight, while the poor Duchess was asleep. Macartney and one Hamilton were the seconds, who fought likewise, and are both fled. I am told that a footman of Lord Mohun's stabbed Duke Hamilton, and some say Macartney did so too. Mohun gave the affront, and yet sent the challenge." A short time afterwards, Colonel Hamilton, the Duke's second, was tried at the Old Bailey, and acquitted. General Macartney surrendered himself to take his trial the following year, when Hamilton swore positively that he was the person who gave the Duke his fatal wound. The jury, however, seem to have placed but little faith in his evidence, for Macartney was merely found guilty of manslaughter, and Colonel Hamilton, to avoid a prosecution for perjury, fled to the Continent, where he died within four months. General Macartney survived till 1730.

The spot of ground, between the Ring and the Serpentine, on which the Duke of Hamilton and Lord Mohun lost their lives, is the same apparently as that which Fielding, in his inimitable novel of "Amelia," mentions as the usual meeting-place of the duellists of the last century, and where probably many a life has been lost. It is here that Fielding fixes the encounter between his hero Booth and the fiery Colonel Bath. Having quarrelled on the fashionable Mall in St. James's Park, the combatants—unaccompanied by seconds, and with no weapons but the sword which every gentleman wore at the period—proceeded forthwith to the secluded spot we have mentioned. "The Colonel," writes Fielding, "bade Booth come along, and strutted forward directly up Constitution Hill to Hyde Park, Booth following him at first, and afterwards walking before him, till they came to that place which may be properly called the field of blood, being that part, a little to the left of the Ring, which heroes have chosen for the scene of their exit out of this world."

It was also near the Ring in Hyde Park that Wilkes fought his memorable duel with Samuel Martin, Secretary to the Treasury, in which the former received the wound from a pistol-ball which so nearly cost him his life.

Swift's journal to Stella reminds us of another interesting passage in that work, connected with Hyde Park. On the 25th of February, 1712, he writes: "I was this morning again with the secretary [Lord Bolingbroke], and we were two hours busy; and then went to the Park—Hyde Park I mean—and he walked to cure his cold, and we were looking at two Arabian horses, sent some time ago to the Lord Treasurer. The Duke of Marlborough's coach overtook us, with his Grace and Lord Godolphin in it; but they did not see us, to our great satisfaction; for neither of us desired that either of those two lords should see us together. There were half a dozen ladies riding like cavaliers to take the air." The Lord Treasurer-here mentioned was Lord Godolphin, and it is not improbable that one of the two Arabian horses which Swift refers to was the famous "Godolphin Arabian."

From the days of Swift and Bolingbroke let us pass to those of Horace Walpole. To Sir Horace Mann Walpole writes on the 17th of November, 1749 :—" Gibberne says you will be frightened at a lamentable history that you will read of me in the newspapers; but pray don't be frightened: the danger, great as it was, was over before I had any notion of it; and the hurt did not deserve mentioning." Walpole, it seems, was passing through Hyde Park, when he was stopped by one M'Lean, a fashionable highwayman of formidable reputation, whose pistol accidentally going off, the ball not only grazed the skin from his cheek-bone, but went out through the roof of the carriage.

"M'Lean," writes Walpole, "had a lodging in *St. James's Street*, over against White's, and another at Chelsea; Plunket, another highwayman, one in *Jermyn Street;* and their faces are as known about St. James's as any gentleman's who lives in that quarter, and who, perhaps, goes upon the road too. M'Lean had a quarrel at Putney bowling-green two months ago with an officer, whom he challenged for disputing his rank; but the captain declined till M'Lean should produce a certificate of his nobility, which he has just received." M'Lean was hanged in October following. To Sir Horace Mann Walpole writes on the 18th: "Robbing is the only thing that goes on with any vivacity, though my friend Mr. M'Lean is hanged. The first Sunday after his condemnation, three thousand people went to see him. He fainted away twice with the heat of his cell. You can't conceive the ridiculous rage there is of going to Newgate; and the prints that are published of the malefactors, and the memoirs of their lives and death set forth with as much parade as Marshal Turenne's."

A little more than a year after M'Lean was hanged, we find his place occupied by one William Belchier, another fashionable highwayman, who resorted to Hyde Park and its lonely vicinity. The evidence given at Belchier's trial, by one William Norton, a thief-catcher, is not a little curious. "The chaise to the Devizes," he says, "having been robbed two or three times, as I was informed, I was desired to go in it, to see if I could take the thief, which I did on the 3rd of June, about half an hour after one in the morning. I got into the postchaise; the postboy told me the place where he had been stopped was near the half-way house between Knightsbridge and Kensington. As we came near the house the prisoner came to us on foot and said, 'Driver, stop!' He held a pistol tinder-box to the chaise and said, 'Your money directly: you must not stay; this minute your money.' I said, 'Don't frighten us; I have but a trifle; you shall have it!' Then I said to the gentlemen—there were three in the chaise—'Give your money.' I took out a pistol from my coat-pocket, and from my breeches-pocket a five-shilling piece and a dollar. I held the pistol concealed in one hand, and the money in the other. I held the money pretty hard. He said, 'Put it in my hat.' I let him take the five-shilling piece out of my hand: as soon as he had taken it I snapped my pistol at him. It did not go off. He staggered back, and held up his hands, and said, 'Oh, Lord! oh, Lord!' I jumped out of the chaise: he ran away, and I after him about six or seven hundred yards, and then took him. I hit him a blow on his back; he begged for mercy on his knees. I took his neck-cloth off, and tied his hands with it, and brought him back to the chaise. Then I told the gentlemen in the chaise that was the errand I came upon, and wished them a good journey, and brought the prisoner to London." When Norton was asked in court by the prisoner what trade he followed, "I keep a shop," he said, "in Wych Street, and sometimes I take a thief."

MAY FAIR, GROSVENOR, PORTMAN, CAVENDISH, AND HANOVER SQUARES.

MAY FAIR.—MAY FAIR CHAPEL.—SINGULAR MARRIAGES.—CURZON STREET.—SOUTH AUDLEY STREET.—GROSVENOR SQUARE.—PORTMAN SQUARE.—CAVENDISH SQUARE.—HANOVER SQUARE.—BOND STREET.—BERKELEY SQUARE.

MAY FAIR, anciently known as Brook Fields, derives its name from a fair which continued to be held in its green meadows from the reign of Charles the Second till the middle of the last century. "May Fair," writes Pennant, "was kept about the spot now covered with May Fair Chapel, and several fine streets. The fair was attended with such disorders, riots, thefts, and even murders, that, in 1700, it was prevented by the magistrates." The site which it occupied was that of the present Curzon Street, Hertford Street, and Chesterfield House and its gardens.

Malcolm, in his "Anecdotes of the Manners and Customs of London," quotes an advertisement which appeared in the London journals of the 27th of April, 1700, which affords a curious picture of this memorable fair. "In Brookfield market-place, at the east corner of Hyde Park, is a fair to be kept for the space of sixteen days, beginning with the 1st of May; the three first days for live cattle and leather, with the same entertainments as at Bartholomew Fair, where there are shops to be let ready built for all manner of tradesmen that usually keep fairs, and so to continue yearly at the same place." In the 'Tatler' of the 24th of May, 1708, we find:—"The downfall of May Fair has sunk the price of this noble creature [the elephant], as well as of many other curiosities of nature. A tiger will sell almost as cheap as an ox; and I am credibly informed a man may purchase a calf with three legs for very nearly the value of one with four. I hear likewise that there is great desolation among the ladies and gentlemen who were the ornaments of the town, and used to shine in plumes and diadems, the heroes being most of them pressed, and the queens beating hemp." May Fair, however, was again revived. Notwithstanding that a part of the ground was built over as early as 1721, we find a donkey race attracting great crowds to the fair in 1736, and as late as 1756 it is mentioned by Maitland as being annually celebrated.

Not the least remarkable feature connected with old May Fair was the celebrated clandestine marriage chapel, presided over by one Keith, where any two persons might be married at a moment's notice, without the consent of parents or guardians, or any other formality than the mutual agreement of the consenting parties. Keith's Chapel stood within a few yards of the present chapel in Curzon Street. "To prevent mistakes," runs one of his advertisements, "the little new chapel in May Fair, near Hyde Park Corner, is in the corner-house opposite to the city side of the great chapel; and within ten yards of it. The minister and clerk live in the same corner-house where the little chapel is: and the licence on a crown stamp, minister and clerk's fees, together with the certificate, amount to one guinea, as heretofore, at any hour till four in the afternoon. And that it may be better known, there is a porch at the door like a country church porch."

Among other singular marriages, the little chapel in Curzon Street witnessed that of the beautiful Elizabeth Gunning to James Duke of Hamilton. To Sir Horace Mann, Horace Walpole writes on the 27th of February, 1752:—" The event that has made most noise since my last, is the extempore wedding of the youngest of the two Gunnings, who have made so vehement a noise. Lord Coventry, a grave young lord, of the remains of the patriot breed, has long dangled after the eldest, virtuously with regard to her honour, not very honourably with regard to his own credit. About six weeks ago, Duke Hamilton, the very reverse of the Earl, hot, debauched, extravagant, and equally damaged in his fortune and person, fell in love with the youngest at the masquerade, and determined to marry her in the spring. About a fortnight since, at an immense assembly at my Lord Chesterfield's, made to show the house, Duke Hamilton made violent love at one end of the room, while he was playing at pharaoh at the other end; that is, he saw neither the bank nor his own cards, which were of three hundred pounds each. He soon lost a thousand. I own I was so little a professor in love, that I thought all this parade looked ill for the poor girl; and could not conceive, if he was so much engaged with his mistress as not to regard such sums, why he played at all. However, two nights afterwards, being left alone with her, while her mother and sister were at Bedford House, he found himself so impatient that he sent for a parson. The Doctor refused to perform the ceremony without licence or ring; the Duke swore he would send for the Archbishop: at last they were married with a ring of the bed-curtain, at half an hour after twelve at night, at May Fair Chapel. The Scotch are enraged; the women mad that so much beauty has had its effect; and, what is more silly, my Lord Coventry declares that now he will marry the other."

Scarcely less remarkable is a marriage which Horace Walpole, in a letter to George Montagu, of the 3rd of September, 1748, mentions as having taken place at Keith's Chapel. "Did you know," he writes, "a young fellow that was called 'handsome Tracy?' He was walking in the Park with some of his acquaintance, and overtook three girls. One was very pretty. They followed them, but the girls ran away, and the company grew tired of pursuing them; all but Tracy. He followed them to Whitehall-gate, where he gave a porter a crown to dog them. The porter hunted them; he the porter. The girls ran all round Westminster and back to the Haymarket, where the porter came up with them. He told the pretty one she must go with him, and kept her talking till Tracy arrived quite out of breath, and exceedingly in love. He insisted on knowing where she lived, which she refused to tell him; and, after much disputing, went to the house of one of her companions, and Tracy with them. He there made her discover her family, a butterwoman in Craven Street, and engaged her to meet him the next morning in the Park; but before night he wrote her four love-letters, and in the last offered two hundred pounds a year to her, and a hundred a year to Signora la Madre. Griselda made a confidence to a staymaker's wife, who told her that the swain was certainly in love enough to marry her if she could determine to be virtuous and refuse his offers. 'Ay,' says she, 'but if I should, and should lose him by it?' However, the measures of the cabinet council were decided for virtue, and when she met Tracy the next morning in the Park, she was convoyed by her sister and brother-in-law, and stuck close to the letter of her reputation. She would do nothing. She would go nowhere. At last, as an instance of prodigious compliance, she told him that if he would accept such a dinner as a butterwoman's daughter could [give him he should be welcome. Away they walked to Craven Street. The mother borrowed some silver to buy a leg of mutton, and they kept the eager lover drinking till twelve at night, when, with a chosen committee, the faithful pair waited on the minister of May Fair. The Doctor was in bed, and swore he would not get up to marry the King, but that he had a brother over the way who perhaps would, and who did. The mother borrowed a pair of sheets, and they consummated at her house, and the next day they went to their own palace."

The streets which occupy the site of old May Fair, though of modern date, present many features of interest.

Curzon Street derives its name from having been built on the property of the Curzons, Earls Howe. In this street lived Pope's friend, Lord Marchmont—

"Where the bright flame was shot through Marchmont's soul."

Here also died, in 1806, George Earl Macartney, celebrated for his embassy to China; here, at No. 14, lodged in his youth Sir Francis Chantrey; No. 1 was for some years the residence of Madame Vestris; at No. 16 lived the late distinguished physician, Sir Henry Halford; at No. 30, on the south side, lived the late Princess Sophia Matilda of Gloucester, and at No. 8, Horace Walpole's accomplished favourites, Miss Mary and Miss Agnes Berry. The Misses Berry had previously resided at No. 26, North Audley Street.

Where Hertford Street—originally called Garrick Street—now stands, there formerly stood a public-house known as the "Dog and Duck," to the north of which was a large pond, a favourite resort of the admirers of the ancient sport of duck-hunting. In this street lived and died in 1792 General John Burgoyne, as celebrated for his defeat at Saratoga as for his comedy of the "Heiress," and in the same house afterwards lived Richard Brinsley Sheridan. At No. 10 died, in 1808, Charles Earl of Liverpool, father of the Premier, and at No. 14 resided the celebrated physician, Dr. Jenner. It was in her drawing-room in Hertford Street that the beautiful Mrs. Horton was married to the Duke of Cumberland, brother of George the Third; and in this street also Mrs. Jordan resided in the days of her dramatic triumphs. In Stanhope Street lived and died Isaac Barré, to whom the authorship of Junius has been sometimes attributed.

In Chesterfield Street, for many years, resided the witty and eccentric George Selwyn. At a small house (No. 4) in this street also lived the celebrated George Brummell, where, with the aid of an excellent cook, and admirable wine, he attracted to his little dining-parlour all the wit, talent, and profligacy of the days of the Regency. Here George the Fourth, when Prince of Wales, is said to have frequently visited him for the purpose of studying the progress of his inimitable toilet; sometimes sending his horses away, and remaining to so late an hour that he was compelled to insist on Brummell's giving him a quiet dinner, which not uncommonly terminated in a midnight debauch. From Chesterfield Street, Brummell removed to 22, South Street. His successor in the occupancy of the house in the former street was Captain Gronow, the author of the well-known "Recollections and Anecdotes."

Chesterfield House, from which Chesterfield Street takes its name, was built by the celebrated Earl of Chesterfield in the reign of George the Second. The staircase, one of the very few marble ones in London, was brought from the magnificent seat of the Duke of Chandos at Canons. Here, in 1773, the Earl died.

From Curzon Street we pass into South Audley Street, in the chapel in which Ambrose Philips, the poet, Lady Mary Wortley Montagu, and the celebrated John Wilkes lie buried. In Bute House, South Audley Street, lived and died the unpopular Minister, John Earl of Bute, near whom was living, about the year 1757, his friend, John Home, the author of "Douglas." At No. 72 in this street resided, at different periods, the two exiled kings of France, Louis the Eighteenth and Charles the Tenth; this being the same house in which, in 1816, Madame D'Arblay mentions her visiting the Duchesse d'Angoulême. It was at No. 77, then the residence of Alderman Sir Matthew Wood, that Queen Caroline took up her abode on the critical occasion of her arrival from the Continent in 1820. In this street also resided the patriot Paoli, and, opposite to Audley Square, the accomplished scholar, Sir William Jones. In Audley Square, Mrs. Jordan resided at one time with her children, and here Spencer Percival, the Minister, was born.

In No. 39, South Street, running out of South Audley Street, lived another Minister, the late Lord Melbourne. No. 31, in this street, overlooking Hyde Park, was the residence of the notorious Egalité, Philip Duke of Orleans. From No. 13, Chapel Street, Brummell effected his sudden flight to France in 1816; and at No. 23, in this street, in 1813, Percy Bysshe Shelley, the poet, was residing.

Between South Audley Street and Park Lane runs a small street, Tilney Street, in which, in 1787, Soame Jenyns breathed his last. No. 6, Tilney Street, overlooking Hyde Park, was long the residence of Mrs. Fitzherbert, the wedded mistress, if not the legal wife, of George the Fourth.

South Audley Street leads us into Grosvenor Square, so called from its having been built on the property of Sir Richard Grosvenor, who died in 1732. It was on the site of this aristocratic square that the rebel citizens of London during the civil war erected, in addition to other fortifications, a redoubt, long known as Oliver's Mount, from which the present Mount Street appears to have derived its name.

In Grosvenor Square lived Erengard de Schulenberg, Duchess of Kendal, the forbidding mistress of George the First, while next door to her, before the erection of Chesterfield House, resided the celebrated Lord Chesterfield and his wife, Melosina Countess of Walsingham, the *reputed* niece of the Duchess, but who, there is every reason to believe, was her daughter by her royal lover.

In this square also lived Bishop Warburton, and here, in 1764, died Lord Chancellor Hardwicke. When, in 1766, the Marquis of Rockingham was driven from the Premiership, he was living in Grosvenor Square, and here also resided another Prime Minister, Lord North. But for the providential discovery of the Cato Street conspiracy, in 1820, the dining-room of No. 39—then as now the residence of the Earls of Harrowby—would have witnessed the slaughter of the unpopular ministers of George the Fourth. The heads of Lords Liverpool and Castlereagh were to have been carried away in two bags. At No. 30, the corner of South Audley Street, lived and died John Wilkes. On the pedestal in the centre of the Square formerly stood a statue of George the First.

At his house in Upper Grosvenor Street died, in 1765, William, Duke of Cumberland, the victor of Culloden. Grosvenor House, formerly Gloucester House (No. 33), was the residence of George the Third's brother, William Henry, Duke of Gloucester, who died here in 1805. It was from the roof of this house that Horace Walpole describes himself as witnessing the awful conflagrations which disgraced and terrified London during the Gordon Riots in 1780.

The beautiful Duchess, formerly Countess of Waldegrave, was Walpole's niece. On his re-entering his drawing-room, it was to greet the Duke and the Ladies Waldegrave, just returned from Ranelagh Gardens.

In Lower Grosvenor Street lived Frederick Prince of Wales's mistress, Miss Vane, whose name is perpetuated in Dr. Johnson's noble satire. No. 23 was the residence of Sir Humphry Davy. Here also breathed her last, in 1730, the frail, the beautiful, and warm-hearted actress, Mrs. Oldfield. Her corpse, having been decorated with fine Brussels lace, "a holland shift with a tucker and double ruffles of the same lace, and a pair of new kid gloves," was conveyed from her house in Grosvenor Street to the Jerusalem Chamber at Westminster, whence, after having lain in state during the day, it was carried at eleven o'clock at night to the Abbey; Lord De la Warr, Lord Hervey, Bubb Dodington, and other gentlemen supporting the pall. In Charles Street, Grosvenor Square, died, in 1785, William Whitehead, the poet-laureate.

Running parallel with Grosvenor Street is Brook Street, so called from a considerable stream or brook which formerly flowed over its site. At No. 57, on the south side, four doors from Bond Street, lived the great musician, Handel.

Upper Brook Street was the scene of one of the most lamentable fires that occurred in London during the last century. To Marshal Conway, Walpole writes on the 6th of May, 1763: "I must tell you of the most dismal calamity that ever happened. Lady Molesworth's house in Upper Brook Street was burnt to the ground between four and five this morning. She herself, two of her daughters, her brother, and six servants perished. Two other of the young ladies jumped out of the two-pair of stairs and garret windows; one broke her thigh, the other (the eldest of all) broke hers too, and has had it cut off. The fifth daughter is much burnt: the French governess leaped from the garret and was dashed to pieces. Dr. Molesworth and his wife, who were there on a visit, escaped; the wife by jumping from the two pair of stairs, and saving herself by a rail; he by hanging by his hands till a second ladder was brought after a first had proved too short. Nobody knows how or where the fire began. The catastrophe is shocking beyond what one ever heard, and poor Lady Molesworth, whose character and conduct were the most amiable in the world, is universally lamented."

It is to the credit of George the Third, that immediately upon hearing of this dreadful calamity, he sent the surviving young ladies a handsome present; ordered a house to be immediately prepared for their reception at his own expense; and not only continued to them a pension which had been enjoyed by their mother, but increased it by two hundred pounds a year.

At No. 18, Upper Brook Street, the Hon. Mrs. Damer, the sculptor, lived, and in the same street, in 1796, died William Gerard Hamilton, better known as "Single-Speech Hamilton."

Crossing Oxford Street, we find ourselves in Portman Square, built about the year 1764, on property anciently belonging to the Knights of St. John of Jerusalem. It derives its name—as does Orchard Street adjoining—from William Henry Portman, Esq., the owner of the estate on which they were built. At the north-west corner stands Montague House, once the residence of the well-known Mrs. Montague, the Madame du Deffand of her day. Here, once a year, she feasted the chimney-sweepers in the garden of the house; here assembled the wit, the rank, and the talent of the last century; and here was the apartment, covered with feather hangings, celebrated by Cowper in well-known verse :—

> "The birds put off their every hue,
> To dress a room for Montague ;
> The peacock sends his heavenly dyes,
> His rainbows and his starry eyes ;
> The pheasant plumes, which round infold
> His mantling neck with downy gold ;
> The cock his arched tail's azure show,
> And river-blanched, the swan his snow," &c., &c.

In Portman Street, Portman Square, Queen Caroline, after her return to England in 1820, was, for a short time, the guest of her Lady of the Bedchamber, Lady Anne Hamilton. Orchard Street is interesting as having been the street in which Sheridan took up his first London abode with his young and beautiful bride, Miss Linley. Here, too, as we learn from his biographer, Moore, he composed his "Rivals" and the "Duenna."

Seymour Street and Wigmore Street lead us into Cavendish Square, most of the streets in the vicinity of which have derived their names either from the Harleys, Earls of Oxford, or from the different families with which they have intermarried. From the earldom of Mortimer and the barony of Harley of Wigmore, we trace the names of Mortimer Street, Harley Street, and Wigmore Street; from the marriage of Edward, second Earl of Oxford and Mortimer, with Henrietta Cavendish, daughter and heiress of John Holles, Duke of Newcastle, we derive Edward Street, Henrietta Street, Cavendish Square, and Holles Street; from the union of their only child, Margaret, to William Bentinck, second Duke of Portland, we trace Margaret Street, Bentinck Street, Duke Street, Duchess Street, and Portland Place; and, lastly, we derive Bulstrode Street from the family seat of the Dukes of Portland, and Welbeck Street from an estate formerly in the possession of the Dukes of Newcastle, which came into the possession of the Harleys by the marriage of the last female descendant of the former to the second Earl of Oxford.

Cavendish Square was built about the year 1718. Here Lady Mary Wortley Montagu resided previously to her long absence from England, and here at the large corner house of the Square and Harley Street, the Princess Amelia, daughter of George the Second, lived and died. In the same house subsequently lived Mr. Hope, the author of "Anastasius," and afterwards Marshal Beresford. No. 32 was successively the residence of two eminent painters, George Romney and Sir Martin Archer Shee: in 1824 the latter was residing at No. 24. The equestrian statue in the square represents the Culloden Duke of Cumberland, and the erect figure on the south side of the square was placed there to the memory of Lord George Bentinck.

With Chandos House, Cavendish Square—the London residence of James Brydges, Duke of Chandos, styled from his magnificent mode of living the "princely Chandos,"—a tragical event is connected. The occasion was a sumptuous entertainment, given by the Duke to celebrate the christening of his infant heir, to whom George the Third and his Queen had consented to become sponsors. The guests, including the royal family, had assembled in the gorgeous apartments; with all due parade the child was being borne to the place appointed for the ceremony of its initiation into the Church, when suddenly an awful transition reversed the scene. Affected, it is said, by the excessive glare of light, the child was seized with convulsions. The ceremony of course was stopped: the guests took their departure to their respective homes, and, before midnight, the infant pride of the princely Chandos had breathed its last. The

Duke, deeply affected by his bereavement, died shortly afterwards, when all his honours became extinct. The grief of the Duchess was probably quite as poignant. She retired from the world, but not from the house which had witnessed the wreck of her fondest hopes, for here she is said to have conceived a melancholy pleasure in residing to the last.

Harley Street and other streets to the north remained unbuilt till many years after the erection of Cavendish Square. Here, in what were then known as Harley Fields, the celebrated George Whitefield was in the habit of preaching in the open air to assembled thousands. In Harley Street lived Sir Philip Francis, the reputed author of the " Letters of Junius," previously to his removal to St. James's Square.

The streets in the vicinity of Cavendish Square furnish the names of several persons of celebrity who formerly resided in them. At No. 7, Bentinck Street, Gibbon the historian composed a considerable portion of his great work, and at No. 24, Holles Street, Lord Byron was born. In Queen Anne Street, No. 47, resided the great landscape-painter, J. M. W. Turner, and in Queen Anne Street East, now Foley Place, lived Richard Cumberland, the dramatic writer, Edmund Malone, the dramatic critic, and Henry Fuseli, the painter.* Martha Blount, beloved and immortalized by Pope, lived in Welbeck Street. In this street Lord George Gordon was residing at the time of the celebrated riots which bear his name; and here died in 1769, at the age of ninety-seven, Edmund Hoyle, author of the famous treatise on the game of whist. In August, 1784, a letter from Mrs. Piozzi to Miss Burney, the novelist, is dated 33, Welbeck Street, Cavendish Square.

* Cunningham's "Handbook of London."

Castle Street, Oxford Market, running parallel with Margaret Street, is interesting from having contained the residences of Dr. Johnson and of Barry the painter, who severally lived here in the days of their distress. Johnson's residence was No. 6, Barry's No. 36. Opposite to Dr. Johnson's humble lodgings resided two sisters of the name of Cotterell. Sir Joshua Reynolds—then scarcely known to fame—was their frequent visitor, and at the house of the maiden ladies commenced the friendship between Johnson and Reynolds, which only terminated with their lives. It was while poor Barry was residing in Castle Street that Edmund Burke ventured to accept an invitation to dine with him at his humble abode. "The windows," we are told, "were mostly broken or cracked, and the tiled roof shewed the sky through many a crevice. There were two old chairs and a single deal table. The fire, however, was bright, and Barry cordial. Presently a pair of tongs were put in Burke's hands, with the remark,—'Be useful, my dear friend, and look to the steaks while I fetch the porter.' The statesman got on admirably with his task, and by the time Barry returned, the steak was done to a turn. 'What a misfortune,' exclaimed Barry, as he entered, 'the wind carried away the fine foaming top as I crossed Titchfield Street.' The friends then sat down to the feast; anecdote and criticism flowed freely; the stars were propitious; no cloud ruffled the painter's mind, and, altogether, Burke used to say he had never spent a happier evening."

In Great Titchfield Street, Marylebone, Cuthbert Shaw the poet—"distinguished alike by his genius, his misfortunes, and his misconduct,"—died in great distress in 1771. In this street, at No. 85, lived at one time Richard Wilson, the landscape - painter, and here, at the house of a brother artist, Joseph Bonomi, died James Barry, in 1806.

In Mortimer Street, Cavendish Square, in 1823, died Joseph Nollekens, the sculptor; at 67, Wimpole Street, Hallam wrote his "History of the Middle Ages;" and from 31, Little Marylebone Street, Cavendish Square, Sir Sidney Smith, the hero of Acre, writes to a correspondent in December, 1788.

Oxford House, the ancient manor house of Marylebone, and the residence at a later period of the Harleys, Earls of Oxford, stood, as late as the year 1791, on the site of Devonshire Mews, New Road. In Devonshire Place, on the east side, lived in 1810, William Beckford, the author of "Vathek." Marylebone is corrupted from St. Mary-on-the-bourne; or, rather, St. Mary-on-the-river; *bourne* being the Saxon name for a river. In the days of Queen Elizabeth, the crown possessed a vast domain in this district, of which the Regent's Park is now probably nearly all that remains. In that reign we find the ambassador from the Emperor of Russia "and other Muscovites" riding through the city of London to Marylebone Park, and there "hunting at their pleasure." The old manor house was probably the ancient hunting-lodge of the royal domain. Having passed from the possession of the Harleys, its gardens became in the reign of Queen Anne celebrated for a fashionable bowling-green, and as the resort of well-dressed gamesters and sharpers. Lady Mary Wortley Montagu, alluding to Sheffield Duke of Buckingham, observes:—

"Some dukes at Mary-bone bowl time away."

Pennant, also, speaking of the Duke's intimacy with the frequenters of Marylebone gardens, writes: "His Grace always gave them a dinner at the conclusion of the season, and his parting toast was, '*May as many of us as remain unhanged next spring, meet here again.*'" Marylebone gardens are perhaps now principally remembered as being the scene of one of Macheath's debauches in the "Beggar's Opera." At a later period they were converted into a place of diversion, resembling the present Cremorne gardens; the amusements consisting of theatrical exhibitions, vocal and instrumental music, and terminating with fireworks. The gardens, which were closed to the public about 1777, stood on the site of the present Beaumont Street, Devonshire Street, and a part of Devonshire Place. No. 17, Devonshire Place, on the east side, is said to have been the site of the orchestra. It may be mentioned, that in the theatre in Marylebone gardens, Charles Dibdin and Bannister made their *début*.

The parish church of St. Marylebone in High Street was rebuilt in 1741 on the site of a former edifice, which had been erected about the year 1400. The parish registers, as we learn from Mr. Peter Cunningham, record the burials of James Ferguson, the astronomer; of James Figg, the prize-fighter,—introduced by Hogarth into the second plate of his "Rake's Progress;" of John Vanderbank, Allan Ramsay, and John Dominick Serres, the painters; of John Michael Rysbraek, the sculptor; of Archibald Bower and William Guthrie, the historical writers, and of Edmund Hoyle, the author of the "Treatise of Whist." In the cemetery on the north side of Paddington Street, lies buried Joseph Baretti, the friend of Dr. Johnson and Sir Joshua Reynolds; and in the cemetery on the south side, William Guthrie and George Canning, the father of the celebrated statesman.

The new church of St. Marylebone, on the south side of Marylebone Road, was built from designs by Thomas Hardwick, father of the eminent architect, Philip Hardwick. Its altar-picture of the Holy Family, painted by Benjamin West, was presented by that artist to the church. Here are buried James Northcote, the pupil and biographer of

Sir Joshua Reynolds, and Richard Cosway, the miniature portrait painter.

At a tavern in High Street, Marylebone, the celebrated Nancy Dawson, when a young girl, was employed in setting up skittles. She died at Hampstead, in 1767, and was buried behind the Foundling Hospital.

In Upper Baker Street, in the last house on the east side, overlooking the Regent's Park, the great actress, Mrs. Siddons, lived and died. In York Place, Baker Street, No. 14, on the east side, William Pitt took up his abode shortly after his resignation of the Premiership in 1801. Hither he removed from Park Place, St. James's. At No. 38, York Place, resided the eminent politician, Joseph Hume.

Hanover Square and the adjoining streets were built about the same time as Cavendish Square; the site on which it stands having been, as late as 1716, still open country. It was at his house in Hanover Square that the once popular poet George Granville, Lord Lansdowne, died in 1735. Here resided Richard Lord Cobham, immortalized by Pope. Here also lived the celebrated circumnavigator of the globe, George Lord Anson; and here, in 1792, at the corner-house of Prince's Street and Hanover Square, a no less celebrated naval commander, George Lord Rodney, breathed his last.

In George Street, Hanover Square, Lady Mary Wortley Montagu passed some of the last months of her long life. From her long residence on the Continent she had imbibed foreign tastes and foreign habits, and consequently the change from the spacious magnificence of an Italian palace, to a small three-storied house in the neighbourhood of Hanover Square, was as striking as it was disagreeable. "I am most handsomely lodged," she said, "for I have two very decent closets and a cupboard on each floor." * "Lady Mary Wortley," writes Walpole, "is arrived. I have seen her: I think her avarice, her dirt, and her vivacity are all increased. Her dress, like her languages, is a galimatias of several countries; the ground-work rags, and the embroidery nastiness. She needs no cap, no handkerchief, no gown, no petticoat, no shoes. An old black laced hood represents the first; the fur of a horseman's coat, which replaces the third, serves for the second; a dimity petticoat is deputy, and officiates, for the fourth; and slippers act the part of the last."† Such is the picture, drawn at the close of life, of the once witty, beautiful, and fascinating Lady Mary Wortley Montagu.

At No. 25, George Street, Hanover Square, died, in 1863, Lord Chancellor Lyndhurst, this being the same house in which his father, the eminent American painter, had previously resided. In St. George's Church in this street were solemnized the remarkable marriage of the Duke of Kingston to the notorious Miss Chudleigh, in 1769; of Lord Nelson's Lady Hamilton (Emma Harte) to Sir William Hamilton, in 1791; and of the Duke of Sussex to Lady Augusta Murray, in 1793.

In Argyll Street, within a short distance of Hanover Square, lived the unfortunate Dr. Dodd, who expiated a life of vanity, hypocrisy, and pleasure on the gibbet. Wraxall mentions his having dined at his table in Argyll Street, when John Wilkes, Sir William Jones, and De Lolme formed the remainder of the company. " Mrs. Dodd," writes Wraxall, " presided, and afterwards received in her drawing-room a large party of both sexes." In Argyll Street lived George Lord Lyttelton, author of the " History of Henry the

* "Works and Letters of Lady M. W. Montagu," edited by Lord Wharncliffe.
† Letter from Horace Walpole to George Montagu, 2nd February, 1762.

Second." Here Mrs. Piozzi, then Mrs. Thrale, was staying during the winter of 1782–3; and here, at No. 30, Madame de Staël resided on the occasion of her visit to England in 1813. In 1824 James Northcote, the painter, was living in Argyll Place.

Before quitting the neighbourhood of Hanover Square, let us cross New Bond Street into Woodstock Street, interesting to the lovers of literary history as the street where Dr. Johnson first resided with his "Tetty," after his arrival in London in search of fortune and fame. "He now [1737] removed," says Boswell, "to London with Mrs. Johnson. His lodgings were for some time in Woodstock Street, near Hanover Square, and afterwards in Castle Street, Cavendish Square." In Woodstock Street the celebrated Prince Talleyrand was residing at the time of the execution of Louis the Sixteenth. In this street also, in 1814, we find the Princess of Wales, afterwards Queen Caroline, setting down Dr. Parr after the opera, on her return to her house in Connaught Place.

Bond Street, it may be remarked, derives its name from Sir Thomas Bond, whose house in Piccadilly we find temporarily occupied by the French ambassador in 1699. The building of Old Bond Street was commenced about the year 1686; that of New Bond Street about the year 1716. In the "Weekly Journal" of the 1st of June, 1717, we read:—"The new buildings, between Bond Street and Marylebone, go on with all possible diligence, and the houses even let and sell before they are built. They are already in great forwardness. Could the builders have supposed their labours would have produced a place so extremely fashionable, they might probably have deviated, once at least, from their usual parsimony by making the way rather wider: as it is at present, coaches are greatly impeded in the rapidity of their course; but this is fortunate for the *Bond Street loungers*, who are by this defect granted glimpses of the fashionable and generally titled fair, who pass and repass from two till five o'clock."

Bond Street is replete with interesting literary associations. From this street we find Richard West dating many of his letters to Gray. Here, at the house of Mrs. Miller, Fielding has placed many of the most pathetic scenes in his "Tom Jones." It was at his lodgings in Bond Street, in 1781, that De la Motte, the spy, was arrested, and hence he was carried to the Secretary of State's office, then in Cleveland Row. In 1766 we find the great Lord Chatham dating his letters from Bond Street. Here Archibald Bower, author of the "History of the Popes," remarkable for his eccentric vices and strange adventures, breathed his last in September, 1766; and lastly, it was here that Gibbon passed many lonely evenings composing his immortal history. "While coaches," he writes, "were rattling through Bond Street, I have passed many a solitary evening in my lodging with my books. My studies were sometimes interrupted by a sigh, which I breathed towards Lausanne; and on the approach of spring I withdrew without reluctance from the noisy and extensive scene of crowds without company, and dissipation without pleasure."*

At Boswell's lodgings in Old Bond Street, in 1769, we find him on one occasion entertaining at dinner Dr. Johnson, Sir Joshua Reynolds, Garrick, Goldsmith, Murphy, Tom Davis the bookseller and actor, and Bickerstaff, the author of "Love in a Village."

It was at his lodgings, No. 41, Old Bond Street, that Lawrence Sterne, the author of "Tristram Shandy," breathed his last on the 18th March, 1768. "I find," writes the late

* Gibbon's Memoirs of his Life and Writings.

Mr. Disraeli, "the moment of his death described in a singular book, the 'Life of a Footman.' I give it with all its particulars. ' In the month of January, 1768, we set off for London. We stopped for some time at Almack's house, in Pall Mall. My master afterwards took Sir James Gray's house in Clifford Street, who was going ambassador to Spain. He now began housekeeping, hired a French cook, housemaid, and kitchen-maid, and kept a great deal of the best company. About this time, Mr. Sterne, the celebrated author, was taken ill at the silk-bag shop in Old Bond Street. He was sometimes called Tristram Shandy, and sometimes Yorick, a very great favourite of the gentlemen's. One day my master had company to dinner, who were speaking about him—the Duke of Roxburghe, the Earl of March, the Earl of Ossory, the Duke of Grafton, Mr. Garrick, Mr. Hume, and Mr. James. "John," said my master, "go and inquire how Mr. Sterne is to-day." I went, returned, and said, "I went to Mr. Sterne's lodging—the mistress opened the door—I inquired how he did. She told me to go up to the nurse. I went into the room, and he was just a-dying. I waited ten minutes; but in five, he said, 'Now is it come!' He put up his hand, as if to stop a blow, and died in a minute." The gentlemen were all very sorry, and lamented him very much.'"

Sterne was interred in the burying-ground belonging to the parish of St. George, Hanover Square, between Connaught Place and Bayswater, where a stone, erected by two Freemasons to his memory, may still be seen. Here also is buried another eminent novelist, Ann Radcliffe, who died in 1823.

In Old Bond Street, on the 11th of October, 1753, died the Countess of Macclesfield, the unnatural mother of Savage, the poet. No. 24, and afterwards No. 29, Old Bond Street, were among the different London abodes of Sir Thomas Lawrence.

To *New* Bond Street almost as much interest is attached as to *Old* Bond Street. At No. 141, Lord Nelson was lodging in 1797; and at No. 148, lodged Lord Camelford at the time of his fatal duel with Best, in March, 1804. Their quarrel took place close by, at the Prince of Wales's Coffee-house (Simme's) in Conduit Street. An "old haunt" of Lord Byron's, in the days of his dissipation, was Stevens's Hotel, No. 18, where he and another brilliant poet, Tom Moore, as the latter informs us, frequently dined together. Long's Hotel, close by (No. 16), was the resort of Sir Walter Scott. " I saw Lord Byron for the last time," writes Sir Walter, "in 1815, after I returned from France. He dined or lunched with me at Long's in Bond Street. I never saw him so full of gaiety and good-humour, to which the presence of Mr. Mathews, the comedian, added not a little. Poor Terry was also present. After one of the gayest parties I ever was present at, my fellow-traveller and I set off for Scotland, and I never saw Lord Byron again."

Such of the great Lord Chatham's letters, in 1766, as are dated from Bond Street, were written by him in what is now the Clarendon Hotel, which was let to him in that year by the Duke of Grafton.

Bruton Street, leading from Bond Street into Berkeley Square, derives its name from Bruton in Somersetshire, formerly the property or seat of John Lord Berkeley, of Stratton. In this street was the London residence of John, the "great" Duke of Argyll and Greenwich, who died in 1743.

"Yes, Sir ! on great Argyll I often wait,
At charming Sudbrook or in Bruton Street."
SIR C. H. WILLIAMS : *Giles Earle and Bubb Dodington.*

"—— Powerful as thy sword, from thy rich tongue
Persuasion flows."—THOMSON.

In Bruton Street lived for many years Richard Brinsley Sheridan, whose house is said to have been so often beset by bailiffs as to render it necessary to introduce the provisions into it by lowering them over the railings into the area. Berkeley Square dates from 1798. Lansdowne House, the principal mansion in the square, was built in 1765, by John Earl of Bute, the celebrated minister and favourite, by whom it was afterwards sold for £22,000 to the first Marquis of Lansdowne, who, as Lord Shelburne, played scarcely a less prominent part in politics than Lord Bute. Many persons of celebrity have been residents in Berkeley Square. Here died Pope's Martha Blount, in 1762. Here, in August, 1762, shortly after removing from George Street, Hanover Square, died Lady Mary Wortley Montagu. At No. 45, the "heaven-born general," Lord Clive, put an end to his existence. Here, at one time, lived Thomas Hope, the author of "Anastasius." Lastly, at No. 11, Horace Walpole resided from 1779 to 1797, and here, in the latter year, he breathed his last.

In Hill Street, died, in 1794, the great lawyer and patriot, Lord Chancellor Camden. Here also, in 1795, before she lost her husband, lived, at one time, the gifted and accomplished Mrs. Montagu. "I had yesterday," writes Hannah More, "the pleasure of dining in Hill Street, Berkeley Square, *at a certain Mrs. Montagu's, a name not totally obscure*. The party consisted of a Mrs. Carter, Dr. Johnson, Solander, and Maty, Mrs. Boscawen, Miss Reynolds, and Sir Joshua, the idol of every company—some other persons of high rank and less wit, and your humble servant—a party that would not have disgraced the table of Lælius, or of Atticus." Mrs. Montagu's friend, the literary Lord Lyttelton, lived in Hill Street; as did also the late Lord Brougham, at No. 5, in 1824, and Thomas Raikes, the fashionable Journal-writer, at No. 13; both on the north side.

Hay Hill is interesting as being the spot where a skirmish took place between the rebels and the royal forces during Sir Thomas Wyatt's insurrection in 1554. Here, after his execution on Tower Hill, the head of Sir Thomas was exposed on the common gibbet; and here three of his most dangerous associates were hanged in chains.

From Hay Hill we pass into Grafton Street, formerly designated Ducking Pond Row. Here Charles James Fox resided when Secretary of State for Foreign Affairs in 1782, and here, at No. 11, lived and died the celebrated Admiral Earl Howe. No. 4, Grafton Street, was long the residence of Lord Brougham, after he had become Lord Chancellor.

In Conduit Street, a few yards from Bond Street, stands a small chapel dedicated to the Holy Trinity, to which a peculiar interest is attached. When James the Second sought to seduce his subjects, and more especially the army, to embrace the Roman Catholic religion, he caused a large wooden chapel to be erected, which, being movable at will, was wheeled to Hounslow Heath, where his army was then lying, and occasionally moved from one part of the camp to the other. When James was subsequently compelled to fly the kingdom, this chapel was brought back to London, and placed in what were then fields, where it remained till 1716, when the present Trinity Chapel was erected on its site.

Conduit Street is connected with several eminent names. It was in Conduit Street, on the 24th of January, 1749, that Charles James Fox first saw the light.* From No. 37, Conduit Street, in the years 1801 and 1802, many of the letters of George Canning are dated. In this street, too, in his praiseworthy attempts to extinguish a fire, another brilliant statesman, William Windham, contracted the dis-

* Earl Russell's "Memorials of Fox."

order which sent him to his grave.* In 1772, Boswell mentions Dr. Johnson drinking tea with him at his lodgings in Conduit Street.

From Conduit Street a narrow passage leads us into Savile Row. Here Henrietta Countess of Suffolk, the celebrated mistress of George the Second, lived after the death of her royal lover; and here the well-known Lady Betty Germaine was residing in 1741. In Savile Row died, in 1830, the Right Hon. George Tierney; and at No. 17, persecuted by duns and threatened by bailiffs, died Richard Brinsley Sheridan, and hence his remains were conveyed to Westminster Abbey.

> "Behold how they flock to the funeral array
> Of him whom they shunned in his sickness and sorrow!
> The bailiff may seize his last blanket to-day,
> Whose pall shall be borne up by nobles to-morrow."

At the south end of Savile Row is Uxbridge House, the work of Vardi, long the residence of the late gallant Marquis of Anglesey. It stands on the site of Queensberry House, so called from its having been the London mansion of Charles, third Duke of Queensberry, and his beautiful Duchess, Katherine Hyde, the " Kitty " of Prior's verse, and rendered still more celebrated by Pope :—

> " If Queensberry to strip there's no compelling,
> 'Tis from a handmaid we must paint a Helen."

It was here that Gay was domesticated and petted by his noble patrons, the Duke and Duchess, and in this house he died. To Pope he writes about two years before his death:— "My melancholy increases, and every hour threatens me with some return of my distemper. Not the divine looks, the kind favours and expressions of the divine Duchess,

* Miss Berry's Journals.

nor the inexpressible goodness of the Duke, can in the least cheer me. The drawing-room no more receives light from those two stars; there is now what Milton says is in hell, 'darkness visible.' Oh that I had never known what a court was!"

Burlington Street, Cork Street, Boyle Street, Clifford Street, and Savile Row, severally derive their names from the Boyles, Earls of Burlington and Cork, and the great heiresses which two of them married, viz., Elizabeth Clifford, daughter of the last Earl of Cumberland, and Dorothy Savile, daughter of the last Marquis of Halifax.

In Cork Street, running parallel with Savile Row, died Dr. Arbuthnot, the courtly physician of Queen Anne, and the friend of Pope, Gay, and Swift. In this street also died Queen Anne's favourite and powerful bedchamber-woman, Mrs. afterwards Lady Masham. Here, too, the well-known Field-Marshal Wade had a miniature residence, designed by Lord Burlington. Lord Chesterfield made the observation, that "since the General surely could not live in it, he had better hire the opposite house in order to look at it." No vestige of it now remains. In Cork Street, Dr. Johnson was a frequent visitor at the house of Mr. Diamond, an apothecary. About the year 1752, we find him dining there nearly every Sunday, accompanied by his blind *protégée*, Mrs. Williams, the poetess.

In Old Burlington Street lived and died Mark Akenside, the author of "The Pleasures of Imagination;" and in Clifford Street, on the north, resided George the Third's physician, Dr. Addington, the father of the respectable Prime Minister, Henry Addington, Viscount Sidmouth. When, in 1814, the Prince of Orange, afterwards King of Holland, was paying his addresses to the Princess Charlotte, he was lodging at his tailor's, No. 8, Clifford Street.

ST. JAMES'S STREET.

ST. JAMES'S STREET.—COLONEL BLOOD.—CLUBS. — COCOA-TREE TAVERN. — THATCHED HOUSE.—DEATH OF GIBBON.—BYRON.

ST. JAMES'S STREET, styled in 1670 the "Long Street," appears to have grown into a regular street between the last days of the Protectorate and the early part of the reign of Charles the Second. It has continued, almost from the days of the merry monarch to the present time, to be the nucleus of fashionable society, and the lounging-place of the witty and the gay. In the days of Queen Anne, it was scarcely less celebrated for the gifted society which frequented its exclusive chocolate-houses, than it is at the present time for the fashionable clubs which are its principal characteristics.

The first event of any interest connected with St. James's Street, is the seizure of the Duke of Ormond's person by the notorious Colonel Blood, on the night of the 6th of December, 1670. The Duke, when Lord Lieutenant of Ireland, had executed some of Blood's accomplices who had been engaged in a treasonable design of surprising Dublin Castle, in revenge for which act, Blood expressed his determination to seize the Duke and hang him at Tyburn. Accordingly, on a dark night, as the Duke was returning from an entertainment in the city, and was passing the bottom of St. James's Street—he was suddenly dragged from his coach by Blood and five of his associates, and immediately mounted on horseback behind one of the party. The Duke, as usual, was accompanied by six footmen, whose habit it was to attend him three on each side of the street, but unfortunately on the present occasion they were accidentally some distance off when Blood and his associates made their attack. The latter had proceeded somewhat further than the present Devonshire House, in the direction of Tyburn, when the Duke contrived to get one of his feet under that of his companion, and though sixty years of age, succeeded in unhorsing him. They both fell in the mud, in which they continued struggling for some seconds, when the Duke's servants, having been alarmed by the outcries of the coachman, fortunately made their appearance. The ruffians thus interrupted, fired two pistols at the Duke, which providentially missed their aim, and then rode off as fast as they could. When the Duke's servants reached the spot, not only was his Grace so exhausted by the struggle as to be unable to speak, but so dark was the night that it was only from the light reflected from the diamonds in his star that they were able to discover the exact spot where he lay.

It was not till the following year, when Blood was captured in his famous attempt to seize the crown jewels, that it became generally known that he was the perpetrator of the insolent attempt on the life of the Duke of Ormond. Both while in confinement in the Tower, as well as while under examination before the Privy Council, he displayed that calm intrepidity which was the constitutional characteristic of this extraordinary man; patiently and sullenly awaiting the ignominious death which he could not fail to look forward to as the consequence of his crimes. While before the Council, his behaviour and language made a forcible impression upon the mind of his sovereign, Charles the Second, who, in a very unprecedented manner, chose to be present. He excited the admiration of the King by his indomitable courage; charmed him with the readiness of his wit, and ingeniously flattered him by the reverence he expressed for his kingly person and office. Though candidly confessing that he was the author of the outrage on the Duke of Ormond, he positively refused to divulge the names of his associates. "I would never," he said, "betray a friend's life, nor be guilty of a falsehood to save my own." When asked what provocation he could have received from the Duke, his answer was, that his Grace had deprived him of his estate and hanged his friends. Again, when asked by Charles how he could have the audacity to make his attempt on the crown jewels—"My father," he replied, "lost a good estate *for* the crown, and I considered it no crime to recover it *by* the crown."—"What," said the King, "if I should give you your life?"—"I shall endeavour," replied Blood, "to deserve it."

Charles apparently would have pardoned him on the spot, but the Duke of Ormond was too powerful a subject not to be consulted on the occasion, and how could Ormond be expected to overlook either the insolent outrage or the attempt on his life? Nevertheless, the Duke submitted to the wishes of his sovereign. "If your Majesty," he said, "can forgive his attempt on the crown, how can I withhold my forgiveness at his attempt on my life?" Blood, accordingly, was not only pardoned, but actually became a favourite at court, had a pension conferred on him, and was subsequently the means of delivering from the hands of justice more than one of his former associates in treason and in crime.*

* For a full account of Blood's extraordinary offences and adventures, see Echard's "History of England," Carte's "Life of the Duke of Ormond," Bishop's Kennett's "Complete History," Stow's "Survey of London," Oldmixon's "History of the Stuarts," and Baxter's "History of his own Life and Times."

Of the famous St. James's Street clubs, the two oldest and most famous are White's and Brooks's, of both of which Mr. Peter Cunningham has given interesting accounts in his admirable "Handbook of London." White's, now Nos. 37 and 38, St. James's Street, stood originally, as the "White's Chocolate House" of Queen Anne's time, on the west side of the street, a few doors from the bottom. This house was burnt down about four o'clock in the morning of the 28th of April, 1733; an event which enabled Hogarth to introduce into the sixth plate of his Rake's Progress the gaming-room of the place, in which the gamblers are represented as so intent upon their play, as to be heedless alike of the flames which are making their way into the apartment, and of the watchmen who are bursting open the doors. Brooks's Club (No. 60), formerly no less famous as a gaming club than White's, owes its name to one Brooks, a wine-merchant, by whom it was at one time farmed. It was originally founded, in 1764, in Pall Mall, on the site of what is now No. 52; the present house in St. James's Street not having been opened till October, 1778. Another fashionable club in St. James's Street in the last century was Weltzie's, so called from Weltzie, its proprietor, who had been house-steward to George the Fourth when Prince of Wales. To the Marquis of Buckingham, his brother William Grenville writes in January, 1780: "The Prince of Wales has taken this year very much to play, and has gone so far as to win or lose £2000 or £3000 in a night. He is now, together with the Duke of York, forming a new club at Weltzie's; and this will probably be the scene of some of the highest gaming which has been seen in town."*

* Weltzie's club stood on the site of Fenton's hotel, on the west side of St. James's Street.

The Cocoa-Tree Tavern—the lounging place of the wits, the dandies, and adventurers of the days of Queen Anne—stood apparently on the site of what in our own time was the Cocoa-Tree Club—No. 64, on the west side of St. James's Street. Addison mentions it as a place of fashionable resort as early as 1710. "Sometimes," he writes, "I am seen thrusting my head into a round of politicians at Wills', and listening with great attention to the narratives that are made in those little circular audiences. Sometimes I smoke a pipe at Child's, and while I seem attentive to nothing but the Postman, [newspaper] overhear the conversation of every table in the room. I appear on Sunday nights at St. James's Coffee-house, and sometimes join the little committee of politics in the inner room, as one who comes there to hear and improve. My face is likewise very well known at the Grecian, the *Cocoa-Tree*, and in the theatres both of Drury Lane and the Haymarket. I have been taken for a merchant upon the Exchange for above these ten years, and sometimes pass for a Jew in the assembly of stock-jobbers at Jonathan's."*

Of the different places here mentioned, Child's coffee-house, the resort of the clergy, was in St. Paul's Churchyard; St. James's, a Whig chocolate-house, stood at the bottom of St. James's Street, the corner house on the west side, opposite the palace; the Grecian stood in Devereux Court, outside Temple Bar; and Jonathan's, the resort of merchants and stock-jobbers, was in Change Alley.

The Cocoa-Tree was a favourite resort of Swift during his occasional visits to London after he had become Dean of St. Patrick's. Prior, the poet, writes to him on the 30th of July, 1717:—"I have been made to believe that we may

* "Spectator," No. I.

see your reverend person this summer in England; if so, I shall be glad to meet you at any place; but when you come to London, do not go to the Cocoa-Tree, but come immediately to Duke Street, where you shall find a bed, a book, and candle; so pray think of sojourning nowhere else."*

Gibbon, the historian, was a member of the Cocoa-Tree after it had been converted into a fashionable club. On the 24th of November, 1762, he inserts in his private journal: " I dined at the Cocoa-Tree with Holt. We went thence to the play (the 'Spanish Friar'), and when it was over returned to the Cocoa-Tree. That respectable body of which I have the honour of being a member, affords every evening a sight truly English. Twenty or thirty, perhaps, of the first men in the kingdom in point of fashion and fortune, supping at little tables covered with a napkin, in the middle of a coffee-room, upon a bit of cold meat or a sandwich, and drinking a glass of punch. At present we are full of king's counsellors and lords of the bedchamber, who, having jumped into the ministry, make a very singular medley of their old principles and language with their modern ones."†

In 1780 we find "a young Mr. Harvey of Chigwell," who had recently come into possession of a large fortune, losing no less a sum than £100,000 at hazard at the Cocoa-Tree.

Gibbon was also a member of White's, Boodle's, and Almack's, to the latter of which he gave the preference. On the 24th of June, 1776, he writes from Almack's : " Town grows empty, and this house, where I have passed many agreeable hours, is the only place which still invites the flower of the English youth. The style of living, though somewhat expensive, is exceedingly pleasant, and, notwith-

* Swift's "Correspondence."
† Gibbon's "Miscellaneous Works."

standing the rage of play, I have found more entertaining, and even rational society here, than in any other club to which I belong."*

· The Cocoa-Tree is connected with another illustrious name, that of Lord Byron, who was also a member of the club. To Moore, the poet, he writes on the 9th of April, 1814: "I am but just returned to town, from which you may infer that I have been out of it; and I have been boxing, for exercise, with Jackson for this last month daily. I have also been drinking, and on one occasion, with three other friends at the Cocoa-Tree, from six till four, yea, until five in the matin. We clareted and champagned till two, then supped, and finished with a kind of regency punch composed of Madeira, brandy, and *green* tea, no *real* water being admitted therein. There was a night for you! without once quitting the table except to ambulate home, which I did alone, and in utter contempt of a hackney-coach and my own *vis*, both of which were deemed necessary for our conveyance."† Lord Byron was at this time residing at the Albany in Piccadilly.

The Thatched House, another celebrated place of entertainment in the days of Queen Anne, stood somewhat lower down, on a part of the ground on which the Conservative and Civil Service Clubs now stand. Swift writes to Stella on the 20th of December, 1711:—"I dined, you know, with our society; and that odious secretary [Lord Bolingbroke] would make me president next week, so I must entertain them this day se'night at the Thatched House Tavern, where we dined to-day. It will cost me five or six pounds, yet the secretary says he will give me wine." Again Swift

* Gibbon's "Miscellaneous Works."
† Moore's "Life of Byron."

writes on the 27th of the same month :—" I entertained our society at the Thatched House Tavern to-day at dinner, but brother Bathurst sent for wine, the house affording none." The "society" alluded to by Swift consisted of a club comprising the most eminent men in rank, literature, and politics at the commencement of the last century. In the Thatched House Tavern, the celebrated literary and dilettanti clubs held for many years their meetings. Both of these clubs were originally founded at the Turk's Head Tavern, in Gerrard Street, Soho; Sir Joshua Reynolds having had the merit of being the proposer and principal promoter of both.

On the 5th of April, 1684, died at his house in St. James's Street, William Lord Brouncker, styled by Bishop Burnet a "profound mathematician," but now principally remembered as having been the first President of the Royal Society. On the 25th of February, 1723, the great architect, Sir Christopher Wren, died in St. James's Street. It was his custom to fall asleep after dinner, and one evening his servant, observing that he had slept longer than usual, entered his apartment and found him dead in his chair.

In a house in St. James's Street, adjoining Brooks's Club, lived, in 1781, Charles James Fox. It was the scene of many of his follies and distresses. Horace Walpole writes to Marshal Conway on the 31st of May, 1781 :—" I had been to see if Lady Ailesbury was come to town. As I came up St. James's Street, I saw a cart and porters at Charles Fox's door; coppers and old chests of drawers loading. In short, his success at faro has awakened his host of creditors; but unless his bank had swelled to the size of the Bank of England, it could not have yielded a sop a piece for each. Epsom, too, had been unpropitious, and one creditor has actually seized and carried off his goods, which did not seem worth removing. As I returned full of this scene, whom should I find sauntering by my own door, but Charles. He came up, and talked to me at the coach window on the Marriage Bill with as much *sang-froid* as if he knew nothing of what had happened."

> "Hark where the voice of battle shouts from far,
> The Jews and Macaronis are at war;
> The Jews prevail, and thundering from the stocks,
> They seize, they bind, they circumcise Charles Fox."
> *Heroic Epistle to Sir William Chambers.*

From the Auckland papers, it appears that at the time Fox was lodging next door to Brooks's Club, his rooms being on the first floor, while his friend James Hare—the "Hare with Many Friends"—occupied the second floor.

St. James's Street witnessed the closing scene of the great historian, Edward Gibbon, on the 16th January, 1794. The account which Lord Sheffield gives of the last moments of his illustrious friend is very interesting. "During the evening," he writes, "he complained much of his stomach, and of a disposition to vomit. Soon after nine he took his opium draught, and went to bed. About ten he complained of much pain, and desired that warm napkins might be applied to his stomach. He almost incessantly expressed a sense of pain till about four o'clock in the morning, when he said he found his stomach much easier. About seven, the servant asked whether he should send for Mr. Farquhar? He answered, No; that he was as well as he had been the day before. About half-past eight he got out of bed, and said he was '*plus adroit*' than he had been for three months past, and got into bed again without assistance, better than usual. About nine he said that he would rise. The servant, however, persuaded him to remain in bed till Mr. Farquhar, who was expected at eleven, should come. Till about that hour he spoke with great facility. Mr. Farquhar came at the time appointed, and he was then visibly dying. When the valet de chambre, after attending Mr. Farquhar out of the room, returned, Mr. Gibbon said—'Pourquoi est-ce que vous me quittez?' This was about half-past eleven. At twelve he drank some brandy and water from a teapot, and desired his favourite servant to stay with him. These were the last words he pronounced articulately. To the last he preserved his senses, and when he could no longer speak, his servant having asked a question, he made a sign to show that he understood him. He was quite tranquil, and did not stir; his eyes half shut. About a quarter before one he ceased to breathe. The valet de chambre observed that Mr. Gibbon did not, at any time, show the least sign of alarm or apprehension of death; and it does not appear that he ever thought himself in danger, unless his desire to speak to Mr. Darell may be considered in that light."*

Lord Sheffield hastened to the bedside of his dying friend, but by the time he arrived in St. James's Street, the great historian had ceased to exist. The house in which Gibbon expired—No. 76, St. James's Street, near the corner of Little St. James's Street,—was pulled down to make room for the present Conservative Club. When Gibbon lodged there it was occupied by Elmsley, the bookseller.

No. 62, higher up the street, was in the last century well-known as Betty's fruit-shop, where men of wit and fashion met to discuss the scandal or politics of the day. Mason has perpetuated her name in the "Heroic Epistle":—

"And patriot Betty fix her fruit-shop there."

To George Selwyn Horace Walpole writes on the 2nd of December, 1765:—" When you have a quarter of an hour awake, and to spare, I wish you would bestow it on me.

* Gibbon's "Miscellaneous Works."

There are no such things as *bon mots* here to send you, and I cannot hope that you will send me your own. Next to them I should like Charles Townshend's, but I don't desire *Betty's*." Walpole, elsewhere describing a party of pleasure at Vauxhall, mentions the circumstance of Betty accompanying them to the gardens with baskets of strawberries and cherries. Her death took place in St. James's Street, on the 30th of August, 1797, at the age of sixty-seven; this being the same street in which she had been born, and which, she used to say, she had never slept out of but twice in her life—once when she paid a visit to a friend in the country, and the second time on the occasion of an Installation of the Knights of the Garter at Windsor. Her real name was Elizabeth Neale.*

In 1758, immediately before the appointment of General Wolfe to command the forces destined to act against Quebec, he was residing in St. James's Street.

On the west side of St. James's Street, in a house of his own, lived, from 1660 to the time of his death in 1687, Edmund Waller, the poet. Here also, "at Mr. Digby's, next door to the Golden Bull," lodged at one time another celebrated poet, Alexander Pope.†

Lord Byron, at the time when the publication of the first and second cantos of "Childe Harold" created so extraordinary a sensation, was lodging at No. 8 in this street. Here it was that, to use his own remarkable words, he "awoke one morning and found himself famous." It was from this house also, that the misanthropic poet departed on the melancholy and well-known occasion of his taking his seat in the House of Lords as a peer of the realm—"in a state," writes Moore, "more lone and unfriended, perhaps, than any youth of his

---

* "Gentleman's Magazine" for 1797, p. 891.
† Cunningham's "Handbook of London."

high station had ever before been reduced to on such an occasion; not having a single individual of his own class, either to take him by the hand as friend or acknowledge him as acquaintance." "I was passing down St. James's Street," writes his relative Dallas, "with no intention of calling, when I saw his chariot at the door, and went in. His countenance, paler than usual, showed that his mind was agitated, and that he was thinking of the nobleman* to whom he had once looked for a hand and countenance in his introduction to the House. He said to me—'I am glad you happened to come in: I am going to take my seat; perhaps you will go with me.' I expressed my readiness to attend him, while, at the same time, I concealed the shock I felt on thinking that this young man, who, by birth, fortune, and talent stood high in life, should have lived so unconnected and neglected by persons of his own rank, that there was not a single member of the senate to which he belonged, to whom he would or could apply to introduce him in a manner becoming his birth. I saw that he felt the situation, and I fully partook of his indignation." The subsequent scene in the House of Lords, though graphically described by Dallas, is too long for insertion. "We returned to St. James's Street," he says, "but he did not recover his spirits."

It was on the east side of St. James's Street that James Gilray, the caricaturist, committed suicide in 1815, by throwing himself from an upper window into the street.

* His relative, Frederick Earl of Carlisle.

THE NEIGHBOURHOOD OF ST. JAMES'S STREET.

BENNETT STREET.—ARLINGTON STREET.—PARK PLACE.—ST. JAMES'S PLACE.
—CLEVELAND ROW.—KING STREET.—ALMACK'S.—LITTLE RYDER STREET.
—BURY STREET.

THE streets diverging from St. James's Street are all of them more or less associated with some person of celebrity, or some event of interest. As we descend towards St. James's Palace, the first opening to the right is Bennett Street, a small avenue leading to Arlington Street. At No. 4, Bennett Street, in the apartments which he occupied on the first floor, Lord Byron composed the "Giaour," the "Bride of Abydos," and the "Corsair." He resided here during a great part of the years of 1813 and 1814, and sometimes in his letters amuses himself with playfully styling it Benedictine Street.

Let us pass into Arlington Street, so called, like Bennett Street, from having been built on property formerly belonging to Henry Bennet, Earl of Arlington, one of the "Cabal" in the reign of Charles the Second. Considering how few are the houses which it contains, the number of persons of note and genius by whom it has been inhabited is remarkable. In Arlington Street, in the reign of William the Third, lived the Duchess of Cleveland, once the beautiful and imperious mistress of the second Charles; and here also, about the same time, lived Mary Fairfax, the amiable and neglected widow of George Villiers, the witty Duke of Buckingham. Here, under the roof of her father, the first Duke of Kingston, resided, in her maiden days of youth, beauty, and genius, Lady Mary Wortley Montagu; and here also, after her marriage with the second Duke of Kingston, lived the notorious Elizabeth Chudleigh. It was to Arlington Street that George the Second, when Prince of Wales, retired to sulk, after his memorable quarrel with his father; here William Duke of Cumberland, the victor of Culloden, dined for the last time; and here, at No. 16—then the residence of the Duke of Rutland—died, in 1827, Frederick Duke of York.

Horace Walpole not inappropriately speaks of Arlington Street as *par excellence* the "ministerial street." Here, for instance, in the last house, overlooking the Green Park, lived the accomplished statesman and scholar, John Lord Carteret, afterwards Earl Granville. On the same side of the street resided a scarcely less eminent statesman and scholar, William Pulteney, Earl of Bath. Next door to Pulteney—on the site of the present No. 17, also overlooking the Green Park—Sir Robert Walpole took up his residence, in 1716. In this house another Prime Minister, Henry Pelham, died in 1754. In Arlington Street, the Duke of Grafton was residing when First Lord of the Treasury, in 1768; and here, in 1779, was residing "Single-Speech" Hamilton, in which year one of the Gothic towers of his house, as we learn from Horace Walpole, fell through the roof and entirely disappeared.

Nor have we yet concluded our list of Arlington Street worthies. At No. 5, on the east side of the street, Sir Robert Walpole resided after his fall from power, and here, in March, 1745, the great minister died. Here his son Horace, who was born in this street, lived till the year

1779; and here many of his charming letters were written. "I was standing," he writes on one occasion, "at my window, after dinner in summer, in Arlington Street, and saw Patty Blount (after Pope's death) with nothing remaining of her immortal charms but her *blue eyes*, trudging on foot with her petticoats pinned up, for it rained, to visit *blameless Bethel*, who was sick at the end of the street." In Arlington Street resided for a short time Charles James Fox, at whose house, in 1804, died William Dixon, Bishop of Down and Connor; and here resided Lord and Lady Nelson at the close of the year 1800 and the beginning of 1801.

As we pass down St. James's Street, the next opening on the west side is Park Place. At No. 9 lived the well-known antiquary, Sir William Musgrave; in this street Hume the historian resided when Under Secretary of State in 1769; and here, in a small furnished house, William Pitt took up his abode on resigning the Premiership in 1801. The following year he removed to another small house, No. 14, York Place, Baker Street.

We next arrive at St. James's Place, built in 1694, a street in which the houses remain nearly the same as they were in the days of Queen Anne. Here, previously to the year 1716, Addison had a house, and in this street occasionally resided Thomas Parnell, the poet, the friend and correspondent of Congreve, Addison, and Steele, of Swift, Pope, Gay, and Arbuthnot. Here also stands the late residence—No. 22, overlooking the Green Park—of a third poet, Mr. Rogers, where Sheridan, Byron, Moore, Southey, Wordsworth, Coleridge, and Campbell have been favoured guests, and in which, at different times, have met all the wit, the beauty, and the talent of the present century. Here he died on the 18th of December, 1855, at the patriarchal age of ninety-two.

In St. James's Place, in a house also overlooking the Green Park, lived the charming Mary Lepel, Lady Hervey, the idol of her contemporaries, and celebrated in verse by Pope, Gay, Voltaire, Arbuthnot, Pulteney, and Lord Chesterfield.

"Now Hervey, fair of face, I mark full well,
With thee, youth's youngest daughter, sweet Lepel."—GAY.

"I am preparing a dwelling," writes Lady Hervey on the 5th of April, 1749, "that will suit better with my purse, though not so well with my inclination. I have paid dear to make that dwelling *look* as like the country as I can; but I have been too much used to grass and green trees to bear the changing them for brick walls and dust." Lady Hervey could scarcely have fixed upon any spot in London which at that time had more the appearance of being in the country. The house in question was afterwards the residence of the Marquis of Hastings, better known as Earl of Moira, and is now divided into two.

In St. James's Place died, in April, 1788, George the Third's venerable favourite, Mrs. Delany, and at No. 13, lived his son's mistress, the beautiful actress, Mrs. Robinson. Here, in December, 1728, died the learned White Kennet, Bishop of Peterborough. Here lived the well-known Secretary of State, James Craggs, immortalised by the praise of Pope, and here also lived the poet's friend, William Cleland, to whom he addressed the verses commencing—

"Few words are best; I wish you well."

It was in "very elegant lodgings" in St. James's Place that John Wilkes was residing in 1756. Here, as we glean from his letters, the Right Honourable Richard Rigby—the jovial politician and *bon-vivant* of the last century—was living in 1760, and from here many of Charles Fox's letters are dated in 1783.

In St. James's Place—No. 25, facing the Green Park—died, on the 23rd of January, 1844, Sir Francis Burdett; his death, it is said, having been caused by grief for the loss of his wife, whose decease had preceded his own by only thirteen days. Close by stands Earl Spencer's noble residence, Spencer House, designed by Vardy.

If St. James's Place is famous for having been the residence of the poets, Cleveland Row and Cleveland Court—at the bottom of St. James's Street—are scarcely less remarkable as having been frequented by the wits. Here resided Colonel John Selwyn—an aide-de-camp of the great Duke of Marlborough, and the father of the memorable wit, George Selwyn—in whose house in Cleveland Row the celebrated personal encounter took place between Sir Robert Walpole, then Prime Minister, and Lord Townshend, one of the Secretaries of State. "My Lord," were Sir Robert's provoking words to his colleague, "for once there is no man's sincerity whom I so much doubt as your lordship's." Lord Townshend, who to many excellent qualities united a fiery and uncertain temperament, immediately seized the First Minister by the throat, when a struggle took place, which was followed by their severally relinquishing their grasp and laying their hands on their swords. Mrs. Selwyn, who was present, had run out in a fright to call in the palace guard, but was prevented by the celebrated Henry Pelham, by whose interposition the friends were subsequently reconciled.* According to Wraxall, Gay is supposed to have introduced this scene into the "Beggar's Opera," under the characters of Peachum and Lockit. Unfortunately, however, for the truth of the anecdote, the fracas between the two ministers of state did not take place till

* Coxe's "Life of Sir Robert Walpole."

the year 1729, whereas the "Beggar's Opera" at that time had had the run of the stage about a year.

The house in which this extraordinary scene took place was subsequently for many years the residence of George Selwyn, who died here on the 25th of January, 1791, penitent and devout. At No. 5, Cleveland Row, the author well remembers visiting a no less brilliant wit, Theodore Hook. But Cleveland Row and Cleveland Court have other eminent names associated with them. In Cleveland Row, for instance, at the Golden Ball, a tailor's—"the last door but one nearest the Green Park Wall"—William Mason, the poet, was lodging in 1767, and here also, in 1782, previously to his splendid victory over De Grasse, lived in great distress the illustrious naval hero, Lord Rodney. In Cleveland Court died, in 1739, Charles Jervas, the painter and correspondent of Pope; and here also, in 1805, died another celebrated wit of the last century, "Gilly" Williams, whose correspondence with his friend George Selwyn during twenty years has been given to the world.

Cleveland Row and Cleveland Court derive their names from Cleveland House, a large mansion which stood close by, but nearer the Green Park. Originally called Berkshire House, from its having been the residence of the Howards, Earls of Berkshire, it was purchased by Charles the Second, and presented to his beautiful mistress, Barbara Duchess of Cleveland. When, in 1691, the Dutch ambassadors arrived in England to congratulate King William and Mary on their coronation, it was to Cleveland House that they were conducted from the tower where they had landed; their *cortège* consisting of no fewer than sixteen of the royal pages and sixty running footmen in magnificent liveries. During the lifetime of the Duchess, a part of the property on which Cleveland House stood was sold by her and converted into smaller houses. The remaining part, in which she continued to reside herself, was afterwards bought by the Duke of Bridgewater, but was pulled down in our own time to make room for the splendid mansion erected near its site by the late Earl of Ellesmere.

Passing up St. James's Street, on the east side is King Street, containing the fashionable rooms opened in 1765 by Almack, the proprietor of the exclusive Almack's Club in Pall Mall. To the Earl of Hertford Horace Walpole writes on the 14th of February, 1765:—" The new assembly room at Almack's was opened the night before last, and they say is very magnificent, but it was empty. Half the town is ill with colds, and many were afraid to go, as the house is scarcely built yet. Almack advertised that it was built with hot bricks and boiling water. Think what a rage there must be for public places, if this notice, instead of terrifying, could draw anybody thither! They tell me the ceilings were dropping with wet; but can you believe me when I tell you the Duke of Cumberland was there? Nay, he had had a levee in the morning, and went to the opera before the assembly! There is a vast flight of steps, and he was forced to rest two or three times. If he died of it, it will sound very silly, when Hercules or Theseus ask him what he died of, to reply—' I caught my death on a damp staircase at a new club-room.'"

In King Street, on the 4th of May, 1749, Charlotte Smith, the novelist and poetess, was born; and lastly, No. 16 in this street is interesting as having been the residence of the present Emperor of the French, at the time of his quitting England to pursue his extraordinary fortunes across the channel.

Somewhat higher up St. James's Street is Little Ryder

Street, where Swift was residing in December, 1712.* Hence we pass into Bury Street, where the unfortunate Letitia Pilkington, the authoress of the well-known autobiography, informs us that she lodged in the time of her necessity. † Swift also had previously resided here in 1710, and from this street many of the most interesting of his letters to Stella are dated. "To-morrow," he writes to her, on the 20th of September, 1710, "I change my lodgings in Pall Mall for one in Bury Street, where I suppose I shall continue while in London;" and again he writes to her on the 29th of the month,—"I lodge in Bury Street, where I removed a week ago. I have the first floor, a dining-room and bed-chamber, *at eight shillings a week, plaguy dear*, but I spend nothing for eating, never go to a tavern, and very seldom in a coach; yet after all it will be expensive."

Another celebrated writer of the days of Queen Anne who lived in Bury Street, was Sir Richard Steele, whose residence, as we learn from himself, was "the third house, right hand, turning out of Jermyn Street." For a long time we find Bury Street the usual residence of Moore, the poet, during his periodical visits to London. In July, 1814, he was lodging at No. 33; and in June, 1817, George Crabbe, the poet, was lodging at 37, Bury Street. In March, 1833, Moore's lodgings were at 15, Duke Street, St. James's.

* "Journal to Stella," 12th December, 1712.
† See her curious "Memoirs of Herself," vol. ii. p. 47.

ST. JAMES'S SQUARE.

ST. JAMES'S SQUARE.—DUKE OF HAMILTON.—FREDERICK PRINCE OF WALES.—JOHNSON AND SAVAGE.—JERMYN STREET.—LORD ST. ALBANS.—SIR WALTER SCOTT.

ST. JAMES'S SQUARE, formerly a part of St. James's Fields, dates from the days of Charles the Second. It was commenced about the year 1676. King Street and Charles Street were named in compliment to that monarch, as Duke Street and York Street were named after his brother the Duke of York, afterwards James the Second. Diverging from the latter street is Appletree Yard—a name which still recalls the days when on its site blossomed the apple-orchards of St. James's Fields.

Fashionable as St. James's Square became as it approached completion, there were still many of the ancient nobility who preferred retaining their old family mansions in districts of London which may now sound strange to fastidious ears. For instance, so late as the year 1783, the Duke of Newcastle lived in Clerkenwell Close, the Earl of Bridgewater in the Barbican, the Earl of Thanet in Aldersgate Street, and Lord Grey of Werk in Charterhouse Close. The Dukes of Norfolk and Beaufort, and the Earls of Bedford and Salisbury, still retained the houses of their forefathers in the Strand; the Marquis of Winchester, and the Earls of Cardigan and Powis resided in Lincoln's Inn Fields, and the Earls of Clare, Anglesea, and Craven in Drury Lane.*

* Chamberlayne's "Angliæ Notitia for 1783."

Among the names of the earliest inhabitants of St. James's Square are those of "Madam Davis" and "Madam Churchill."* Of these two ladies, the former was the beautiful actress, Mary Davis, whom Charles the Second fell in love with, and induced to quit the stage and become his mistress. The latter was Arabella Churchill, mistress of James the Second when Duke of York, a lady principally remarkable as having been the sister of the great Duke of Marlborough and the mother of James Duke of Berwick. The residences of both ladies in 1677 were on the west side of the square. In this square also resided another mistress of James the Second, Catherine Sedley, a lady of more wit than beauty, and of more indelicacy than either. When James—worn out by the reproaches of his young wife, Mary of Modena, and by the exhortations of the priests—determined on separating from his celebrated mistress, he created her Baroness of Darlington and Countess of Dorchester, and transferred her from her apartments in the royal palace of Whitehall to the house which we find her subsequently occupying in St. James's Square. "I imagine your Countess of Dorchester," runs a letter dated April 6th, 1686, "will speedily move hitherwards, for her house is furnishing very fine in St. James's Square, and a seat taken for her in the new consecrated St. Anne's Church." †

"Yet Vane could tell what ills from Beauty spring,
And Sedley cursed the form that pleased a king."

On the west side of St. James's Square, and one of its earliest inhabitants, resided the poet, wit, and philanthropist, Charles Earl of Dorset, Rochester's—

"——best good man with the worst-natured muse."

Here also lived William Bentinck, Earl of Portland, the

* Cunningham's "London;" Art. St. James's Square.
† The Ellis Correspondence.

Dutch favourite of William the Third, and here his body lay in state previously to its interment in Westminster Abbey.

In the "New View of London," published in 1708, St. James's Square is described as "a very pleasant, large, and beautiful square, mostly inhabited by the prime quality; all very fine spacious buildings, except that side toward Pall Mall." At this period there were residing here, on the north side, the Dukes of Northumberland and Ormond, and the Earl of Pembroke—on the east side, the Earls of Sunderland and Kent, and Lords Ossulston and Woodstock—and, on the west side, the Duke of Norfolk and Lord Torrington.

The Norfolk family subsequently removed to the east side of the square. The site of Ormond House, the residence of the great Duke of Ormond, is pointed out by its stabling which stood at the back of it, and which still stands in Ormond Yard, running to the west out of York Street. On the site of the east corner house of York Street and the square (No. 8) lived and died, in 1704, Henry Sidney, created Earl of Romney, the "handsome Sidney" of De Grammont's Memoirs. Close by, also on the north side (No. 6), is Bristol House, in which, or on its site, have resided the Hervey family from the time of Charles the Second. In 1677, for instance, it was the residence of John Hervey, the patron of the poet Cowley, and the friend of the accomplished Robert Sydney, Earl of Leicester. "He was one," writes Burnet, "whom the king (Charles II.) loved personally, and yet upon a great occasion he voted against that which the king desired, so the king chid him severely for it. Next day, another important question falling in, he voted as the king would have him; so the king took notice of it at night, and said, 'You were not against me to-day.'—'No, sir,' he replied, 'to-day I voted against my conscience.'" At a later date Bristol House was the residence of John Lord Hervey, the "Spores" of Pope's verse, and the husband of Mary Lepel.

To his house in St. James's Square were conveyed the remains of the unfortunate James Duke of Hamilton, after he had been killed in his sanguinary duel with Lord Mohun. The duke's body, it will be remembered, was brought home in his coach while the Duchess was asleep. "They have removed the poor Duchess," writes Swift, "to a lodging in the neighbourhood, where I have been with her two hours, and am just come away. I never saw so melancholy a scene. She has moved my very soul. The lodging was inconvenient, and they would have removed her to another; but I would not suffer it, because it had no room backward, and she must have been tortured with the noise of the Grub Street screamers mentioning her husband's murder in her ears."*

Sir Robert Walpole lived at one period of his life in St. James's Square, while, nearly opposite to him, on the other side of the square, lived the celebrated Lord Chesterfield. Here, too, lived Pope's accomplished friend, Allen Earl Bathurst.

On the east side of St. James's Square stands Norfolk House (No. 21), the residence of the Dukes of Norfolk. The present house, which was built in 1742, stands on the site of an old mansion, the residence, up to the year 1683, of Henry Jermyn, Earl of St. Albans, the reputed husband of Henrietta Maria, Queen of Charles the First. When, in 1737, George the Second, in consequence of the misconduct of his eldest son, Frederick Prince of Wales, issued his peremptory order to him to remove with his family from St. James's Palace, we find the disgraced Prince taking up his

* "Journal to Stella," November 15th, 1712.

abode in Norfolk House, which thenceforth became the rallying-point of the Opposition, and the centre of political intrigue. Thus it was that, on the 4th of June, 1738, Norfolk House came to be the birthplace of King George the Third. So suddenly, it appears, had the Princess been taken in labour that the Archbishop of Canterbury, Dr. Potter, was the only great personage of State who arrived in time to be present at the birth. "The identical bed," writes Wraxall, "in which the Princess of Wales was delivered, is now at the Duke of Norfolk's seat of Worksop, in the county of Nottingham; and it forcibly proves the rapid progress of domestic elegance and ease within the last eighty years. Except that the furniture is of green silk, the bed has nothing splendid about it, and would hardly be esteemed fit for the accommodation of a person of ordinary condition in the present times."*

On the same side of the Square as Norfolk House, is the residence of Viscount Falmouth (No. 2), the iron street-posts in front of which are cannon captured by the gallant Admiral Boscawen in Anson's naval action off Cape Finisterre.

On the west side of St. James's Square either stand, or have lately stood, the residences of many persons eminent in modern times. For instance, in the north-west corner house (No. 11), now the Windham Club, resided at different times the amiable statesman and scholar, William Windham— John Duke of Roxburghe, from whose "Bibliotheca" the Roxburghe Club took its rise—and Lord Chief Justice Ellenborough. The adjoining house (No. 12), now the London Library, was the residence of Jeffrey Lord Amherst, when Commander-in-Chief. On the site of No. 13 stood Lichfield House, formerly the residence of Athenian Stuart, and since

* "Wraxall's Memoirs," vol. ii., p. 5, 3rd edition.

famous as the scene of the "Lichfield House Compact" between the Whigs and Daniel O'Connell. It was to this house—at which the Prince Regent happened to be dining at the time—that, on the 20th of June, 1815, the captured French eagles, just arrived from Waterloo, were brought to him in triumph, and from its balcony it was that he displayed them to the huzzaing crowd below. On the site of the present East India United Service Club stood Nos. 14 and 15, the one the residence of Sir Philip Francis and the other of Lord Chancellor Thurlow. It was at the drawing-room windows of No. 14 that Queen Caroline—to whom, during the days of her memorable trial, the house had been lent by Lady Francis—used to display herself to the crowds that daily came to swell her tumultuous progresses to the House of Lords. Curiously enough, No. 16, the next house but one to her, was at this time the residence of one of the Queen's most formidable enemies, Lord Castlereagh, who, at its threshold, was more than once in danger from the fury of the populace.

It was round St. James's Square, as Dr. Johnson told Sir Joshua Reynolds, that he walked one night for hours with his unfortunate friend, Savage the poet; neither of them having a shilling in the world with which to procure a bed. The statue in the centre of the square, it may be mentioned, is that of King William the Third.

From St. James's Square we pass eastward into Charles Street, interesting from its having been for a time the residence of Edmund Burke. Here it was that Crabbe addressed to him that touching letter, and was admitted to that affectionate interview which happily so entirely revolutionized the poet's fortunes. Another eminent inhabitant of Charles Street was John Hoppner the portrait painter, who died here, at No. 18, in 1810.

Jermyn Street and St. Albans' Place—running out of Charles Street—derive their names from the before-mentioned Henry Jermyn, Earl of St. Albans', the garden of whose mansion in St. James's Square extended so far back as to cover the site of the present Waterloo Place. In Jermyn Street, as we learn from his correspondence, Sir Isaac Newton was residing in 1699. Here Gray, the poet, usually took up his abode during his occasional visits to London, and from here, in a letter dated the 3rd of August, 1768, he informed his correspondent, Mr. Nicholls, that the king had conferred upon him the Professorship of History at the University of Cambridge. The house in which he lodged was at the east end of the street.

In some slight degree Jermyn Street is connected with the breaking out of the great French Revolution. For instance, on the 24th of September, 1789, not long after the capture of the Bastille, one of Lord Auckland's correspondents writes to him: "Saintefoy has been out of town these few days, but I believe he is shortly to return to Grenier's Hotel, in Jermyn Street, the grand resort of the illustrious fugitives from France, where among others is Madame de Boufflers and the Countess Emilie."*

In Jermyn Street we find Richard Brinsley Sheridan occupying a house in 1793; and here, in the earlier period of his professional career—in a house opposite to St. James's Church—lived Sir Thomas Lawrence.

No. 76, Jermyn Street, formerly the St. James's Hotel, was the scene of almost the latest sufferings, and received nearly the last sigh, of Sir Walter Scott. When that great man, by his own particular wish, was hurried back from the shores of the Mediterranean to breathe his last at his beloved Abbotsford, it was here that he passed the three

* "Auckland Correspondence," vol. ii., p. 352.

melancholy weeks which intervened between his arrival in London and his departure for the banks of the Tweed.* "When we reached the hotel," writes Mr. Lockhart, "he recognized us with many marks of tenderness, but signified that he was totally exhausted; so no attempt was made to remove him farther, and he was put to bed immediately. To his children, all assembled once more about him, he repeatedly gave his blessing in a very solemn manner, as if expecting immediate death; but he was never in a condition for conversation, and sunk either into sleep or delirious stupor upon the slightest effort." The account of Fergusson, who was seldom absent from Sir Walter's pillow during his sojourn in Jermyn Street, is extremely interesting. "When I saw Sir Walter," he says, "he was lying in the second-floor back room of the St. James's Hotel in Jermyn Street, in a state of stupor, from which, however, he could be roused for a moment by being addressed, and then he recognized those about him, but immediately relapsed. I think I never saw anything more magnificent than the symmetry of his colossal bust, as he lay on the pillow with his chest and neck exposed. During the time he was in Jermyn Street he was calm but never collected, and in general either in absolute stupor or in a waking dream. He never seemed to know where he was, but imagined himself to be still in the steamboat. The rattling of carriages, and the noises of the street,

* Just before Sir Walter Scott set out for the Continent, in hopes of regaining that health which never returned to him, he dined with the late Mr. Murray in Albemarle Street. For some time he joined cheerfully in conversation, but suddenly a thought seemed to strike him, and an expression of melancholy passed over his face. After a short pause he said, "It is singular that both Fielding and Smollett should have died in foreign countries;" evidently reflecting on his own shattered state of health, and foreseeing that the fate of his two illustrious brother novelists might in all probability be his own.

sometimes disturbed this illusion, and then he fancied himself at the polling of Jedburgh, where he had been insulted and stoned. . . . . At length his constant yearning to return to Abbotsford induced his physicians to consent to his removal; a consent which, the moment it was notified to him, seemed to infuse new vigour into his frame. It was on a calm clear afternoon of the 7th of July that every preparation was made for his embarkation on board the steamboat. He was placed on a chair by his faithful servant Nicholson, half-dressed, and loosely wrapt in a quilted dressing-gown. He requested Lockhart and myself to wheel him towards the light of the open window, and we both remarked the vigorous lustre of his eye. He sat there silently gazing on space for more than half an hour, apparently wholly occupied with his own thoughts, and having no distinct perception of where he was, or how he came there. He suffered himself to be lifted into his carriage, which was surrounded by a crowd, among whom were many gentlemen on horseback, who had loitered about to gaze on the scene. His children were deeply affected, and Mrs. Lockhart trembled from head to foot, and wept bitterly. Thus surrounded by those nearest to him, he alone was unconscious of the cause or the depth of their grief, and while yet alive seemed to be carried to his grave."*

On the 7th of July, 1832, Sir Walter embarked on board the steam-vessel for Scotland. On the 11th his eye once more brightened up as it caught the familiar waters of the Tweed, and when at length he recognized the towers of his own Abbotsford, he sprang up in the carriage with a cry of delight. On the 21st of September the mighty master of romance and song had ceased to exist.

* Lockhart's "Life of Sir W. Scott."

From the interesting researches of Mr. Peter Cunningham we further learn that, from 1675 to 1681, the great Duke of Marlborough, then the young and handsome Colonel John Churchill, lived on the south side of Jermyn Street, about five doors from St. James's Street; that, in the years 1681-83, Frances Stuart, *la Belle Stuart* of De Grammont's Memoirs, was residing on the north side near Eagle Passage; that, in 1683, three doors from the Duchess, lived Simon Verelst, the painter; and, lastly, that in Jermyn Street, in 1721, died Secretary Craggs, the friend of Addison and Pope.

In Jermyn Street died, in 1809, Sir George Baker, physician in ordinary to George the Third.

PALL MALL.

FORMER STATE OF PALL MALL.—SIR THOMAS WYATT.—MURDER OF THYNNE. —CHARLES THE SECOND'S MISTRESSES.—BEAU FIELDING'S STRANGE ADVENTURE.—SCHOMBERG HOUSE.—STAR AND GARTER.—DUKE OF BUCKINGHAM'S RESIDENCE.—CARLTON HOUSE.

PALL MALL—sometimes styled Catherine Street in the reign of Charles the Second—derives its name from a foreign game, so called from *Palla* a ball, and *Maglia* a mallet or racket, which was introduced into England some time before the middle of the seventeenth century. Up to the time of the Restoration, when Charles the Second formed a new Mall in St. James's Park, the game used to be played on the site of the present street, on each side of which a row of elm trees then extended. So late, in fact, as about the year 1660, the tract of ground on which Pall Mall, St. James's Square, and Piccadilly now stand, consisted of open fields; St. James's Street alone being partially built. The only buildings to be seen west of Charing Cross were a small church, the name of which is not remembered,—the conduit, a small Gothic structure, which stood nearly on the site of St. James's Square,—and a house of public refreshment.

It was along the site of the present Pall Mall that Sir Thomas Wyatt marched his troops on the 6th of February, 1554. The Earl of Pembroke, who advanced to oppose him at the head of the royal forces, planted his artillery on the high ground where Hay Hill and Piccadilly now stand, when a piece of the Queen's ordnance, we are told, slew three of Wyatt's followers in a rank, and after carrying off their heads passed through the wall into the Park. "The same night," writes Stow, "about five of the clock, a trumpeter went about and warned all horsemen and men of arms to be at St. James's Fields, and all footmen to be there by six of the clock on the next morning. The Queen's scout, upon his return to the Court, declared Wyatt's being at Brentford, which sudden news made all the Court wonderfully afraid. Drums went through London at four of the clock in the morning, commanding all soldiers to armour, and so to Charing Cross. Wyatt, hearing the Earl of Pembroke was come into the field, stayed at Knightsbridge until day, where his men being very weary with travel of that night and the day before, and also partly feebled and faint, having received small sustenance since their coming out of Southwark, rested. There was no small ado in London; and likewise the Tower made great preparation of defence. By ten of the clock the Earl of Pembroke had set his troop of horsemen on the hill in the highway, above the new bridge over against St. James's; his footmen were set in two battles, somewhat lower and nearer Charing Cross, at the lane turning down the brick wall from Islington ward, where he also placed certain other horsemen; and he had planted his ordnance upon the hill side. In the mean season, Wyatt and his company planted his ordnance upon a hill beyond St. James's, almost over against the Park corner; and himself, after a few words spoken to his soldiers, came down the old lane on foot, hard by the court gate at St. James's, with four or five ancients, his men marching in good array."

In the mean time, "the great ordnance shooting off freshly

on both sides," Wyatt advanced from Hyde Park Corner, apparently down Constitution Hill, passing along by the wall towards Charing Cross. "At Charing Cross," continues Stow, "there stood Sir John Gage, Lord-Chamberlain, with the Guard, and a number of others, being almost a thousand; the which, upon Wyatt's coming, shot at his company, but at the last fled to the Court gates, which certain pursued, and forced with shot to shut the Court gates * against them. In this repulse, the said Lord Chamberlain and others were so amazed, that many cried treason in the Court, and had thought that the Earl of Pembroke, who was assaulting the tail of his enemies, had gone to Wyatt, taking his part against the Queen. There was running and crying out of ladies and gentlemen, shutting of doors and windows, and such a shrieking and noise as was wonderful to hear. The noise of women and children," adds Stow, "when the conflict was at Charing Cross was so great, that it was heard at the top of the White Tower, and also the great shot was well discerned there out of St. James's Fields." On the leads of St. James's Palace stood the Marquis of Northampton, Sir Nicholas Penn, Sir Thomas Pope, and others, anxious spectators of the conflict. Wyatt passed on to Ludgate, but his followers, finding that no persons of consequence joined him, insensibly deserted him, and he was at length seized by Sir Maurice Berkeley near Temple Bar. He was beheaded on Tower Hill, on the 11th of April, 1554, and his quarters were set up in different parts of the metropolis. His head was fixed to the public gallows on Hay Hill, whence it was shortly afterwards stolen by some of his relatives or friends.

The next incident of interest connected with Pall Mall is the murder, on the 12th of February, 1682, of Thomas

* The gates apparently of Whitehall Palace.

Thynne, the princely Lord of Longleat, and the "Issachar" of Dryden's "Absalom and Achitophel." The scene of this celebrated tragedy was nearly opposite to the entrance of the present Opera arcade, in those days apparently a dark and retired spot. The story is well known. Elizabeth, heiress of Jocelyn Percy, eleventh Earl of Northumberland, had been married when a mere child to Henry Cavendish, Earl of Ogle, son and heir of. Henry Duke of Newcastle, who died in 1680, leaving her a "virgin widow" at an early age. Shortly afterwards she was contracted by her grandmother, the old Countess of Northumberland, to Thynne, on the condition, however, that, on account of her extreme youth, a twelvemonth should elapse before the consummation of the marriage. In the mean time Count Konigsmark, an elder brother of the reputed lover of the ill-fated Sophia Dorothea of Zell, had conceived the daring project of marrying the heiress of the Percys, and, as a preliminary step, decided on the murder of Thynne. With this purpose in view he engaged the services of three foreign adventurers—Captain Vratz, a German; Lieutenant Stern, a Swede; and Borotski, a Pole; who, on a winter's evening, between seven and eight o'clock, posted themselves on horseback at a spot where they had ascertained that the equipage of Thynne would shortly pass. As soon as the coach appeared in sight, the three men rode up to the window, and by their imposing attitude easily compelled the coachman to stop. Only one shot was fired, which was from a musketoon by Borotski; but so sure was the aim, that as many as five bullets entered the body of his unfortunate victim. "I happened," writes Reresby in his Memoirs, "to be at Court that evening, when the King, hearing the news, seemed greatly concerned at it, not only for the horror of the action itself, which was shocking to his natural disposition, but also for fear the turn the anti-court party might give thereto. I left the Court, and was just stepping into bed when Mr. Thynne's gentleman came to me to grant him an hue and cry, and immediately at his heels comes the Duke of Monmouth's page, to desire me to come to him at Mr. Thynne's lodgings, sending his coach for me, which I made use of accordingly. I found there his Grace, surrounded by several lords and gentlemen, Mr. Thynne's friends, and Mr. Thynne himself mortally wounded with five shots from a blunderbuss."

The following epigram, in allusion to the assassination of Thynne, appears to have been much in vogue at the time :—

"Here lies Tom Thynne of Longleat Hall,
Who never would have miscarried,
Had he married the woman he lay withal,
Or lain with the woman he married."

"Two anecdotes," says Horace Walpole, "are attached to these lines. Miss Trevor, one of the maids of honour to Catherine of Portugal, wife of Charles the Second, having discovered the Duke of Monmouth in bed with a lady, the Duke excited Mr. Thynne to seduce Miss Trevor. She was 'the woman he lay withal.' 'The woman he married' was the great heiress to whom he was affianced when he was killed by Count Konigsmark in Pall Mall." With some difficulty the Count and his three auxiliaries were taken into custody, Captain Vratz being the last who was captured, in the house of a Swedish doctor in Leicester Fields. They were severally tried at Hicks's Hall, when Konigsmark, after some hesitation, was acquitted. The remaining three were found guilty, and, on the 10th of March, 1682, suffered the full penalty of the law at the scene of their offence in Pall Mall.

From a small tract* drawn up by the celebrated Bishop Burnet, who attended the criminals in their last moments, it appears that Stern and Borotski admitted the justice of their punishment and died penitent. Vratz, however, persisted to the last in affirming that he had no worse intention than to challenge Thynne to single combat, adding that the fact of Borotski having fired the fatal shot was altogether from a misapprehension of his orders. On Burnet attempting to impress him with a due sense of the heinousness of his crime, "he considered it to be sufficient," he said, "if he confessed his sins to God," adding that he "thought it was a piece of popery in the Bishop to press him to confess." He expressed his firm conviction that he should be "received into eternal happiness," stating it to be his opinion of the next state, that the only punishment of the damned would be their exclusion from the presence of God, and their seeing others happier than themselves. To Dr. Horneck, another clergyman who attended him, he expressed even more extraordinary opinions. "He was confident," he said, "that God would consider a gentleman, and deal with him suitably to the condition and profession he had placed him in, and that he would not take it ill if a soldier, who lived by his sword, revenged an affront offered him by another."

Burnet had more than once warned him against a false affectation of courage, which must necessarily desert him in his last moments. When, however, finally met on the scaffold in Pall Mall, "he smiled on me," says the Bishop, "and said that I should see it was not a false bravery, but that he was fearless to the last. It is certain that never man died with more resolution and less signs of fear, or the

* "An Account of the Deportment of Captain Vratz, Lieutenant Stern, and George Borotski, the murderers of Thomas Thynne, Esq., both in the prison and at the execution."

least disorder. His carriage, both in the cart as he was led along, and at the place of execution, was astonishing. He was not only undaunted, but looked cheerful and smiled often. When the rope was put about his neck, he did not change colour nor tremble; his legs were firm under him. He looked often about on those that stood in balconies and windows, and seemed to fix his eyes on some persons. Three or four times he smiled. He would not cover his face as the rest did, but continued in that state, often looking up to heaven, with a cheerfulness in his countenance, and a little motion of his hands." "The Captain," writes Reresby in his "Memoirs," "died without the least symptom of fear; and seeing me in my coach as he passed by in the cart, he made a bow to me with the most steady countenance, as he did to several of the spectators he knew, before he was turned off." Stern, on the scaffold, complained that he died for a man's fortune whom he never spoke to, for a woman whom he never saw, and for a dead man whom he never had a sight of.*

One of the first inhabitants of Pall Mall appears to have been Nell Gwynn, whose residence, in 1670, was on the north side of the then unfinished street. "Nell Gwynn's house," writes Pennant, "is the first good one on the left hand of St. James's Square as we enter from Pall Mall. The back room was, within memory, entirely of looking-glass, as was said to have been the ceiling. Over the chimney was her picture; and that of her sister was in a third room." In 1671 she removed to the south side of the street, where she resided till the time of her death, in a house, overlooking St. James's Park, which had been built for her on a spot of ground granted her by her royal lover, Charles the Second. On the 7th of March, 1771, Mr. Ewin writes

* Scott's Dryden.

to Granger the historian, "My friend, Dr. Heberden, has built a fine house in Pall Mall, on the palace side; he told me it was the only freehold house on that side; that it was given by a long lease by Charles the Second to Nell Gwynn, and upon her discovering it to be only lease under the Crown, she returned him the lease and conveyance, saying she had always *conveyed free* under the crown, and always would; and would not accept it till it was conveyed free to her by an act of parliament, made on and for that purpose. Upon Nelly's death it was sold, and has been conveyed free ever since."* The house in question—in which the light-hearted actress toyed with the Merry Monarch and laughed at his gay courtiers—stood on the site of the present No. 79, Pall Mall, and is said to be still the only freehold residence on the Park, or south side of the street. Here, in 1687, she died.

Pall Mall is not very reputably connected with three other mistresses of Charles the Second—Mary Knight, famous for the lustre of her beauty and the exquisite sweetness of her voice—the lovely and eccentric Hortense Mancini, Duchess of Mazarine, and the Duchess of Cleveland. The Viscountess de Longueville, who resided in the days of William the Third at the house of her father in Pall Mall, well remembered the celebrated Monsieur de St. Evremond —"a little old man in his black silk coif"—being carried every morning by her window in a sedan-chair to the house of the Duchess of Mazarine. He always took with him a pound of butter, made in his own little dairy, for her grace's breakfast.† The death of the Duchess, in 1699, appears to have caused great distress to St. Evremond. In a letter to M. Silvester, he writes:—" Had the poor Duchess of Maza-

* "Granger's Letters."
† Oldys, MS. notes to Langbaine.

rine been alive, she would have had peaches, of which I should not have failed to have shared; she would have had truffles, which we should have shared together; not to mention the carps of Newhall."

The extraordinary salutation with which the Duchess of Cleveland greeted the poet William Wycherley, in Pall Mall, is well known. Wycherley, then perhaps the handsomest man of the day, had just risen into reputation by the success of his comedy, " Love in a Wood, or St. James's Park," which was first acted in 1672. He was passing along Pall Mall, when he encountered the equipage of the Duchess of Cleveland, to whom he was entirely unknown. To his astonishment she thrust her head out of the carriage window, and exclaimed—" You, Wycherley, you are a son of a ———." The poet was at first somewhat confused, but remembering the stanza in a song introduced into his " Love in a Wood,"—

> " Where parents are slaves,
>   Their brats cannot be any other ;
> Great wits and great braves,
>   Have always a punk for their mother ;"

—he considered the greeting of the Duchess as a compliment to his wit, and immediately drove after her carriage into the Park.

In Pall Mall, in 1683, was born the fascinating actress, Mrs. Oldfield.

One would like to be able to point out in this interesting street the house of the celebrated Beau Fielding—the " Orlando the Fair" of the 'Tatler,'—to which the beautiful opera singer, the Margarita, was summoned to sing " Ianthe the Lovely," previously to his passing his wedding-night with the fictitious widow of Waddon Hall. In the romance of real life there is scarcely a story more amusing or more remarkable than that of this spoiled and handsome coxcomb. Having ruined himself by the splendour of his equipages and his addiction to the gaming-table, he proposed to repair his broken fortunes by uniting himself to a wealthy wife. The lady on whom his choice fell was a rich widow, a Mrs. Deleau, with whom he had no previous acquaintance. Having taken the preliminary step of parading his handsome person before her windows, he contrived to make the acquaintance of a Mrs. Charlotte Villars, a woman of indifferent repute, to whom, on his receiving her assurance that she was on intimate terms with the widow, he guaranteed the sum of five hundred pounds to be paid to her in the event of Mrs. Deleau becoming his wife. Thus commissioned, Mrs. Villars succeeded in securing the services of a young woman, named Mary Wadsworth, who is said to have somewhat resembled the widow in person, and whose part she carefully instructed her how to play. The rest of the scene is laid in Fielding's apartments in Pall Mall, to which he was told that the coy widow had at length consented to be conducted in order to become his wife. "He desired," runs the evidence of Mrs. Villars in the State Trials, "that I would bring her to his lodgings on Lord Mayor's day, at night, which I did about nine o'clock, in a mourning-coach. Mr. Fielding was not at home, but came immediately. When he came in he fell upon his knees and kissed her, and expressed abundance of fond expressions. He asked her why she stayed so long, and whether she loved singing. He said he would send for Margarita to come up. When she came up, Mr. Fielding bade her sing the two songs he loved; which she did: the one was 'Charming Creature,' and the other, 'Ianthe the Lovely.' After which Mr. Fielding sent for two pints of wine, and some plum-cakes." The evidence of the beautiful Margarita,* the *prima donna* of her day, is no less curious. "I remember," she says, "Mr. Fielding sent for me to his lodgings in Pall Mall. I sang several Italian songs, and one English, and that was 'Ianthe the Lovely.' He desired me to sing that song, 'Ianthe the Lovely,' for he said he had the original of it, and had translated it out of the Greek."

The further evidence of Mrs. Villars affords a curious picture of a clandestine marriage in the days of Queen Anne. "The priest," she says, "called for water, salt, and rosemary, to make holy water. Boucher (Fielding's man-servant) brought up water and salt, but could get no rosemary. Mr. Fielding and I received it at the dining-room door. Then Mr. Fielding locked the door, and took the key on the inside. Mr. Fielding asked Mrs. Wadsworth whether it should be done in the bed-chamber or dining-room. Mrs. Wadsworth agreed it should be in the bed-chamber. There were none present but Mr. Fielding, Mrs. Wadsworth, the priest, and myself. The priest made holy water, and blessed it. Then he set Mrs. Wadsworth at the right of Mr. Fielding. The priest stood before them, and read the ceremony in Latin, as I understood; and Mrs. Wadsworth said she was not yet satisfied he was a priest. Says Mr. Fielding to her, 'Do you think, my dear, that I would have anybody to do this business but the holy father?' Mrs. Wadsworth was well satisfied till he came to that part—'Wilt thou have this

---

* The Margarita is mentioned by Swift in a letter to Stella from Windsor : "We have a music-meeting in our town to-night. I went to the rehearsal of it, and there was Margarita and her sister, and another drab, and a parcel of fiddlers ; I was weary, and would not go to the meeting, which I am sorry for, because I heard it was a great assembly."—"Journal to Stella," 6th June, 1711. "According to Mrs. Manley, the Earl of Nottingham purchased the favours of the Margarita for £4000, and afterwards bought her silence for a similar sum."—"New Atlantis," vol. i. pp. 187, 188.

woman to thy wedded wife?' She desired it might be spoken in English by him. He did so. Mr. Fielding said, 'Yes, with all my heart.' He asked the lady, then, if she would have this gentleman for her husband. She said, 'Yes,' faintly. 'But,' says Mr. Fielding, 'you must speak it so earnestly as I do; you must say with all my heart and soul;' which she did. Then the priest blessed the ring, and gave it to Mr. Fielding to put on the lady's finger. He said something in Latin, but what it was I know not. Then we went into the dining-room. Boucher brought up wine, and when all had drunk, the priest was discharged."

Last, and not the least curious, is the evidence of Fielding's servant, Boucher. "My master," he said, "ordered me to be at home and get clean sheets, wax candles, and sconces, and fires in both the rooms. He told me some ladies would be there that night, and ordered me, if he was not at home when they came, to tell them that he would be there presently. Accordingly they came, and he was not at home, but in a little time he came, and went up to them. Some little time after that he came down stairs in great haste, and said, 'Boucher, go and speak a dish of pickles.' I did so, and brought over a cloth, and the rest of the things, and left them in the window. I stayed by the stairs till he came back in a hackney-coach with a priest along with him, in a long gown and long beard, and a fur cap. I knew him to belong to the Emperor's envoy. Then I was ordered to set the table, and glasses, and wine, and things of that kind upon the sideboard. I waited at table all the while. When supper was over, Mr. Fielding ordered me to go down and fetch water, salt, and rosemary. I went and got water and salt, but could get no rosemary. Then I was ordered to go down, and they were locked in about three-quarters of an hour. When this was over, the priest went away. Presently after, says Mr. Fielding—' Take the sheets from my bed, and lay them on the other bed for Mrs. Villars, and see that none lie there.' Mrs. Villars, in the mean time, put the lady to bed. When I came down to tell them of it, I saw the lady's clothes on a stool in the chamber, and Mrs. Villars folding them up and laying them in another room. I then lighted Mrs. Villars to bed, and then went to bed myself. In the morning I was called to make a fire. I then perceived this lady and Mr. Fielding in bed together. The fire being made, I was ordered to get a hackney-coach. Mrs. Villars dressed the lady hastily, and she was carried away in the hackney-coach."

It could have been no great length of time before Fielding detected the audacious trick which had been played upon him, inasmuch as a little more than a fortnight afterwards he married the celebrated Duchess of Cleveland, then verging on old age. On the 4th of December, 1706, after a lapse of about a year, he was tried for bigamy at the bar of the Old Bailey, and having been found guilty, was sentenced to be burnt in the hand, but was subsequently pardoned. His marriage with the Duchess of Cleveland was formally annulled in the Arches Court on the 23rd of May, 1707.

Schomberg House, Nos. 81 and 82, Pall Mall, is still one of the most striking-looking objects in the street. It was built by the Duke of Schomberg in the reign of William the Third, apparently by Charles, the second Duke, the son of the celebrated German favourite of William, who fell at the battle of the Boyne at the age of eighty-one. Schomberg House, as appears by a letter dated the 31st of October, 1760, from Horace Walpole to Montagu, subsequently became the residence of the celebrated William Duke of Cumberland, the victor of Culloden. It was afterwards inhabited by John

Astley the painter—commonly called "Beau Astley"—who divided it into three different residences, reserving the centre for himself, which he fitted up in a very whimsical manner. In this centre part subsequently resided Richard Cosway, the well-known miniature painter, and here after he had outlived his ninetieth year, "he used," we are told, "to hold up his palsied right hand, that had painted lords and ladies for upwards of sixty years, and smile with unabated good-humour at the vanity of human wishes."* In the west wing of Schomberg house, now no longer standing, lived the celebrated painter Thomas Gainsborough.

The following curious notice of Pall Mall in 1703 is from the pen of Defoe:—"I am lodged in the street called Pall Mall, the ordinary residence of all strangers, because of its vicinity to the Queen's Palace, the Park, the Parliament House, the theatres, and the chocolate and coffee-houses, where the best company frequent. If you would know our manner of living, 'tis thus: we rise by nine, and those that frequent great men's levees find entertainment at them till eleven, or, as at Holland, go to tea-tables. About twelve, the *beau-monde* assembles in several coffee or chocolate houses; the best of which are the Cocoa-Tree,† and White's chocolate houses, St. James's, the Smyrna, Mrs. Rockford's, and the British coffee-houses; and all these so near one another, that in less than an hour you see the company of them all. We are carried to these places in sedan chairs, which are here very cheap, a guinea a week, or a shilling per hour; and your chairmen serve you for porters to run on errands, as your gondoliers do at Venice."

---

* "London Magazine," vol. vi. p. 410.

† From a lease in the author's possession, dated 1760, and signed by the Duke of York, it appears that a house on the south side of Pall Mall was then known as the Cocoa-Tree Chocolate House.

The sign of the Star and Garter, immediately opposite Schomberg House, still points out the site of the fashionable tavern which bore the same name in the days of Queen Anne. It was here that the celebrated club of which Swift was a member occasionally assembled, and which consisted of the most eminent men of rank and genius in that remarkable period. To Stella Swift writes on the 20th of March, 1711-12: "I made our society change their house, and we met together at the Star and Garter in the Pall Mall; Lord Arran was president. The other dog was so extravagant in his bills, that for four dishes and four, first and second course, *without wine or dessert*, he charged twenty-one pounds six shillings and eightpence to the Duke of Ormond." This sum is not a little exorbitant, if we remember that Swift mentions a party of *nine* as constituting a large meeting at the club, and especially when we consider the difference of prices between the early part of the last century and the present day. In 1763 we find a club still held at the Star and Garter, consisting of George Selwyn, Gilly Williams, and other men of wit and fashion of the last century.*

At the Star and Garter took place the famous duel between William, fifth Lord Byron, great-uncle to the poet, and Mr. Chaworth, on the 26th of January, 1765. Horace Walpole writes to the Earl of Hertford the next day : "The following is the account nearest the truth that I can learn of the fatal duel last night. A club of Nottinghamshire gentlemen had dined at the Star and Garter, and there had been a dispute between the combatants whether Lord Byron, who took no care of his game, or Mr. Chaworth, who was active in the association, had most game on their manor. The company, however, had apprehended no consequences, and

* "Selwyn Correspondence."

parted at eight o'clock; but Lord Byron, stepping into an empty chamber, and sending the drawer for Mr. Chaworth, or calling him thither himself, took the candle from the waiter, and bidding Mr. Chaworth defend himself, drew his sword. Mr. Chaworth, who was an excellent fencer, ran Lord Byron through the sleeve of his coat, and then received a wound fourteen inches deep into his body. He was carried to his house in Berkeley Street, made his will with the greatest composure, and dictated a paper which, they say, allows it was a fair duel, and died at nine this morning." The duel seems to have produced a long feud between the neighbouring families of Byron and Chaworth, nor was it apparently till the great poet succeeded as the lord of Newstead Abbey, that a Byron was again received as a cherished guest at Annesley Hall. The romantic love of Lord Byron for the heiress of the Chaworths is well known, and the feud which had divided the families is more than once referred to in his writings. In "The Dream," the most pathetic and one of the most beautiful of his compositions, he says of his first love:

> "Her sighs were not for him; to her he was
> Even as a brother—but no more; 'twas much,
> For brotherless she was, save in the name
> Her infant friendship had bestowed on him;
> Herself the solitary scion left
> Of a time-honoured race. It was a name
> Which pleased him, and yet pleased him not—and why?
> Time taught him a deep answer."

And he says in prose, scarcely less beautiful: "Our union would have healed feuds in which blood had been shed by our fathers; it would have joined lands broad and rich; it would have joined at least *one* heart and two persons not ill matched in years,—and—and—and—what has been the result?"

In Pall Mall stood the Smyrna Coffee House, a fashionable resort of the wits of the reign of Queen Anne, but the site we are unable to point out.

On the south side of Pall Mall, now occupied by a portion of the War Department, stands the former mansion of the Grenvilles, Earls Temple, and Dukes of Buckingham, in which so often have assembled the wit, the rank, the beauty, and the talent of a past age. It was here that an event occurred, which, though consisting merely of a private and disreputable quarrel, Horace Walpole thought proper to record in his "Correspondence," and Sir Nathaniel Wraxall in his "Memoirs." The hero was George,[*] eldest son of the celebrated John Lord Hervey, the effeminate son of an effeminate father. Horace Walpole writes to Sir Horace Mann on the 25th of February, 1750: "About ten days ago, at the new Lady Cobham's assembly, as Lord Hervey was leaning over a chair talking to some women, and holding his hat in his hand, Lord Cobham came up and spit in it—yes, spit in it! and then, with a loud laugh, turned to Nugent and said, 'Pay me my wager.' In short, he had laid a wager that he committed this absurd brutality, and that it was not resented. Lord Hervey, with great temper and sensibility, asked if he had any further occasion for his hat.—'Oh! I see you are angry!'—'Not very well pleased.' Lord Cobham took the fatal hat and wiped it, made a thousand foolish apologies, and wanted to pass it for a joke. Next morning he rose with the sun, and went to visit Lord Hervey; so did Nugent: he would not see them, but wrote to the spitter (or, as he is now called, Lord Gob'-em) to say that he had affronted him very grossly before company, but

---

[*] He afterwards succeeded as second Earl of Bristol; was Ambassador to Spain in 1758, and Lord Lieutenant of Ireland in 1766. He died unmarried in 1775.

having involved Nugent in it, he desired to know to which he was to address himself for satisfaction. Lord Cobham wrote him a most submissive answer, and begged pardon both in his own and Nugent's name. Here it *rested* for a few days, till, getting wind, Lord Hervey wrote again to insist on an explicit apology under Lord Cobham's own hand, with a rehearsal of the excuses that had been made to him. This too was complied with, and the *fair conqueror* shews all the letters."*

But Pall Mall is associated with brighter names than any we have yet recorded. Here, on the south side of the street, in 1681, lived Sir William Temple, and next door to him, in 1683, lived the Hon. Robert Boyle, the natural philosopher. Here Swift had lodgings in 1710, previous to his removal to Bury Street. Here Lord Bolingbroke had a house after his return from exile; and here he renewed his intrigues against his old enemy, Sir Robert Walpole. Gay the poet writes to Swift on the 22nd October, 1726: "I hear that Lord Bolingbroke will be in town at his house in Pall Mall next week," and about a fortnight afterwards we find Pope, Gay, and Arbuthnot assembled together at the table of the noble philosopher.† Pall Mall also is associated with another illustrious name, that of Addison, who, in the reign of Queen Anne, appears to have been a frequenter of the then fashionable tavern, the "George," in this street. In a letter, dated 29th February, 1708, we find him inviting Swift to dine with him here at two o'clock in the afternoon, and he mentions that Sir Richard Steele is to be of the party.‡ In 1772, Gibbon dates his letters from Pall Mall; and from No. 25,

---

* See Walpole's "Letters," vol. ii. p. 319, ed. 1840, and Wraxall's "Memoirs," vol. i. p. 188.
† "Swift's Correspondence."
‡ Ibid.

Pall Mall, Sir Walter Scott dates many entries in his Diary.

Two other literary names, though of less interest, are associated with Pall Mall. One is that of Robert Dodsley—the footman, poet, dramatist, and publisher—who opened a bookseller's shop here in 1735, with the sign of the "Tully's Head," the lounging-place of Pope, Young, Akenside, Gray, Joseph and Thomas Warton, Horace Walpole, and Burke. The other is that of the unfortunate Letitia Pilkington, who in her girlhood had been the sprightly favourite of Swift, and whose indiscretions appear to have been at least equal to her wit. With a capital, it is said, of only five guineas, she opened a small shop in Pall Mall for the sale of pamphlets. Distress conducted her to the Marshalsea prison, and an addiction to spirituous liquors, contracted by her in her days of penury and misfortune, brought her to an untimely grave. She died at Dublin in 1750, in her thirty-eighth year.

In Pall Mall resided for many years the charming actress Mrs. Abingdon; and here also lived the well-known Bubb Dodington, the "Bubo" of Pope's verse. Persons familiar with Richard Cumberland's Memoirs will readily perhaps picture to themselves the old courtier setting out from his house in Pall Mall for his fantastic villa at Hammersmith; his cumbrous coach—the same probably which had formerly been his ambassadorial equipage at Madrid—being drawn by "six fat unwieldy black horses, short-docked, and of colossal dignity."

Only a few more casual incidents and names connected with Pall Mall remain to be noticed before passing on to other localities. To Sir Horace Mann, for instance, Horace Walpole writes on the 8th of January, 1786—"The mail from France was robbed last night in Pall Mall at half an hour past eight; yes! in the great thoroughfare of London, and within call of the guard at the Palace." To apartments in Pall Mall it is that Fielding conducts Tom Jones and Nightingale on their being compelled to quit Mrs. Miller's lodgings in Bond Street. Here, at the house of a "Mr. John's in Pall Mall,"* lodged, in 1733, the ill-fated Charles Radcliffe, brother of the young Earl of Derwentwater, who was executed in 1716, and who was himself destined to be beheaded on Tower Hill on the 8th of December, 1746. Lastly, at the Royal Hotel, in Pall Mall, resided the French Admiral, the Count de Grasse, while a prisoner in England after his capture by Lord Rodney in the great naval action of 1782.

Besides William Duke of Cumberland, Pall Mall is associated with the names of more than one other Prince of the House of Brunswick. No. 86, formerly the Ordnance Office and now a part of the War Department, was built for Edward Duke of York, who died at Monaco in 1767, and here subsequently resided another brother of George the Third, Henry Frederick Duke of Cumberland, who died in 1790. At her house in Pall Mall, on the 6th of September, 1766, the beautiful Maria Countess of Waldegrave was privately married by her chaplain to a third brother of the King, William Henry Duke of Gloucester.

Another royal residence which formerly stood in Pall Mall was Carlton House, the site of which, and of its once fair and sequestered pleasure-grounds, is pointed out by the familiar names of Carlton House Terrace, and Carlton Gardens. Carlton House was built in 1709, by Henry Boyle, Baron Carlton, from whom it descended to his nephew, Richard Boyle, Earl of Burlington, who bestowed it upon his mother, the Countess Dowager. By this lady it was

* "Gentleman's Magazine" for 1746.

sold in 1732 to Frederick Prince of Wales, father of George the Third, and from this time occasionally became that Prince's residence. Here it was, in 1751, that he was attacked by the illness which was the immediate cause of his death. He had been unwell for some days with pleurisy, but had sufficiently recovered to be able to attend the King to the House of Lords, on his return from which he was imprudent enough, though much heated, to change his clothes for a light unaired dress, in which on a very inclement day he travelled to Kew. In the evening he returned to Carlton House, and, being extremely fatigued, lay down for three hours in a cold room on the ground floor opening into the garden. In vain Lord Egmont remonstrated with him that the indulgence was a very dangerous one. The result was a return of his malady, which carried him off at Leicester House on the 20th of March, 1751, in his forty-ninth year. At Carlton House it was, on the day following the accession of his son, George the Third, that the latter presided at his first council; and here, on that occasion, the powerful Whig Ministers of the late King had the mortification of listening to a speech from the throne, which, instead of being of their composition, was only evidently the work of the new King and his then favourite adviser, Lord Bute. "Is there anything wrong in point of *form?*" inquired the King, significantly; "on which," writes the Duke of Newcastle, "we all bowed, and went out of the closet."* After the death of Frederick Prince of Wales, Carlton House became the occasional residence of his widow, Augusta of Saxe Gotha, and under its roof, on the 9th of February, 1772, she died. Its last occupant was George the Fourth, when Prince of Wales, during whose Regency its

* Harris's "Life of the Earl of Hardwicke," v. iii. p. 214.

costly saloons were the scene of many a gorgeous revel and of many interesting political episodes. Carlton House was demolished in 1826, when the columns which formed its portico were transferred to the National Gallery in Trafalgar Square.

Pall Mall, it may be mentioned, was the first street in London that was lighted with gas; the night of its first exhibition being the 28th of January, 1807.

ST. JAMES'S PALACE.

SITE OF ST. JAMES'S PALACE.—ERECTED BY HENRY THE EIGHTH.—THE RESIDENCE OF QUEEN MARY, HENRY PRINCE OF WALES, CHARLES THE FIRST, MARY DE MEDICIS, CHARLES THE SECOND, JAMES THE SECOND, WILLIAM THE THIRD, GEORGE THE FIRST, GEORGE SECOND, AND DAUGHTER.

ON the site of St. James's Palace stood, coeval with the Norman Conquest, a hospital dedicated to St. James, founded for the reception of "fourteen sisters, maidens that were leprous, living chastely and honestly," to whom five brethren were afterwards added for the purpose of performing divine service. Thus it continued to stand till the year 1532, when Henry the Eighth, having taken a fancy to the site from its vicinity to the Palace of Whitehall, gave, in exchange for it, Chattisham and other lands in Suffolk, at the same time settling pensions on the sisterhood, who were thus compelled to seek an asylum elsewhere. "I find," writes Lord Herbert of Cherbury, "that our King, having got York House, now Whitehall, upon the Cardinal's conviction in a *præmunire*, did newly enlarge and beautify it, buying also the hospital and fields of St. James, and building the palace there, for which purpose he compounded with the sisters of the house for a pension during their lives."* According to Stow, it was "a goodly manor," which the King, in the words of Holinshed,

* Lord Herbert's "Life and Reign of King Henry VIII."

converted into a "fair mansion and park." He further inclosed it with a wall of brick. As Henry commenced building the palace in the same year in which he married Anne Boleyn, it seems not improbable that he intended it to be the residence of his beautiful consort. On each side of the great gateway of the palace, facing St. James's Street, may still be seen a small arched doorway, each of which is ornamented with the "love-knot" and blended initials of Henry the Eighth and the ill-fated Anne.

In 1558, Queen Mary—the "Bloody Mary" of our childish recollections—breathed her last in St. James's Palace. "'Tis said," writes Bishop Godwin, "that in the beginning of her sickness, her friends, supposing King Philip's absence afflicted her, endeavoured by all means to divert her melancholy. But all proved in vain; and the Queen, abandoning herself to despair, told them she should die, though they were yet strangers to the cause of her death; but if they would know it hereafter, they must dissect her, *and they would find Calais at her heart;* intimating that the loss of that place was her death wound."

The circumstance which,—far more than the absence of her husband, or the death of Charles the Fifth,—appears to have affected the mind of the dying Queen, was one to which Bishop Godwin obscurely alludes—namely, her disappointment at finding herself afflicted with a dropsical disorder, when she had fondly hoped that the alteration in her personal appearance gave a promise of her producing an heir to the throne. There are extant among the State Papers several copies of a very curious circular letter, intended to be transmitted to the different European courts, in which blanks are left to be filled in with the words "son," or "daughter," immediately after the Queen's *accouchement.* From St. James's the body of the deceased Queen was carried in great state to Westminster Abbey. "Her funeral," says Bishop Kennet, "was celebrated on the 13th and 14th of December, with a pomp suitable to her quality. Her body was brought from St. James's, where she died, in a splendid chariot, with her attendants and ceremony usual on such occasions, and so by Charing Cross to Westminster Abbey. It was met at the church door with four bishops, and the Lord Abbot mitred. Her body being brought into the church lay all night under the hearse with watch. On the next day, December 14th, was the Queen's mass, and White, Bishop of Winchester, made her funeral sermon."

During the reign of James the First, St. James's Palace was set apart as the residence of the gifted, the accomplished and precocious Henry Prince of Wales—the Marcellus of his age—who kept his court here with considerable magnificence, combined with sobriety and discretion, during the lifetime of his father. In 1610, as Arthur Wilson informs us, his household amounted to no fewer than four hundred and twenty-six persons, of whom two hundred and ninety-seven were in the receipt of regular salaries. Here the youthful Prince constantly entertained the learned, the young, the gallant, and the beautiful of both sexes; retaining about his person a number of young gentlemen whose spirit of chivalry and literary tastes assimilated with his own. According to his faithful follower, Sir Charles Cornwallis, although the most beautiful women of the court and city were invited to his entertainments, he could never discover the slightest inclination on the Prince's part to any particular beauty. Such was his popularity, that his levees at St. James's were much more numerously attended than those of the King himself; a preference of which James was so jealous as to make use of the remarkable words—"Will he bury me alive?" It was at St. James's Palace, on the 6th of November, 1612, after a long illness which he bore with exemplary piety and resignation, that the young Prince, when only in his nineteenth year, breathed his last. "On Sunday, the 25th of October," we are told, "he heard a sermon, the text in Job, 'Man that is born of woman is of short continuance, and is full of trouble.' After that he presently went to Whitehall, and heard another sermon before the King, and after dinner, being ill, craved leave to retire to his own court, where instantly he fell into sudden sickness, faintings, and after that a shaking, with great heat and headache, that left him not whilst he had life." The Archbishop of Canterbury and the Dean of Rochester remained by his bedside, and prayed with him during his illness. According to Cornwallis, "he bore his sickness with patience, and as often recognition of his faith, his hopes, and his appeals to God's mercy, as his infirmity, which afflicted him altogether in his head, would possibly permit."

When Charles the First, on the death of his brother, became Prince of Wales, he not only occasionally resided at St. James's, but here, with the assistance of Sir Kenelm Digby, he commenced forming his fine collection of statues, which was dispersed during the civil troubles. Although his interest in the place seems to have ceased with his accession to the throne, we nevertheless find his beautiful consort, Henrietta Maria, giving it the preference to Whitehall as the place of her confinements. Here were born her second and third sons, Charles and James—successively kings of England—and here also she was confined with her second daughter, Elizabeth,—that interesting child over whom Charles wept his last tear in their interview in St. James's Palace on the day previous to his execution.

When, in 1638, the intrigues of Cardinal Richelieu drove Mary de Medicis from the court of her son Louis the Thirteenth, and France no longer afforded her a safe asylum, her daughter Henrietta invited her to England, and St. James's Palace was fixed upon as the place of her residence. Unfortunately for her, however, the spirit of Puritanism was at this time in the ascendant, and accordingly the arrival of a popish Princess in the metropolis not only roused the fury of the bigoted populace, but it was with the greatest difficulty that the military were enabled to force an entrance for the widow of Henry the Fourth of France into the palace of her son-in-law. Before the court-yard gates of St. James's had closed upon the equipage of the exiled Queen, three individuals had been killed in the riots to which her arrival had given occasion.

By many persons the chief interest which attaches itself to St. James's Palace will be derived from its association with the last days of the unfortunate Charles the First—from its having witnessed the insults inflicted upon him by a brutal soldiery, from its having been the scene of his last pathetic interview with his beloved children, and from its having been through its portal that he walked to his execution at Whitehall.

It was only a few days before his memorable trial in Westminster Hall, that Charles was brought from Windsor to St. James's in a coach, surrounded by a strong guard of military; the insolent fanatical preacher, Hugh Peters, riding in triumph in front of the cavalcade. On his arrival at St. James's, his first step was to retire to his own chamber, where he passed some time in prayer and in the perusal of the Bible. For about a fortnight he was treated with some slight respect for his exalted rank. Although the principal nobility, his favourite servants, and his domestic chaplains were excluded from his society, he was still attended with some degree of former state. He dined publicly in the presence-chamber; the gentlemen of his household waited on him at his meals, and the cup as usual was presented to him on the knee. But even this mockery of respect, for such it was, was continued only for a few days. In accordance with a mandate decreed by one of the councils of the army, all state ceremony about his person was suddenly dispensed with, and the number of his domestics, and even the dishes supplied to his table, were diminished. When this unfeeling and parsimonious curtailment, combined with the absence of many familiar faces, was first remarked by Charles, the observation which escaped him was a just as well as a sad one. "There is nothing," he said, "more contemptible than a despised Prince." From this time, not only was his restricted meal brought into his presence by common soldiers, but, according to Lord Clarendon, a guard was forced upon him night as well as day; the soldiers actually smoking and drinking in his bedchamber as if they had been among their own comrades in the guard-room. The King, according to the same high authority, was confined entirely to his sleeping apartment, where he was compelled to perform his devotions, and whatever Nature required of him, in the presence of his rude jailers.

On the 19th of January, 1649, the day previous to his trial, Charles was conveyed in a sedan-chair through St. James's Park, to his usual bedchamber at Whitehall. There he slept while his trial lasted, till its termination on the 24th, when he was reconducted to St. James's, where he passed the three remaining days of his life. On the day previous to his execution took place the affecting interview between Charles and his young children, the Princess Elizabeth and the Duke of Gloucester, the particulars of which are too well known to require recapitulation. He was watching their departure with a father's grief, when, just as the door of his apartment was about to shut them out for ever from his sight, he moved hastily from the window where he was standing, and folding them passionately in his arms, again kissed and blessed them, and bade them farewell. The remainder of the day he passed in prayer and meditation; the night in a calm sleep; his faithful attendant Herbert lying, by the King's orders, on a pallet-bed on the floor by the side of his own.

Shortly after the death of Charles, St. James's Palace received as a prisoner the gay and gallant courtier, Henry Rich, Earl of Holland, the reputed lover of Henrietta Maria. Hence he was carried to the place of his execution in front of the entrance to Westminster Hall, where he was beheaded on the 9th of March, 1649, less than six weeks after the death of his royal master. The Duke of Hamilton and the brave and noble-minded Lord Capel suffered the same day, and on the same scaffold.

Charles the Second was born at St. James's on the 29th of May, 1630, and here, on the 2nd of July following, he was christened in the Chapel Royal with all due solemnity. " The gossips," we are told, " were the French king, the Palsgrave, and the Queen-mother of France: the deputies, the Duke of Lennox, Marquis Hamilton, and the Duchess of Richmond, which last was exceedingly bountiful. The ordnance and chambers at the Tower were discharged; the bells did ring; and at night were in the streets plenty of flaming bonfires. The Duchess was sent for by two Lords, divers knights and gentlemen, six footmen, and a coach with six horses plumed, all the Queen's; and alighted, *not without the gate, but within the court.* Her retinue were six women, and gentlewomen I know not how many: but all, of both sexes, were clad in white satin, garnished with crimson, and crimson silk stockings.*

* "Desiderata Curiosa."

During the reign of Charles the Second, St. James's appears to have been principally set apart as the residence of his brother, the Duke of York. Later, however, we find the beautiful mistress of Charles, Hortense Mancini Duchess of Mazarine—the formidable rival of the Duchess of Portsmouth—residing within its walls. Captivated by her wit and beauty, Charles not only allowed her to occupy apartments in the palace, but conferred on her a pension of £4000 a year.

> "When through the world fair Mazarine had run,
> Bright as her fellow-traveller, the sun;
> Hither at length the Roman eagle flies,
> As the last triumph of her conquering eyes."—WALLER.

James the Second, like his brother Charles, gave the preference to Whitehall as a residence, and consequently during his reign St. James's Palace was comparatively speaking deserted. With the earlier history, however, of the bigoted monarch, it had been intimately associated. Here, on the 15th of October, 1633, he was born; here, nine days after his birth, he was christened by the Archbishop of Canterbury; and here his infancy was passed with his younger brother the Duke of Gloucester, and his interesting sister the Princess Elizabeth.

When, at the surrender of Oxford to the Parliamentary forces in 1646, James fell into the hands of Fairfax, it was in St. James's Palace that he found himself a prisoner, and from its well-guarded walls that he effected his somewhat romantic escape. Having on two previous occasions been discovered when making attempts to escape, he was now watched with the closest care, though happily to little purpose. The principal persons in his secret were Colonel Bamfield and a Mr. George Howard, by whom the necessary preparations were made for his flight. "All things," we are told, "being in readiness, the Duke went to supper at his usual hour, which was about seven, in the company of his brother and sister, and when supper was ended they went to play at hide and seek with the rest of the young people in the house. At this childish sport the Duke had accustomed himself to play for a fortnight together every night, and had used to hide himself in places so difficult to find, that they were commonly half an hour in searching for him; at the end of which time he came out to them of his own accord. This blind he laid for his design, that they might be accustomed to miss him, before he really intended his escape; by which means, when he came to practise it in earnest, he was secure of gaining that half-hour before they could reasonably suspect he was gone.

"His intention had all the effect he could desire; for that night, as soon as they began their play, he pretended, according to his custom, to hide himself. But instead of so doing he went first into his sister's chamber, and there locked up a little dog that used to follow him, that he might not be discovered by him; then, slipping down a pair of back stairs, which led into the inmost garden, having found means beforehand to furnish himself with a key of a back door from the said garden into the park, he there found Bamfield, who was ready to receive him, and waited there with a footman, who brought a cloak, which he threw over him, and put on a periwig. From thence they went through the Spring Garden, where one Mr. Tripp was ready with a hackney-coach, which carried them to Salisbury House."

Here, on a pretence of business, the fugitives alighted from the coach, and having waited till the driver was out of sight, proceeded on foot down Ivy Lane to the river's side, where they hired a boat, which landed them on the south side of London Bridge. Hence they hastened to the house of one

Loe, a surgeon, where a Mrs. Murray was expecting them with a suit of female apparel, in which she speedily attired the Duke. Bamfield had hired a large row-barge with a cabin in it, in which they proposed to proceed down the river below Gravesend, where a Dutch vessel which was ready to sail at a moment's notice waited for them. An accident, however, occurred which very nearly frustrated their plans. The owner of the barge, taking it into his head that the Duke was some disguised person of high rank, peeped through a cranny in the cabin door, where he perceived the young prince, one of whose legs was on the table, tying his garters in so unfeminine a manner that his suspicions were completely aroused. Fortunately a marked change in the man's manner, and the disinclination which he expressed to proceed further than Gravesend, betrayed the state of the case to Bamfield, who, with little difficulty, contrived to purchase the owner's silence by a considerable sum of money. Thus they were enabled to reach Gravesend, on approaching which town they extinguished their lights, and, lest the sound of the oars might betray them, floated past the town with the tide. In due time they fell in with the vessel which was expecting them, and after a prosperous voyage arrived in safety at Middleburg in Holland.*

After the Restoration, James, as Duke of York, kept his court at St. James's, and here several of his children were born. Here, also, his first wife, Anne Hyde, breathed her last. For some time it had been whispered that she had forsaken the Protestant faith, but it was not till she was on her death-bed that she expressed herself "convinced and reconciled" to the Church of Rome, and received the sacraments of that faith. Her dying requests to the Duke, her

* "Stuart Papers."

husband, were not to stir from her bedside till life had departed; and secondly, should any Protestant bishops attempt to enter her apartment, to explain to them that she died immovably fixed in the Roman Catholic faith, and consequently how useless it would be to disturb her last moments with controversial discussions. Nevertheless an attempt made by Dr. Blandford, Bishop of Worcester, to obtain admittance to her sick-chamber proved successful. On being ushered into her apartment, he found the Queen of Charles the Second, Catherine of Braganza, seated by the bedside of the expiring Duchess. "Blandford," says Burnet, "was so modest and humble that he had not presence of mind enough to begin prayers, which probably would have driven the Queen out of the room; but that not being done, she pretended kindness, and would not leave her. He happened to say, 'I hope you continue still in the truth,' upon which she asked—'*What is truth?*' And then her agony increasing, she repeated the word 'Truth, Truth, Truth,' often." A few minutes afterwards she expired. Her death took place on the 31st of March, 1671, at the age of thirty-three.

At St. James's, after the death of his first wife, James appears to have constantly resided with his second duchess, the young and interesting Mary of Modena; and here, after his accession to the throne, occurred, on the 10th of June, 1688, that memorable event, the birth of James Edward, afterwards known as the "Old Pretender." Needless perhaps it is to remind the reader that not only was the fact of the queen's pregnancy openly called in question by the king's enemies, but it was further insisted that, in order to rear up a popish heir to the throne, James had caused a spurious new-born infant to be introduced into the queen's bed in a warming-pan. "The young prince," writes Pennant, "was born in the room now called the old bedchamber; at present the ante-chamber to the levee room. The bed stood close to the door of a back stairs, which descended to an inner court. It certainly was very convenient to carry on any secret design; and might favour the silly warming-pan story, was not the bed surrounded by twenty of the Privy Council, four other men of rank, twenty ladies, besides pages and other attendants."

Although William the Third, with one exception only, never held his court for any length of time at St. James's, the old palace is nevertheless associated with his history and with that of his queen. Here Mary was born on the 30th of April, 1662, and here, in her own bedchamber, she was married to her Dutch consort at eleven o'clock at night, on the 4th of November, 1677; Charles the Second gave the bride away, the Duke and Duchess of York being among the number present.

After William's successful invasion of England, in 1688, St. James's was the place where he took up his abode on his arrival in London, and where he continued to reside till his elevation to the throne. His court at St. James's after his accession would seem to have been as gloomy as his manner to the English nobility is said to have been ungracious. For instance, Carte, the historian, was assured, in 1724, by a Mr. Dillon, that in his youth he had frequently attended at St. James's when the King dined in public, and that on those occasions he had only once known an instance of an English nobleman being invited to the royal table. Usually, he said, the Duke of Schomberg, and other Dutch general officers were the King's guests; Schomberg invariably sitting at the King's right hand, while the great officers of the royal household were compelled to stand, as state menials, behind the King's chair. Dillon further added, that on the several occasions of his being present when the King dined in public at St. James's, he never, as far as he remembered, had heard him utter a word. On his asking Keppel whether his master was always so silent, the reply was, that the King could talk enough at night when seated round a bottle of wine with his private friends.

Queen Anne was born in St. James's Palace on the 6th of February, 1665, and here, in the Chapel Royal, on the 28th of July, 1683, she was married to Prince George of Denmark. Here she kept her court during the latter part of the reign of King William, and here she was residing when Bishop Burnet brought her the tidings of her accession to the throne. When the death of her beloved husband at Kensington associated that place too painfully with the memories of the past, it was to St. James's Palace that the widowed Queen retired to indulge her grief.

George the First, on his accession to the throne, was conducted, immediately on his arrival in London, to St. James's Palace. "This is a strange country," he remarked afterwards: "the first morning after my arrival at St. James's, I looked out of the window, and saw a park with walks and a canal, which they told me were mine. The next day Lord Chetwynd, the ranger of my park, sent me a fine brace of carp out of my canal; and I was told I must give five guineas to Lord Chetwynd's servant for bringing me my own carp, out of my own canal, in my own park."*

Like Charles the Second, George the First and George the Second made no scruple of establishing their mistresses under the same roof with themselves. From Horace Walpole we learn that the apartments of George the First's ungainly mistress, the Duchess of Kendal, were on the ground-floor at St. James's, looking into the garden; apartments

---

* Walpole's "Reminiscences."

which, after the King's death, were successively inhabited by the Countesses of Yarmouth and Suffolk, the celebrated mistresses of his son and successor. Shortly before his death, George the First established a young mistress at St. James's, Anne Brett, a daughter of the repudiated Countess of Macclesfield by her second husband, and a sister of the unfortunate Savage, the poet. Her apartments also were on the ground floor of the palace, overlooking the garden, adjoining those of the King's granddaughters, the Princesses Anne, Amelia, and Elizabeth. When the King departed on his last journey to Hanover, whence he never returned, Miss Brett, we are told, ordered a door to be opened from one of her apartments into the palace garden. The Princess Anne, unwilling to have such a companion in her walks, ordered the wall to be built up again. The command was imperiously reversed by Miss Brett, but while the dispute was still at issue, the news arrived of the King's death, and at once put an end to the short reign of the haughty courtezan.

George the Second, when Prince of Wales, appears for a time to have lived on tolerably amicable terms with his father at St. James's. In 1717, however, the bedchamber of the Princess of Wales became the scene of a remarkable *fracas* which could scarcely fail to occasion an estrangement between the father and son. The Princess having been recently delivered of a child, it was the Prince's proposal to the King that his Majesty and the Bishop of Osnaburgh should stand godfathers to the infant, a selection apparently as unexceptionable as could well have been made. The King, however, notwithstanding the annoyance it was likely to occasion his son, chose to select as his fellow-sponsor Thomas Duke of Newcastle, a nobleman personally obnoxious to the Prince. Hence arose the *fracas* to which we have alluded, an account of which was imparted to Horace Walpole by Lady Suffolk, who, as woman-in-waiting on the Princess, happened to be present. "Lady Suffolk," writes Walpole, "painted the scene to me exactly. On one side of the bed stood the godfathers and godmother; on the other the Prince and Princess's ladies. No sooner had the Bishop closed the ceremony, than the Prince, crossing the feet of the bed in a rage, stepped up to the Duke of Newcastle, and holding up his hand and forefinger in a menacing attitude, said :—' You are a rascal, but I shall find you :' meaning, in broken English, I shall find a time to be revenged. What was my astonishment," continued Lady Suffolk, "when going to the Princess's apartment the next morning, the yeomen in the guard-chamber pointed their halberds at my breast, and told me I must not pass. I urged that it was my duty to attend the Princess; they said, 'No matter, I must not pass that way.' In one word, the King had been so provoked at the Prince's outrage in his presence, that it had been determined to put a still greater insult on his Royal Highness. His threat to the Duke was pretended to be understood as a challenge, and to prevent a duel he had been actually put under arrest! As if a Prince of Wales could stoop to fight with a subject! The arrest was soon taken off, but at night the Prince and Princess were ordered to leave the palace."

The child who was the innocent cause of the quarrel between the Prince and his father, was christened George William, and survived its birth scarcely three months, dying on the 6th of February, 1718. Singularly enough, it fell to the lot of the Duke of Newcastle, as Lord Chamberlain, to superintend the funeral obsequies of the deceased child; a circumstance which induced the observation that the Duke twice had the honour of introducing the royal infant into the Church; once into the bosom, and once into the bowels of it.*

On the 20th of November, 1737, Queen Caroline, the strong-minded consort of George the Second, died at St. James's of an illness with which, eleven days previously, she was seized while walking in the garden of the palace. During the interval which preceded her dissolution, though enduring almost intolerable agony, not only did her fortitude remain unshaken, but her gentleness and courtesy to those who surrounded her sick-bed, drew tears from every eye. Expressing herself resigned to the will of God, and grateful for his dispensations, she recommended her servants, in the most pathetic manner, to the care and protection of her heart-broken husband. "How long can this last?" was her inquiry of one of her physicians shortly before her dissolution; and on his answering, "Your Majesty will soon be eased of your pains,"—" The sooner the better," she said. Some minutes before she expired, the weeping bystanders, at her request, knelt down and prayed for her; she herself faintly joining them in repeating the Lord's Prayer, at the conclusion of which she waved her hand, and, endeavouring to give utterance to some indistinct expression, expired.

At St. James's, on the 26th of April, 1736, Frederick Prince of Wales was married to the Princess Augusta of Saxe Gotha. A mutual antipathy between the sovereign and the heir to the throne seems to have been an hereditary failing in the house of Hanover; accordingly, when Frederick in his turn came to quarrel with his father, George the Second, St. James's could scarcely fail to become associated with their unhappy squabbles. It was apparently with no other feeling but to spite his father, that Frederick, when his young Princess was actually in the very pains of labour

* Biog. Brit., Supplement.

with her first child, hurried her away in the middle of the night from Hampton Court, where every preparation had been made for her lying-in, to an unaired bed at St. James's. So destitute, in fact, was the palace of attendants and accommodation, that Frederick and his mistress, Lady Archibald Hamilton, were compelled to air the sheets. Before the arrival at the palace of the Prime Minister, the Archbishop of Canterbury, and the different officers of state, the Princess had given birth to a child. When, on the following morning, Queen Caroline arrived at St. James's from Hampton Court, it was, as may be readily imagined, in no very gentle terms that she upbraided her son for his unmanly conduct. The Prince's sulkiness on that occasion—his addressing no single word to his mother on his offering her his arm to re-conduct her to her coach—and lastly, on his finding a crowd of people assembled at the gateway of the palace—his servility in kneeling in the dirt to the Queen and kissing her hands— are incidents which Walpole has related with his usual graphic minuteness. "Her majesty's indignation," he writes, "must have shrunk into contempt."

On the 14th of March, 1734, took place in the Chapel Royal, St. James's, the marriage of the Princess Anne, daughter of George the Second, to William Prince of Orange, a man, the hideousness of whose appearance is said to have been only exceeded by some monster in a pantomime, or some ogre in a fairy tale. In giving him her hand, the Princess seems to have been entirely influenced by a feminine love of power and rule. To her mother she once observed— "I would die to-morrow to be a Queen to-day." Again, when her father warned her affectionately on the subject of her lover's repulsive appearance, adding that it was not yet too late to recede—"I would marry him," said she, "even if he were a baboon." Fortunately however, the Prince, as we learn from Lord Chesterfield, had many "great and good" qualities, and, accordingly, the Princess not only grew extremely fond of her husband, but is said to have been sensitively jealous of his attentions to other women.

A much more interesting personage than the Princess of Orange, was her amiable and feminine sister, the Princess Caroline, of whose hopeless love for the celebrated John Lord Hervey but little secret seems to have been made at that time. After his death she confined herself to two rooms in [one of the inner courts of St. James's Palace, where, excluded from the view of all passing objects, she admitted the visits only of a very few of her nearest relations and most cherished friends. In this seclusion she almost entirely occupied herself with her religious duties; dispensing nearly the whole of her income in acts of charity and generosity, and calmly preparing for her end. Her constant prayer was for death. When urged to accede to some proposition to which she was extremely averse, "*I would not do it,*" she said, "*to die!*" Her death took place at St. James's on the 28th of December, 1757, in the forty-fifth year of her age.

Another daughter of George, the no less gentle and amiable Princess Mary, was married on the 8th of May, 1740, in the Chapel Royal, to Frederick, hereditary Prince of Hesse-Cassel. Shortly after their marriage he carried his charming wife with him to his German dominions, where, after having had more than thirty years of her life embittered by his unceasing brutalities, she expired on the 14th of June, 1771.

It was in the Chapel Royal, St. James's, on the 8th of September, 1761, that George the Third was married to the Princess Charlotte of Mecklenburgh-Strelitz. Here, on the 12th of August, 1762—with the Archbishop of Canterbury in the same room with her, and with the Duke of Devonshire and eight other lords in an adjoining room with the door open—the young Queen gave birth to her first child, afterwards King George the Fourth. Lastly, in the Chapel Royal, on the 8th of April, 1795, the latter Prince was married to the ill-fated Caroline of Brunswick. In the reign of William the Third, the standards captured by him at the battle of the Boyne hung in the Chapel Royal, St. James's.

When Peter the Great was in this country, in William's reign, he is said to have remarked to his brother-monarch, that were he King of England he would convert Greenwich Hospital into a palace, and St. James's Palace into a hospital. Notwithstanding, however, its sombre and unsightly appearance, St. James's is said to be the most commodious for the purposes of a court of any palace in Europe. It should be noticed that, on the 21st of June, 1809, a fire broke out in St. James's Palace, which destroyed the whole of the east wing of the inner court.

Before we pass from St. James's Palace into its no less interesting Park, there is one illustrious name of which mention should on no account be omitted. In Stable Yard, on the site of the Duke of Sutherland's present stately mansion, stood Godolphin House, in which Charles Fox resided during the earlier stages of his last and fatal illness. " The garden of the house in Stable Yard," writes his secretary and biographer, Trotter, "was daily filled with anxious inquirers: the foreign ambassadors, or ministers, or private friends of Mr. Fox, walked there, eager to know his state of health, and catch at the hope of amendment. As he grew worse, he ceased to go out in his carriage, and was drawn in a garden-chair, at times, round the walks. I have myself drawn him whilst the Austrian Ambassador, Prince Stahremberg, conversed with him. His manner was as easy, and his mind as penetrating and vigorous as ever; and he transacted business in this way, though heavily oppressed by his disorder, with perfect facility." Among the distinguished persons who came to manifest their sympathy for the suffering statesman, we find the Dukes of York and Clarence, Sheridan and Grattan, Lord Sidmouth, Earl Grey, and Rogers, the poet. The Prince of Wales is said to have visited and sat with him almost every day. It was at Godolphin House, after Fox's death at the Duke of Devonshire's villa at Chiswick, that his remains lay, previously to their interment, on the 10th of October, 1806, in Westminster Abbey. The Annual Register at this time mentions Godolphin House as "the elegant mansion of the Duke of Bedford at St. James's."

ST. JAMES'S PARK.

ORIGINAL ENCLOSURE.—CHARLES GOING TO EXECUTION.—CROMWELL.—SKATING.—GAME OF PALL MALL.—CHARLES THE SECOND.—QUEEN ANNE.—MARLBOROUGH HOUSE.—THE MALL.—SPRING GARDENS.—BUCKINGHAM HOUSE.

ST. JAMES'S PARK was originally enclosed by Henry the Eighth shortly after his purchase of the hospital of St. James and the fields attached to it. The wall, or rather paling, of the park, formerly ran where the houses on the south side of Pall Mall now stand. Charles the Second removed it to its present boundary, and, under the direction of the celebrated French gardener, Le Notre, planted the avenues of trees as we now see them. Birdcage Walk, on the south side of the park, derives its name from the cages in which Charles kept his ducks, for which he had constructed a decoy close by. In the park too, small as were its dimensions, he formed a ring-fence for deer. "This day," writes Pepys in August, 1664, "for a wager before the King, my Lord of Castlehaven, and Arran, a son of my Lord of Ormond's, they two alone did run down a stout buck in St. James's Park." Charles also formed the present canal, and in his reign Duck Island took its name from being the breeding-place of the numerous waterfowl with which the park was stocked. The *government* of Duck Island was once enjoyed, with a small salary, by the celebrated St. Evremond. Pennant is mistaken when he speaks of it as "the first and last government," inasmuch as at an earlier period we find it conferred by Charles the Second on Sir John Flock, a man of good family,' and a companion of the King during his exile. To Sir Horace Mann, Horace Walpole writes on the 9th of February, 1751: —" My Lord Pomfret is made ranger of the Parks, and, by consequence, my lady is queen of the *Duck Island.*" This little island, which stood at the west end of the canal, disappeared on the occasion of some alterations being made in the Park in 1770.

Another interesting feature of St. James's Park which disappeared about the same time, was Rosamond's Pond, situated opposite to James Street, Westminster, close to the present Buckingham Palace. Its romantic aspect, the irregularity of the ground, the trees which overshadowed it, and the view of the venerable abbey, not only rendered it, we are told, a favourite resort of the contemplative, but its secluded situation is said to have tempted a greater number of persons to commit suicide, especially unfortunate females, than any other place in London.

St. James's Park is replete with historical associations, not the least interesting of which is the fact of Charles the First having passed through it on foot, on the morning of his execution, from his bedchamber in St. James's Palace to the scaffold at Whitehall. Colonel Hacker having knocked at his door and informed him that it was time to depart, Charles took Bishop Juxon by the hand, and bidding his faithful attendant Herbert bring with him his silver clock, intimated to Hacker, with a cheerful countenance, that he was ready to accompany him. As he passed through the palace garden into the Park, he inquired of Herbert the hour of the day, bidding him at the same time keep the clock for *his* sake. The procession was a remarkable one. On each side of the King marched a line of soldiers, while before him and behind him were a guard of halberdiers, their drums beating and colours flying. On his right hand was Bishop Juxon, and on his left hand Colonel Tomlinson, both bareheaded. There is a tradition that during his walk he pointed out a tree, not far from the entrance to Spring Gardens, which he said had been planted by his brother Henry. He was subjected to more than one annoyance during his progress. One ruffianly fanatic officer in particular, inquired of him, with insulting brutality, whether it was true that he had been cognizant of his father's murder. Another fanatic—a "mean citizen," as he is styled by Fuller—was perceived to walk close by his side, keeping his eyes constantly fixed on the King with an expression of particular malignity. Eventually, however, the man was pushed away by the more feeling among the King's persecutors. As the guards were marching at a slow pace, the King desired them to proceed faster. "I go," he said, "to strive for a heavenly crown, with less solicitude than I have formerly encouraged my soldiers to fight for an earthly one." On reaching the spot where the Horse Guards now stands, Charles ascended a staircase which then communicated with Whitehall Palace, and passing along the famous gallery which at that time ran across the street, was conducted to his usual bedchamber, where he remained till summoned by Hacker to the scaffold. "This day," according to a contemporary MS., "his Majesty died upon a scaffold at Whitehall. His children were with him last night: to the Duke of Gloucester he gave his George; to the Lady Elizabeth his ring off his finger. He told them his subjects had many things to give *their* children, but that was all he had to give them. This day, about one o'clock, he came from St. James's in a long black cloak and grey stockings. The Palsgrave came through the Park with him. He was faint, and was forced to sit down and rest him in the Park. He went into Whitehall the usual way out of the Park; and so came out of the Banqueting House upon planks, made purposely, to the scaffold. He was not long there, and what he spoke was to the two Bishops, Dr. Juxon and Dr. Morton. To Dr. Juxon he gave his hat and cloak. He prayed with them; walked twice or thrice about the scaffold; and held out his hands to the people. His last words, as I am informed, were—'To your power I must submit, but your authority I deny.' He pulled his doublet off himself, and kneeled down to the block himself. When some officer offered to unbutton him, or some such like thing, he thrust him from him. Two men, in vizards and false hair, were appointed to be his executioners. Who they were is not known. Some say he that did it was the common hangman; others, that it was one Captain Foxley, and that the hangman refused. The Bishop of London hath been constantly with him since sentence was given. Since he died, they have made proclamation that no man, upon pain of I know not what, shall presume to proclaim his son Prince Charles, King; and this is all I have yet heard of this sad day's work."

During the Protectorate we find repeated notices of the "Lord Protector" as either walking in, or "taking the air in St. James's Park in a sedan." It was in St. James's Park, for instance, on a "fair evening" in November, that Whitelock, the Memorialist, as he himself informs us, happened to encounter the Protector, who, after having "with more than ordinary courtesy desired him to walk aside with him," began to sound him on the subject of his contemplated assumption of the sovereign power. "What," he said, "if a man should take upon him to be king?" "I think," replied Whitelock, "that remedy would be worse than the disease." On the 12th of April, 1657—the day before the Parliament actually offered Cromwell the title of king— we find him making a similar attempt in St. James's Park to tamper with the principles of those uncompromising republicans, Fleetwood and Desborough. "He drolled with them," we are told, "about monarchy; said that it was but a feather in a man's cap, and wondered that men would not please children, and permit them to enjoy their rattle." Fleetwood and Desborough were both near connections of the great Protector; the former having married his daughter, and the latter his sister. In vain, however, he appealed to their feelings, their prejudices, their ambition. The conversation terminated by both tendering him their commissions. They were resolved, they said, never to serve a *King*; they saw the evils which would follow the elevation of their kinsman to the throne; adding, that, though they certainly would not bear arms against him, they felt it a duty hereafter to decline carrying them in his service. Cromwell, it seems, laughed off the affair; called them "a couple of precise, scrupulous fellows," and took his leave.

It was apparently not on every occasion of Cromwell's presenting himself in St. James's Park that his countenance wore this hilarious aspect. "Some say," writes the Marquis of Ormond, on the 13th of March, 1656, "that the Protector is many times like one distracted; and in these fits he will run round about the house and into the garden, or else ride out with very little company, which he never doth when composed and free from disorder. Friday last a friend met him in St. James's Park with only one man with him, and in a distempered carriage. If any people offered to deliver him petitions or the like, he refused, and told them he had other things to think of. Fleetwood was in the Park at the same time, but walked at a distance, not daring to approach him in his passion, which, they say, was occasioned by some carriage of Lambert's. This you may give credit to."*

During the memorable storm which raged round Cromwell's death-bed in the neighbouring Palace of Whitehall, many of the ancient trees in St. James's Park were uprooted. Waller has celebrated the occasion in his fine monody on the death of Cromwell:—

> "We must resign ! Heaven his great soul doth claim,
> In storms as loud as his immortal fame.
> His dying groans ; his last breath shakes our isle,
> And trees uncut fall for his funeral pile.
> About his palace their broad roots are tost
> Into the air. So Romulus was lost ;
> And Rome in such a tempest lost her King,
> And from obeying, fell to worshipping."

In the pages of Pepys will be found many curious notices of St. James's Park from the time that Charles the Second commenced his improvements there under the direction of Le Notre, till the Mall became the established loungingplace of the merry monarch and his gay court. We will select some scattered passages from the "Diary" of the gossiping chronicler:—"1660, July 22nd. Went to walk in the inward Park, but could not get in; one man was basted by the keeper for carrying some people over on his back through the water."—"Sept. 16th. To the Park, where I saw how far they had proceeded in the Pall Mall, and in making a river through the Park, which I had never seen before since it was begun."—"Oct. 11th. To walk in St. James's Park, where we observed the several engines at work to draw up water, with which sight I was very much pleased."—"1661, April 2nd. To St. James's Park, where I

---

* Carte's "Collection of Original Letters."

saw the Duke of York playing at Pall Mall, the first time that ever I saw the sport."—"August 4th. Walked into St. James's Park (where I had not been a great while), and there found great and very noble alterations."—" 1662, July 27th. I went to walk in the Park, which is now every day more and more pleasant by the new works upon it."— "December 15th. To the Duke, and followed him into the Park, where, though the ice was broken, he would go slide upon his skates, which I did not like, but he slides very well."

Fourteen days before the date of the last extract Evelyn inserts in his "Diary :"—" 1662, December 1st. Saw the strange and wonderful dexterity of the sliders on the new canal in St. James's Park performed before their majesties by divers gentlemen and others with skates, after the manner of the Hollanders, with what a swiftness they pause, how suddenly they stop in full career upon the ice." From these extracts it is evident that the art of skating had been acquired by Charles and his gay followers during the time that the former held his exiled court in the Low Countries, and that it was introduced by them into England at the Restoration. From a passage in Swift's "Journal to Stella," it would seem that more than half a century afterwards the art was still comparatively unknown. In January, 1711, he writes:—" Delicate walking weather, and the canal and Rosamond's Pond full of the rabble, sliding, and with skates, if you know what that is."

In the time of the Commonwealth, when the ground to the north of St. James's Park consisted of open fields, the game of pall mall, as has been already stated, was played on the site of the present Pall Mall. After Charles the Second, however, had removed the boundary of the Park to its present site, the game was played between the avenue of trees nearest to St. James's Palace, adjoining the present carriage-road; a fact established by a curious print in the supplementary volume to Lord Lansdowne's works printed by Walthoe in 1732, and also by a letter from Sheffield Duke of Buckingham to the Earl of Shrewsbury, in which he vaunts the advantages of his newly-erected mansion, the precursor of the present Buckingham Palace. "The avenues to this house," he writes, "are along St. James's Park, through rows of goodly elms on one hand, and gay flourishing limes on the other; that for coaches, this for walking, with the Mall lying betwixt them." Of the game itself we know little more than that it consisted of striking a ball through an iron ring suspended from a hoop. From Pepys we learn that the ground was kept with great care. "1663, May 15th. I walked in the Park discoursing with the keeper of the pall mall, who was sweeping it, and who told me that the earth is mixed that do floor the mall, and that over all there is cockle-shells powdered and spread to keep it fast, which, however, in dry weather turns to dust and deads the ball." The person who had the care of the ground was called the "King's Cockle Strewer."

Charles the Second, in the early part of his reign, was not only frequently to be seen playing at pall mall in St. James's Park, but, according to some adulatory lines of Waller, was extremely expert at the game.

> "Here a well-polished mall give us the joy,
> To see our Prince his matchless force employ ;
> His manly posture and his graceful mien,
> Vigour and youth in all his motions seen ;
> His shape so lovely, and his limbs so strong,
> Confirm our hopes, we shall obey him long.
> No sooner has he touched the flying ball,
> But 't is already more than half the mall ;
> And such a fury from his arm has got,
> As from a smoking culverin it were shot."

Charles, as is well known, took a considerable interest in the numerous birds with which St. James's Park was stocked, and delighted [in feeding his favourites with his own hands. Pepys, for instance, mentions his passing an hour in the Park, seeing the King and the Duke of York "come to see their fowl play;" while Colley Cibber, in his "Apology," writes, "The King's indolent amusement of playing with his dogs, and feeding his ducks, in St. James's Park, which I have seen him do, made the common people adore him." Charles was one day taking his accustomed walk in the Park, when he encountered Prince Rupert, whom he invited to accompany him. "The King," writes Coke, who overheard their conversation, "told the Prince how he had shot a duck, and such a dog fetched it; and so they walked on till the King came to St. James's House, and there the King said to the Prince, 'Let's go and see Cambridge and Kendal,' the Duke of York's two sons, who then lay a-dying. But upon his return to Whitehall he found all in an uproar; the Countess of Castlemaine, as it was said, bewailing above all others, that she should be the first torn to pieces." It appears that the startling news of the Dutch fleet having sailed up the Medway had just been received at the palace.

The dalliance-scene between Charles the Second and Nell Gwynn in St. James's Park, as described by Evelyn in his Diary, is perhaps as well remembered as any passage in that valuable work. It must be remembered that at this time the garden of her house in Pall Mall extended as far back as the new wall erected by Charles in the Park. "1st March, 1671. I thence walked with him [the King] through St. James's Park to the garden, where I both saw and heard a very familiar discourse between [the King] and Mrs. Nelly, as they called an impudent comedian; she looking out of her garden on a terrace at the top of the wall, and [the King] standing on the green walk under it. I was heartily sorry at this scene." Thence the King walked to the Duchess of Cleveland, another lady of pleasure and curse of our nation." Strype, writing of Pall Mall, observes —" The houses on the south side have a pleasant prospect into the King's garden; and besides they have small gardens behind them which reach to the wall; and to many of them there are raised mounts, which give them the prospect of the said garden and of the Park." It was doubtless standing on the mount in her garden that Nell Gwynn conversed with her royal lover. It should be mentioned that under the Park wall ran what was called the "Green Walk," and afterwards the "Jacobite Walk," along which it probably was that Charles walked with Prince Rupert, and in which we have seen him standing while talking to the "impudent comedian."

Among other persons with whom we find Charles the Second conversing familiarly in the Mall at different times, may be mentioned Dryden the poet, and Thomas Hobbes the philosopher.

With the following graphic description by Pepys of a court cavalcade returning to Whitehall in 1663, we will conclude our notices of St. James's Park in the reign of Charles the Second. "July 13. I met the Queen-mother walking in the Pall Mall, led by my Lord St. Albans; and finding many coaches at the gate, I found upon inquiry that the Duchess is brought to bed of a boy; and hearing that the King and Queen are rode abroad with the ladies of honour to the Park, and seeing a great crowd of gallants staying here to see their return, I also stayed, walking up and down. By-and-by the King and Queen, who looked in this dress (a white laced waistcoat and a crimson short petticoat, and her hair dressed *à la négligence*) mighty pretty; and the King rode hand in hand with her. Here also my Lady Castlemaine rode amongst the rest of the ladies; but the King took no notice of her; nor when she alighted did anybody press (as she seemed to expect and stayed for it) to take her down, but was taken down by her own gentleman. She looked mighty out of humour, and had a yellow plume in her hat (which all took notice of), and yet is very handsome but very melancholy; nor did anybody speak to her, or she so much as speak or smile to anybody."

From that most interesting series of Letters, Swift's "Journal to Stella," we learn that in the days of Queen Anne the Mall in St. James's Park was the favourite resort of Swift, and that here many of the most remarkable men of the Augustan age of England were the frequent companions of his walks. "1711, Feb. 8.—I walked in the Park to-day in spite of the weather; as I do every day when it does not actually rain." "March 21.—The days are now long enough to walk in the Park after dinner, and so I do whenever it is fair. This walking is a strange remedy. Mr. Prior walks to make himself fat, and I to bring myself down; he has generally a cough, which he only calls a cold: we often walk round the Park together." "May 15.—My way is this: I leave my best gown and periwig at Mrs. Vanhomrigh's, then walk up the Pall Mall, out at Buckingham House, and so to Chelsea, a little beyond the Church. I set out about sunset, and get there in something less than an hour: it is two good miles, and just 5748 steps. When I pass the Mall in the evening, it is prodigious to see the number of ladies walking there; and I always cry shame at the ladies of Ireland, who never walk at all, as if their legs were of no use but to be laid aside." "1712, March 9.—I walked in the Park this evening, and came home early to avoid the Mohocks."

"March 16.—Lord Winchilsea told me to-day at court, that two of the Mohocks caught a maid of old Lady Winchilsea's at the door of their house in the Park, with a candle, who had just lighted out somebody. They cut all her face and beat her without any provocation." "December 27.—I met Mr. Addison and Pastoral Philips on the Mall to-day, and took a turn with them; but they both looked terribly dry and cold."

Another remarkable person mentioned by Swift as having been his companion in his walks in the Mall, was the young and accomplished Secretary of State, Henry St. John, afterwards Lord Bolingbroke. For instance, on the 24th of August, 1711, Swift writes: "Lord Radnor and I were walking the Mall this evening, and Mr. Secretary met us and took a turn or two and then stole away, and we both believe it was to pick up some wench, and to-morrow he will be at the cabinet with the Queen: so goes the world!" Nor was this the only occasion of Bolingbroke's immorality having displayed itself in St. James's Park. "I have spoken to an old man," says Goldsmith, "who assured me that he saw him and one of his companions run naked through the Park in a fit of intoxication; but then it was a time when public decency might be transgressed with less danger than at present." "His youth," writes Lord Chesterfield, "was distinguished by all the tumult and storm of pleasures, in which he most licentiously triumphed, disclaiming all decorum."

St. James's Park is connected with the name of another illustrious subject of Queen Anne, that of the great Duke of Marlborough. At the time when he was in the zenith of his unpopularity, we find a Mrs. White writing to a Mrs. Mason: —" On the birthday of the Queen, the Duke of Marlborough was in a chair in St. James's Park, with the curtains drawn. The mob, that believed it to be the Prince Eugene, huzzaed the chair; but the Duke modestly drew back the curtains and put himself out, and with a sign showed his dislike to the salutation. The mob, finding their mistake, and that it was he, cried out, 'stop thief,' which was a thorough mortification to him. His daughters that day, to show their contempt of the Court, were in wrapping-gowns in a window at St. James's, to see the company pass, two of them, and the other two drove through the Pall Mall four times, in the worst of mob-dress they could put themselves. *The Duke was in a black suit that day, and his son-in-law, the Duke of Montague, was at Court in a plain coarse red coat, with a long shoulder-knot, in ridicule of the day;* but the Queen had the satisfaction to see the most splendid Court that ever was, and crowded more than ever by all the church, nobility, and gentry. My Lord Marlborough finds his levees much thinner than they were, and daily less and less."*

On the site of Marlborough House and of the German Chapel, St. James's, was formerly "The Friary," so called from its containing the chapel and lodgings of the Friars who formed part of the establishment of Charles the Second's Queen, Catherine of Braganza. Here, too, Catherine had a garden in which Charles had planted an acorn gathered from the famous Boscobel oak, which, at the time that Marlborough House was built, had grown into a flourishing young tree. Pepys, who, in January, 1667, was conducted over the Friary by Queen Catherine's almoner, Cardinal Howard, has left us an interesting account of his visit. "I saw," he writes, "the dortoire [dormitory], and the cells of the priests, and we went into one, a very pretty little room, very clean, hung with pictures and set with books. The priest was in his cell, with his hair-clothes to his skin, bare-legged with a sandall only on, and his little

* Macpherson's "Original Papers."

bed without sheets, and no feather-bed; and yet I thought soft enough."—" Queen Catherine," writes Sarah Duchess of Marlborough, "had given her interest in the ground to the sisters of Lord Feversham, her chamberlain : for full twenty years these two Frenchwomen lived in it. I had the house of the Countess du Bois,* and where Queen Catherine's priests lived, having obtained the promise of the Queen [Anne] *before* the death of the Queen Dowager, Catherine of Braganza, of the site in St. James's Park, upon which my house now stands."†

Marlborough House, built after designs by Christopher Wren, was erected at an expense of upwards of £40,000. It originally consisted of only two stories; the present upper story having been added by George, fourth Duke of Marlborough, who also added the large apartment on the ground-floor. There are few persons, perhaps, who pass by Marlborough House without calling to mind some remarkable passage in the history of the great warrior and of his beautiful and high-spirited duchess of which this interesting mansion was the scene. Here it was that the remains of the illustrious Duke were removed from Windsor Park, where he died; and hence they were conveyed in great state to Westminster Abbey. The cavalcade moved from Marlborough House along St. James's Park, and up Constitution Hill to Hyde Park Corner, thence through Piccadilly and Pall Mall, by Charing Cross to Westminster. At the entrance to the Abbey, the body was received with a blaze of torches; the funeral ceremony being rendered the more impressive from the fine voice and digni-

* Countess de Duras ? Queen Catherine's Chamberlain was Lewis de Duras, Earl of Feversham, K.G., naturalized in 1666. From his intimacy with Queen Catherine, he was commonly called the "King Dowager." He died in 1709.

† Strickland's "Lives of the Queens of England," vol. viii., 295-6.

fied delivery of Bishop Atterbury, then Dean of Westminster, who performed the service.

It had been the wish of the imperious Duchess after her husband's death to improve the present insignificant entrance in Pall Mall, by purchasing and pulling down the adjoining house in that street, and thus form a fine approach immediately in front of the mansion. Unfortunately, the house which she was desirous of purchasing for this purpose was, to her infinite vexation, bought by her enemy Sir Robert Walpole, who by this means entirely frustrated her design. In addition to the heavy offence thus given her, it was to Sir Robert that the Duchess attributed her exclusion from the right which she had enjoyed in the reign of Queen Anne of driving in St. James's Park—an exclusion the more irritating to her, inasmuch as the privilege had been accorded to the widow of Sheffield Duke of Buckingham, as well as to another Court lady, Mrs. Dunch, a daughter, we imagine, of James the Second's mistress, Arabella Churchill. To Dr. Hare, the Duchess writes in 1726, "What makes this the more extraordinary, is that Sir Robert Walpole told me himself that the Duchess of Buckingham had wrote so impertinent a letter to the King that she was not to be allowed to go through the Park. Yet after that she was allowed to go through every part of the Park, as much as the Royal Family does, and what I aimed at was only to go sometimes, when my health required it, to take the air. Mrs. Dunch has been likewise permitted the same favour, who lives at Whitehall. When I found the Duchess of Buckingham went through—being so ill that I could not bear the jolting of a coach upon the stones when I wanted to take the air—I wrote to the Princess to obtain this favour for me. She wrote to me in half an hour, with a great deal of goodness, and would not send me a refusal till she had tried several times, and there is no doubt but Sir Robert knew this, who might have prevented me troubling her Royal Highness at all—as it was natural for any man that had any gentlemanlike qualities—by asking the King's leave long before anything of this happened."*

If these allusions to the exclusiveness of St. James's Park in the reign of George the First are curious, still more remarkable is it to find the Queen of King George the Second entertaining a serious intention of excluding the public altogether from the Park, and converting it into a private garden to be attached to St. James's Palace. When this project was first contemplated by her, she inquired of Sir Robert Walpole what he considered would be the cost of the undertaking? "*Madam*," was the significant reply, "*only three crowns.*"

A curious anecdote, in connection with Marlborough House and its imperious mistress, has been bequeathed to us by Horace Walpole. When, in 1734, the Prince of Orange arrived in England for the purpose of espousing the Princess Anne, daughter of George the Second, a large boarded gallery was erected for the convenience of the company in the court-yard of St. James's, between the windows of the principal drawing-room and the German Chapel. The ceremony having been delayed in consequence of the Prince having been seized with illness, and the physicians having ordered him to Bath for the benefit of his health, the gallery remained for several weeks darkening the windows of Marlborough House. Alluding to this circumstance, the Duchess observed with some humour to one of her friends—" I wonder when my neighbour George will take away his *orange-chest.*" According to Walpole, the gallery nearly resembled

* "Private Correspondence of the Duchess of Marlborough."

the article to which the Duchess compared it. It was at Marlborough House that the celebrated Duchess breathed her last in 1744.

In the year 1817, Marlborough House was purchased by the Crown as a residence for the Princess Charlotte and Prince Leopold of Saxe Coburg. Unhappily the Princess died before it was ready for her occupation, but here her widowed husband lived for some years. Here, too, Queen Adelaide resided after the death of William the Fourth.

The Mall in St. James's Park continued to be the most fashionable promenade in London as late as 1750, if not till a much later period. In a letter to George Montagu, dated June 23, 1750, Horace Walpole describes the gay scene in his happiest manner. "I had a card," he writes, "from Lady Caroline Petersham to go with her to Vauxhall. I went accordingly to her house, and found her and the little Ashe, or the *Pollard Ashe*, as they call her. They had just finished their last layer of red, and looked as handsome as crimson could make them. We issued into the Mall to assemble our company, which was all the town, if we could get it; for just so many had been summoned, except Harry Vane, whom we met by chance. We mustered the Duke of Kingston, with whom Lady Caroline says she has been toying for these seven years; but, alas! his beauty is at the fall of the leaf; Lord March, Mr. Whithead, a pretty Miss Beauclerc, and a very foolish Miss Sparre. These two damsels were trusted by their mother, for the first time of their lives, to the matronly care of Lady Caroline. As we sailed up the Mall with all our colours flying, Lord Petersham, with his hose and legs twisted to every point of crossness, strode by us on the outside, and repassed again on the return. At the end of the Mall she called to him. He would not answer: she gave a familiar spring, and, between laugh and confusion, ran up to him—'My Lord, my Lord! why, you don't see us!' We advanced at a little distance, not a little awkward in expectation how all this would end, for my Lord never stirred his hat, or took the least notice of anybody. She said—'Do you go with us, *or are you going anywhere else?*'—'I don't go with you, I am going *somewhere else;*' and away he stalked, as sulky as a ghost that nobody will speak to first."

The "Spring Garden," with its fashionable bowling-green and ordinary, its springs of excellent water, and its "thickets contrived to all advantages of gallantry," was situated at the east end of the Mall in St. James's Park, into the "spacious walks" of which it opened. Even at the present day every house in what is called "Spring Garden Terrace" has its separate well. The garden itself would seem to have been laid out about the end of the reign of James the First.

The bowling-green in Spring Gardens was the frequent resort of the unfortunate Charles the First. When his celebrated favourite, the first Villiers Duke of Buckingham, was in the height of his unpopularity, Charles was one day sauntering with him in the Spring Gardens, watching his favourite game of bowls, when they were approached by a Scotchman, who for some time had been narrowly watching them. Of all the company, the haughty Buckingham was the only person who retained his hat on his head in the presence of his sovereign. The Scotchman, having first of all kissed the Duke's hand, suddenly snatched off his hat, exclaiming, "Off with your hat before the King." Buckingham, we are told, instantly gave the Scotchman a kick, and probably in his wrath would have proceeded to further lengths had not the King interposed. "Let him alone, George," he said, " he is either mad or fool." "No, sir," said the offender, " I am a sober man, and if your Majesty would give me leave, I will tell you *that* of this man which many know and none dare speak."*

About six years after this singular occurrence, we find the amusements in the Spring Gardens suppressed by royal command. " The bowling-green in the Spring Gardens," writes Mr. Garrard to the Earl of Strafford in 1634, " was put down one day by the King's command; but by the intercession of the Queen it was reopened for this year; but hereafter it shall be no common bowling-place. There was kept an ordinary of six shillings a meal (where the King's proclamation allows but two elsewhere), continual bibbing and drinking under all trees; two or three quarrels every week. It was grown scandalous and insufferable; besides, my Lord Digby, being apprehended for striking in the King's garden, he said he took it for a common bowling-place."

The Spring Gardens could have remained closed only a few years, [since, in 1649, we find Evelyn " treating divers ladies of his relations" here. However, very shortly after the death of Charles the First, the public were again excluded from them. "Lady Oliver Gerrard," writes Evelyn, "treated us at Mulberry Garden, now the only place of refreshment about the town for persons of the best quality to be exceedingly cheated at, Cromwell and his partisans having shut up and seized on Spring Garden, which till now had been the usual rendezvous for ladies and gallants at this season." We have already mentioned that Charles the First, when on his way to the scaffold, pointed out a tree in Spring Gardens as having been planted by his brother Henry. There is a tradition also, that, on the same melancholy occasion, he stopped to drink a glass of water at one of the springs.

* Disraeli's " Curiosities of Literature."

On, or near, the site of these celebrated gardens many eminent persons have from time to time resided. For instance, in the days of the Commonwealth, we find no less illustrious an individual than John Milton, lodging "at one Thomson's, next door to the Bull Head Tavern at Charing Cross, opening into the Spring Garden."

Here, in the reign of Charles the Second, lived Philip, second Earl of Chesterfield, the Lord Chesterfield of De Grammont's Memoirs, while near him, at the same time, lived Prince Rupert, who, in 1782, died at his house in Spring Gardens. Here, at the latter end of the reign of Queen Anne, Colley Cibber was residing; and here, in 1723, died the celebrated dramatic writer, Mrs. Centlivre, whose genius and strange adventures have rendered her name familiar to posterity. Here resided Augusta Duchess of Brunswick, the venerable sister of George the Third, who died in England in 1813. Here, on Sunday, the 3rd of November, 1807, at the house of James Earl of Malmesbury, the diplomatist, Pitt had translated to him from a Dutch newspaper the terrible tidings of General Mack's capitulation at Ulm. "I observed but too clearly," writes Lord Malmesbury, "the effect it had on Pitt, though he did his utmost to conceal it." At a house no longer standing, then No. 13, George Canning was residing in 1800. At No. 2, New Street, Spring Gardens, Sir Astley Cooper was residing in 1824; and at No. 22, Joseph Jekyll, the wit.

On the site of the present Buckingham Palace and its pleasure-grounds extended the well-known Mulberry Garden, a fashionable place of entertainment in the reigns of the First and Second Charles, and frequently mentioned by the dramatists of the seventeenth century. It derived its name from the ground having been planted with mulberry-trees by order of James the First, in 1609; that monarch having been desirous of encouraging the production of silk in England, for which purpose he caused ship-loads of mulberry-trees to be imported from France into this country. Twenty years afterwards we find letters patent issued to Walter, Lord Aston, granting him the "custody and keeping of the garden, mulberry-trees, and silkworms, near St. James's, in the County of Middlesex;" but the speculation turned out a failure, the result of which was the conversion of the ground into a place of public recreation.

> "The fate of things lies always in the dark :
> What Cavalier would know St. James's Park ?
> For Locket's stands where gardens once did spring,
> And wild ducks quack where grasshoppers did sing ;
> A princely palace on that space does rise,
> Where Sedley's noble muse found mulberries."
> DR. KING's *Art of Cookery*, 1709.

The Mulberry Garden is said to have been the favourite resort of the immortal Dryden, where he used to eat mulberry tarts with his mistress, Mrs. Anne Reeve.

> "Nor he, whose essence, wit, and taste, approved,
> Forget the *mulberry-tarts* which Dryden loved."
> *Pursuits of Literature.*

Near the Mulberry Garden—"without the gate of St. James's Park"—stood Tart Hall, built in 1638, by Nicholas Stone, for Alathea, Countess of Arundel. After her death it became the residence of her second and ill-fated son, William Stafford, one of the victims of the perjuries of Titus Oates during the Popish plot of 1680. From this nobleman, Stafford Place and Stafford Row, Pimlico—which stand on the site of part of the garden—derived their names.

On the site of the present Buckingham Palace stood Arlington House, the residence of Henry Bennet, Earl of

Arlington, already mentioned as having been one of the famous *Cabal* in the reign of Charles the Second.

Arlington House was subsequently purchased and afterwards pulled down by the no less celebrated John Sheffield, Duke of Buckingham, who erected on its site, in 1703, the large red brick mansion which has been displaced by the present Buckingham Palace. Here it was that the Duke died, and hence his remains were conveyed with great magnificence to Henry the Seventh's Chapel at Westminster.

After the death of the Duke, Buckingham House became the residence of his widow, the fantastic Catherine Darnley, illegitimate daughter of James the Second by the celebrated Catherine Sedley, Countess of Dorchester. Here it was, on each successive anniversary of the execution of her grandfather, Charles the First, that she was accustomed to receive her company in the great drawing-room of Buckingham House; herself seated in a chair of state, clad in the deepest mourning, and surrounded by her women, as black and dismal-looking as herself. Here, too, it was that this eccentric lady breathed her last. "Princess Buckingham," writes Horace Walpole, "is dead or dying. She sent for Mr. Anstis, and settled the ceremonial of her burial. On Saturday she was so ill that she feared dying before the pomp was come home. She said, ' Why don't they send the canopy for me to see ? Let them send it though all the tassels are not finished.' But yesterday was the greatest stroke of all. She made her *ladies* vow to her that if she should lie senseless, they would not sit down in the room before she was dead." By her own directions she was buried with great pomp in Henry the Seventh's Chapel, where there was formerly a waxen figure of her, adorned with jewels, prepared in her lifetime by her own hands. In 1761, Buckingham House was purchased by the Crown for twenty-one thousand pounds, and settled upon Queen Charlotte for her life, from which time it was commonly called the "Queen's House." Here George the Third and his consort constantly resided when in London; here he admitted Dr. Johnson to his famous interview; and here the Queen gave birth to all her numerous offspring with the exception of George the Fourth. The King had not been long married when he and the Queen had reason to complain of the threatened invasion of their domestic privacy by the erection of houses on the tract of ground on which Grosvenor Place now stands. Twenty thousand pounds was all that was demanded for the ground in question, and yet, notwithstanding it would have added another healthy area to the metropolis, Mr. Grenville, the most parsimonious of ministers, refused to sanction the expenditure.* Its present value, it is needless to add, is incalculable. Old Buckingham House stood till the year 1825, when it was taken down and the present palace erected by Nash on its site. Here we may cursorily mention, that in Grosvenor Place died, on the 14th of June, 1801, the celebrated American renegade, General Benedict Arnold.

James Street, Buckingham Gate, overlooking St. James's Park, is not without interest. It was in one of the houses in this street that the well-known historian, Bishop Kennet, expired; and in another that the secret interview took place between the great Duke of Marlborough and the Lord Treasurer Oxford, at the time when the discovery of the disgraceful negotiations between the Duke and the French King placed the life of the Duke in the hands of the English minister. According to the account given of their secret interview by Erasmus Lewis, the faithful secretary of Lord Oxford, to Carte, the historian—"They had a meeting at Thomas Harley's house, in James Street, Westminster;

* Walpole's "Reign of George III.," vol. ii., p. 160.

Oxford coming to the street door in his coach, the Duke of Marlborough in a chair to the garden door opening into the Park. It was then resolved that the Duke of Marlborough should go abroad."—"It is known," writes Dalrymple, on the authority of Gordon, the principal of the Scots College at Paris, "that there was a private meeting between the Duke and Lord Oxford, at Mr. Thomas Harley's house, to which the Duke came by a back-door; immediately after which he quitted England." Such is an episode in the secret history of the circumstances which led to the memorable exile of the great Duke of Marlborough towards the close of the reign of Queen Anne.

At No. 11, James Street, Buckingham Gate, lived Richard Glover, the author of "Leonidas;" at No. 2, now no longer standing, resided Henry Pye, the poet laureate; and, lastly, at No. 6, died William Gifford, the translator of "Juvenal," and editor of the "Quarterly Review." The remains of Gifford were interred in Westminster Abbey.

The ground between James Street and Tothill Street, Westminster, was formerly known as Petty France. Here it was, on quitting his residence in Scotland Yard, that Milton removed to a "garden house," opening into St. James's Park. In the winter, when the leaves are off the trees, the back of the house, with the stone upon it, inscribed—

"SACRED TO MILTON, PRINCE OF POETS"

may be seen from Birdcage Walk. In this house it was that Milton lost his second wife, who died in childbed, and to whose death we owe one of the most beautiful of his sonnets—

"Methought I saw my late espoused saint,
Brought to me, like Alcestis, from the grave," &c.

Here, too, it was that the great poet became totally blind.

Milton resided in Petty France from 1652 till within a short time before the Restoration of Charles the Second, when, foreseeing the danger which awaited him in the event of a change of dynasty, he sought refuge in the house of a friend in Bartholomew Close. Here he remained concealed till he found himself included in the general amnesty, when he removed to a house in Holborn, near Red Lion Square, and shortly afterwards to Jewin Street.

Close to Milton's residence and overlooking its garden, is a detached house, in which the celebrated Jeremy Bentham lived and died.

Between Storey's Gate and the new public offices stands the residence—also overlooking St. James's Park—of the infamous Judge Jeffreys, a house easily recognisable from its having a flight of stone steps leading from it into the Park, as well as from its having a chapel adjoining. Both the steps and the chapel are associated with Jeffreys's occupation of the house; the former, it is said, having been constructed by the especial favour and permission of James the Second, and the latter having been the great room in which he transacted judicial business out of term. This house, the entrance to which is in Duke Street, Westminster, was subsequently purchased by the Government from the son of Lord Jeffreys, and in the reign of William the Third was used as the Admiralty Office.

Through Storey's Gate—so called from its having been near the residence of one Edward Storey, in the reign of Charles the Second—we pass into Westminster.

KING STREET, WESTMINSTER,—ST. MAR-GARET'S CHURCH.

WESTMINSTER, KING STREET.—RESIDENCE OF SPENSER, CAREW, LORD DORSET, CROMWELL.—GREAT PLAGUE.—MRS. OLDFIELD.—DOWNING STREET. —GARDINER'S LANE.—CANNON ROW.—ST. MARGARET'S CHURCH.—THE SANCTUARY.

THE old city of Westminster—with its venerable Abbey, and its gloomy and narrow streets, once the residence of peers, courtiers, and poets—constitutes, perhaps, the most interesting district of the great metropolis. We have the Sanctuary, too, famous in history—the beautiful but mouldering cloisters of the old Abbey—the Almonry, anciently called the Eleemosynary, where the monks distributed alms to the poor, and where Caxton, under the auspices of Bishop Islip, established the first printing-press in England; and, lastly, we have still left to us Westminster Hall, with all its host of historical associations.

Previously to the building of the present Parliament Street, King Street constituted the only thoroughfare between the cities of London and Westminster; yet such was its miserable state that on the days on which the sovereign opened or dissolved Parliament, faggots had to be thrown into the ruts in order to render the motion of the ponderous state-coach at all endurable. Curious then it is, in glancing over the "New View of London," published in 1708, to find King Street dignified as "*the most spacious street and principal for trade* in Westminster, being between the Gate at the south end of the Privy Garden and Abbey Yard." It may be mentioned that the Gate in question was one which spanned King Street, immediately to the north of where Downing Street now stands; forming originally a part of the palace of Whitehall. In the reign of Charles the First it contained the apartments of the beautiful and intriguing Mary Countess of Buckingham, the mother of the great favourite, George Villiers, Duke of Buckingham, who, dying in the "Gatehouse Whitehall" in 1632, her body was conveyed hence with great pomp to Westminster Abbey, where it was laid beside the murdered remains of her ill-fated son.

King Street is replete with interesting associations. Either in this gloomy thoroughfare, or in the streets which till lately diverged from it, not only have there lived or died many illustrious persons whose names are familiar to us in the literary or historical annals of our country, but through this mean thoroughfare the majority of our kings since the Conquest have passed either to their coronations or to their last homes in Westminster Abbey.

The first illustrious name with which King Street is associated appears to be that of Charles Lord Howard of Effingham, the great High Admiral, at the time of the setting out of the Spanish Armada. Here, too, in the reign of Elizabeth, lived for a short time, and died, the great poet, Edmund Spenser. When, in 1598, Tyrone's rebellion burst forth in Ireland, the political opinions of the poet rendered him so obnoxious to the infuriated insurgents, that his only safety lay in immediate flight. He had scarcely, however, turned his back on his beloved home at Kilcolman, when the rebels took possession of it, and, having carried off his goods, set fire to the house, in the flames of which an infant child, whom he had been compelled to leave behind him, unhappily perished. Ruined and broken-hearted, the great poet flew to England, taking up his abode on his arrival in London in a small inn or lodging-house in King Street, Westminster. The circumstances of his end are painful to reflect upon. According to Drummond of Hawthornden, whose informant was Ben Jonson—" The Irish, having robbed Spenser's goods, and burnt his house and a little child new born, he and his wife escaped, and after, he died for lack of bread in King Street, and refused twenty pieces sent to him by my Lord of Essex, and said, he was sorry he had no time to spend them." Such was the end of that great poet of whom Dryden said—" No man was ever born with a greater genius or had more knowledge to support it "—whom Thomson, the author of " The Seasons," confessedly took as his model— whom Joseph Warton ranked in erudition next to Milton— whom Milton himself was not ashamed to confess as his original—by reading whom Cowley tells us that he was " made a poet "—and, lastly, whose " Fairy Queen " Pope tells us he had not only read " with a vast deal of delight " when he was only twelve years old, but read with no less pleasure after the lapse of nearly half a century. " The armorial shield of the Spensers," are the famous words of Gibbon, " may be emblazoned with the triumphs of a Marlborough, but I exhort them to look upon the 'Fairy Queen' as the proudest jewel in their coronet."

The poet, as we have seen, died in a miserable lodging-house *of absolute want of bread;* but, as is often the fate of genius, the breath had scarcely departed from his body, when the great, the titled, and the powerful came forward to do honour to his memory, and to shower laurels on his grave. His remains were carried in state from King Street to Westminster; the expenses of his funeral being defrayed by the great favourite, the Earl of Essex. " His hearse," writes

Camden, "was attended by poets and mournful elegies; and poems, with the pens that wrote them, were thrown into his tomb;" and, lastly, the celebrated Anne Countess of Dorset, erected the monument over his grave.

One would like to be able to point out the house in King Street in which once resided Thomas Carew, the most graceful poet of the reign of Charles the First, and afterwards the faithful adherent of his unfortunate master. There it was that Ben Jonson, Sir William Davenant, May, the translator of Lucan's "Pharsalia," and Sir John Suckling were his frequent guests. His burial-place is unknown, and even the year of his death is a disputed point; yet the beautiful song—

"He that loves a rosy cheek,
Or a coral lip admires," &c.

will, perhaps, continue to be read and appreciated as long as the English language endures.

In King Street, too, lived the witty and accomplished Charles Lord Buckhurst, afterwards Earl of Dorset, a nobleman who had been as notorious in his youth for his wild frolics and debauchery, as he was afterwards distinguished for all the virtues and graces which throw a dignity over human nature—

"For pointed satire I would Buckhurst choose,
The best good man with the worst-natured muse."

A high compliment this from Rochester, who also said of his friend—" I know not how it is, but my Lord Dorset can do anything, and yet is never to blame." "He was the first nobleman," writes Horace Walpole, " in the voluptuous Court of Charles the Second, and in the gloomy one of King William. He had as much wit as his first master, or his contemporaries Buckingham and Rochester, without the royal want of feeling, the Duke's want of principles, or the Earl's want of thought."—"Lord Dorset," writes Bishop Burnet, "was so lazy, that though the King seemed to court him to be a favourite, he would not give himself the trouble that belonged to that post." Lord Dorset is now, perhaps, best remembered from his famous song, addressed to the ladies of the gay court of Charles the Second, which was composed by him at sea on the day before the great sea-fight in 1665, in which Opdam, the Dutch Admiral, was blown up with all his crew :—

"To all you Ladies now on land,
We men at sea indite ;
But first would have you understand
How hard it is to write :
The Muses now, and Neptune too,
We must implore to write to you,
With a fa, la, la, la, la," &c.

A melancholy interest attaches itself to King Street as being the thoroughfare through which the unfortunate Charles the First was conducted on the first and last days of his memorable trial in Westminster Hall. On both of these occasions his conveyance was a sedan-chair, by the side of which his faithful follower, Herbert—the only person who was allowed to attend him—walked bareheaded. As he returned through King Street, after his condemnation, the inhabitants, we are told, not only shed tears, but, unawed by the soldiers who lined the street, offered up audible prayers for his eternal welfare.

It is curious to find that at the time of Charles's execution Oliver Cromwell was residing in King Street. It was from this house, six months after the death of the King, that Cromwell departed to prosecute his memorable campaign in Ireland. "This evening, about five of the clock," runs one of the newspapers of the day, "the Lord Lieutenant of Ireland began his journey by the way of Windsor, and so to Bristol. He went forth in that state and equipage as the like hath hardly been seen; himself in a coach with six gallant Flanders mares, whitish grey, divers coaches accompanying him, and very many great officers of the army; his life-guard, consisting of eighty gallant men, the meanest whereof a commander or esquire, in stately habit, with trumpets sounding almost to the shaking of Charing Cross had it been now standing. Of his life-guard many are colonels, and, believe it, it's such a guard as is hardly to be paralleled in the world." The house which was believed to have been the residence of Cromwell stood on the north side, and has only within the present century been razed to the ground.

Not many years after the death of Charles, the Protector was passing through King Street in his coach on his way from Whitehall to Westminster, when an incident occurred, of which Richard Lord Broghill, afterwards Earl of Orrery, who was in the coach with Cromwell at the time, gave the following account to his chaplain and biographer, Morrice. "At one particular time it happened the crowd of people was so great that the coach could not go forward, and the place was so narrow, that all the halberdiers were either before the coach or behind it, none of them having room to stand by the side. While they were in this posture Lord Broghill observed the door of a cobbler's stall to open and shut a little, and at every opening of it his lordship saw something bright, like a drawn sword or a pistol. Upon which my lord drew out his sword with the scabbard on it, and struck upon the stall, asking who was there. This was no sooner done, but a tall man burst out with a sword by his side, and Cromwell was so much frightened that he called his guard to seize him; but the man got away in the crowd. My lord thought him to be an officer in the army of Ireland, whom he remembered Cromwell had disgusted; and his lordship apprehended he lay there in wait to kill him. Upon this Cromwell forbore to come any more that way, but a little time after sickened and died."

The next occasion on which Cromwell passed through King Street was to his grave in Westminster Abbey. The funeral procession was a magnificent one. On each side of King Street, which was strewed with gravel, was drawn up a line of soldiers in "red coats and black buttons," with their regimental colours enclosed in cypress. The hearse, adorned with plumes and escutcheons, was drawn by six horses in trappings of black velvet. On it reclined a recumbent waxen effigy of the late Protector, habited in the robes of royalty, with a crown on its head and the globe and sceptre in its hands. At the head and feet of the figure were placed two seats, on each of which sat a gentleman of the bedchamber. Over the hearse itself extended a velvet pall borne by several persons of distinction; and in this solemn state the body was conducted to the great western entrance of the Abbey, where it was received by the clergy with the usual ceremonials.

During the great plague in 1665, King Street was one of the places visited by the giant pestilence. Its vicinity to the palace of Whitehall—the appalling sight of the red cross, and the words "Lord have mercy upon us," painted upon the doors—terrified the neighbouring inhabitants of the palace, and Charles the Second departed with his voluptuous court to breathe the purer air of Oxford. "This day," on the 20th of June, writes Pepys, "I informed myself that there died four or five at Westminster of the plague, in several houses, upon Sunday last, in Bell Alley, over against the Palace Gate;" and on the following day he writes: "I find all the town going out of town, the coaches and carriages being all

·full of people going into the country." Again, on the 28th, he writes : " In my way to Westminster Hall, I observed several plague-houses in King Street and the palace ;" and on the 29th : " To Whitehall, where the court was full of waggons and people ready to go out of town. This end of the town every day grows very bad of the plague."—" For some weeks," writes Lingard, " the tide of emigration flowed from every outlet towards the country : it was checked at last by the refusal of the Lord Mayor to grant certificates of health, and by the neighbouring townships, which rose in their own defence, and formed a barrier round the devoted city."

The October Club, founded in the reign of William and Mary, held their meetings, first at the Bell and afterwards at the Crown, in King Street.

King Street is intimately connected with the strange fortunes of the beautiful and accomplished actress, Mrs. Oldfield, who in her girlhood was employed here as a sempstress. She was the daughter of a Captain Oldfield, formerly an officer in the Life Guards, whose extravagance had reduced his widow to such a state of penury that she had to seek an asylum in the house of her sister, Mrs. Voss, who kept the Mitre Tavern in St. James's Market, apparently the Mrs. Voss once well known as the mistress of Sir Godfrey Kneller. The chief enjoyment of the young girl was in reading plays, and as she was one day entertaining her relations at the Mitre with reading aloud to them, the musical sweetness of her voice caught the ear of an occasional frequenter of the tavern, the celebrated dramatic writer, George Farquhar, who, after listening at the door for a few moments, entered the apartment. Struck with her surpassing grace and beauty, and the peculiar talent which she displayed for the stage, Farquhar, in conjunction with Sir John Vanbrugh, introduced her to Rich, the patentee of Drury Lane; the result was that, at the age of sixteen, she made her appearance in public as Candiope in Dryden's play of "Secret Love," with a salary of *fifteen shillings a week!* Fortunately it was a time extremely favourable for the *début* of a young actress. Mrs. Cross had just eloped from the theatre with a gay baronet; Mrs. Verbruggen had recently died in childbed; and Mrs. Barry and Mrs. Bracegirdle had just retired from the stage. Miss Oldfield subsequently performed the character of Lady Surewell in Farquhar's comedy of the "Constant Couple," in which she was so successful that the play had a run of fifty-one nights. By this time she had grown so much in favour with the public, that we are told Rich increased her salary *to twenty shillings a week!* "Had her birth," writes Walpole, speaking of her performance of Lady Betty Modish in the "Careless Husband," "placed her in a higher rank of life, she had certainly appeared in reality—what in this play she only excellently acted—an agreeable gay woman of quality, a little too conscious of her natural attraction. Women of the first rank might have borrowed some part of her behaviour without the least diminution of their sense of dignity." It may be mentioned that the young actress had scarcely appeared on the stage, when her wit and beauty captivated the heart of the handsome and accomplished Arthur Maynwaring, by whom she had a son, who bore the baptismal and surname of his father, and who afterwards followed his mother to the grave as chief mourner. Maynwaring dying in 1712, of a cold caught by him in visiting the Duchess of Marlborough at St. Albans, Mrs. Oldfield shortly afterwards placed herself under the protection of General Charles Churchill, the son of an elder brother of the great Duke of Marlborough.

> "None led through youth a gayer life than he,
> Cheerful in converse, smart in repartee;
> Sweet was his night and joyful was his day,
> He dined with Walpole, and with Oldfield lay."
>
>   SIR C. HANBURY WILLIAMS.

By General Churchill she had also one son, who married Lady Mary Walpole, a natural child of Sir Robert, for whom he obtained the rank of an Earl's daughter. Mrs. Oldfield died on the 23rd of October, 1730, at the age of forty-seven. Her contemporaries considered her deserving of burial in Westminster Abbey, and accordingly thither her body was borne through the very street in which she had formerly lived a humble sempstress. Her pall was not only supported by persons of distinction, but her remains were suffered to lie in state in the Jerusalem Chamber. Her grave is towards the west end of the south aisle of the Abbey, between the monuments of Craggs and Congreve, near the Consistory Court, a circumstance which induced a bystander at her interment, to scribble the following lines on a piece of paper which he was indecent enough to throw into the grave:

> "If penance in the Bishop's court be feared,
> Congreve, and Craggs, and Oldfield will be scared,
> To find that, at the Resurrection-day,
> They all so near the Consistory lay."

Downing Street derives its name from Sir George Downing, Secretary to the Treasury in the reign of Charles the Second. Here stood the residence of the ancient family of the De Veres, Earls of Oxford, of whom Aubrey de Vere, the twentieth and last Earl, died here on the 18th of March, 1703, and hence his remains were conveyed to Westminster Abbey, where they were interred in St. John the Baptist's Chapel. Here stands the official residence of the First Lord of the Treasury, conferred by George the Second on his favourite minister, Sir Robert Walpole, and on his successors in that high office for ever. Here, to the residence of an officer of Parliament, the great Lord Chatham was carried from the House of Lords after his memorable fainting-fit in the House in 1778. Here lived Gibbon's friend, Lord Sheffield, whose guest in Downing Street the great historian repeatedly mentions his having been. Lastly, in 1763, here lodged Dr. Johnson's biographer, James Boswell.

Diverging from King Street, parallel with Downing Street, formerly ran Axe Yard, the name of which was afterwards changed to Fludyer Street. A part of the new Public Offices now occupies its site. It was in Axe Yard that the misfortune happened to the celebrated Sir William Davenant which cost him his nose, and which afforded so much food for merriment to his brother poets in the reign of Charles the First. Sir John Suckling, alluding to Davenant having been selected to succeed Ben Jonson as poet laureate, says in his " Session of the Poets " :—

> " Surely the company would have been content,
> If they could have found any precedent ;
> But in all their records, in verse or in prose,
> There was not one *Laureate without a nose.*"

In the same poem, Suckling attributes the loss of Davenant's nose to

> "——————— a foolish mischance,
> That he had got lately travelling in France."

Anthony Wood, however, a more curious researcher, tells us in his " Athenæ Oxonienses,"—" The said mischance, which Sir John mentions, happened to Davenant through a dalliance with a handsome black girl in Axe Yard in Westminster, on whom he thought when he spoke of Dalga in his 'Gondibert,' which cost him his nose ; and thereupon some wits were too cruelly bold with him and his accident, as Sir John Mennes, Sir John Denham, &c."

In 1659–60, we find the celebrated Samuel Pepys residing in Axe Yard; and here, after the name had been changed to Fludyer Street, resided James Macpherson, the translator of Ossian's Poems, with whom Sir Nathaniel Wraxall mentions his having on more than one occasion dined in this street.

In Gardiner's Lane, which formerly ran parallel with Axe Yard, the celebrated engraver, Wentzel Hollar, in 1677, breathed his last. His end was such as has too often been the fate of genius. After all his indefatigable labours, and when he was on the verge of his seventieth year, not only was an execution put into his house in Gardiner's Lane, but he narrowly escaped becoming the inmate of a jail. His only desire, we are told, was the liberty of dying in his bed, and to be removed to no other prison but his grave. According to the "Biographia Britannica," Hollar was interred in the burial-ground of New Chapel, Westminster. Aubrey, however, writes—" He died on our Lady Day (25th Martii), 1677, and is buried in St. Margaret's Churchyard, at Westminster, near the north-west corner of the tower.*

Gardiner's Lane leads us into Duke Street, where, as has been already mentioned, stood the house of the infamous Lord Jeffreys, No. 25. Here, for many years, in a house immediately facing Charles Street, lived the celebrated poet and politician, Matthew Prior. It was at this house he requested his friend Swift, in July, 1717, to take up his quarters instead of at the Cocoa-Tree. Prior, too, writes to Swift on the 5th of May, 1719: "Having spent part of my summer very agreeably in Cambridgeshire, with dear Lord Harley, I am returned without him to my own

* Aubrey's "Letters of Eminent Men."

palace in Duke Street, whence I endeavour to exclude all the tumult and noise of the neighbouring Court of Requests, and to live *aut nihil agendo aut aliud agendo*, till he comes to town."

At his house in Park Street, close by, died, on the 27th of March, 1699, the celebrated divine, Edward Stillingfleet, Bishop of Worcester; and here also resided the great critic, Richard Bentley. In this street the late Lord Palmerston was born in 1784.

Running parallel with King Street and Parliament Street is Cannon Row, sometimes called Channel Row. According to Stow, it derives its name from the Canons of St. Stephen's Chapel, who were anciently lodged here, while others seem inclined to trace it to a branch, or *channel*, of the Thames which, in former times, ran between the north end of the Row and Privy Gardens. Here stood the magnificent residence of Anne Stanhope, the second and turbulent wife of the great Protector, Duke of Somerset. Here, in the reign of Queen Elizabeth, was the inn or palace of the Stanleys, Earls of Derby. Close by was the mansion of Henry, second Earl of Lincoln, who sat in judgment on Mary Queen of Scots, and who was one of the peers deputed by Queen Elizabeth to arrest the Earl of Essex in his house. Here, in the reign of James the First, the Sackvilles, Earls of Dorset, had their town residence; and, lastly, here, in the time of Queen Elizabeth was the mansion of the great family of the Cliffords, Earls of Cumberland. Anne Clifford, Countess of Dorset, informs us that here, on the 1st of May, 1589, she was begotten by her most valiant father, George Earl of Cumberland, on the body of her most virtuous mother, Margaret, daughter of Francis Earl of Bedford. This great heiress—who married, first, Richard Sackville, Earl of Dorset, and who subsequently became the wife of Walpole's "memorable simpleton," Philip Herbert, Earl of Pembroke and Montgomery—is now, perhaps, best remembered from her famous letter to Sir Joseph Williamson, Secretary of State to Charles the Second, when applied to by him to nominate a member of Parliament for the borough of Appleby :—

"I have been bullied by a usurper; I have been neglected by a court; but I will not be dictated to by a subject: your man sha'n't stand.
"ANNE DORSET,
"Pembroke and Montgomery."

It may be mentioned that in the reign of William and Mary there ran a private way from Whitehall Palace through Privy Gardens and Channel Row to [New Palace Yard.' Thus, on the morning of Queen Mary's coronation we find her—arrayed in her robes of state, and wearing a circlet of gold round her head—conveyed in a sedan-chair from Whitehall to the Court of Wards at Westminster, where she rested herself till summoned to take her part in the ceremony. Without a special order from the Lord Chamberlain, it would seem that the privilege of using this route was confined to the royal family."*

Channel or Cannon Row is connected by a curious anecdote with the last days of Charles the First. On one of the nights which intervened between his trial and his execution, the unfortunate King took a ring from his finger, and delivering it to his affectionate follower, Herbert, desired him to proceed with it to a certain house in Channel Row, where he was to deliver it to the lady of the house, without saying a word. This person proved to be Lady Wheeler,

* Strickland's "Lives of the Queens of England."

the King's laundress. Having obtained the watch-word from Colonel Tomlinson who commanded the guard, Herbert proceeded, on a dark night, to the house which the King had designated, where he readily gained admission to its mistress. The result was her placing in his hands a small cabinet closed with three seals, which she charged him to deliver to the same person from whom he had received the ring. The next morning, in Herbert's presence, the King broke the seals, when the cabinet was found to contain a number of diamonds and jewels, most of them set in broken insignia of the Order of the Garter. "This," said the King, "is all the wealth which I have it in my power to bequeath to my children."

In Derby House, the name of which is still retained in Derby Street, were lodged, in the reign of James the First, the suite of the Queen's brother, Ulric, Duke of Holstein, during his visit in England in 1604. The Duke himself, it appears, was lodged in Whitehall Palace, having "twenty dishes of meat allowed every meal; certain of the guard bringing him the same, and attending therewith."* In Derby House died, in 1643, the celebrated republican politician, John Pym. "Over against" Derby House, on the site of Manchester Buildings stood Manchester House, once the residence of the Montagu's, Earls of Manchester. In Manchester Buildings, Thurtell, the murderer of William Weare at Gill's Hill in Hertfordshire, at one time kept a gaming-house.

At the bottom of King Street, under the shadow of the magnificent Abbey, stands the interesting parish church of St. Margaret's, Westminster, originally built by Edward the Confessor. The Abbey had previously been used as the parish church, to the great inconvenience of the monks, to

* Lodge's "Illustrations of English History," vol. iii., p. 106.

relieve whom the Confessor caused a small church to be built under the wing of the magnificent pile which now overshadows it. St. Margaret's was rebuilt in the reign of Edward the First, and again in the reign of Edward the Fourth. What remains of the ancient building is extremely beautiful; especially the altar recess, which, with its groined roof, its panelled niches, and fresco designs, has been much and deservedly admired. But the gem of St. Margaret's is its magnificent east window, unquestionably one of the most beautiful specimens of painted glass in Europe—which was executed by order of the magistrates of Dort as a present to King Henry the Seventh. The subject of the three middle compartments is the Crucifixion. In a compartment on the right hand Arthur Prince of Wales is depicted on his knees with his patron saint, St. George, standing in full armour above him; while on the left side is his bride, Catherine of Aragon, with the figure of St. Catherine, and the instruments of her martyrdom, over the young princess's head. When, after the lapse of five years from the commencement of this admirable work of art, it was ready for erection, King Henry was no more. Its subsequent history is very interesting. By Henry the Eighth it was presented to Waltham Abbey, where it remained set up until the dissolution of that monastery, when it was preserved from destruction by the last Abbot, who sent it to New Hall, in Essex, a seat of the Butlers, Earls of Ormond. In the course of the next century it passed successively, with the property of New Hall, into the possession of the Earl of Wiltshire, father of Anne Boleyn, of Thomas Radcliffe, Earl of Sussex, the first George Villiers, Duke of Buckingham, Oliver Cromwell, and General Monk. When the civil wars broke out it was in the possession of Monk, who, dreading lest it might fall a sacrifice to the blind zeal of the bigoted Puritans, caused it to be carefully taken to pieces and buried in the garden at New Hall. Here it remained till the Restoration, when, having reverted to the second Duke of Buckingham, it was dug up and restored to its former position in the chapel. Some years afterwards, when the chapel at New Hall fell to ruins, the window was again taken down, and remained for a considerable time packed up in boxes, till purchased by Mr. Conyers for his chapel at Copthall, in Essex. From the son of this gentleman it was purchased, in 1758, for four hundred guineas, by the committee appointed for repairing and beautifying St. Margaret's, and was forthwith placed in its present position.

In addition to its beautiful window, St. Margaret's is replete with interest.

Essentially the church of the House of Commons, it was here, in the reign of Charles the First, that Hugh Peters, Philip Nye, and other nonconformist divines preached their Fast-Day Sermons and other homilies in the presence of Cromwell, Ireton, Bradshaw, Praise-God Barebones, and their fellow-democrats of the day.

Either in St. Margaret's Church, or in its adjoining churchyard, rest the remains of many eminent persons. Here lies the honoured dust of William Caxton, who first introduced printing into England, and who for years pursued his priceless labours in the precincts of the adjoining Abbey. In the chancel lies the body of the celebrated satirical poet John Skelton, poet laureate to Henry the Eighth, who, in spite of his unpolished verse and his buffooneries in the pulpit, is described by Erasmus, in one of his letters to Henry the Eighth, as *Britannicarum literarum lumen et decus*—" the light and glory of English literature." Anthony Wood tells us " he was guilty of many crimes, *as most poets* *are.*" At length Skelton was bold enough to point his satire at Cardinal Wolsey. The officers of that powerful minister were immediately on his track, but happily he succeeded in keeping out of their clutches by taking refuge in the Sanctuary at Westminster. Here he was treated with great kindness by Abbot Islip, and here he breathed his last in 1529, only a short time before the fall of the great Cardinal.*

Close to the grave of Skelton lie the remains of a brother poet, Thomas Churchyard, of whose chequered fortunes we would gladly know more particulars than have been handed down to us. With no other accomplishment, as far as we are aware, than being able to play the lute, he quitted his father's roof at the age of seventeen, and, with only a small sum of money in his pocket, made his appearance at the court of Henry the Eighth. Anthony Wood tells us, that as long as his money lasted he continued a "roysterer," but his means being soon exhausted, he gladly obtained admission into the household of the accomplished Henry Howard, Earl of Surrey. Unhappily the early death of his noble patron again threw him upon the world, with no better prospect apparently than that of becoming a soldier of fortune ; soon, however, growing tired of the military profession, he travelled into foreign countries, and on his return took up his abode at Oxford for the purpose of pursuing his studies at his ease. But it was not in the nature of the restless poet to remain quiet in stirring times. Accordingly, on the breaking out of the war with Scotland, he hastened to that country; was taken prisoner in an engagement with the enemy—probably in the battle of Pinkey—and when, at the conclusion of the war, he obtained his release, he returned to the Court "very poor and bare, spoiled of all,

* Chalmers. "Warton's Hist. of Eng. Poetry."

and his body in a very sickly and decayed condition." Fortune, however, once more smiled on him. He was taken into the household of Elizabeth's great favourite, Robert Dudley, Earl of Leicester, shortly after which he married a rich widow, Mrs. Catherine Browning. His marriage proving in every respect an unhappy one, the poet again took up arms, was wounded and taken prisoner in the wars in the Low Countries, but fortunately found means to escape. After walking for several days through an enemy's country, he at length contrived to reach England, where, being still poor and restless, he was once more compelled to set off for the wars. Again he was taken prisoner, and having been tried and condemned to death as a spy, would have been sent to execution but for the intercession of a noble lady who obtained permission for him to return to his own country. Of his subsequent history we know little, except that his end, like that of most poets, was one of penury and privation. There was formerly a monument to his memory in the porch of St. Margaret's Church, of which Camden has preserved the inscription, but the monument itself has long since disappeared.

In the chancel, near the high altar of St. Margaret's, lie the headless remains of Sir Walter Raleigh, who was executed close by in Old Palace Yard. Either in the same grave, or in its immediate vicinity, rests the body of James Harrington, the well-known author of the "Oceana." According to Toland, Harrington's biographer, the grave of the great political writer is "on the south side of the altar," *next* to that of Sir Walter Raleigh. Here also was buried Milton's second wife, and "late espoused saint," Catherine Woodcock, upon whose death, in giving birth to a daughter, the great poet composed the beautiful sonnet to which we have already had occasion to refer. Less than a year had elapsed since she had stood with him at the altar of this very church as his bride.

The only other persons of particular note who appear to have been interred in St. Margaret's church are the fair and frail Lady Denham, the wife of Sir John Denham, the poet; Sir John Cutler, the miser, rendered memorable by Pope; and the gallant cavalier, Sir Philip Warwick, the faithful attendant of Charles the First in his misfortunes, and the author of some interesting memoirs of his unfortunate master. With the exception of a tablet erected to the memory of Caxton by the Roxburghe Club, and a brass tablet which records that Sir Walter Raleigh lies buried in the church, St. Margaret's contains no memorial of the resting-places of the many remarkable persons whom we have mentioned as having been interred within its walls. Nevertheless in the church are many old and curious monuments of persons less known to fame, and among them memorials of more than one faithful adherent of our Tudor sovereigns.

Before quitting St. Margaret's church we must not omit to mention that it was at the altar that the celebrated Edward Hyde, Earl of Clarendon, was married to his second wife, Frances, daughter of Thomas Aylesbury, with whom—as the great Chancellor himself informs us—he lived " very comfortably in the most uncomfortable times, and very joyfully in those times when matter of joy was administered, for the space of five or six and thirty years."* By this wife Lord Clarendon was the father of Anne Hyde, Duchess of York, who became the mother of Mary and Anne, successively Queens of England.

* Life of Himself.

Three other eminent persons whose marriages took place here were Edmund Waller, the poet, Samuel Pepys, the delightful diarist, and Thomas Campbell, the poet.*

Much would one like to know the spot in St. Margaret's churchyard where rest the remains of the great and gallant Admiral Blake. The parliament having voted him a public funeral, he was buried with great magnificence in Henry the Seventh's chapel. At the Restoration, however, to the great disgrace of the government, his body was taken up and flung into a pit in St. Margaret's churchyard. At the same time were removed and thrown into the same hole, the bodies of Oliver Cromwell's mother—of Thomas May, the translator of Lucan and the historian of the Commonwealth—and of the celebrated Dr. Dorislaus, assistant to the high court of justice which tried Charles the First.

* Cunningham's "Handbook of London."

WESTMINSTER.

THE SANCTUARY.—PERSONS WHO TOOK REFUGE THERE.—THE GATEHOUSE.
—ITS HISTORY.—TOTHILL STREET.—THE STREETS OF OLD WESTMINSTER.
—WESTMINSTER SCHOOL.—REMARKABLE PERSONS EDUCATED THERE.

THE famous Sanctuary—a place of refuge for criminals apparently from the time of Edward the Confessor—stood chiefly on the ground on which Westminster Hospital and the Guildhall now stand. The church which belonged to it, which was in the form of a cross, and of great antiquity, was pulled down about 1750 to make room for a market which was afterwards held on its site. Dr. Stukeley, the antiquary, who remembered its destruction, informs us that its walls were of vast strength and thickness, and that it was not without difficulty that it was demolished. The open space to the north of Westminster Abbey still bears the name of "Broad Sanctuary."

When Edward the Fourth, in 1470, was compelled to fly the kingdom at the approach of the king-maker Warwick, it was to the Sanctuary at Westminster that his beautiful Queen, Elizabeth Grey, flew for refuge, and within its precincts that she was delivered of her eldest son, afterwards Edward the Fifth, whose subsequent tragical fate in the Tower is so well known.

> "I'll hence forthwith unto the Sanctuary,
> To save at least the heir of Edward's right.
> There shall I rest secure from force and fraud.

> Come, therefore, let us fly, while we may fly,
> If Warwick take us, we are sure to die."

Thirteen years afterwards, when the designs of Richard Duke of Gloucester against the life and authority of his young nephew were but too apparent, the Queen, with her young son, the Duke of York, again flew for refuge to the Sanctuary at Westminster. Her eldest was already in the hands of the usurper.

> "Ay me, I see the downfall of our house!
> The tiger now hath seized the gentle hind;
> Insulting tyranny begins to jut
> Upon the innocent and aweless throne.
> Welcome, destruction, death, and massacre!
> I see, as in a map, the end of all.
> . . . . . .
> Come, come, my boy; we will to Sanctuary."

Richard, anxious by all means to get the young Duke of York in his power, and enraged at his prey slipping through his hands, would with little scruple have taken the young Prince from the Sanctuary by force, but that he was opposed at the council-table by Cardinal Bourchier Archbishop of Canterbury, and Rotherham Archbishop of York, who boldly protested against the sacrilege of the measure. The church of Westminster, and its Sanctuary, said the two prelates, had been consecrated five hundred years since by St. Peter himself, who descended from heaven in the night, attended by multitudes of angels. No King of England, they added, had ever dared to violate that Sanctuary, and such an attempt would certainly draw down upon the whole kingdom the just vengeance of God. It was at length agreed that before having resort to more violent measures the two primates should wait on the Queen in the Sanctuary, and endeavour by persuasion to induce her to comply with Gloucester's wishes. The scene between Gloucester's creature, the Duke of Buckingham, and Cardinal Bourchier is admirably dramatized by Shakspeare:—

> "*Buck.* ————— Lord Cardinal, will your grace
> Persuade the Queen to send the Duke of York
> Unto his princely brother presently?
> If she deny, Lord Hastings, go with him,
> And from her jealous arms pluck him perforce.
> *Card.* My Lord of Buckingham, if my weak oratory
> Can from his mother win the Duke of York,
> Anon expect him here; but if she be obdurate
> To mild entreaties, God in heaven forbid
> We should infringe the holy privilege
> Of blessed *sanctuary!* not for all this land
> Would I be guilty of so deep a sin.
> *Buck.* You are too senseless-obstinate, my Lord,
> Too ceremonious and traditional:
> Weigh it but with the grossness of this age,
> You break not sanctuary in seizing him.
> The benefit thereof is always granted
> To those whose dealings have deserved the place,
> And those who have the wit to claim the place:
> This prince hath neither claimed it nor deserved it;
> And therefore, in mine opinion, cannot have it:
> Then, taking him from thence that is not there,
> You break no privilege nor charter there.
> Oft have I heard of sanctuary men;
> But sanctuary children ne'er till now.
> *Card.* My Lord, you shall o'errule my mind for once.
> Come on, Lord Hastings, will you go with me?
> *Hast.* I go, my Lord."
>
> King Richard III., act iii., sc. 1.

There seems to be little doubt that at the time when Cardinal Bourchier and the Archbishop of York waited on the unfortunate Queen in the Sanctuary, they were severally fully satisfied of Gloucester's good faith, and consequently it was not unnatural that they should use both argument and entreaty to induce her to give up her beloved child. For a long time she remained obstinate, till finding herself unsupported in her opposition, and being assured that force would in all probability be used should she persist in her obduracy, she at last complied, and produced her son to the two prelates. At the moment of parting she is said to have been struck with a strange presentiment of his future fate; but it was now too late to retract. Overcome with feelings which only a mother can experience, she caught the child in her arms, wetted him with her tears, and at last reluctantly delivered him to the Cardinal, who immediately conducted him to the Protector. Richard, we are told, no sooner caught sight of his young nephew, than he ran towards him with open arms, and kissing him, exclaimed— "Now welcome, my Lord, with all my heart." The sequel of the melancholy history is too well known to require recapitulation.

The neighbourhood of the Sanctuary is intimately connected with the early, as well as with the closing, history of Ben Jonson. When a scholar at Westminster School, he must often have wandered in its precincts; in a house overlooking St. Margaret's Churchyard he died; and in the neighbouring Abbey he lies buried. "Long since, in King James's time," writes Aubrey, "I have heard my uncle Danvers say, who knew him, that Ben Jonson lived without Temple Bar, at a comb-maker's shop, about the Elephant and Castle. In his later time he lived in Westminster, in the house under which you pass as you go out of the churchyard into the old palace, where he died. He lies buried in the north aisle, in the path of square stone (the rest is lozenge), opposite to the scutcheon of Robertus de Ros, with this inscription only upon him, in a pavement-square, blue marble, about fourteen inches square—O RARE BEN JONSON!

—which was done at the charge of Jack Young, afterwards knighted, who, walking there when the grave was covering, gave the fellow eighteenpence to cut it."*

In 1780, Edmund Burke was residing in the "Broad Sanctuary," Westminster.

At the end of Tothill Street, facing the towers and the great western entrance of the Abbey, stood the famous Gatehouse—built in the reign of Edward the Third—anciently a prison under the jurisdiction of the Abbots of Westminster. Formerly, when malefactors were conducted to this prison, it was the custom, in order to prevent their touching the Sanctuary, which would have insured them their liberty, to bring them by a circuitous route down a small lane running parallel with Great George Street, which from this circumstance obtained the name of Thieving Lane. It was in the Gatehouse, Westminster, that one of the sweetest of love-poets, Richard Lovelace—so celebrated for his misfortunes and the beauty of his person—suffered imprisonment for his loyalty to his unfortunate master, Charles the First. Here it was, too, that he composed his beautiful song, " To Althea, from prison."

> "Stone walls do not a prison make,
> Nor iron bars a cage ;
> Minds innocent and quiet take
> That for an hermitage.
> If I have freedom in my love,
> And in my soul am free,—
> Angels alone, that soar above,
> Enjoy such liberty."

In the Gatehouse, Westminster, died the celebrated dwarf, Sir Jeffery Hudson, whose name is immortalized in the pages of one of the greatest writers of fiction in modern

* Aubrey's "Letters of Eminent Men."

times. He was born in 1619, at Oakham, in Rutlandshire, "the least man in the least county." In his tenth year he was presented to the Duchess of Buckingham by his father, a tall and broad-shouldered yeoman, who had charge of the "baiting-bulls" of George Villiers, the first Duke. The Duchess had him dressed in satin, and attended by two tall footmen; yet, notwithstanding his elevation, her Grace —when some time afterwards Charles the First and Henrietta Maria paid a visit to the Duke and Duchess at Burghley-on-the-hill—made no scruple of having the little fellow served up in a cold pie for their majesties' diversion. Immediately on his stepping out he was presented by the Duchess to the Queen, in whose service he afterwards remained, and on whom he was twice painted in attendance by Vandyke. On the breaking out of the Civil Wars he obtained a commission as captain of horse, and subsequently accompanied his royal mistress to France, where he remained till the Restoration. Fuller says of him, that "though a dwarf, he was no dastard." On one occasion, having been teased beyond bearing by a young courtier named Crofts, Sir Jeffery challenged his persecutor to single combat, when, to his annoyance, Crofts appeared on the ground with a squirt in his hand. A real meeting was the result; it being agreed that they should fight on horseback with pistols, when, at the first shot, Sir Jeffery shot his antagonist dead. In 1682 he was most absurdly implicated by Titus Oates in the still more absurd Popish Plot, and in consequence was committed to the Gatehouse, where he died shortly afterwards, in his sixty-third year.

Tothill Street derives its name from an extensive meadow called Tothill-field, or, as Fabyan describes it in 1238, "a fielde by Westmynster, lying at ye west end of ye church." On the occasion of the magnificent rejoicings which took place in the ancient palace of Westminster at the Coronation of Queen Eleanor, consort of Henry the Third, we find "royal solemnities and goodly joustes" kept up during eight days in Tothill-fields. In the year 1248, when the dislike which Henry bore the citizens of London induced him to endeavour to injure their trade by diverting their profits into other channels, we find him adopting the expedient of granting a licence to the Abbot of Westminster for holding an annual fair, afterwards called St. Edward's Fair, for fifteen days in Tothill-fields. "To the end," writes Holinshed, "that the same should be more haunted with all manner of people, the King commanded by proclamation that other fairs holden in that season should not be kept, nor that any wares should be shewed within the city of London, either in shop or without; but that such as would sell should come for that time unto Westminster. This was done, but not without great trouble and pains to the citizens, who had not room there but in booths and tents, to their great disquieting and disease for want of necessary provision, being turmoiled too pitifully in mire and dirt, through occasion of rain." About this period the spacious mansion of John Mansell, Priest, King's Counsel, and Lord High Chancellor of England, was probably the only one in Tothill-fields. Here, in 1256, we find him entertaining, with great magnificence, Henry the Third and his Queen, the King of Scotland, and a great number of the wealthy citizens of London.

In the latter part of the reign of Queen Elizabeth, if we may judge from the fact of Lord Dacres and Lord Grey having severally had houses here, Tothill Street must have been a fashionable quarter of the town. The name of the former nobleman is still preserved in Dacre Street, near the west end of Tothill Street. We must not omit to mention that the celebrated actor, Thomas Betterton, the son of an under-cook to Charles the First, was born in Tothill Street, in 1635.

If the reader is not unwilling to trust himself among gloomy streets and dingy alleys, and amidst a somewhat lawless population, he will be repaid by making a short circuit round the old city of Westminster. Diving into Little Dean Street, out of Tothill Street, we stand on the site of the old Almonry, where, as we have already mentioned, the monks were accustomed to distribute their alms, and where, under the protection of the Abbot, Caxton set up the first printing-press which was established in England, and printed his first book,—"The Game and Play of the Chesse." Close by, between the east end of Orchard Street and Dean's Yard, stood the Little Almonry, interesting as having been the spot where the celebrated James Harrington lived for many years, and where he apparently died. Aubrey has not only pointed out the spot with great minuteness, but has also left us a curious picture of the great political writer as he appeared at the close of life. "His durance in prison," says Aubrey, "was the cause of derilation or madness, which was not outrageous, for he would discourse rationally enough, and he was very facetious company; but he grew to have a fancy that his perspiration turned to flies, and sometimes to bees; and he had a versatile timber house built in Mr. Hart's garden, opposite to St. James's Park, to try the experiment; he would turn it to the sun, and sit towards it; then he had his fox-tails to chase away and massacre all the flies and bees that were to be found there, and then shut the chasses. Now this experiment was only to be tried in warm weather, and some flies would lie so close in the crannies and the cloth with which the place was hung, that they would not presently show themselves. A quarter of an hour after, perhaps, a fly or two, or more, might be drawn out of the lurking-holes by the warmth, and then he would cry out, 'Do you not see it is evident that these come from me ?' 'Twas the strangest sort of madness that ever I found in any one: talk of anything else, his discourse would be very ingenious aud pleasant. Anno , . . . he married his old sweet-heart, Mistress . . . . . Daynell, a comely and discreet lady. It happening so, from some private reasons, that he could not enjoy his dear in the flower of his youth, he would never lie with her; but loved and admired her dearly : for she was *vergentibus annis* when he married her, and had lost her sweetness. In his conversation he was very friendly, facetious, and hospitable. For above twenty years before he died he lived in the Little Almonry, in a fair house on the left side, which looks into the Dean's Yard, Westminster. In the upper story he had a pretty gallery, which looked into the yard, (over . . . . Court,) where he commonly dined, and meditated, and took his tobacco." In 1708 we find Lord Ashburnham, as well as the Bishops of Lincoln and Rochester, residing in Dean's Yard.

Leading from Tothill Street is York Street, formerly called Petty France from the number of French refugees who settled here on the revocation of the Edict of Nantes by Louis the Fourteenth. In like manner, York Street derives its name from the Archbishops of York, whose London residence was situated here in the days of Queen Anne.

In York Street (No. 19) is the front or street entrance to Milton's House, which has been already mentioned as having opened at the back into St. James's Park, and where he lived for about eight years. According to tradition, the cotton-willow-tree in the garden was planted by the great poet. The house in the present century was occupied by William Hazlitt.

Down the Broadway to the right is the "New Chapel," built originally in the time of Charles the First, at the expense of the Rev. George Davell, one of the prebendaries of Westminster, as a chapel of ease for the inhabitants of Petty France and of the neighbouring streets. During the Civil Wars it was converted into a stable for the horses of the Republican troopers, but was again fitted up as a chapel at the Restoration. Within its walls was buried, "privately but decently," the body of the memorable Colonel Blood.

Adjoining the burying-ground of New Chapel, to the westward, was the Artillery Ground, a name still preserved in "Artillery Brewery," which stands on part of its site. In the dreadful days of the raging of the Great Plague in 1665 —when the red cross and the words "Lord, have mercy upon us" were painted on the doors of half the houses in London, and when the dead-cart went its round in the still night, and the tinkle of the bell and the cry of "Bring out your dead" alone broke the awful silence—it was into a vast pit in this locality that the frequent dead-carts discharged their noisome cargoes by the fitful light of the torches borne by the buryers of the dead. The Pest House in Tothill Fields, and that in the fields beyond Old Street, appear to have been the two principal ones in the neighbourhood of the metropolis.

Passing along Strutton Ground, we turn down Great Peter Street, from the east side of which diverges St. Anne's Lane, in which one of the sweetest poets, Robert Herrick, resided after the Restoration of Charles the Second. The poet himself writes :—

> "To Richmond, Kingston, and to Hampton Court,
> Never again shall I with finny oar
> Put from, or draw unto the faithful shore;
> And, landing here, or safely landing there,
> Make way to my beloved Westminster."

In St. Anne's Lane also resided the celebrated musical composer, Henry Purcell, who died in 1695.

Continuing our route down Great Peter Street, the corner house of this street and Tufton Street was that to which Blood is said to have retired after he made his famous attempt on the crown jewels in the Tower. Whether or no this be the case, certain it is that the house in which Blood latterly lived, and in which he breathed his last, was in Bowling Street, a continuation of Tufton Street. He was attended in his last illness by a clergyman, who found him sensible but reserved, and to whom he declared that he had no fear of death.

Bowling Street leads us into Great College Street, of which we find more than one notice in Gibbon's interesting "Memoir of his Life and Writings." Speaking, for instance, of his return from the Continent in 1758, he writes—"The only person in England whom I was impatient to see was my aunt Porten, the affectionate guardian of my tender years. I hastened to her house in College Street, Westminster, and the evening was spent in the effusions of joy and confidence." Once more the great historian mentions his passing through Westminster, on the occasion of the last visit which he paid to his beloved Lausanne. "As my post-chaise," he says, "moved over Westminster Bridge, I bade a long farewell to the *fumum et opes, strepitumque Romœ.*"

Near to College Street is the fantastic-looking church of St. John the Evangelist, with its four belfries, one at each corner. This church, of which Sir John Vanbrugh has usually had the discredit, but the real architect of which was a person of the name of Archer, was commenced in 1721, and completed in 1728. Perhaps its chief feature of interest is its connection with the fortunes of Charles Churchill, the poet, who, previously to his resorting to satire for a livelihood, was curate and lecturer of St. John's. In Vine Street, close by, Churchill was born.

To the east of the church of St. John the Evangelist is Millbank, deriving its name from a mill which at one time stood here. Here, formerly, stood the mansion of the Mordaunts, Earls of Peterborough, in whose family it remained till the time of Charles Mordaunt, the third Earl, whose talents and eccentricities have rendered his name so famous. "Here, in my boyish days," writes Pennant, "I have often experienced the hospitality of the late Sir Robert Grosvenor, its worthy owner, who enjoyed it by the purchase, by one of his family, from the Mordaunts."

Before concluding our notices of the old city of Westminster, let us stroll into Dean's Yard, and dwell a short time on the ancient and interesting school, where so many of the most celebrated men in the literary annals of our country passed the earliest, perhaps the happiest, part of their lives. The ground on which Westminster School now stands was entirely occupied by the apartments of the Abbot, the dormitories of the monks, the refectory, the granary, and other monastical buildings. The dormitory of the King's scholars stands on the site of the old granary, built by Abbot Littlington, who died in 1386, while the hall in which they dine was formerly the refectory of the old abbots. Considerable portions of the walls of the old monastic buildings may still be traced.

That, so early as the time of the Saxon kings, there existed, on or near this spot, a school under the direction of the monks, there can be doubt. Ingulphus, Abbot of Crowland, speaks of his having been educated at it—of the disputations which he had here with the Queen of the Confessor—and of the presents which she made him in money in his boyish days. It was not, however, till 1560, a few years after the dissolution of the monasteries, that Queen Elizabeth founded the present institution for the classical education of forty boys, who are still designated as King's or Queen's scholars.

One of the earliest head-masters of Westminster School was the celebrated antiquary and historian, William Camden. According to Aubrey, whose authority was William Bagshawe, one of the under-masters of the school, Camden's lodgings were in the " the gatehouse by the Queen's scholars' chambers in Dean's Yard;" whence he used to wander forth, when his pupils were at play, to copy the inscriptions on the ancient tombs of Westminster Abbey, an occupation much more congenial to the gifted antiquary, than impressing on his pupils the necessity of learning hard words, or in flagellating the idle or the dull. Ben Jonson was one of Camden's pupils, and not only did he love and revere his old master, but must have afforded him infinite gratification when, at the early age of twenty-four, he dedicated to him, in a most affectionate address, his first, and perhaps the most admirable of his dramatic productions—" Every Man in his Humour." " It is a frail memory," he says, " that remembers but present things;" and Jonson adds—" Now I pray you to accept this—such wherein neither the confession of my manners shall make you blush, nor of my studies repent you to have been the instructor. And for the profession of my thankfulness, I am sure it will, with good men, find either praise or excuse. Your true lover,— BEN JONSON."

Glancing at the two great schools of Eton and Westminster, one would have imagined that Eton, from its rural and romantic situation, its vicinity to Windsor Castle, and its picturesque playing-fields—

> "Whose turf, whose shade, whose flowers among,
> Wanders the hoary Thames along
> His silver-winding way—"

possessed all the qualities usually thought requisite to engender or to stimulate poetical genius; while, on the other hand, Westminster, from its confined situation and dingy atmosphere, would almost seem to be an antidote to poetical fire. Eton, moreover, would seem to possess no particular advantages in the way of producing orators or statesmen; while Westminster, from its vicinity to the Houses of Parliament, and the liberty allowed the students of attending the debates, holds out every incitement to young ambition if gifted with oratorical talent. In both cases, however, the result has been exactly the opposite to what we should naturally have expected. Eton has produced but three poets of any note: Waller, Gray, and Shelley—for Lord Lyttelton and West are beings of an inferior order—yet she has made up for this deficiency in poetical talent by rearing no fewer statesmen of celebrity than Harley Earl of Oxford, Lord Bolingbroke, Sir Robert Walpole, the great Lord Chatham, Lord North, Fox, Canning, the Duke of Wellington, and the late Marquis Wellesley. On the other hand, Westminster has produced not a single illustrious statesman, while we find that more than half of our greatest poets were educated within her classical walls.

The following list of eminent persons who have been educated at Westminster School may very possibly be an imperfect one, but, such as it is, it may not be unacceptable to those who take an interest in this celebrated institution. The dates prefixed to the several names are those of birth, thus enabling the reader to form a tolerable conjecture who were contemporaries. Those from Adam Littleton to the Duke of Newcastle, inclusive (1627–1693), were brought up

WESTMINSTER SCHOOL.

under the celebrated Dr. Busby, who was nearly fifty-five years head-master of the school, and who could at one time boast that of the bench of bishops as many as sixteen had been educated by him.

1533. Richard Hakluyt, collector of voyages.
1574. Ben Jonson.
1588. Giles Fletcher, poet.
1593. George Herbert, poet.
1602. William Heminge, son of the dramatic writer and fellow-actor with Shakspeare.
1604. Jasper Mayne, poet and divine.
1605. Thomas Randolf, dramatic poet.
1606. Richard Busby, afterwards head-master.
1611. William Cartwright, poet and divine.
1612. Sir Harry Vane, republican statesman, beheaded in 1662.
1612. Sir Arthur Haselrigge, the republican statesman and regicide.
1618. Abraham Cowley, poet.
1627. Adam Littleton, philosopher and divine.
1630. The Marquis of Halifax, statesman and author.
1631. John Dryden, poet.
1632. John Locke, philosopher.
1632. Sir Christopher Wren, the great architect.
1633. Robert South, divine.
1636. Thomas Sprat, Bishop of Rochester, poet.
1648. Dr. Humphrey Prideaux, historian and divine.
1648. Elkanah Settle, poet.
1652. Nathaniel Lee, dramatic poet.
1660. Kennet, Bishop of Peterborough, historian.
1662. Francis Atterbury, Bishop of Rochester.
1663. George Smaldridge, scholar and divine.
1663. William King, poet.
1664. Matthew Prior, poet and statesman.
1665. Richard Duke, poet.
1668. Sir Richard Blackmore, poet and physician.
1668. Edmund Smith, poet.
1673. Nicholas Rowe, dramatic poet.
1675. Sir John Friend, philosopher and physician.
1677. Vincent Bourne, Latin poet.
1681. Barton Booth, the celebrated actor.
1685. Aaron Hill, poet and dramatic author.
1693. Thomas Pelham, Duke of Newcastle, statesman.
1700. John Dyer, poet.
1703. Bishop Newton, author of the "Dissertation on the Prophecies."

1706. Isaac Hawkins Browne, poet.
1721. Thomas Sheridan, author and actor.
1730. Thomas King, comedian.
1731. William Cowper, poet.
1731. Charles Churchill, poet.
1732. Warren Hastings.
1732. Richard Cumberland, dramatic writer.
1733. Robert Lloyd, poet.
1733. George Colman, the elder, dramatic writer and scholar.
1736. John Horne Tooke, political and philosophical writer.
1737. Edward Gibbon, historian.
1774. Robert Southey, poet, historian, and biographer.

It was from his house in Great George Street, Westminster, in 1763, that the celebrated John Wilkes was carried before the two Secretaries of State, the Earls of Halifax and Egremont, by whom he was committed to the Tower. At No. 25, in this street—now the Institution of Civil Engineers—Lord Byron's body lay in state for two days in July, 1824. At No. 15, during the last years of his life, resided Lord Chancellor Thurlow, and here, in 1806, he died.

OLD PALACE OF WESTMINSTER.

ITS EARLY REGAL BUILDERS AND TENANTS.—EDWARD THE SECOND AND GAVESTON.—DEATH SCENE OF HENRY THE FOURTH.—HENRY THE EIGHTH THE LAST RESIDENT.—COURT OF REQUESTS.—PAINTED CHAMBER.—GUN- POWDER PLOT.—ST. STEPHEN'S CHAPEL.—OLD AND NEW PALACE YARD.

THE earliest notice we discover of the existence of a royal residence at Westminster, is in the reign of Canute, who is mentioned as having held his court here in 1035. It has even been suggested that it was from one of the windows of this palace that the perfidious Saxon traitor, Duke Edric, was thrown, by order of Canute, into the Thames. The palace of the Dane was burnt down a few years afterwards in the reign of Edward the Confessor, who on its site erected a far more magnificent structure. Every trace of Canute's palace has ceased to exist, but possibly a part of the foundations of the Confessor's structure still remains; indeed, but for the fatal fire which took place on the 16th of October, 1834, we should still be able to wander into the Court of Requests and the Painted Chamber, in the former of which, according to tradition, was the banqueting room, and the latter the sleeping apartment of the "meek Confessor." Scarcely necessary, perhaps, is it to remark, that Old Palace Yard points out where stood the palace of the Confessor, and New Palace Yard the site of the additions made by the early Norman kings. From the windows of the former, the Confessor could watch the progress made towards the completion of the glorious Abbey, an object in which he took the deepest interest. "He pressed on the work," writes Sulcardus, "very earnestly, having appropriated to it a tenth of his entire substance in gold, silver, cattle, and all other possessions."

In 1085 we find William the Conqueror holding his court at Whitsuntide in the palace of Westminster, on which occasion he received the homage of his subjects, and knighted his youngest son, afterwards Henry the First. Here William Rufus held his court in 1099, and here, the following year, he kept the festival of Whitsuntide within the magnificent Hall which had recently risen under his auspices. During the reign of Henry the First, the Confessor's palace appears to have been the constant residence of that monarch, as well as that of his pious and gentle consort, Matilda, daughter of Malcolm the Third, King of Scotland, and niece to Edward Atheling. During Lent, the good Queen—bare-footed and clothed in a garment of horse-hair—was frequently to be seen crossing the Old Palace Yard to the "Old Chapter House," where she performed her devotions and washed the feet of the poor. Dying in Westminster Palace on the 1st of May, 1118, she was buried within the walls of the Chapter-house, the former scene of her piety and humble virtues.

King Stephen and Henry the Second were severally crowned at Westminster, and both, at different times, held their courts in the Old Palace. Here Richard Cœur de Lion held a magnificent court on the occasion of his coronation in September, 1189, and here it was, when seated at dinner in the "Little Hall," at Westminster, that the news was brought to him that King Philip of France had invaded his Norman Duchy and besieged Verneuil. Starting from table in a violent rage, he swore passionately that he would never "turn away his face" till he had met the French King and given him battle, a threat which he followed up by immediately setting off for Portsmouth, where he embarked for Normandy. On the return of the lion-hearted King to his dominions, in 1197, after having dispossessed his brother John of the throne, we find him crowned a second time at Westminster. After the death of his brother, King John was not only crowned in the Abbey, but during his reign we find him more than once keeping Christmas at Westminster.

Henry the Third, the successor of King John, made great additions to the palace of the Confessor. During his reign, also, we find numerous notices of his having kept divers festivals at Westminster. Here, especially, in 1235, took place the interesting betrothment of Isabella, the King's sister, to the Emperor Frederic. "In February, 1235," writes Matthew Paris, "two ambassadors from the Emperor arrived at Westminster to demand in marriage for their master the Princess Isabella, the King's sister. The King summoned a council of the Bishops and great men of the kingdom, to consider the proposals of the Emperor, to which, after three days' consultation, an unanimous consent was given. The ambassadors then entreated that they might be permitted to see the Princess. The King sent confidential messengers for his sister to the Tower of London, where she was kept in vigilant custody, and they most respectfully brought the damsel to Westminster into the presence of her brother. She was in the twenty-first year of her age, exceedingly beautiful, in the flower of youthful virginity, becomingly adorned with royal vestments and accomplishments, and thus she was introduced to the imperial envoys. They, when they had for a while delighted themselves with beholding the virgin, and judged her to be in all things worthy of the imperial bed, confirmed by oath the Emperor's proposal of matrimony, presenting to her, on the part of their master, the wedding ring. And when they had placed it on her finger, they declared her to be Empress of the Roman empire, exclaiming altogether—' *Vivat Imperatrix, vivat !*' "

In due time, the Emperor despatched the Duke of Louvaine and the Archbishop of Cologne, with a suitable train, to escort the fair bride to Germany. By King Henry they were received with all due honours, and, previously to their departure with his beautiful sister, he entertained them on the 6th of May with great magnificence at Westminster.

The following year, Henry married Eleanor, daughter of Raymond Earl of Provence, on which occasion, as well as on that of the coronation of the new queen, the ceremonials seem to have surpassed in splendour anything which up to that time had been witnessed in England. At the palace of Westminster, Queen Eleanor was delivered, on the 16th of June, 1239, of her first son, afterwards King Edward the First, styled from the place of his birth, Edward of Westminster. Here, in 1260, we find King Henry entertaining Alexander King of Scotland, and here apparently Henry died. Among other curious entries of expenditure in this reign, and which show the simplicity of the times, we find, in April, 1222, the sum of 3s. 8d. paid to purchase *rushes* for the King's "two chambers at Westminster;" and again in December following, 3s. 4d. for *rushes* for the King's Great Chamber.

Edward the First, like his predecessors, made Westminster his residence. Here, during the Christmas of 1277, he entertained Llewellyn Prince of Wales, and here, the following year, we find Alexander the Third, King of Scotland, paying homage to him for the lands which he held under the English crown. Here, in 1294, John Baliol, King of Scotland, was Edward's guest, shortly after which we find the King "royally entertaining in his palace of Westminster the four noble envoys of the King of Aragon," with whom he was carrying on a secret negotiation for assistance in the war which he was meditating against the French King.

At the early period of our history of which we are writing, it was customary for the kings of England to keep their treasury within the precincts of the Abbey of Westminster; a circumstance only so far of importance that, in 1303, during the absence of Edward the First in Scotland, the door of the apartment in which the treasure was kept was forcibly entered, the chests and coffers were broken open, and treasure to the amount, it was computed, of a hundred thousand pounds abstracted. Suspicion at first falling on the ecclesiastic establishment, the Abbot, forty-eight monks, and thirty-two other persons connected with the Abbey were arrested by order of the King, and sent to the Tower. They were subsequently tried by the King's justices and acquitted, though apparently without the real perpetrators of the daring robbery being ever discovered.

On the accession of Edward the Second, the old palace of Westminster became, under the auspices of the King's handsome Gascon favourite, Piers Gaveston, the perpetual scene of feasting, dancing, and all kinds of riotous merriment. "Within a while," writes Holinshed, "the young King gave himself up to wantonness, passing his time in voluptuous pleasure and riotous excess, and Piers, as though he had sworn to make the King forget himself and the state to which he was called, furnished his court with companions of jesters, ruffians, flattering parasites, musicians, and other vile and naughty ribalds, that the king might spend both days and nights in jesting, playing, banqueting, and such other filthy and dishonourable exercises." Yet the time was not far distant when the one was to suffer an excruciating death under the hands of an assassin, and the other to die by the axe of the executioner!

> "Weave the warp, and weave the woof,
> The winding-sheet of Edward's race;
> Give ample room and verge enough
> The characters of hell to trace.
> Mark the year, and mark the night,
> When Severn shall re-echo with affright,
> The shrieks of death, through Berkeley's roof that ring,
> Shrieks of an agonizing king."

True it is that the extravagances and debaucheries of the young king were checked for a time by his marriage with the beautiful Isabella, daughter of Philip le Bel, King of France.

> "She-wolf of France, with unrelenting fangs,
> That tear'st the bowels of thy mangled mate," &c.

But her influence over him lasting but a short time, he soon relapsed into his former reckless career of frolic and vice.

On more than one occasion we find Westminster associated with the fortunes of Edward the Second and his unworthy favourite. It was here, for instance, that Gaveston gave such offence to the haughty barons of England, by not only wearing the crown jewels at Edward's coronation, but by walking immediately before the King in the procession as the bearer of the crown. Here, too, it was, in the refectory hall of the monks, that the barons, headed by the first prince of the blood, Thomas Earl of Lancaster, bound themselves by a solemn oath to drive the obnoxious favourite out of the kingdom; and, lastly, here it was, on Edward recalling his minion from exile, that the confederated barons presented themselves with their armed retinues before the King's palace and again exacted Gaveston's expatriation. The last occasion on which Edward met his beloved favourite was at

York, in the month of January, 1312, whither the young King had proceeded after having kept his Christmas at the palace of Westminster. Five months afterwards, on the 19th of June, Gaveston was led forth by Guy Earl of Warwick, from the dungeons of his famous castle of that name, to be beheaded on Blacklowe Hill, in its immediate neighbourhood. It may be mentioned that Gaveston in the days when he had basked in the rays of royal sunshine, had sneered at Warwick by the name of the "Black Dog of Arderne." "The Black Dog of Arderne," had been Warwick's oath, "will make him feel his teeth."

On the 1st of February, 1327, Edward the Third, then in his fifteenth year, was crowned in Westminster Abbey, and the same day was knighted in the palace by his cousin, Henry Earl of Lancaster, the double ceremony being followed by a magnificent banquet in Westminster Hall. Ten years afterwards we find the young King knighting and conferring the Dukedom of Cornwall and the Earldom of Chester on his infant son, Prince Edward, afterwards so celebrated as the Black Prince. The ceremony, which took place in the palace of Westminster, was followed by magnificent banquetings and rejoicings. Edward himself girded the sword to the side of his child, then only six years old, after which ceremony the little Prince, in virtue of his having become possessed of the palatinate of Chester, conferred knighthood on twenty persons of noble family. It may be mentioned that this was the first instance of the creation of a duke in England.

In April, 1341, a scene took place in Westminster Palace, which was singularly characteristic of the age. John de Stratford, Archbishop of Canterbury, having fallen under the displeasure of Edward the Third, was summoned before the Court of Exchequer to answer certain charges brought against him. Insisting, however, on his exalted rank, he not only refused to plead before any other tribunal but that of Parliament, but, setting the King's authority at defiance, flew to the sanctuary at Canterbury, where, "with the dreadful ceremony of bell, book, and candle, the bells ringing dolefully, and the candles being suddenly extinguished with a stench," he hurled anathemas at his enemies, and on any who might attempt to violate his present asylum. Here the Archbishop remained till the assembling of Parliament at Westminster, when, accompanied by the Bishops of London and Chester, and "a great company of clergymen and soldiers," he presented himself, armed with all the terrors of the Church, at the gates of the palace. Having been forbidden to enter the Parliament Chamber by Sir William Atwood, Captain of the King's Guard, the Archbishop took the Cross from the hands of one of the attendant priests, and raising it aloft, pronounced a solemn protest against his exclusion. He would never, he said, stir from the spot till the King admitted him to his seat in Parliament, or explained the reason why he was excluded. Some of the bystanders denouncing him "as a traitor who had deceived the King and betrayed the realm," the Archbishop turned passionately round to them. "The curse of God," he exclaimed, "and of His Blessed Mother, and of St. Thomas, and mine also, be upon the heads of those who inform the King so!—Amen, Amen!" Some of the barons now repaired to the King, and successfully using their good offices, induced him to consent to the Archbishop's admission into the Parliament chamber, where, after some discussion, his case was referred to a tribunal consisting of four bishops, four earls, and four barons. "On the 19th of April following," writes Barnes, "being a Thursday, the King came into St. Edward's Chamber, commonly called the Painted Chamber, before whom, in sight of all the Lords and Commons, the Archbishop humbled himself, and required his gracious pardon; which, upon the whole Parliament's general suit and entreaty, his Majesty granted."

On the 24th of May, 1357, John King of France, whom the Black Prince had recently taken prisoner at the battle of Poictiers, was entertained by Edward the Third in Westminster Palace with great splendour. Edward, apprized that his gallant son might shortly be expected in London with his august prisoner, had previously sent to the Lord Mayor to prepare the City pageants in honour of the monarch, and on the day of King John's arrival he anxiously awaited him, seated in great state in Westminster Hall. So soon as the French monarch made his appearance, Edward descended from his throne, and after having embraced him with great courtesy and show of affection, led him to a magnificent banquet which had been prepared for him.

In 1358 Edward the Third kept his Christmas with great splendour at Westminster, on which occasion we find his two illustrious captives, John King of France and David King of Scotland, seated at table with him at the same time. The English and French monarchs seem to have lived on the most friendly terms; the latter, who was lodged in the Savoy Palace in the Strand, "going as often as he pleased, privately by water, to visit King Edward at his palace of Westminster."

Were it from no other circumstance, the old Palace of Westminster would be interesting as the spot where Edward the Black Prince breathed his last. He expired on the 8th of June, 1376, in the "Great Chamber," and was buried at Canterbury.

"Is the sable warrior fled?
Thy son is gone: he rests among the dead."

The King survived the melancholy event only twelve

months; dying on the 21st of June, 1377, at the Palace of Sheen, or Richmond; abandoned in his last moments by his beautiful mistress Alice Piers, as well as by "the other knights and esquires who had served him, allured more by his gifts than his love."

"Mighty victor, mighty lord,
   Low on his funeral couch he lies!
No pitying heart, no eye, afford
   A tear to grace his obsequies!"

The unfortunate Richard the Second constantly resided at Westminster; Froissart further informing us that it was in the chapel of the palace, on the 14th of January, 1382, that the young King was married to the Princess Anne of Bohemia, sister of the Emperor Wenceslaus. Their nuptials were solemnized with tournaments and other extraordinary rejoicings. "At her coming to the city of London," writes Holinshed, "she was met on Blackheath by the Mayor and citizens of London in most honourable wise, and so with great triumph conveyed to Westminster, where, all the nobility of the realm being assembled, she was joined in marriage to the King, and shortly after crowned by the Archbishop of Canterbury with all the glory and honour that might be devised."

It was in the palace of Westminster, on the 3rd of May, 1389, that the famous scene occurred, when Richard, then in his twenty-second year, suddenly declared, before the assembled barons, his determination to be no longer a puppet in the hands of his uncle, the Duke of Gloucester, but to govern, by his own authority, his kingdom and household. Turning to the Duke, he inquired of him his age. "Your highness," replied Gloucester, "is in your twenty-second year."—"Then," rejoined the young King, "I am of years sufficient to govern my own house and family, and also my kingdom. Every one at the age of twenty-one is held capable of managing his own affairs; and wherefore should I be deprived of a privilege that may be claimed by the meanest subject of my realm?" He then removed the Duke of Gloucester and the Earl of Warwick from the council; displaced the Bishop of Hereford from the office of Treasurer; the Earl of Arundel from that of Lord Admiral, and having demanded the great seal from the Chancellor, Thomas Arundel Archbishop of York, placed it in his bosom and quitted the apartment.

On the 7th of June, 1394, Richard lost his young and beloved queen, Anne of Bohemia; an event which so deeply affected him, that he caused the apartments at Sheen which she had inhabited, and where she died, to be razed to the ground. The grief, however, of the royal widower so far yielded to circumstances that, sixteen months afterwards, on the 31st of October, 1396, he married at Calais Isabella, daughter of Charles the Sixth, King of France, then only in her eighth year, immediately after which he conducted her to Westminster, where her arrival was celebrated with extraordinary rejoicings. This was the same year, it may be mentioned, in which John of Gaunt, Duke of Lancaster, contracted his eventful marriage with Catherine Swinford.

On the deposition of the unfortunate Richard, and the accession of Henry Duke of Lancaster as Henry the Fourth, the latter, on the 12th of October, 1399—attended by a cavalcade of six thousand horse—proceeded in great state from the Tower to Westminster, where he formally took possession of the palace of the Confessor. The streets through which he passed were hung with tapestry, and the conduits flowed with red and white wine. Henry himself, magnificently attired, was naturally the observed of all observers,——

> "Great Bolingbroke,
> Mounted upon a hot and fiery steed
> Which his aspiring rider seemed to know,

> With slow but stately pace kept on his course,
> Whilst all tongues cried—'God save thee, Bolingbroke!'
> You would have thought the very windows spake,
> So many greedy looks of young and old
> Through casements darted their desiring eyes
> Upon his visage, and that all the walls
> With painted imagery had said at once,
> 'Jesu preserve thee! welcome, Bolingbroke!'
> Whilst he, from the one side to the other turning,
> Bareheaded, lower than his proud steed's neck,
> Bespake them thus,—'*I thank you, countrymen:*'
> And thus still doing, thus he passed along."
>
> *King Richard II.*, act v., sc. 2.

When age had dimmed the eye and disease had enfeebled the frame of the once haughty and magnificent Bolingbroke —when, moreover, the dissipated career of his son, the Prince of Wales, afterwards Henry the Fifth, and the charges of treason brought against that Prince by his enemies, added anguish of mind to the tortures of the King's body, it was in the Presence Chamber at Westminster that the repentant son knelt for the forgiveness and blessing of his father. Attended to Westminster by a large body of friends and retainers, the Prince entered with them into the great Hall, and having given them strict injunctions to advance no further into it than to its central fireplace underneath the lantern, he proceeded almost alone into the interior of the palace, where he sent, with all humility, a message to the King, entreating him to grant him an audience. Henry, at this time, was not only confined to his sick chamber, but was lying, we are told, so "greevouslie diseased," that the powerful monarch who had waded through bloodshed to a throne, and who with his own hand had slain thirty-six persons on the memorable field of Shrewsbury, shrank with a nervous abhorrence from an interview with his own son. At length, however, having stipulated that the interview should take place "in the presence of three or four persons in whom he had much confidence," Henry consented to be borne from his own apartment to the Presence Chamber where, seated in an easy chair, with a severe countenance he demanded of his son the object of his visit. The future victor of Agincourt fell reverently on his knees, and insisting passionately on his innocence of any design against his father's life or government, drew his dagger, and presenting it to the King, implored him, if he had the least suspicion of his undutifulness, to deprive him at once of life. "I have this day," he said, still kneeling, "made myself ready by confession and receiving of the Sacrament; and I beseech you, most redoubted lord and dear father, for the honour of God, to ease your heart of all suspicion as you have of me, and to despatch me here before your knees with this same dagger; and in thus ridding me of life, and yourself from all suspicion, here, in the presence of these lords, and before God at the day of the general judgment, I faithfully protest clearly to forgive you." Deeply affected by the evident and passionate sincerity of the Prince's manner, the sick monarch threw his arms round his son's neck, and with many tears assured him that he would never again give credit to the insinuations of his maligners.

There occurred one more memorable interview at Westminster Palace between the dying monarch and his gallant son; the interview which followed the King's discovery that the person who had removed the crown from his pillow was no other than his forgiven son and expectant heir.

"*King Henry.* Where is the crown? who took it from my pillow?
Warwick. When we withdrew, my liege, we left it here.
King Henry. The Prince hath ta'en it hence: go, seek him out.
 Is he so hasty that he doth suppose
 My sleep my death?
 . . . . .

Re-enter Prince Henry.

Lo, where he comes. Come hither to me, Harry.
Depart the chamber, leave us here alone.
Prince Henry. I never thought to hear you speak again.
King Henry. Thy wish was father, Harry, to that thought:
I stay too long by thee, I weary thee.
Dost thou so hunger for mine empty chair
That thou wilt needs invest thee with my honours
Before thy hour be ripe? Oh foolish youth!
Thou seek'st the greatness that will overwhelm thee.
Stay but a little; for my cloud of dignity
Is held from falling with so weak a wind
That it will quickly drop: my day is dim.
Thou hast stolen that which after some few hours
Were thine without offence; and at my death
Thou hast sealed up my expectation:
Thy life did manifest thou lovedst me not,
And thou wilt have me die assured of it.
Thou hidest a thousand daggers in thy thoughts,
Which thou hast whetted on thy stony heart,
To stab at half an hour of my life.
What! canst thou not forbear me half an hour?
Then get thee gone and dig my grave thyself,
And bid the merry bells ring to thine ear
That thou art crowned, not that I am dead.
Let all the tears that should bedew my hearse
Be drops of balm to sanctify thy head:
Only compound me with forgotten dust;
Give that which gave thee life unto the worms.
Pluck down my officers, break my decrees;
For now a time is come to mock at form:
Harry the Fifth is crowned."

King Henry IV., part 2, act iv., sc. 5.

The old chroniclers, whom Shakspeare has followed, differ but little in the accounts which they give of the removal of the crown by Prince Henry. The King, it appears, had for some time been subject to fits which were usually followed by a lethargy, on one of which occasions it was that the Prince, entering his bedchamber and conceiving him to be dead, carried away the crown which was " set on a pillow at the bed's head," or, according to Monstrelet, " on a cushion by the bedside." The King, it is added, on awaking, and being informed that the Prince was the person who had taken the crown, ordered him to be summoned to his presence, and demanded of him an explanation of his conduct. "Sire," is said to have been the Prince's reply, " to mine and all men's judgments you seemed dead in this world; wherefore I, as your next and apparent heir, took the crown as mine own, and not as yours." "Well, fair son," replied the King with a deep sigh, "what right I had to it, and how I enjoyed it, God knoweth." "My liege," returned the Prince, "if you die King, I shall have the garland, and trust to keep it by the sword, as you have done, against all mine enemies." "Well," said the exhausted King, "I leave all things to God, and pray him to have mercy on me."

It was not long after this memorable interview between the father and son, that the King, whilst performing his devotions at the shrine of St. Edward in Westminster Abbey, was seized with a fit and carried by his attendants into the Jerusalem Chamber. Happily he had strength enough to address some earnest words of parting advice to Prince Henry before he expired.

Henry the Fifth was crowned at Westminster on the 9th of April, 1413, and, like most of his predecessors, made the palace of the Confessor his constant residence when in London. Hither he returned in triumph after his splendid victory at Agincourt, in 1415 ; the Lord Mayor and Aldermen— "gorgeously horsed, with rich collars and great chains"— attending him through the City to the palace-gates. Here, the following year, he entertained with magnificent jousts and tournaments the Emperor Sigismund, and Albert Duke of Holland. Hither, in 1421, he conducted in great state his fair queen, Katherine, daughter of Charles the Sixth, whom he had recently married in France ; and lastly, the same year, we find him here entertaining the chivalrous, the accomplished, and unfortunate James the First of Scotland. At the Queen's coronation feast James is mentioned as being seated at her left hand.

✦ King Henry, dying in the Château de Vincennes, near Paris, on the 31st of August, 1422, he was succeeded by his infant son, the unfortunate Henry the Sixth, then only eight months old. During the early part of this reign we find but few notices of the old palace. Here, however, in 1444, he was united in marriage to the high-spirited Margaret of Anjou, and here on the 13th of October, 1453, the intrepid Queen was delivered of her eldest son, the ill-fated Prince Edward; the same child whom she subsequently held in her arms when, a fugitive after the battle of Hexham, she encountered the robber in the forest; the same prince who, in 1471, is said to have been so inhumanly butchered by the Dukes of Clarence and Gloucester after the battle of Tewkesbury:—

> —— "Then came wandering by
> A shadow like an angel, with bright hair
> Dabbled in blood;—and he shrieked out aloud,
> Clarence is come,—false, fleeting, perjured Clarence,—
> That stabbed me in the field by Tewkesbury;—
> Seize on him, furies, take him to your torments."

In 1450, "in a tower within the palace of Westminster," was imprisoned the once powerful subject, Edward de la Pole, Duke of Suffolk. He was subsequently tried by his peers in the King's chamber, and having been sentenced to banishment, was on his way across the channel to France when he was intercepted by his enemies, who, after cutting off his head on the side of a boat, threw his body into the sea. In the same year, we find the King holding his court at Westminster, and hence, on the breaking out of the insurrection of Jack Cade, he flew for refuge to Kenilworth.

It was during the temporary reconciliation between the

rival houses of York and Lancaster, in 1459, that the apparently trifling circumstance of a "fray" between one of the King's servants and a retainer of the "king-maker," Earl of Warwick, led to the shedding of the most illustrious blood in the kingdom. The quarrel, it seems, took place while Warwick was attending the King in council; his retainers remaining in the court-yard of the palace. "A fray," writes Holinshed, "was made upon a yeoman of the Earl of Warwick's by one of the King's servants, in the which the assailant was sore hurt, but the Earl's man fled. Hereupon the King's menial servants, seeing their fellow hurt, and the offender escaped, assembled together and watched the Earl when he returned from the council-chamber towards his barge, and suddenly set on him, the yeomen with swords, the black guard with spits and fireforks. After long fight, and many of the Earl's men maimed and hurt, by help of his friends he got a wherry, and so escaped to London."

In July, the following year, the old palace witnessed a still more extraordinary scene. The result of the battle of Northampton having delivered the person of the unfortunate Henry the Sixth into the hands of his enemies, his kinsman, Richard Plantagenet, Duke of York—who claimed the throne as representative of Edward the Third,—naturally took advantage of so favourable an opportunity of asserting his rights. Accordingly, attended by a numerous body of his friends and their retainers—a naked sword being borne before him, and trumpets sounding defiance—he proceeded to Westminster, where the Parliament was then assembled. "At his coming to Westminster," writes Holinshed, "he entered the palace, and passing forth directly through the Great Hall, stayed not till he came to the chamber where the King and Lords used to sit in the Parliament time, commonly called the Upper House, a chamber of the peers, and being there entered, stept up into the throne room, and there, laying his hand upon the cloth of the estate, seemed as if he meant to take possession of that which was his right (for he held his hand so upon that cloth a pretty good while), and after withdrawing his hand, turned his face towards the people. Beholding their pressing together, and marking what countenance they made whilst he thus stood and beheld the people, supposing they rejoiced to see his presence, the Archbishop of Canterbury (Thomas Bourchier) came to him, and after due salutations, asked him if he would come and see the King; with which demand he seeming to take disdain, answered briefly, and in a few words thus, 'I remember not that I know any within this realm, but that it beseemeth him rather to come and see my person, than I go and see his.' The Archbishop, hearing his answer, went back to the King, that lay in the Queen's lodging. The Duke also departed, and went to the most principal lodging that the King had within all his palace, breaking up the locks and doors, and so lodged himself therein, more like to a king than a duke."

These extraordinary proceedings, followed by the declaration of the Peers in the Duke of York's favour, no sooner reached the ears of Queen Margaret, than that heroic princess—trembling for the rights of her young son, and indignant at her husband's degradation—flew to arms, and having in a short time collected an army of twenty thousand men, gave battle to the Duke of York, at Wakefield. The result is well known. The Queen's troops proving successful, and the Duke of York having been killed on the field of battle, his head, by Margaret's orders, was severed from his body, and, with a paper crown placed upon it in derision, was fixed on the gates of York.

Margaret's triumph, however, was of short duration. The

same year was fought the battle of Mortimer's Cross, when the young Earl of March, afterwards Edward the Fourth, revenged the death of his father, the late Duke of York, by completely defeating his adversaries, leaving nearly four thousand of them dead on the field of battle.

Marching to London with his victorious troops, his handsome person, his affability, his personal courage, and numerous accomplishments, soon earned for him the suffrages of the people; and accordingly, at a great assemblage, at Baynard's Castle, of peers, prelates, and magistrates, it was declared that King Henry, by violating his faith in joining the Queen's army, had forfeited his claims to the throne, and that it had consequently become the right of the son of the late Duke of York. As may be supposed, no time was lost by Edward in establishing his authority. On the following day, the 4th of March, 1461, he was conducted in solemn state, and amidst the cheers of the populace, through the city to Westminster. On entering the great Hall he took his seat on the throne, holding the sceptre of Edward the Confessor in his hand, after which he repaired to the Abbey, where, after he had performed his devotions at the shrine of St. Edward, the assembled nobles, one by one, knelt to him and did homage to him as King Edward the Fourth.

In May, 1465, we find Edward celebrating the coronation of his beautiful consort, Elizabeth Grey, with great rejoicings at Westminster, and here, on the 11th of February, 1466, she presented him with their first-born child, Elizabeth, afterwards the Queen of Henry the Seventh. Here, on the 15th of January, 1478, took place, in St. Stephen's Chapel, the interesting marriage of her second son, Richard Duke of York, with Anne Mowbray, heiress of John Duke of Norfolk—the espousals of a bridegroom in his sixth year to a bride only three years old. After the ceremony a banquet took place in St. Edward's chamber, at which the courtiers drained the wine-cup to the happiness of the infant couple—a happiness, however, which it was destined they should never enjoy. The bride died in childhood; while the bridegroom shared the fate of his brother, Edward the Fifth, in the dungeon-rooms of the Tower.

> "The bridegroom bore a royal crown
> Amid the shining hair,
> That like a golden veil fell down
> In tresses soft and fair.
>
> The bearing of the noble child
> His princely lineage told;
> Beneath that brow so smooth and mild
> The blood of warriors rolled.
>
> All coyly went the sweet babe-bride,
> Yet oft with simple grace
> She raised, soft-stepping by his side,
> Her dark eyes to his face.
>
> And playfellows who loved her well,
> Crowns of white roses bore,
> And lived in after years to tell
> The infant bridal o'er."*

At Westminster, on the 9th of April, 1483, the gallant and amorous Edward the Fourth breathed his last. His remains were interred at Windsor, where, in 1789, his body was discovered undecayed; his dress being nearly perfect, and the lineaments of his face but little changed.

With the short story of the unfortunate Edward the Fifth the palace of Westminster is not very intimately associated. It was in one of its apartments, however, when a mere infant, that his father, King Edward the Fourth, had created him, with unusual state and ceremony, Prince of Wales, Duke of Cornwall, and Earl of Chester. There had then

---
* Verses by Mrs. Acton Tindal, quoted in Miss Mitford's "Recollections of a Literary Life."

knelt and sworn fealty to him as the heir to the throne, his uncles the Dukes of Clarence and Gloucester, the Archbishops of Canterbury and York, eight prelates, and all the principal nobility of the realm; yet scarcely twelve years were destined to elapse before one of those uncles had become his murderer, and scarcely one of the remaining prelates and barons continued true to the obligation by which they had so solemnly bound themselves.

The Duke of Gloucester having by his talent and his crimes invested himself with the regal power, was proclaimed king on the 20th of June, 1483, by the title of King Richard the Third. The same day he proceeded in great state to Westminster Hall, where, surrounded by the prelates and nobles of the realm, he took his seat on the throne of the Plantagenets and addressed the assembled multitude. "He declared," writes Holinshed, "that he would take upon him the crown in that place there, where the king himself sitteth and ministereth the law, because he considered that it was the chiefest duty of a king to minister the laws. Then, with as pleasant an oration as he could, he went about to win unto him the nobles, the merchants, the artificers; and, in conclusion, all kind of men, but especially the lawyers of the realm."

Richard's court at Westminster would seem to have been far from the gloomy one that might be supposed. "Too much attention," according to the chronicler of Croyland, was at one time "given to gaiety and dancing." Here, at all events, he kept his last Christmas with great magnificence; enlivening the old palace of the Confessor with a succession of banquets and balls. At the Feast of the Epiphany, he is especially mentioned as presiding at a splendid feast in Westminster Hall, wearing the crown on his head. At Westminster, in the preceding reign, he had married his present queen, Anne Neville, daughter of the "Kingmaker," Earl of Warwick, and here, on the 16th of March, 1485, at the early age of twenty-eight, she died. Her husband honoured her with a magnificent funeral in Westminster Abbey, and is said to have been so affected by her death as to have shed tears.

On the 22nd of August, 1485, took place the death of King Richard, on the field of Bosworth, two months after which, on the 30th of October, his victorious rival, the Earl of Richmond, was solemnly crowned at Westminster by the title of King Henry the Seventh. Here Henry seems to have constantly kept his court, yet with the exception of the rejoicings attending his coronation, and those which followed his marriage with Elizabeth, daughter of Edward the Fourth, we find the old palace presenting no particular feature of interest during his reign.

The last of our monarchs who kept his court at Westminster was Henry the Eighth, in the earlier period of whose reign the old palace appears to have been the constant scene of tournaments, masques, and all kinds of pageantries and "solemnities." Alluding to the marriage of the young King with Catherine of Aragon, Hall, the chronicler, writes— "On Shrove Sunday the King prepared a goodly banquet in the Parliament Chamber for all the ambassadors which were then here out of divers realms and countries. The banquet being ready, the King, leading the Queen, entered into the chamber. Then the ladies, the ambassadors, and other noblemen followed in order. The King caused the Queen to keep the estate, and then sat the ambassadors and ladies, as they were marshalled by the King, who would not sit, but walked from place to place, making cheer to the Queen and the strangers. Suddenly the King was gone. Shortly after, his Grace, with the Earl of Essex, came in apparelled

after the Turkish fashion in long robes of bawdkin powdered
with gold; hats on their heads of crimson velvet, with great
rolls of gold, girded with two swords, called scimitars, hanging by great bawdricks of gold. Next came the Lord
Henry, Earl of Wiltshire, and the Lord Fitzwalter, in two
long gowns of yellow satin, traversed with white satin, and
in every bend of white was a bend of crimson satin, after
the fashion of Russia, with furred hats of grey on their
heads; either of them having an hatchet in their hands,
and boots with *pykes* turned up. And after them came Sir
Edward Howard, then Admiral, and with him Sir Thomas
Parr, in doublets of crimson velvet, *voyded* low on the back
and before to the *cannell-bone*, laced on the breasts with
chains of silver; and, over that, short cloaks of crimson satin,
and on their heads hats after the dancer's fashion, with
pheasants' feathers in them. These were apparelled after
the fashion of Prussia. The torch-bearers were apparelled
in crimson satin and green, like Moors, their faces black.
And the King brought in a *mommarye*. After that the
King, the Queen, and ladies, such as would, had played, the
said mummers departed, and put off the said apparel, and
soon after entered into the chamber in their usual apparel.
And so the King made great cheer to the Queen, ladies, and
ambassadors. The supper or banquet ended and the tables
avoyded, the Queen with the ladies took their places in their
degrees. Then began the dancing, and every man took
much heed to them that danced. After the King's grace
and the ladies had danced a certain time, they departed
every one to his lodging."

In February, 1511, in celebration of the Queen's delivery
of a son, we find the old palace the scene of a truly magnificent tournament, the King on this occasion riding forth
on horseback from under a gorgeous pavilion " of cloth of

gold and purple velvet embroidered, powdered with fine gold." The principal combatants were the King, the Marquis of Dorset, the Earl of Wiltshire, Sir Charles Brandon, and Sir Thomas Boleyn, among whom, we are told, "his Grace attained the prize." After evening song, the bevy of "gorgeous dames and barons bold" repaired to one of the halls of the palace, richly hung for the occasion, where a magnificent banquet had been provided, at which Henry knighted the celebrated Irish chieftain, Shan O'Neal. Then followed a masque, in which the King appeared in a purple satin suit, brocaded with "posies," after which, writes Holinshed, "the minstrels, which were disguised, danced; and the lords and ladies danced, that it was a pleasure to behold."

From this period the old palace of the Confessor ceases to be associated with the domestic history of the Kings of England. In 1512, a considerable portion of it was destroyed by fire, from which time till the palace of Whitehall passed from the hands of Cardinal Wolsey into those of Henry, we find the King holding his court either at Baynard's Castle, Bridewell, or the Tower.

Among the many interesting vestiges of the old palace of Westminster, of which the fatal fire of 1834 was the destroyer, was the celebrated Painted Chamber; the same apartment, it is said, in which Edward the Confessor, with Editha, his queen, and his unfortunate successor King Harold watching by his bed-side, breathed his last. As early as the reign of Edward the Third we find it designated as "*Le Chambre de Peinte*," a name explained under very interesting circumstances in 1800, when, on the removal of some old tapestry and wainscoting, there was discovered on the walls a series of ancient paintings, to which the apartment evidently owed its appellation. Considering their antiquity they possessed considerable merit. They represented for the most part the Battles of the Maccabees; the Seven Brethren; the delivery of the ring and the message from St. John the Evangelist to Edward the Confessor, and lastly the canonization of the royal saint.

When, in 1337, a war seemed to be impending between England and France, it was in the Painted Chamber that Edward the Third received in great state the Cardinal ambassadors delegated by Pope Benedict the Twelfth to negotiate a reconciliation between the two countries. Here, in the time of the Norman kings, the opening of the new Parliaments usually took place, and here, during the latter part of the reign of Edward the Third, the Commons of England held their debates.

In the Painted Chamber took place the memorable scene of the regicides affixing their signatures to the death-warrant of Charles the First; Oliver Cromwell, it is said, besmearing with the pen with which he had just signed the document, the face of Henry Marten, who sat next him, and who retorted the miserable jest. Here, too, it was that, partly by force and partly by jest and argument, Cromwell induced the well-known Colonel Ingoldesby to add his signature to those of the other regicides. "As soon," writes Lord Clarendon, "as Cromwell's eyes were on him, he ran to him, and taking him by the hand, drew him by force to the table, and said, 'Though he had escaped him all the while before, he should now sign that paper as well as they;' which he, seeing what it was, refused with great passion, saying he knew nothing of the business, and offered to go away. But Cromwell and others held him by violence, and Cromwell, with a loud laughter, taking his hand in his, and putting the pen between his fingers, with his own hand writ Richard Ingoldesby, he making all the resistance he could."

In the Painted Chamber lay in state the body of Elizabeth

Claypole, the favourite daughter of Oliver Cromwell, previously to its interment in Westminster Abbey. Here also was the temporary resting-place—between the Palace of Whitehall and Henry the Seventh's Chapel—of the remains of the "merry monarch," Charles the Second. Here lay in state after death, Queen Anne's consort, Prince George of Denmark. Here also lay in state the body of the great Earl of Chatham, as did afterwards that of his scarcely less celebrated son, William Pitt.

At the south end of the old Court of Requests was the Prince's chamber, sometimes designated the "Old Robing Room," from our sovereigns having been in the habit of robing themselves here when they attended Parliament. The foundations as well as the walls of this apartment were apparently of the time of the Confessor, although the ornamental part was generally attributed to the reign of Henry the Third. It was to the Prince's chamber that Lord Chatham was first carried after he was seized with his memorable and fatal illness in the House of Lords. Here anciently hung some curious tapestry, representing the birth of Queen Elizabeth; her mother, Anne Boleyn, being delineated as in bed, with a nurse holding the royal infant on one side of it, and Henry and his courtiers standing at some distance.

Immediately between the north end of the old Court of Requests and the south end of Westminster Hall, appears to have run the white hall, or great chamber of the ancient palace, memorable from having been the scene of many remarkable events in the history of our country, but more especially as having been the apartment in which, according to tradition, Edward the Black Prince breathed his last.

At the east end of the Painted Chamber stood the *old* House of Lords, the foundations of which were also of the time of the Confessor. This was the ancient "Parliament

Chamber," so often mentioned in the annals of the old palace, beneath which was the vault, known as Guy Fawkes's cellar, in which the conspirators associated in the Gunpowder Plot concealed the barrels of powder with which they proposed to destroy the King and Parliament.

St. Stephen's Chapel, in which the Norman kings were accustomed to offer up their devotions, was originally founded by King Stephen, but was afterwards twice rebuilt during the reigns of the first three Edwards. When at length, after a labour of seventeen years, St. Stephen's was completed, it could boast an elaborateness and magnificence of decoration which rendered it a model of architectural perfection as a specimen of the purest style of Gothic architecture. The walls were covered with oil paintings, of great richness and beauty; the windows were gorgeously illuminated; and, lastly, all the internal fittings, the ornaments, the jewels, the hangings of the altar, and the vestments of the priests, corresponded in beauty and costliness with its architectural splendour.

A few years after the suppression of the monasteries, this interesting chapel was converted into the House of Commons, at which time its fine roof was concealed by a false ceiling, and its unique oil-paintings by a wooden wainscoting. Its beautiful crypt, or under-chapel, still remains to us, but St. Stephen's itself, with its host of historical associations, has passed away for ever.

Old and New Palace Yards are severally replete with historical associations. In the former Guy Fawkes, with his associates Thomas Winter, Ambrose Rookwood, and Robert Keyes, were hanged, drawn, and quartered; but the spot is principally interesting from its having witnessed, on the 29th of October, 1618, the execution of Sir Walter Raleigh. Though suffering severely from illness, he maintained his dignity and fortitude to the last. "I desire," were his words to the bystanders, "you will bear with me withal; and if I shew any weakness, I beseech you to attribute it to my malady, for this is the hour in which it is wont to come." Having concluded his well-known beautiful prayer—"Now," he said, "I am going to God." Taking up the axe, he felt its edge, and said smilingly—"This is a sharp medicine, but it will cure all diseases." The executioner inquiring in what manner he proposed to lay his head upon the block—"So the heart be straight," he said, "it is no matter which way the head lieth." Having lain down, and the executioner hesitating to strike the blow, "What dost thou fear?" he said, "strike, man!" His head was then severed from his body by two blows.

In the time of the Commonwealth stood in Old Palace Yard a place of entertainment well known by the singular denomination of "Heaven." Butler speaks of it in his "Hudibras" as "false 'Heaven' at the end of the Hall;" and Pepys mentions his dining there in 1659-60. "I sent a porter," he says, "to my house for my best fur cap, and so I returned and went to 'Heaven,' where Luellin and I dined."

At his house in Old Palace Yard died the younger Edmund Calamy in 1732.

Before quitting Old Palace Yard, we must not omit to mention that when the celebrated poet Geoffrey Chaucer held the appointment of Clerk of the Works at Westminster, in the reign of Richard the Second, his residence stood on the spot where Henry the Seventh's Chapel now stands, and here apparently he died. By a curious writ, dated the 13th of July, 1389, the poet was appointed Clerk of the Works at the palace of Westminster, the Tower of London, the Mews near Charing-Cross, and other places, with a salary of two shillings a day.

NEW PALACE YARD.

In New Palace Yard anciently stood two objects of some interest, one a handsome conduit or fountain, which, according to Stow, on the occasion of great triumphs was "made to run with wine out of diverse spouts;" and the other, facing the entrance to the Hall, a lofty tower, called the Clock Tower, built out of the proceeds of a fine of eight hundred marks imposed upon Ralph Hengham, Chief Justice of the King's Bench, in the reign of Edward the First. The old Tower was pulled down in 1715, when its ancient bell was granted to the Dean and Chapter of St. Paul's Cathedral, and some time afterwards was recast. On it was inscribed the following doggrel distich,—

> Tertius aptavit me rex, Edwardque vocavit,
> Sancti decore Edwardi signaretur ut hora,

signifying that the King gave the bell and called it Edward, in order that it might give notice of the hours to the neighbouring Abbey of St. Edward the Confessor. In the reign of Queen Elizabeth, we find the name of the bell changed to that of Tom of Westminster.—

> "Hark! Harry, 'tis late, 'tis time to be gone,
> For Westminster Tom, by my faith, strikes one."

In New Palace Yard, on the east side, stood the old buildings of the Exchequer, containing the despotic and terrible Star Chamber, with its thousand dark but interesting associations. The name is generally supposed to have been derived from the *stars* with which the ceiling was anciently decorated; though according to Blackstone it was so called from the *Starra* (corrupted from the Hebrew Shetar), or Jewish covenants, which were deposited here by Richard the First.

When, in September, 1498, the unsuccessful attempt of Perkin Warbeck on the city of Exeter delivered him into the merciless hands of Henry the Seventh, it was decided, in order to complete his humiliation, to expose him in the stocks before the great entrance to Westminster Hall. "Incontinently," writes Holinshed, "Perkin was brought to the court at Westminster, and was one day set fettered in a pair of stocks before the door of Westminster Hall, and there stood a whole day, not without innumerable reproaches, mocks, and scornings; and the next day he was carried through London, and set upon a like scaffold in Cheapside, by the Standard, with like gins and stocks as he occupied the day before, and there stood all day, and read openly his own confession, written with his own hand." The following year, having been arrested in an unlucky attempt to escape from the Tower, the unfortunate youth was hanged at Tyburn on the 23rd of November; the companion of his flight, the Earl of Warwick, being beheaded on Tower Hill a few days afterwards.

At the Court of King's Bench, Westminster, in 1612, Robert Crighton, Lord Sanquhar, was tried for the murder of one Turner, a fencing-master, and, having been found guilty, was hanged two days afterwards "opposite to the gate of Westminster Hall."

In front of Westminster Hall, on the same spot on which Perkin Warbeck sat in the stocks, perished on the scaffold at the same time James, first Duke of Hamilton, the devoted adherent of Charles the First; the gay and handsome Earl of Holland, and the gallant and high-minded Lord Capel. On the 9th of March, 1649, less than six weeks after the decapitation of their royal master, the three prisoners were conducted from St. James's Palace to the residence of Sir Robert Cotton, at the upper end of Westminster Hall, a house of some note from so many great or unfortunate men having at different times partaken of its melancholy hospitality in their last passage to the grave. The Judges, it may be mentioned, were sitting in the Hall at the time of the execution, and from their seats had a full view of the scaffold.

The Duke of Hamilton was the first who was brought forth. Entertaining hopes of a reprieve to the last, he was observed to linger as he passed through the hall, till the Earl of Denbigh coming up to him, and whispering in his ear that there was no hope, he forthwith mounted the scaffold, and submitted himself with great fortitude and composure to the stroke of the executioner.

Next came the once gay and graceful Holland, his steps tottering and his cheeks blanched, the effects of recent and severe illness. According to Walker, in his "History of Independency,"—" After some divine conference with Mr. Bolton for near a quarter of an hour, and having spoken to a soldier that took him prisoner and others, he embraced Lieutenant-Colonel Beecher, and took his leave of him. After which he came to Mr. Bolton, and having embraced him, and returned him many thanks for his great pains and affection to his soul, he prepared himself for the block; whereupon, turning to the executioner, he said—' Here, my friend, let my clothes and my body alone; there is ten pounds for thee; that is better than my clothes. . I am now fit, and when you take up my head, do not take off my cap.' Then taking farewell of his servants, he kneeled down and prayed for a pretty space with much earnestness. Then going to the front of the scaffold, he said to the people—' God bless you all; God give all happiness to this kingdom, to this people, to this nation.' Then laying himself down, he seemed to pray with much affection for a short space; and then lifting up his head, seeing the executioner by him, he said—'Stay while I give the sign;' and presently after, stretching out his hand, and saying—'Now! now!' just as the words were coming out of his mouth, the executioner at one blow severed his head from his body."

The last who was summoned to the fatal stage was Lord Capel, who, as he passed through Westminster Hall greeted with a serene countenance his several friends and acquaintance. Having ascended the scaffold, he inquired whether the other lords had addressed the people bare-headed. Being informed that such was the case, he took off his hat, and delivered that fine and well-known appeal which, more than any other circumstance at the time, tended to weaken the respect of the people for their Republican leaders. "Like Samson," writes Heath, "he did the Philistines more harm by his death than he had done by his life." Lord Capel's demeanour at the last afforded a beautiful picture of dignified innocence and Christian fortitude. According to Lord Clarendon—"After some prayers very devoutly pronounced upon his knees, he submitted himself, with an unparalleled Christian courage, to the fatal stroke, which deprived the nation of the noblest champion it had." Even Cromwell, though he refused to save his life, did justice to his talents and unbending probity.

At the time of the Restoration there was held at Miles's Coffee House, in Old Palace Yard, a club called the Rota, of which the celebrated James Harrington was the founder. "Here," writes Aubrey, "we had a balloting box, and balloted how things should be carried by way of Tentamens. The room was every evening full as it could be crammed. Mr. Cyriack Skinner, an ingeniose young gentleman, scholar to John Milton, was chairman." Pepys, who was a member of the Rota, more than once mentions the "admirable discourse" which he heard there.

New Palace Yard, from the convenience which its open

space afforded, was frequently the scene where criminals were exposed on the pillory. Here it was that the celebrated Titus Oates was pilloried in the reign of James the Second. In the last century, also, when the celebrated John Wilkes had the boldness to republish his famous No. 45 of "The North Briton," so obnoxious to George the Third and his ministers, it was in the New Palace Yard that his publisher, Mr. John Williams, a bookseller in Fleet Street, was made to stand in the pillory on the 14th of February, 1765. The result, however, proved to be very different from what the ministers either hoped, or perhaps anticipated; the mob, instead of pelting the offender with filth and stones, hailed his appearance on the pillory with repeated cheers. Moreover, the spectators not only presented him with two hundred guineas—which they had subscribed among themselves, but, after having erected a gibbet, on which they suspended a boot and Scotch bonnet, in ridicule of the Prime Minister, Lord Bute, carried off the delinquent in triumph in a hackney-coach correspondingly numbered 45.

New Palace Yard was anciently surrounded by a wall, in which there were four gates: one on the east leading to Westminster Stairs; another to the north, where Bridge Street now stands; a third on the west, taken down in 1706, and a fourth leading into Old Palace Yard, which was demolished in 1731.

WESTMINSTER HALL.

ITS ERECTOR.—THE HALL FOR THE CORONATION AND BANQUETINGS OF THE ENGLISH KINGS.—EXTRAORDINARY SCENES AND REMARKABLE TRIALS WHICH HAVE OCCURRED THERE FROM THE TIME OF WILLIAM RUFUS TILL THE PRESENT DAY.

WESTMINSTER HALL is one of the most interesting apartments in Europe. To an Englishman it is unquestionably so. Who is there, indeed, whose philosophy is so cold, or whose heart is so dead to every poetical or romantic feeling, as to be able to stand, without deep emotion, on the threshold of the colossal banqueting-room of the Norman Kings, associated as it is in our minds with so many scenes of gorgeous splendour, so many events of tragical interest? Here our early monarchs sat personally in judgment on their subjects. Here, on its vastest scale, was displayed the rude but magnificent hospitality of the Middle Ages. Here a long line of sovereigns—the Norman, the Tudor, the Plantagenet, the Stuart, and the Guelph—have sat at their gorgeous coronation banquets. Here Edward the Third embraced his gallant son, when the "sable warrior" returned from the bloody field of Poictiers conducting a monarch as his captive; and here were the trial-scenes of the young and accomplished Essex, the stately Strafford, and the ill-fated Charles the First!

Westminster Hall, it is almost needless to remark, was originally erected by William Rufus to serve as a banqueting-hall to the palace of the Confessor. It was completed in 1099, in which year we find the King keeping his court beneath its roof. "In this year," writes Matthew Paris, "King William, on returning from Normandy into England, held, for the first time, his court in the new Hall at Westminster. Having entered to inspect it, with a large military retinue, some persons remarking that it was too large, and larger than it should have been, the King replied that 'it was not half so large as it should have been,' and that it was only a *bed-chamber* in comparison with the building which he intended to make." This same year, according to Stow, William Rufus kept his Whitsuntide in the Palace of Westminster, where he feasted in his new banqueting-hall " very royally."

Henry the First, King Stephen, Henry the Second, Richard the First, and King John were severally crowned in the Abbey of Westminster, and therefore, in all probability, kept their coronation feasts in the old Hall. Here also Henry, the eldest son of Henry the Second, was crowned in the lifetime of his father, and here, at the banquet which followed in Westminster Hall, occurred one of those incidents which the old chroniclers delight to record. "The King," writes Holinshed, "upon that day served his son at the table as sewer, bringing up the boar's head with trumpets before it, according to the usual manner. Whereupon the young man, conceiving a pride in his breast, beheld the standers-by with a more stately countenance than he had wont. The Archbishop of York, who sat by him, marking his behaviour, turned unto him, and said,—'Be glad, my good son, there is not another prince in the world hath such a sewer at his table.' To this the new King answered, as it were disdainfully,—'Why dost thou marvel at that? My father in doing it thinketh it not more than becometh him; he, being of princely blood only on the mother's side, serveth me that am a King born, having both a King to my father, and a Queen to my mother.' Thus the young man, of an evil and perverse nature, was puffed up with pride by his father's unseemly doing."

In January, 1236, on the occasion of the marriage of Henry the Third with Eleanor, daughter of Raymond Earl of Provence, and her subsequent coronation, we find the royal bridegroom giving a magnificent banquet in Westminster Hall. "At the nuptial feast," writes Matthew Paris, " were assembled such a multitude of the nobility of both sexes; such numbers of the religious, and such a variety of stage-players, that the city of London could scarcely contain them. In the procession, the Earl of Chester bore before the King the sword of Edward the Confessor. The High Marshal of England (the Earl of Pembroke) carried a rod before the King, both in the church and in the hall; making way for the King, and arranging the guests at the royal table. The Barons of the Cinque Ports bare a canopy over the King, supported on five spears. The Earl of Leicester held water for the King to wash before dinner, and the Earl of Warenne officiated as the royal cup-bearer in lieu of the Earl of Arundel, who was a youth not yet knighted. Master Michael Belet had the office of butler; the Earl of Hereford was Marshal of the King's household; William de Beauchamp was almoner. The justiciary of the forests removed the dishes from the King's table; the citizens of London poured the wine abundantly into precious cups; the citizens of Winchester had oversight of the kitchen and napery. The chancellor, the chamberlain, the marshal, and the constable, took their seats with reference to their offices; and all the barons in the order of their creation. The solemnity was resplendent with the clergy and knights, properly placed; but how shall I describe the dainties of the table, and the abundance of diverse liquors; the quantity of game, the variety of fish, the multitude of jesters, and the attention of the waiters? Whatever the world pours forth of pleasure and glory was there especially displayed."

Such was a royal banquet in the thirteenth century! The same year the King entertained six thousand poor men, women, and children in Westminster Hall and in the adjoining apartments of the palace.

Three other entertainments of note are recorded to have been given by Henry the Third in Westminster Hall during his reign. The first was in 1241, when he entertained with great magnificence the Pope's legate, Otho. The second took place on the fifth of January following, when he feasted a vast assemblage of guests, consisting chiefly of the citizens of London, who, it appears, were summoned to attend by a royal edict, subject to a penalty of one hundred shillings if they absented themselves. The last entertainment which we have to mention was given in 1244, in honour of the marriage of his brother, Richard Earl of Cornwall, with Cincia of Provence, sister of the Queens of France and England. According to Matthew Paris, as many as thirty thousand dishes were prepared for the nuptial banquet.

It was in Westminster Hall, on the 3rd of May, 1253, that Henry the Third, in the presence of his barons, subscribed to one of those awful oaths to respect the ancient charters of the realm, which his pecuniary necessities more than once impelled him to take, but which, in the days of returning prosperity, he as often disregarded. The scene must have been a very impressive one. Besides the King and his barons, there were assembled in the Hall, prelates, mitred abbots, and other churchmen of high dignity, each clad in his ecclesiastical robes and bearing a lighted taper. Then, in the midst of a solemn silence, the Archbishop of Canterbury arose from his seat, and in the most awful language invoked the curse of heaven on whomsoever might infringe, or advise the King to infringe, the charters of the realm. At the moment when the frightful anathema was passing his lips, the torches were thrown smoking and stinking on the ground, and the voice of the Archbishop rose to a louder pitch. "Thus," he said, "be extinguished, and stink, and smoke in hell, all those who dare to violate the charters of the kingdom!" After a short pause, the King himself arose, and, with his hand on his heart, exclaimed, in a no less solemn manner, "So may God help me, I will inviolably observe all these things, as I am a man and a Christian, and a knight, and a crowned and anointed King." Possibly, Henry may have been sincere at the moment, but how indifferently he kept his solemn oath, history has left us a melancholy record.

The only other incident of any interest connected with Westminster Hall in the reign of Henry the Third, was an affray arising out of an ancient feud, which took place in 1269, between John de Warenne, Earl of Surrey, and Sir Alan la Zouche, one of the King's justices, in which each of these powerful subjects appears to have taken a personal part with his retainers. Sir Alan, being closely pressed by his enemies, flew towards the King's chamber, which he had almost reached, when he fell pierced by the swords of his pursuers. De Warenne flew to, and fortified his castle of Reigate, but subsequently, having been induced to submit to the King's mercy, escaped with fine and penance. Sir Alan, however, less fortunate, died shortly afterwards from the effect of his wounds.

On the death of Henry the Third, on the 16th of November, 1272, we find his son proclaimed with all due honours in Westminster Hall, as King Edward the First. Here also, on the 19th of August, 1274, on the occasion of his coronation and marriage with Eleanor of Castile, the young and chivalrous monarch celebrated the double ceremony with extraordinary magnificence; Alexander King of Scotland gracing the nuptial ceremony with his presence. "The King of Scotland," writes the old chronicler, Henry de Knyghton, "was accompanied by one hundred knights on horseback, who, as soon as they had dismounted, turned their steeds loose for any one to catch and keep that thought proper. Then came Edmund Earl of Cornwall, the King's nephew, and the Earls of Gloucester, Pembroke, and Warenne, each having in their company an hundred illustrious knights, wearing their lord's armour; and when they had alighted from their palfreys, they also set them free, that whoever chose might take them unquestioned. And the aqueduct in Cheapside poured forth white wine and red, like water, for those who would to drink at pleasure."

Edward the Second having been crowned at Westminster—viz., on the 25th of February, 1308,—Westminster Hall was apparently the scene of the magnificent banquetings and rejoicing with which that event, as well as his marriage, the same year, with Isabella, the beautiful daughter of Philip le Bel, King of France, was celebrated. Here, in August, 1321, we find the assembled barons of England signed a sentence of banishment on the King's obnoxious favourites, the Spencers; and, lastly, in Westminster Hall—a few months before Berkeley Castle echoed with the shrieks of the agonizing king—the barons proclaimed him incapable of governing the realm, and announced to the assembled people the accession of his son in his room.

Edward the Third was knighted and crowned at Westminster on the 1st of February, 1327, and the same day kept his coronation feast with great magnificence in the

Hall. Here, as has been already mentioned, on the 24th of May, 1357, he received and magnificently entertained his son, the Black Prince, together with his illustrious prisoner, John King of France, whom the "sable warrior" had recently taken prisoner at the battle of Poictiers. Willingly Edward and his gallant son would have consoled the French King for his misfortunes, but the reply of the royal captive was in the touching words of the Psalmist. "How," he said, with a mournful smile, "shall we sing in a strange land?"

Richard the Second, on his accession, proceeded in magnificent state from the Tower to Westminster, where he took possession of the palace of his ancestors. "On arriving at Westminster," we are told, "with the Princes, nobles, and many others of his lieges, he entered the great Hall of the palace, and going up to the high marble table, he asked for wine, which being brought he drank of it, as did others standing around him. The King then retired with the Princes and his family to his chamber, where he supped royally, and, having bathed becomingly, retired to rest." The following day, the 16th of July, 1377, Richard was crowned with great state in the Abbey, after which he partook of the usual banquet in the Hall; the nobility, the prelates, and the great officers of state being seated at different tables. "During the entertainment," we are told, "the Lord Steward, the Constable, and the Earl Marshal, with certain knights deputed by them, *rode* about the Hall on noble coursers, to preserve peace and order among the people. All that time, the Earl of Derby stood at the King's right hand, holding the principal sword drawn from its scabbard. The Earl of Stafford performed the office of chief carver. Dinner being finished, the King arose and went to his chamber, with the prelates, great men, and nobles before mentioned. Then the great men, knights, and lords passed the remainder of the day until supper-time in shows, dances, and solemn minstrelsy; and having supped, the King and the others retired to rest, fatigued with their exertions in the ceremonies of this magnificent festival." Sir John Dymoke, as possessor of the manor of Scrivelsby, in Lincolnshire, claimed to be the King's champion, and in this capacity rode into Westminster Hall in full armour. "Having furnished himself," writes Walsingham, "with the best suit of armour save one, and the best steed save one, from the King's armoury and stable, he proceeded on horseback, with two attendants, the one bearing his spear and the other his shield, to the Abbey gates, there to await the ending of the mass. But the Lord Marshal, the Lord Seneschal, and the Lord Constable, being all mounted on their great horses, went to the knight, and told him that he should not have come so soon, wherefore he had better retire, and laying aside his weighty armour rest himself until the proper time." The champion, it appears, took their advice by withdrawing till the King took his seat at the banquet in the Hall.

When, in 1387, the associated barons, headed by the King's uncle, Thomas of Woodstock, Duke of Gloucester, took up arms against the unfortunate Richard the Second, it was in Westminster Hall that they assembled with their armed retainers, waiting for an interview with their sovereign. "The King," writes Holinshed, "when he heard they were come, apparelled himself in his kingly robes, and, with his sceptre in his hand, came into the great Hall at Westminster. The lords, as soon as they had sight of him, made him their humble obeisance, and went forward till they came to the nether steps going up to the King's seat of state, where they made their second obeisance; and then the King gave them countenance to come nearer to him." This display of courtesy, however, was but the prelude to a storm; the barons loudly denouncing Robert de Vere, Duke of Ireland, and others of the King's council, as traitors to their sovereign and their country; and concluding by throwing down their gauntlets on the floor, and offering to prove the truth of what they asserted by single combat. With some difficulty they were pacified by Richard, who solemnly promised to summon a Parliament, when their grievances should be taken into full consideration. At the same time his indignation at the barons having the boldness to appear in arms in his presence was excessive. "Have I not armed men," he said, "sufficient to have beaten you down, compassed about like a deer in a toil, if I would? Truly, in this behalf I make no more account of you than of the vilest scullion in my kitchen." During this remarkable scene we find the haughty barons, including even the King's uncle, the Duke of Gloucester, kneeling the whole time before the King.

On the 30th of September, 1399, the day after Richard had formally renounced the crown in the Tower of London, Westminster Hall witnessed a far more memorable scene than the foregoing. The Hall, we are told, was "hung and trimmed sumptuously;" the prelates and barons were in their respective places; the throne alone was vacant! Then, in the midst of a profound silence, the Archbishop of York arose and read aloud the renunciation of the King. His abdication having been accepted by the Parliament, there again ensued a solemn silence, when Henry Bolingbroke, Duke of Lancaster, rising from his seat, and making the sign of the cross on his forehead and breast, cried aloud—" In the name of the Father, the Son, and the Holy Ghost, I, Henry of Lancaster, challenge this realm of England, and the crown, with all the members and appurtenances, as that I am descended by right line of the blood, coming from the good lord King Henry the Third; and through the right that God, of his grace, hath sent me, with help of my kin and of my friends to recover it; the which realm was in point to be undone for default of governance, and undoing of good laws." This speech was followed by loud cries of, "Long live Henry the Fourth!" In proof of Richard having resigned the regal authority to him, Henry produced the signet-ring of the abdicated monarch; when, the assembly having unanimously admitted his rights, the Archbishop of Canterbury approached him and led him to the vacant throne.

To the ill-fated Richard the Second we are indebted for the magnificent old hall as it now stands. Under his auspices it was greatly strengthened and beautified; the present matchless roof having been added, and the exterior coated with thick walls of stone. With the exception of the Hall of Justice at Padua, Westminster Hall is said to be the largest apartment unsupported by pillars in the world. As a specimen also of scientific construction, its massive timber roof has the reputation of being unrivalled.

The coronation of Henry the Fourth took place at Westminster on the 12th of October, 1399, after which he presided at a sumptuous banquet in the Hall; the two archbishops and several of the other prelates sitting at the same table with him, and Dymoke, the champion, entering the hall " mounted upon a goodly steed, barbed, with crimson housings;" the herald who accompanied him vociferating the usual challenge.

Henry the Fifth, the victor of Agincourt, was also crowned at Westminster, but of the consequent feastings and ceremonies in the Hall we find no particular record. In 1421, however, on the occasion of the coronation of his Queen, Katherine daughter of Charles the Sixth of France, the ceremony in the Abbey was followed by a sumptuous entertainment in Westminster Hall; the Queen sitting on a throne " at the marble table at the upper end of the hall," with the Archbishop of Canterbury seated on one side of her, and the King of Scotland on the other. The menial offices were performed by the principal nobility; the Duke of Gloucester, as "over-looker," standing bare-headed before the Queen, while on her right knelt the Earl of March holding a sceptre, and on her left the Earl Marshal. During the ceremony the Earl of Worcester is described as riding up and down the hall " on a great courser," to preserve order.

Henry the Sixth, when only in his tenth year, was crowned at Westminster, and here, in 1460, took place the memorable scene when the assembled prelates and nobles declared that having forfeited his crown, it had descended by right to the Earl of March, whom with loud shouts they hailed as King Edward the Fourth.

During the reigns of Edward the Fourth, and of his son and successor, Edward the Fifth, Westminster Hall is but rarely mentioned; but not so with the reign of Richard the Third. It was here, on the day of his being proclaimed King, that Richard made his famous speech, which he hoped would win for him the suffrages of his subjects; and here also, on the 6th of July, 1483, we find him presiding at the magnificent banquet which followed his coronation. The procession which attended him from the Abbey to the Hall must have been gorgeous in the extreme. First issued forth the trumpets and clarions, the serjeants at arms, and the heralds, bearing the King's heraldic insignia; then followed the bishops and abbots, with their mitres on their heads, and their croziers in their hands; the Bishop of Rochester carry-

CORONATION OF RICHARD THE THIRD.

ing the cross before Cardinal Bourchier, Archbishop of Canterbury; then came the Earl of Northumberland carrying the sword of state; the Duke of Suffolk with the sceptre; the Earl of Lincoln with the globe and cross; and the Earls of Kent and Surrey, and Lord Lovel, carrying other swords of state. Next came the Duke of Norfolk bearing the crown, and immediately after him followed Richard himself, dressed in robes of purple velvet. On each side of him walked the Bishops of Bath and Durham. His train was held up by the Duke of Buckingham, and the gorgeous canopy over his head by the Barons of the Cinque Ports. The procession was closed by a long train of Earls and Barons.

After the procession of the King came that of the Queen. Her sceptre was borne by the Earl of Huntington; the Viscount Lisle carrying the sceptre and dove, and the Earl of Wiltshire her crown. Then came the Queen herself, having "on her head a circlet of gold, with many precious stones set therein." On each side of her walked the Bishops of Exeter and Norwich. The Countess of Richmond, mother of Henry the Seventh, supported her train. After the Queen came her sister Catherine, Duchess of Suffolk, walking in the procession by herself, and then a long train of ladies, followed by a train of knights and esquires.

At the banquet in the Hall, the King and Queen were served on dishes of gold and silver; Lord Audley performed the office of state carver, Thomas Lord Scrope of Upsal that of cup-bearer; Lord Lovel during the entertainment standing before the King, and "two squires lying under the board at the King's feet." As soon as the second course was put on the table, "the King's champion, Sir Robert Dymoke, rode into the hall, his horse trapped with white silk and red, and himself in white harness; the heralds of arms standing upon a stage among all the company. Then the King's champion rode up before the King, asking, before all the people, if there was any man would say against King Richard the Third, why he should not pretend to the crown. And when he had so said, all the Hall cried 'King Richard,' all with one voice. And when this was done anon one of the Lords brought unto the champion a covered cup full of red wine, and so he took the cup and uncovered it, and drank thereof; and when he had done, anon he cast out the wine and covered the cup again; and, making his obeisance to the King, turned his horse about, and rode through the Hall, with his cup in his right hand, and that he had for his labour." No single untoward accident seems to have marred the harmony or splendour of the day. When at length evening set in, the vast Hall was illuminated by a great light of wax torches and torchets, apparently the signal for the King and Queen to retire. Accordingly, wafers and hippocras having been previously served, Richard and his consort rose up and departed to their private apartments in the palace.

When, about this time, the widowed Queen of Edward the Fourth consented, at the instance of Cardinal Bourchier, Archbishop of Canterbury, to deliver up her second son to the tender mercies of Richard, it was in the centre of the Hall that the Duke of Buckingham received the Cardinal and the weeping child. At the door of the Star Chamber they were met by Richard; who, running towards his nephew with open arms, kissed him, we are told, with a great show of affection.

Although the palace of Westminster appears to have been constantly the residence of Henry the Seventh, the Hall presents but few features of particular interest during his reign. It was the scene, however, of his coronation feast, and also of his nuptial banquet on the occasion of his marriage with Elizabeth, eldest daughter of Edward the Fourth.

In June, 1509, Henry the Eighth solemnized at Westminster the two events of his coronation and of his marriage with Catherine of Aragon, and considering his taste for splendour the old Hall was doubtless on these occasions the scene of extraordinary revellings and rejoicings. A few years afterwards a very different scene took place in Westminster Hall. According to Stow, "a great heart-burning and malicious grudge had grown among the Englishmen of the city of London against strangers; the artificers finding themselves much aggrieved because such a number of strangers were permitted to resort hither with their wares, and to exercise handicrafts, to the great hindrance and impoverishing of the King's liege people." Hence the rising of the London apprentices, and the formidable riots which ensued on "Evil May Day," 1547.

For these riots one John Lincoln, the reputed leader of those who had taken a part in it, and about twelve other persons had been hanged; while many of the remainder would probably have shared their fate but for the intercession of the Queen and Henry's sisters, the Queens Dowager of France and Scotland, who refused to rise from their knees before the King till he had promised to spare their lives. At length the residue of the rioters of "Evil May Day" was brought before the King for judgment. "Thursday, the 22nd of May," writes Hall, "the King came into Westminster Hall, for whom, at the upper end, was set a cloth of estate, and the place hanged with arras: with him went the Cardinal [Wolsey], the Duchess of Norfolk and Suffolk, &c. The Mayor and Aldermen were there, in their best livery, by nine of the clock. Then the King commanded that all the prisoners should be brought forth. Then came in the poor younglings and old false knaves, bound in ropes, all along, one after another, in their shirts, and every one a halter about his neck, to the number of four hundred men and eleven women. And when all were come before the King's presence, the Cardinal rose, laid to the Mayor and commonalty their negligence, and to the prisoners he declared they had deserved death for their offence. Then all the prisoners together cried, 'Mercy, gracious lord, mercy!' Then the Lords altogether besought his Grace for mercy, at whose request the King pardoned them all. And then the Cardinal gave unto them a good exhortation, to the great gladness of the hearers. And when the general pardon was pronounced, all the prisoners shouted at once, and altogether cast up their halters into the hall roof, so that the King might perceive they were none of the discreetest sort." In the crowd were several of the leaders of the riot who had hitherto contrived to evade justice, but who no sooner perceived the favourable turn which affairs were taking, than they "suddenly stripped them into their shirts, with halters," and mingling with the other offenders received pardon with the rest.

On the 19th of May, 1521, Westminster Hall witnessed the trial scene of the once all-powerful Edward Stafford, Duke of Buckingham, Lord High Constable of England, and lineal descendant of King Edward the Third. It was conducted in solemn state before the Duke of Norfolk, sitting as Lord High Steward, and twenty-two other peers. Having been found guilty of high treason, and sentence of death having been passed upon him, the Duke, in a calm and dignified manner, addressed the court:—"My Lord of Norfolk," he said, "you have said as a traitor should be said to; but I was never any. I nothing malign you for what you have now done to me, and may the Eternal God forgive

SIR THOMAS MORE.

you my death, as I do. I shall never sue to the King for life; howbeit, he is a gracious Prince, and more grace may come from him than I desire. I beseech you, my Lords, and all my fellows, to pray for me."

> "I have this day received a traitor's judgment,
> And by that name must die : yet, Heaven bear witness,
> And if I have a conscience, let it sink me,
> Even as the axe falls, if I be not faithful !
> The law I bear no malice for my death ;
> 'T has done, upon the premises, but justice :
> But those that sought it I could wish more Christians :
> Be what they will, I heartily forgive 'em :
> Yet let 'em look they glory not in mischief,
> Nor build their evils on the graves of great men ;
> For then my guiltless blood must cry against 'em.
> For further life in this world I ne'er hope,
> Nor will I sue, although the King have mercies
> More than I dare make faults. You few that loved me,
> And dare be bold to weep for Buckingham,
> His noble friends and fellows, whom to leave
> Is only bitter to him, only dying,
> Go with me, like good angels, to my end ;
> And, as the long divorce of steel falls on me,
> Make of your prayers one sweet sacrifice,
> And lift my soul to Heaven.—Lead on, o' God's name."
> *Henry VIII.*, act ii., sc. 1.

The Duke was re-conducted to the Tower, and three days afterwards was beheaded on Tower Hill, attended by the lamentations of the people.

In July, 1535, the trial of the wise and witty Sir Thomas More, for denying the King's supremacy, took place in Westminster Hall. Notwithstanding the eloquence of his defence, he was found guilty, and sentenced to be hanged, drawn, and quartered ; a sentence which the King afterwards commuted for decapitation, which was carried into effect, on Tower Hill on the sixth of the month.

Edward the Sixth was crowned in Westminster Abbey on the 20th of February, 1547, and after the ceremony partook of his coronation feast in the old Hall. It was near the close of his reign, on the 1st of December, 1552, that his uncle, the great Protector, Duke of Somerset, was brought from the Tower to Westminster Hall, to undergo his memorable trial on charges of treason and felony. "The Lord Treasurer, the Marquis of Winchester," writes Hayward, "sat as High Steward, under a cloth of state, on a bench mounted three degrees; the peers, to the number of twenty-seven, sitting on a bench one step lower." He was acquitted of the charge of treason, but having been found guilty of the felony, the object of his enemies was fully answered, and he was condemned to death. On the 22nd of the following month, the Duke was led forth to Tower Hill, where he submitted himself to the stroke of the executioner with a dignified fortitude and resignation.

The next trial of any importance which we find taking place in Westminster Hall, was that of Charles, seventh Baron Stourton, who was arraigned here on the 26th of February, 1557, for the foul murder of two gentlemen, William and John Hartgill, father and son, his neighbours in Somersetshire. Having been found guilty and sentenced to be hanged, he was placed on a horse's back with his arms pinioned behind him, and his legs tied under the horse's belly, and thus conveyed by slow stages to Salisbury, in the market-place of which town the sentence was carried into effect. The only distinction made between him and an ordinary malefactor was his being hanged with a silken halter.

Queen Mary was crowned in Westminster Abbey, and in all probability kept her coronation feast in Westminster Hall, as subsequently did her sister and successor, Queen Elizabeth, on the 15th of January, 1559. "She dined," says Holinshed, "in Westminster Hall, which was richly hung, and everything ordered in such royal manner as to such a regal and most solemn feast appertained."

During the reign of Queen Elizabeth more than one state trial of deep interest took place in Westminster Hall. That of Thomas Howard, Duke of Norfolk, who died for his romantic attachment to Mary Queen of Scots, presented an imposing and magnificent scene. The trial took place on the 16th of January, 1572, George Talbot, Earl of Shrewsbury, presiding as Lord High Steward of England. "A scaffold," writes Camden, who was present at the trial, "was erected in the midst of the Hall, reaching from the gate to the upper end, where there was a tribunal built, with seats on both sides; such a sight as had not been seen full eighteen years." It was in vain that the Duke entreated to be allowed the aid of counsel. Counsel, answered the Lord Chief Justice, was never allowed to criminals charged with high treason. "Then," said the Duke, "to-day I must plead for my life, my estate, my children, and, which is above all, my honour. If I die innocent, God will be sure to avenge my cause." The Clerk of the Crown then asked him, "Thomas Duke of Norfolk, art thou guilty of the crimes with which thou art charged, or no?" The Duke answered, "Not Guilty;" then said the Clerk, "How wilt thou be tried?" to which the Duke replied, "To God and to these Peers I commend my cause."

The Duke having been found guilty, the Lord Steward asked him if he had anything to offer why sentence should not be passed upon him, to which he replied—"God's will be done: He will judge between me and my false accusers." Silence being again proclaimed, and the edge of the axe having been turned towards the Duke, Barham, the Queen's Serjeant-at-Law, rose from his seat, and called upon the High Steward in the Queen's name to pass sentence. With tears in his eyes, the Lord Steward then proceeded to pronounce the dreadful sentence of the law. " Forasmuch," he said, " as thou, Thomas Duke of Norfolk, hast been charged with high treason, hast pleaded not guilty, and hast submitted thyself to the judgment of thy peers; this court adjudgeth thee to be carried back from hence to the Tower; then to be laid upon an hurdle, and drawn through the city to the gallows, there to be hanged; and being half dead, to be cut down, thy bowels taken out, and after thy head is cut off, to be quartered; thy head and body to be disposed of according to the Queen's pleasure ; and God have mercy upon thy soul." To these frightful details the Duke listened without any visible emotion. "Sentence is passed upon me," he said, "as upon a traitor: I have none to trust but God and the Queen. I am excluded from your society, but hope shortly to enjoy the heavenly. I will fit myself to die. Only one thing I crave : that the Queen would be kind to my poor children and servants, and take care that my debts be paid." The Duke was beheaded on Tower Hill, on the 2nd of June, 1572. He died pious and undaunted on the same spot where his father, the accomplished Earl of Surrey, had been decapitated twenty-six years previously.

Another interesting trial in this reign, at which Camden was present, was that of Robert Devereux, Earl of Essex, the ill-fated favourite of Queen Elizabeth, who was tried in Westminster Hall, with his friend, Henry Wriothesley, Earl of Southampton, on the 19th February, 1601. The Peers having unanimously pronounced a verdict of guilty, the Clerk of the Crown inquired of the prisoners, as usual, if they had anything to offer why judgment should not be passed upon them. Southampton addressed them in a modest, pathetic, and effective appeal, while Essex contented himself with generously pleading the cause of his friend. As for his own life, he said, he valued it not. His only desire was to lay down his life with the sincere conscience of a good Christian and a loyal subject; and though he was unwilling that he should be represented to the Queen as a person who despised her clemency, yet he trusted he should make no cringing submissions for his life. "And you, my lords," he concluded, "though you have condemned me in this tribunal, yet I most heartily entreat you, that you will acquit me in your opinion of having entertained any ill intentions against my Prince."

The edge of the axe being now turned towards the prisoners, the High Steward passed on them the dreadful sentence of the law. Eventually Southampton not only escaped with his life, but, on the accession of James the First, obtained the Order of the Garter and other honours. Essex was less fortunate. He was beheaded in the courtyard of the Tower six days after his condemnation; displaying on the scaffold the same unaffected courage and calm dignity which he had exhibited at his trial in Westminster Hall.

James the First and his consort, Anne of Denmark, were crowned in Westminster Abbey, after which they sat at their coronation banquet in the Hall. Two years afterwards the old Hall witnessed a very different scene, the trial of the handsome Sir Everard Digby, Guy Fawkes, and the other conspirators engaged in the memorable Gunpowder Plot, who were conveyed by water from the Tower to be tried by a special commission in Westminster Hall.

Scarcely less remarkable trials were those of the celebrated favourite, Robert Carr, Earl of Somerset, and his Countess, who were arraigned before the bar of the House of Lords in Westminster Hall on the 24th and 25th of May, 1616, for the murder of Sir Thomas Overbury.

The Countess was the first who was tried; presenting the extraordinary spectacle of a young, noble, and beautiful woman being arraigned before her peers for a foul and unnatural murder. The Lord Chancellor, who acted as Lord High Steward, rode into Westminster Hall on *horseback*. At the bar she stood pale and trembling, and during the reading of the indictment kept her face covered with her fan. Pleading guilty to the crime with which she was charged, she at the same time beseeched the Peers to intercede for her with the King, and this she did with so many tears and with such evident anguish of mind, that the bystanders, forgetting the horror of her crime in the touching sight of beauty in distress, were unable to refuse her their commiseration.

The following day, the Earl—dressed in "a plain black satin suit, his hair curled, his face pale, his beard long, and his eyes sunk in his head, and decorated with the George and Garter —was brought before the same tribunal. The Peers bringing in a verdict of guilty against him, he was sentenced with his Countess to be reconducted to the Tower, and thence to be carried to the place of execution, where they were to be hanged like common criminals. They received, however, at different times, several reprieves; till, at last, in 1624, about four months previous to the death of James, they received a full pardon for their crime. The guilty pair during the remainder of their lives resided together in a private and almost obscure condition. Their former passionate love was converted into abhorrence, and though inmates of the same house, they lived entirely separated and estranged. Such was the end of these two persons—both of them gifted with extraordinary beauty of person, and of exalted rank—whose marriage, only a few years previously, had been solemnized in the King's Palace of Whitehall with greater splendour than had ever been witnessed in England at the espousals of a subject!

Charles the First was crowned in Westminster Abbey on the 2nd of February, 1626, and afterwards dined in the Hall, attended by the usual ceremonies. It was probably in order to denote the purity of his intentions, that he wore a robe of white satin. It was an age in which faith was placed in omens, and accordingly when, during the coronation ceremonial, the golden dove fell from the sceptre, it may readily be imagined that the superstitious attached no small importance to the circumstance. Moreover, the text selected by Senhouse, Bishop of Carlisle, for the sermon,—Rev. ii. 10, "Be thou faithful unto death, and I will give thee a crown of life," &c.—was considered far more suitable for a funeral sermon than adapted to the gorgeous ceremonial of a coronation.

On the twenty-second of March, 1641, Westminster Hall witnessed the memorable trial of Thomas Wentworth, Earl of Strafford. At the upper end of the Hall was placed a throne for the King, and by the side of it a chair for the Prince of Wales, afterwards Charles the Second, who occupied it in his robes though only in his eleventh year. On each side of the throne, which was vacant, were erected temporary closets covered with tapestry, in one of which sat some French noblemen who were then in England, and in the other the King and Queen and several ladies of the court. In front of this box was a curtain which had been placed there for the purpose of screening the royal party from observation, but Charles no sooner entered the box than he tore it down with his own hands. The Queen and her ladies, we are told, were observed constantly taking notes during the trial.

Beneath the throne, on seats covered with green cloth, sat

the Peers in their parliamentary robes; and near them the judges, on "sacks of wool," in their scarlet gowns. Lower down were ten ranges of seats for the members of the House of Commons. A bar covered with green cloth ran across the centre of the Hall, behind which were placed a table and desk for the convenience of the prisoner, together with a chair which he could make use of if he felt fatigued. Close to him stood Sir William Balfour, the Lieutenant of the Tower. Strafford's four secretaries sat on a desk behind him; and on one side of them were the witnesses for the prosecution. On each side of the Hall were galleries filled with the rank and beauty of the land.

The trial of Strafford lasted from the 22nd of March to the 17th of April. On each day of the trial he was brought by water from the Tower, guarded by six barges containing a hundred soldiers. On his landing at Westminster stairs he was received by a hundred of the train bands, who conducted him into the Hall, and afterwards stood as guards at the doors. Strafford and the Peers usually arrived about eight o'clock in the morning; the King generally preceding them by about half an hour. Principal Baillie, who was present, speaks of the scene as "daily the most glorious assembly the isle could afford." "All being set," he writes, "the chamberlain and black rod went out and brought in my Lord Strafford. He was always in the same suit of black. At the entry he made a low curtsey; proceeding a little, he gave a second; when he came to his desk, a third; then, at the bar, the fore-face of his desk, he kneeled. Rising quickly, he saluted both sides of the house, and then sat down. Some few of the lords lifted their hats to him. This was his daily carriage."

On the last day of his trial Strafford was attended by his young children, who were allowed to stand by his side at the bar. Regarding them with looks of deep affection, and pointing towards them, he thus concluded his beautiful address to his judges:—"My lords, I have now troubled your lordships a great deal longer than I should have done, were it not for the interest of these pledges which a saint in heaven has left me." Here his feelings overcame him, and compelled him to pause for a few seconds. "I should be loath, my lords—what I forfeit for myself is nothing; but I confess, that my indiscretion should forfeit for them, it wounds me very deeply. You will be pleased to pardon my infirmity. Something I should have said, but I see I shall not be able, and therefore I will leave it. And now, my lords, for myself; I thank God I have been, by His good blessing towards me, taught that the afflictions of the present life are not to be compared with that eternal weight of glory that shall be revealed to us hereafter. And, my lords, even so with all humility and all tranquillity of mind, I do submit myself clearly and freely to your judgments, and whether that righteous judgment shall be to life or to death—

Te Deum laudamus, Te Deum confitemur."

Even the enemies of Strafford beheld his dignified demeanour and listened to his lofty eloquence with admiration. Sir William Pennyman, after giving his evidence against him, burst into tears; and even Whitelocke, the chairman of the committee of the House which had drawn up the impeachment against him, seems to have been affected almost to enthusiasm. "Never," he writes, "did any man ever act such a part, on such a theatre, with more wisdom, constancy, judgment, and temper, and with a better grace in all his words and actions, than did this great and excellent person; and he moved the hearts of all his auditors, some few excepted, to remorse and pity." On the 12th of May following, Strafford was beheaded on Tower Hill, displaying on the scaffold the same grace and dignity, and the same humble submission to the will of heaven, which, amidst the assembled thousands in Westminster Hall, had drawn the tear from the eye of beauty, and had thrilled the heart even of the most acrimonious republican.

It must have been an extraordinary scene when, on the 9th of January, 1649, a sergeant-at-arms rode into the middle of Westminster Hall, and, after a loud flourish of drums and trumpets, proclaimed to the astonished crowd that the Commons of England had determined on bringing King Charles the First to a solemn trial. Twelve days afterwards the old hall witnessed the amazing spectacle of a great nation sitting in judgment on its sovereign. At the upper end of the hall, on benches raised one above the other, and covered with scarlet, sat the King's judges, about seventy in number. In the middle of them, on a raised chair of state covered with crimson velvet and with a desk in front of it, sat the President, Bradshaw. Immediately in front of Bradshaw, though with a considerable space between them, was the chair, covered also with velvet, provided for the King. Between Charles and Bradshaw stood a large table covered with a rich Turkey carpet, on which the mace and sword of justice were laid, and at which two clerks of the court were seated. On either side of the hall were galleries for the convenience of the spectators; and behind, and on the right and left hand of the King, were arranged the soldiers and officers of the court; Cooke, the solicitor for the self-styled people of England, standing on the King's right hand. A strong bar ran across the centre of the Hall, behind which were crowded the populace in a dense mass; while, for the protection of the judges, the leads and windows of the Hall were filled with soldiers.

At the entrance of the King into the Hall he was received from the custody of Colonel Hacker by the sergeant-at-arms, who conducted his Majesty to his chair, in which he seated himself without either taking off his hat, or otherwise acknowledging any respect for the court. Some minutes afterwards, however, he rose from his chair, and turning himself round, fixed his eyes steadily on the guards and the dense mass of people behind him. While the indictment was being read he sat calm and unmoved, except only when some more absurd or daring allegation was laid to his charge, when he was occasionally observed to smile.

During the proceedings a well-known incident occurred which created a considerable sensation in the Hall. The name of Fairfax, the Lord General, having been called over, a female voice exclaimed from one of the galleries—" He has more wit than to be here." Again, when the proceedings were stated to be on behalf of the people of England, the same mysterious voice called out with increased energy— " No, not the hundredth part of them! It is false—where are they?—Oliver Cromwell is a traitor!" The utmost confusion was the consequence, which may be presumed to have increased when Colonel Axtell threatened to order the soldiers to fire into the gallery whence the voice had proceeded. It was soon discovered that the offender was the Lady Fairfax, the wife of the general, who was instantly compelled to retire.

On entering the Hall on the second day, Charles seems to have been much affected by the soldiers receiving him with loud cries for "justice," which, however, he afterwards attributed, and perhaps with reason, to their having been instigated by their officers. "Poor souls," he said, "for a little money they would do as much against their commanders." It was on this day also—according to the evidence given by

Sir Purbeck Temple at the trial of Colonel Axtell—that the soldiers "did fire powder in the palms of their hands, that did not only offend his Majesty's smell, but enforced him to rise up out of his chair, and with his hand to turn away the smoke; *and after this he turned about to the people and smiled upon them, and those soldiers that so rudely treated him.*" As he was quitting the Hall, one of the common soldiers, of a kinder nature than his fellows, exclaimed,—"God bless you, sir!" The man's officer, overhearing the benediction, struck him severely on the head with his cane. "Methinks," said the King, "the punishment exceedeth the offence." One person was actually brutal enough to spit at the meek monarch. "My Saviour," said Charles, as he quietly wiped his face, " suffered more than this for me."

On the third day of the trial nothing remarkable happened, except the rather singular coincidence of the gold head of the King's walking-cane falling off, which Charles himself, who was singularly superstitious even for the age he lived in, regarded as an ill omen.

On the fourth and last day of this memorable trial, Bradshaw entered Westminster Hall in his scarlet gown, a signal to the King that his doom was fixed, and that before another sun had set sentence would be pronounced. Silence having been commanded, Bradshaw delivered a tedious tirade, in which the King was accused of being the author of "all the late unnatural, cruel, and bloody wars; of all the murders, rapines, burnings, spoils, desolations, damages, and mischief, occasioned by and committed during the said wars;" for which "treasons and crimes," this court, said the President, "doth adjudge that he, the said Charles Stuart, as a tyrant, traitor, murderer, and public enemy, shall be put to death by severing his head from his body." Charles listened calmly to the reading of the sentence, at the conclusion of which he requested permission to address a few words to his judges, which, however, was refused.

"*Bradshaw.*—Sir, you are not to be heard after the sentence.
Charles.—No, sir?
Bradshaw.—No, sir, by your favour. Guards, withdraw your prisoner.
Charles.—I may speak after the sentence, by your favour, sir. I may speak after the sentence, ever. By your favour——
Bradshaw.—Hold!
Charles.—The sentence, sir; I say, sir, I do——
Bradshaw.—Hold!
Charles.—*I am not suffered to speak! expect what justice the people will have.*"

Before he could say more, the King was hurried off by the guards.

On the 26th of June, 1657, Westminster Hall witnessed the extraordinary scene of the installation of Oliver Cromwell as Lord Protector of the Commonwealth of Great Britain and Ireland, on the same spot on which a few years before he had sat in judgment on his unfortunate sovereign. The ceremony was conducted with as much splendour as if it had been the coronation of one of the ancient Kings. On a raised platform, under a splendid canopy, sat the subverter of monarchy, on the same throne on which the Tudors and Plantagenets had taken their coronation oaths, and which had been brought from the Abbey for the purpose. Before him was set a table, covered with pink-coloured Genoa velvet, fringed with gold, on which were placed the Bible, the sword, and the sceptre of the Commonwealth. On each side of the Hall were erected temporary galleries, in which sat the Protector's family, the spectators, and the members of the House of Commons; Sir Thomas Widdrington, the Speaker, being the only person honoured with a seat near the Protector. As soon as the oath was taken, the heralds, after a flourish of trumpets, proclaimed him, with all the usual formalities, Lord Protector of England, Scotland, and Ireland. Exactly three years afterwards, the head of Cromwell,—a ghastly object,—was affixed to a pole on the roof of that very apartment in which he now sat in all the pomp and pride of usurped power. By the side of that of Cromwell were also affixed on poles the heads of Ireton and Bradshaw.

In the time of Cromwell, and up to a later period, we find Westminster Hall used as a fashionable lounging-place, where the gay and idle assembled to discuss the news and gossip of the day. Here, too, books, and apparently all kinds of articles, were exposed for sale. Pepys especially mentions, in 1660, buying, "among other books, one of the life of our Queen, which I read at home to my wife, but it was so sillily writ that we did nothing but laugh at it." As late as the middle of the last century, Westminster Hall, except when required for state purposes, appears to have presented the appearance rather of a bazaar than a banqueting-hall. On each side of it were arranged book-shelves and stalls, on which books, mathematical instruments, prints, and even articles of ladies' dress were exposed for sale.

On the 8th of May, 1660,—to the great disgust and abhorrence of the old Puritan and Republican party,—Charles the Second was proclaimed by the heralds King of Great Britain and Ireland in front of Westminster Hall; the members of the House of Commons standing by bare-headed. On the 23rd of April the following year, Charles was solemnly crowned in the Abbey, and the same day kept his coronation feast with great magnificence in the same old hall in which, twenty-one years previously, he had listened, a mere child, to the dying eloquence of the ill-fated Strafford. Since that time how many revolutions of fortune had the old hall witnessed! Since then, the King's unfortunate father, the princely Hamilton, the gay and graceful Holland, and the virtuous and high-minded Lord Capel—each surrounded by guards and preceded by the fatal axe—had severally passed forth from its massive portal, never to cross its threshold again. Since then the mighty Cromwell had sat there arrayed in purple and ermine, and now he was beneath the gibbet at Tyburn. The empire, too, of the second Cromwell had not only come and gone, but he, who a few months previously had received a greater number of fulsome addresses from the people of England than had ever congratulated the accession of a legitimate sovereign, was now a prescribed fugitive in a foreign land. Yet many of these men had been gifted with rare virtues or were of exalted talent; whereas it was the fate of Charles, without any merit of his own, to sit unchallenged at the gay and gorgeous banquet, bandying wit and repartee with the frolic Buckingham, or exchanging looks of love and gallantry with the bright eyes which glanced down on the young monarch from the silken galleries above.

James the Second, on the 23rd of April, 1685, was crowned in Westminster Abbey with his consort, the young and lovely Mary of Modena, after which he partook of a "most sumptuous and magnificent" banquet in the hall. At the coronation of the misguided monarch more than one incident occurred which his subjects regarded as ominous of future ill, and which, to say the least, were remarkable coincidences. At the moment, for instance, when the Tower guns announced that the King was crowned, the royal standard was blown from the White Tower; the canopy, also, over the King's head was observed to be unaccountably rent, and in one of the London churches a window in which the royal arms were beautifully painted fell down without any apparent cause. Moreover, at one moment, not only was the crown observed to totter on the King's head, but it seems it would have dropped to the ground had not Henry Sidney, the brother of the high-minded patriot, Algernon Sidney, stepped forward and prevented its falling. "It was not the first occasion," he said, "that his family had supported the Crown."

During the short and dark reign of James the Second, the only incident of great interest associated with Westminster Hall is the memorable trial of the Seven Bishops —the most important, perhaps, that ever took place under its venerable roof. On the day of their trial, the 29th of June, 1688, the Bishops were conducted from the Tower to Westminster by water; the banks of the river on both sides being crowded with an immense mass of anxious spectators, who followed the barge with their eyes, and audibly offered up their prayers for the persecuted fathers of the Church. On being arraigned at the bar in Westminster Hall, the venerable appearance of the aged prelates, the position in which they stood as the meek but undaunted champions of the civil and religious liberties of their fellow-countrymen, as well as the crowded thousands who filled the hall, presented one of the most imposing scenes of which we can form any notion. After having sat up all night, the jury again made their appearance in the hall before the anxious and excited audience. The wished-for verdict of "Not Guilty" having been returned, the roof of the old hall rang with such a universal shout of joy as had rarely been heard within its walls. The same shout was echoed through the cities of Westminster and London, and in a short time was re-echoed by the army on Hounslow Heath, where the King was dining with the general, Lord Feversham, in his tent, and for the moment startled the infatuated monarch.

William the Third and his consort, Queen Mary, were crowned in Westminster Abbey, on the 11th of April, 1689, and afterwards banqueted in the hall with the usual pomp and ceremony, Dymoke, the champion, making the customary challenge. "It was as usual," writes Reresby, "a splendid sight: the procession to the Abbey was quite regular, though not so complete in the number of nobility as at the two last solemnities of the same kind. Particular care was had of the House of Commons, who had a place prepared for them to sit in, both in the church and in the hall."

It was in this reign that Peter the Great of Russia paid a visit to England, and, among other places, was conducted by the Marquis of Carmarthen to Westminster Hall. It happening to be term time, the vast area was—as usual at such seasons—crowded with lawyers in their wigs and gowns. Peter appeared to be struck with the sight, and inquired who these persons could possibly be. Being informed by Lord Carmarthen that they were all persons of the legal profession, he appeared quite confounded. "Lawyers!" he exclaimed, "why I have only *two* in all my dominions, and I believe I shall hang one of them the moment I get back."

On the 23rd of April, 1702, Queen Anne was crowned in Westminster Abbey, after which the banquet in the hall was solemnized with the customary splendour and rejoicings; her consort, Prince George of Denmark, sitting on her right hand under the same canopy. Two years afterwards, Westminster Hall was decorated with the trophies won by the great Marlborough at the battle of Blenheim. They consisted of no fewer than one hundred and twenty-one standards, and one hundred and seventy-nine colours. During the Commonwealth the trophies which had hung in the old hall were the banners captured from Charles the First at the battle of Naseby, and from Charles the Second at the battles of Worcester and Dunbar.

It was in the reign of Queen Anne that the second Protector, Richard Cromwell, was compelled, at a very advanced age, to visit London for the purpose of giving his evidence in the Court of Queen's Bench, Westminster. While waiting in the hall to be called as a witness, he was induced to stroll into the House of Lords, on the throne of which, half a century before, he had sat as the foremost personage in the realm. While standing there—absorbed probably in strange, if not painful associations—a stranger, mistaking him for a mere country gentleman attracted there by curiosity, inquired of him if he had ever before beheld such a scene? "*Never*," replied the old man, pointing to the throne, "*since I sat in that chair!*" When, subsequently, Richard Cromwell entered the Court of Queen's Bench, his venerable appearance, and the exalted position which he had once filled, appear to have excited an extraordinary sensation. The judge not only ordered him to be conducted into a private apartment where refreshments were in readiness, but directed a chair to be brought into court for his convenience, and insisted that on account of his age he should remain covered. It was in vain that the counsel on the opposite side objected to the indulgence of the chair. "I will allow no reflections to be made," said the judge, "but that you go to the merits of the cause." It was to the credit of Queen Anne that she had the good feeling to appreciate and to express her approbation of the conduct of the presiding judge.

The only other incident of any interest connected with Westminster Hall in the reign of Queen Anne, was the trial of the celebrated Dr. Sacheverell, which took place here before the Peers on the 27th of February, 1710. The lenient sentence passed on him, that he was to abstain from preaching for three years, was regarded by the people as a triumph, and was hailed by them with acclamations almost as loud as those which had attended the acquittal of the Seven Bishops.

The first two of our German sovereigns, George the First and Second, were crowned and feasted at Westminster, if with less popular enthusiasm, at least with as much magnificence as had attended the coronation ceremonials of the Plantagenets or the Stuarts. In the former reign, the first event of any interest connected with the old Hall was the arraignment under its roof on the 10th of January, 1716, of the Rebel Lords, the Earls of Derwentwater, Nithisdale, and Carnwath, and the Lords Widdrington, Kenmure, and Nairn. The area behind the bar was crowded with thousands of spectators; the peers and judges sat in their robes; the galleries were filled with the rank and beauty of the land; the Commons of Great Britain, with great solemnity, presented the articles of impeachment at the bar of the House of Lords; while the prisoners were led into the Hall with the usual formalities, surrounded by soldiers, and with the back of the axe turned towards them. The peers having returned a verdict of guilty, on the 9th of February these unfortunate noblemen were again brought to the bar in Westminster Hall to receive their sentence. The appearance and demeanour of the young and gallant Derwentwater excited the warmest commiseration in the vast audience. "The terrors of your Lordships' just sentence," he said, in reply to the question whether he had anything to advance why judgment should not be pronounced upon him, "which at once deprives me of my life and estate, and completes the misfortunes of my wife and innocent children, are so heavy upon my mind, that I am scarcely able to allege what may extenuate my offence, if anything can do it. I have confessed myself guilty; but, my lords, that guilt was rashly incurred without any premeditation." Lord Nairn also pathetically pleaded the cause of his wife and twelve children. It was to no purpose, as far at least as the former was concerned.

The Lords Derwentwater and Kenmure were beheaded on the same scaffold on Tower Hill, on the 24th of February, 1716; the Earl of Nithisdale, by means of his heroic Countess, contrived to escape from the Tower in female attire; and the Earl of Carnwath, and Lords Widdrington and Nairn, after remaining in prison till 1717, were released by the Act of Grace, with the forfeiture of their titles and estates.

The only other event of any interest connected with Westminster Hall in the reign of George the First, was the arraignment, on the 24th of June, 1717, of the celebrated statesman, Robert Harley, Earl of Oxford, for high crimes and misdemeanours, on which occasion the King, the royal family, and the foreign Ambassadors were present. On the 1st of July the prisoner was called to the bar in Westminster Hall, when, no prosecutors appearing, he was unanimously acquitted, and, after an imprisonment of upwards of two years in the Tower, was restored to his liberty.

In the reign of George the Second, on the 28th of July, 1746, took place in Westminster Hall the trial for high treason of those gallant and devoted followers of the fortunes of Charles Edward, the Earls of Cromartie and Kilmarnock and Lord Balmerino. They were conducted from the Tower to Westminster in three coaches, attended by a strong guard of foot soldiers, and as soon as the peers had assembled in Westminster Hall, and proclamation had been made for their appearance, they were brought to the bar, preceded by the gentleman gaoler carrying the axe with the back part towards them. The usual formal compliments having passed between the prisoners and the peers, the indictments were read with all the customary formalities. "I am at this moment," writes Walpole on the 1st of August, 1746, "come from the conclusion of the greatest and most melancholy scene I ever yet saw! You will easily guess it was the trials of the rebel Lords. As it was the most interesting sight, so it was the most solemn and fine. A coronation is a puppet-show, and all the splendour of it idle, but this sight at once feasted one's eyes and engaged all one's passions. It began last Monday. Three parts of Westminster Hall were enclosed with galleries, and hung with scarlet; and the whole ceremony was conducted with the most awful solemnity and decency, except in the one point of leaving the prisoners at the bar amidst the idle curiosity of some crowd, and even with the witnesses who had sworn against them, while the Lords adjourned to their own house to consult. No part of the royal family was there, which was a proper regard to the unhappy men, who were become their victims. One hundred and thirty-nine Lords were present, and made a noble sight on their benches *frequent and full!*"

According to Walpole, the first appearance of the prisoners shocked him; their behaviour melted him. "For Lord Balmerino," he writes, "he is the most natural brave old fellow I ever saw; the highest intrepidity, even to indifference. At the bar he behaved like a soldier and a man; in the intervals of form, with carelessness and humour. He pressed extremely to have his wife, his pretty Peggy, with him in the Tower. Lady Cromartie only sees her husband through the grate, not choosing to be shut up with him, as she thinks she can serve him better by her intercession without. She is big with child, and very handsome; so are her daughters. When they were to be brought from the Tower in separate coaches, there was some dispute in which the axe must go·

Old Balmerino cried—'Come, come, put it with me.' At the bar, he plays with his fingers upon the axe, while he talks to the gentleman-gaoler; and one day somebody coming up to listen, he took the blade and held it like a fan between their faces. During the trial a little boy was near him, but not tall enough to see; he made room for the child and placed him near himself." One of his reasons for pleading not guilty, as Balmerino gallantly affirmed, was that so many ladies might not be disappointed of their show.

"While the Lords were withdrawn," writes Walpole, "the Solicitor-General Murray officiously and insolently went up to Lord Balmerino, and asked him how he could give the Lords so much trouble, when his solicitor had informed him that his plea could be of no use to him. Balmerino asked the bystanders who this person was; and being told, he said, 'Oh, Mr. Murray! I am extremely glad to see you; I have been with several of your relations; the good lady, your mother, was of great use to us at Perth.' Are you not charmed with this speech? How just it was! As he went away, he said, 'They call me Jacobite; I am no more a Jacobite than any that tried me; but if the Great Mogul had set up his standard, I should have followed it, for I could not starve.'"

Being found guilty by the unanimous verdict of their Peers, the prisoners were recalled to the bar, and having been informed by the Lord Steward, that on the day following the next, sentence would be passed upon them, they were reconducted to the Tower, with the edge of the axe turned towards them. Accordingly, on the 30th of July they were again brought to the bar of Westminster Hall to receive judgment, but in consequence of a technical objection raised by Lord Balmerino, the court was once more adjourned to the 1st of August, in order to enable him to obtain the assistance of counsel. On that day, the Peers again assembled in Westminster Hall, when the prisoners were called upon with the usual formalities to state if they had any objection to raise why sentence of death should not be passed upon them. They all answered in the negative. The Lord Steward then addressed them in a pathetic speech, at the conclusion of which he passed on them the dreadful sentence which the law awards for the crime of high treason. Then, the prisoners having been removed, the Lord Steward broke his staff, and declared the commission to be dissolved.

Eight months afterwards the same imposing spectacle was exhibited in Westminster Hall, on the occasion of the trial of the celebrated Lord Lovat, who, after a long life of craft and profligacy, stood a prisoner before his Peers, at the almost patriarchal age of eighty. To Sir Horace Mann Walpole writes, on the 20th of March, 1747: "I have been living at old Lovat's trial, and was willing to have it over before I talked to you of it. It lasted seven days. The evidence was as strong as possible; and after all he had denounced, he made no defence. . . . The old creature's behaviour has been foolish, and at last indecent. I see little of parts in him, nor attribute much to that cunning for which he is so famous. It might catch wild Highlanders, but the art of dissimulation and flattery is so refined and improved, that it is of little use now where it is not very delicate. When Sir Everard Falkner," adds Walpole, " had been examined against Lovat, the Lord High Steward asked the latter if he had anything to say to Sir Everard, he replied, ' No; but that he was his humble servant, and wished him joy of his young wife.' The two last days he behaved ridiculously, joking, and making everybody laugh even at the sentence. He said to Lord Ilchester, who sat near the bar,

'*Je meurs pour ma patrie, et ne m'en soucie guère.*' When he withdrew, he said—'Adieu, my lords, we shall never meet again in the same place.' He says he will be hanged, for that his neck is so short and bended, that he should be struck in the shoulders. I did not think it possible to feel so little as I did at so melancholy a spectacle; but tyranny and villany, wound up by buffoonery, took off all edge of concern. The foreigners were much struck."

This extraordinary man, notwithstanding his buffoonery at his trial, his vices, and the exceeding infamy of his career, died with a dignity which would have done credit to an ancient Roman. "Old Lovat," writes Walpole on the 10th of April, " was beheaded yesterday, and died extremely well, without passion, affectation, buffoonery, or timidity: his behaviour was natural and intrepid." With the executioner he jested on the subject of his melancholy occupation, and died with the beautiful line of Horace on his lips—"*Dulce et decorum est pro patriâ mori.*"

George the Third, with his consort, Charlotte of Mecklenberg-Strelitz, was crowned at Westminster on the 22nd of September, 1761, and afterwards sat at his coronation banquet in the Hall with his young bride, attended by all the formalities and ceremonials which had been dignified by the custom of past ages. Looking down from one of the galleries, sat one, who, in a disguised habit, and with his face half concealed, was no unconcerned spectator of that gorgeous scene. This person was no other than the young hero of Preston Pans and Falkirk; he who had rendered himself the idol of the rude and devoted Highlanders; he who, by the right of legitimate descent, was entitled to sit upon that very throne which he now had the mortification to behold occupied by another. The fact of Charles Edward having been present at the coronation of George the Third, was related by Earl Mareschal to Hume, the historian, only a few days after the ceremony had taken place. "I asked my lord," says Hume, "the reason for this strange fact. 'Why,' says he, 'a gentleman told me that saw him there, and that he even spoke to him, and whispered in his ears these words, Your royal highness is the last of all mortals whom I should expect to meet here. It was curiosity that led me, said the other, but I assure you that the person who is the object of all this pomp and magnificence is the man I envy the least.' *What if the Pretender had taken up Dymoke's gauntlet?*"

We have already perhaps lingered at too great length on the scenes which have taken place in Westminster Hall, but to those who delight in graphic descriptions of the manners and customs of past times, the picture is one of almost equal interest, whether it be borrowed from the pages of an ancient monkish chronicler, or from a gossiping writer of modern times; whether from the grave chronicles of Fabian and Matthew Paris, of Hall and Holinshed, or the charming pages of Horace Walpole. With respect to the coronation of George the Third, Walpole, on the 24th of September, 1761, writes to his friend, George Montagu:— "For the coronation, if a puppet show could be worth a million, that is. The multitudes, balconies, guards, and processions, made Palace Yard the liveliest spectacle in the world. The Hall was the most glorious. The blaze of lights, the richness and variety of habits, the ceremonial, the benches of peers and peeresses, frequent and full, was as awful as a pageant can be; and yet for the King's sake and my own I never wish to see another, nor am impatient to have my Lord Effingham's promise fulfilled. The King complained that so few precedents were kept for their proceedings. Lord Effingham owned the Earl Marshal's office had been strangely neglected; but he had taken such care for the future, that the 'next coronation' would be regulated in the most exact manner imaginable. The number of peers and peeresses present was not very great. Some of the latter, with no excuse in the world, appeared in Lord Lincoln's gallery, and even walked about the hall indecently in the intervals of the procession. My Lady Harrington, covered with all the diamonds she could borrow, hire, or seize, and with the air of Roxana, was the finest figure at a distance. She complained to George Selwyn that she was to walk with Lady Portsmouth, who would have a wig and a stick. 'Pooh,' said he, 'you will only look as if you were taken up by the constable.' She told this everywhere, thinking the reflection was on my Lady Portsmouth. Lady Pembroke alone, at the head of the countesses, was the picture of majestic modesty; the Duchess of Richmond as pretty as Nature and dress, with no pains of her own, could make her; Lady Spenser, Lady Sunderland, and Lady Northampton, very pretty figures; Lady Kildare still beauty itself, if not a little too large. The ancient peeresses were by no means the worst party. Lady Westmoreland still handsome, and with more dignity than all. The Duchess of Queensberry looked well, though her locks are milk white; Lady Albemarle very genteel; nay, the middle age had some good representatives in Lady Holdernesse, Lady Rochford, and Lady Strafford, the perfectest little figure of all. My Lady Suffolk ordered her robes, and I dressed part of her head, as I made some of my Lord Hertford's dress, for you know no profession comes amiss to me, from the tribune of the people to a habit maker. Don't imagine that there were not figures as excellent on the other side; old Exeter, who told the King he was the handsomest man she ever saw; old Effingham, and a Lady Say and Sele, with her hair powdered, and her tresses black, was an excellent contrast to the handsome. Lord B—— put on rouge upon his wife and the Duchess of Bedford in the Painted Chamber. The Duchess of Queensberry told me of the latter, that she looked like an orange peach, half red and half yellow. The coronets of the peers and their robes disguised them strangely. It required all the beauty of the Dukes of Richmond and Marlborough to make them noticed. One there was, though of another species, the noblest figure I ever saw, the high constable of Scotland, Lord Errol; as one saw him in a space capable of containing him, one admired him. At the wedding, dressed in tissue, he looked like one of the giants in Guildhall new gilt. It added to the energy of his person, that one considered him acting so considerable a part in that very Hall where so few years ago one saw his father, Lord Kilmarnock, condemned to the block. The champion acted his part admirably, and dashed down his gauntlet with proud defiance. His associates, Lord Effingham, Lord Talbot, and the Duke of Bedford were woeful. Lord Talbot piqued himself on backing his horse down the hall, and not turning its rump towards the King, but he had taken such pains to dress it to that duty, that it entered backwards, and at his retreat the spectators clapped, a terrible indecorum."

On the 16th of April, 1765, the fifth Lord Byron was tried before his peers in Westminster Hall for the manslaughter of William Chaworth, Esq. The circumstances under which Lord Byron killed his neighbour and friend we have already related in our notices of Pall Mall. The duel, originating in a most trifling dispute, took place in the Star and Garter Tavern in that street; the combatants fighting with swords in a solitary apartment, without witnesses or seconds, and by the light of a single candle. Fortunately for Lord Byron, Mr.

Chaworth was able before he died to exonerate his antagonist from blame, and to declare the duel to have been a fair one. To the Earl of Hertford Horace Walpole writes—" Lord Byron has not gone off, but says he will take his trial, which, if the coroner brings in a verdict of manslaughter, may, according to precedent, be in the House of Lords, and without the ceremonial of Westminster Hall. George Selwyn is much missed on this occasion, but we conclude it will bring him over." The following month Gilly Williams writes to George Selwyn:—" I suppose Byron has told you himself that he intends to surrender as soon as Westminster Hall is ready for him. It will be a show for a day to the Queen and the foreign ministers, but cannot possibly be attended with any ill consequences to the culprit." Lord Byron was found guilty by his peers, by a majority of one hundred and fourteen against four, but claiming the privilege of the peerage under a statute passed in the reign of Edward the Sixth, he was discharged.

On the 15th of April, 1776, the notorious and once beautiful Duchess of Kingston underwent her trial in Westminster Hall, for having married Evelyn Pierrepoint, Duke of Kingston, her first husband, Augustus, third Earl of Bristol, being still alive. "Garrick," writes Hannah More, "would have me take his ticket to go to the trial of the Duchess of Kingston, a sight which for beauty and magnificence exceeded anything which those who were never present at a coronation or trial by peers can have the least notion of. Mr. Garrick and I were in full dress by seven. You will imagine the bustle of five thousand people getting into one hall; yet, in all this hurry we walked in tranquilly. When they were all seated, and the king-at-arms had commanded silence on pain of imprisonment—which however was very ill observed—the gentleman of the black rod was commanded to bring in his prisoner. Elizabeth, calling herself Duchess Dowager of Kingston, walked in, led by black rod and M. La Roche, courtsying profoundly to her judges. The peers made her a slight bow. The prisoner was dressed in deep mourning; a black hood on her head, her hair modestly dressed and powdered, a black silk sacque with crape trimmings, black gauze, deep ruffles, and black gloves. The counsel spoke about an hour and a quarter each. Dunning's manner is insufferably bad; coughing and spitting at every three words, but his sense and expression pointed to the last degree. He made her grace shed bitter tears. The fair victim had four virgins in white behind the bar. She imitated her great predecessor, Mrs. Rudd, and affected to write very often, though I plainly perceived she only wrote as they do their love epistles on the stage, without forming a letter. The Duchess has but small remains of that beauty of which kings and princes were once so enamoured. She looked much like Mrs. Pritchard. She is large and ill-shaped. There was nothing white but her face, and had it not been for that, she would have looked like a bale of bombazeen. There was a great deal of ceremony, a great deal of splendour, and a great deal of nonsense. They adjourned upon the most foolish pretences imaginable, and did nothing with such an air of business as was truly ridiculous. I forgot to tell you the Duchess was taken ill, but performed it badly." The writer adds in a subsequent letter, "I have the great satisfaction of telling you, that Elizabeth, calling herself Duchess Dowager of Kingston, was this very afternoon undignified and unduchessed, and very narrowly escaped being burned in the hand." The Duchess claimed the privilege of the peerage, under the statute of the first of Edward the Sixth, and was accordingly discharged without punishment. The subsequent history of the eccentric Duchess is well known.

One of the most remarkable trials which have taken place in Westminster Hall, or perhaps in any country or age, was that of Warren Hastings, whose arraignment for alleged tyranny over the native princes and the dusky population of Hindostan, took place on the 12th of February, 1788. This great man had recently returned from his dominion over the vast empire of the East, leaving behind him a name which was revered even where it was most dreaded. When he reached his native country he was still in the prime of life; eager to take that share in the great political struggles of the day for which his genius so well adapted him, and expecting that his brilliant services in the East would be repaid with those honours and rewards which they so well merited. But a different fate awaited him. He had scarcely set his foot in England, when he not only found himself assailed in all quarters as a tyrant and despot, but was called upon to resist, almost alone and unsupported, a united and powerful party, at the head of which were arrayed the giant intellects of Burke, Sheridan, and Charles James Fox. With such men as these for his prosecutors, Westminster Hall presented, time after time, a scene of surpassing interest as well as grandeur. " The grey old walls," are the famous words of Lord Macaulay, " were hung with scarlet. The long galleries were crowded by an audience such as has rarely excited the fears or the emulation of an orator. There were gathered together from all parts of a great, free, enlightened, and prosperous empire, grace and female loveliness, wit and learning, the representatives of every science and of every art. There were seated round the Queen the fair-haired young daughters of the House of Brunswick. There the ambassadors of great kings and commonwealths gazed with admiration on a spectacle which no other country in the world could present. There Siddons, in the prime of her majestic beauty, looked with emotion on a scene surpassing all the imitations of the stage. There the historian of the Roman Empire thought of the days when Cicero pleaded the cause of Sicily against Verres, and when, before a senate which still retained some show of freedom, Tacitus thundered against the oppressor of Africa. There were seen, side by side, the greatest painter and the greatest scholar of the age. The spectacle had allured Reynolds from that easel which has preserved to us the thoughtful foreheads of so many writers and statesmen, and the sweet smiles of so many noble matrons. It had induced Parr to suspend his labours in that dark and profound mine from which he had extracted a vast treasure of erudition, a treasure too often buried in the earth, too often paraded with injudicious and inelegant ostentation, but still precious, massive, and splendid. There appeared the voluptuous charms of her to whom the heir of the throne had in secret plighted his faith. There too was she, the beautiful mother of a beautiful race, the Saint Cecilia, whose delicate features, lighted up by love and music, art has rescued from the common decay. There were the members of that brilliant society, which quoted, criticised, and exchanged repartees under the rich peacock-hangings of Mrs. Montagu. And there the ladies, whose lips, more persuasive than those of Fox himself, had carried the Westminster election against palace and treasury, shone round Georgiana Duchess of Devonshire. The sergeants made proclamation, Hastings advanced to the bar and bent his knee. The culprit, indeed, was not unworthy of that great presence; he had ruled an extensive and populous country, and made laws and treaties, had sent forth armies, had set up and pulled down princes; and in his high place he had so borne himself, that all had feared him, most had loved him, and that hatred itself could deny him no title to glory except virtue. He looked like a great man, and not like a bad man. A person small and emaciated, yet deriving dignity from a carriage which, while it indicated deference to the court, indicated also habitual self-possession and self-respect, a high and intellectual forehead, a brow pensive but not gloomy, a mouth of inflexible decision, a face pale and wan but serene, on which was written, as legibly as under the picture in the council-chamber at Calcutta, *Mens æqua in arduis;* such was the aspect with which the great proconsul presented himself to his judges."

The trial, or rather persecution, of Warren Hastings not only lasted nine years; but when the verdict of acquittal was at length pronounced, it was when the vigour of life had passed away, and when, having expended his fortune in the struggle, he found himself, comparatively speaking, a ruined man.

The only other event of any interest associated with Westminster Hall—the last occasion also on which it presented the striking splendour of ancient times—was the coronation banquet of George the Fourth, which was solemnized on the 1st of August, 1820. At the magnificent banquet, the King sat on a gorgeous throne on a raised dais, immediately under the great window at the south end of the Hall. At long ranges of tables were seated the guests, including the peers and the knights of the different Orders, in their robes. Every ceremonial was adopted which had been in use in the days of the Tudors and Plantagenets; and lastly, the champion Dymoke rode into the fine old Hall attended by the Duke of Wellington as High Constable of England, and the Marquis of Anglesea as Lord High Steward, both of them also on horseback. The total expense of the coronation ceremony of George the Fourth, the pageant of a day, was estimated at one hundred and fifty thousand pounds.

WESTMINSTER ABBEY.

EARLY PLACES OF WORSHIP ON ITS SITE.—ERECTION OF THE PRESENT EDIFICE.—SCENES AND CEREMONIES IN IT.—POETS' CORNER.—CHAPELS OF ST. EDMUND, ST. NICHOLAS, ST. PAUL, EDWARD THE CONFESSOR, ISLIP, HENRY THE SEVENTH.—CLOISTERS.—JERUSALEM CHAMBER.—CHAPTER HOUSE.

WILLINGLY would we enter into a detailed history of Westminster Abbey—of its ancient monuments, its architectural magnificence, and its host of romantic and historical associations—but that the character of the present work compels us to restrict ourselves to a brief account of the venerable pile, and of the principal objects of interest which it contains. Perhaps there is no other religious structure in the world which awakens so many heart-stirring emotions, or which can boast so many exquisite specimens of ancient art, or so many interesting monuments to the illustrious dead. Who is there who has ever found himself beneath the roof of Westminster Abbey without being struck with feelings of admiration and awe? Who is there who has ever wandered among its tombs of departed kings and warriors, of statesmen and poets, without becoming the moralist of the hour? "When I look," writes Addison, "upon the tombs of the great, every emotion of envy dies within me: when I read the epitaphs of the beautiful, every inordinate desire goes out; when I meet with the grief of parents upon a tombstone, my heart melts with compassion; when I see the tomb of the parents themselves, I consider the vanity of grieving for those whom we must quickly follow; when I see kings lying by those who deposed them, when I consider rival wits placed side by side, or the holy men that divided the world with their contests and disputes, I reflect with sorrow and astonishment on the little competitions, factions, and debates of mankind. When I read the several dates of the tombs, of some that died yesterday, and some six hundred years ago, I consider that great day when we shall all of us be contemporaries, and make our appearance together." Such are the reflections which many have felt in wandering through Westminster Abbey, but which none have so beautifully described.

The earliest notice which we discover of there having been a place of worship on the site of the present Westminster Abbey, is about the year 184, when King Lucius is reported to have embraced Christianity. Usher, moreover, informs us, on the authority of Fleta, that even at this early period it was "specially deputed for the burial of kings, and as a treasury or repository of their royal ornaments."

According to the old monkish writers, the church built by King Lucius continued to be a place of Christian worship, either till the persecution of the Christians in Britain in the reign of the Emperor Diocletian, or till the irruption into the island of a large body of Pagan Saxons, about the fifth or sixth century, when it was converted into a temple of Apollo. In this state it is said to have remained till about the year 616, when, having been thrown down by an earthquake, Sebert, King of the East Saxons, erected a new church on the ruins of the Pagan temple; Mellitus, Bishop of London, instigating him to persevere in his pious work. In connection with the completion of the new church, there exists a curious legend which for centuries obtained universal credence. Previously to its consecration, but after every preparation had been made for the ceremony, St. Peter, to whom the church was intended to be dedicated, is said to have descended on a stormy night on the Lambeth side of the river, and to have prevailed upon one Edric, a fisherman, to ferry him over to the opposite side. Desiring the fisherman to wait for him, the Saint proceeded in the direction of the Abbey, which was shortly afterwards miraculously illuminated; the voices of angels at the same time singing choral hymns. The next day, it is further stated, the chrism, and droppings of the wax candles were found in the church. On his return to the fisherman, St. Peter desired him to tell the Bishop that the church had no need of further consecration. The Saint further desired Edric to cast his nets into the water, which having done, he drew them out again loaded with a miraculous draught of salmon. St. Peter told him also, that neither he nor his successors should ever want salmon so long as they presented every tenth to his new church. So late, it appears, as the end of the fourteenth century the fishermen still continued to bring salmon to the high altar, and had periodically the honour of sitting at the same table with the prior.

As regards the pleasant legend that a temple of Apollo stood on the site of the present Westminster Abbey, it may very possibly be as much without foundation as the legend of St. Peter appearing to Edric the fisherman. Respecting the antiquity of the site as a place of Christian worship, all that we know with certainty is the fact that there existed here a church and monastic establishment in the early part of the seventh century, which were pulled down by Edward the Confessor for the purpose of erecting on their site a structure worthy of the religion to which it was dedicated.

18—2

The Confessor, taking the deepest interest in the new pile, "pressed on the work," writes Sulcardus, "very earnestly, and appropriating to it a tenth of his entire substance in gold, silver, cattle, and all other possessions." This church, which was commenced in 1049 and completed in 1066, appears to have been one of the first built in England in the shape of a cross, setting an example, according to Matthew Paris, which was afterwards much followed in the construction of other churches. Not content with its architectural adornment, the pious Confessor filled it with all kinds of relics. Here, says Dort, were "part of the place and manger where Christ was born; some of the frankincense offered to him by the Eastern Magi; of the table of our Lord; of the bread which he blessed; of the seat where he was presented in the Temple; of the wilderness where he fasted; of the gaol where he was imprisoned; of his undivided garment; of the sponge, lance, and scourge with which he was tortured; of the sepulchre, and cloth that bound his head." Here, also, were preserved the veil and some of the milk of the Virgin; the bladebone of St. Benedict; the finger of St. Alphage; the head of St. Maxilla; and half the jawbone of St. Anastasia.

It had been the intention of the Confessor to consecrate his new church with an extraordinary display of magnificence, for which purpose he had summoned the prelates and his principal nobles to assemble on Innocents' Day, 1065. On the night, however, before Christmas Day, he was seized with his fatal illness, and being unable to quit his chamber, his consort, Queen Editha, was compelled to preside at the ceremony. The Confessor was buried within his own church; William the Conqueror bestowing a rich pall on his resting-place, and Henry the Second subsequently erecting a magnificent tomb over his remains.

From the circumstance of our finding the unfortunate successor of the Confessor, King Harold, proceeding from York to Westminster after his accession, the probability seems to be that he was crowned in the Abbey, as has been every successive sovereign of England from the time of the Conquest to the present day. It was in the old Abbey that William the Conqueror solemnly returned thanks after his victory over King Harold at the battle of Hastings, and here, on Christmas Day following, he was crowned by the side of the tomb of the Confessor. Here, in September, 1189, Richard the First was crowned in the presence of the "assembled archbishops, bishops, earls, barons, and a great number of knights;" and here, on the 27th of May, 1199, the crown was placed on the head of his brother, King John, "after the manner then used, with great solemnity, and no less rejoicing of all such as were present."

Henry the Third, too, was crowned in the Abbey, when only ten years old, wearing, we are told, on his head merely a plain circlet of gold, in consequence of the crown worn by his predecessors, as well as the rest of the regalia, having been lost by King John in the Wash between Lincolnshire and Norfolk. Whether the church built by the Confessor had fallen to decay, or whether Henry the Third was desirous of erecting a more magnificent structure on its site, seems to be uncertain. At all events, in the year 1245, the latter monarch commenced the demolition of the old edifice, and, on the 13th of October, 1269, a great portion of the beautiful Abbey as it now stands—namely, the eastern part, with the choir, to some distance beyond the transept—was opened for divine service. At the time of Henry's death the work had proceeded no further than the fourth arch west of the middle tower, and even the vaulted roof of this part was not completed till 1296. Edward the First continued the good work which his predecessor had commenced; but it was not till after the Restoration of Charles the Second that the two present towers were built, and, moreover, the centre tower is still wanting.

At the same time that the finished portion of the new church was opened for divine worship, King Henry removed the remains of Edward the Confessor from their original resting-place into the present "chapel at the back of the high altar, and there laid them in a rich shrine," which he had piously caused to be erected for their reception. The ceremony was performed with great solemnity and splendour; the King and many of his nobles, clothed in white garments, passing the preceding night within the walls of the Abbey, watching and performing their devotions. According to a passage in Wykes's Chronicle, "The King, being grieved that the reliques of St. Edward were so poorly enshrined, and not elevated, resolved that so great a luminary should be placed on high as a candlestick to enlighten the church. He therefore, on the 3rd of the Ides of October, the day of St. Edward's first translation, summoned the nobility, magistrates, and burgesses of the realm to Westminster, to attend this solemn affair. At that time, the coffin being taken out of the old shrine, the King and his brother, the King of the Romans, carried it upon their shoulders in view of the whole church; his son Edward, Edmund Earl of Lancaster, the Earl Warenne, and the Lord Philip Basset, with as many other nobles as could come near to touch it, supporting it with their hands to the new shrine, which was of gold adorned with precious stones, and placed in an exalted situation." At the conclusion of the ceremony the King gave a magnificent banquet in the neighbouring palace.

Another remarkable religious ceremony which took place

in Westminster Abbey in this reign, was on St. Edward's day, 1247, on the occasion of King Henry presenting to the Abbey Church some of the blood which was asserted to have trickled from the wounds of our Saviour on the Cross, and which had been sent him from Jerusalem by the Knights Templars and Hospitallers. It may be mentioned that the genuineness of the holy relic was attested by the Patriarch of Jerusalem, and the Archbishop, Bishops, and Abbots of the Holy Land. Having previously sent summonses to his nobles and prelates to attend him, Henry, on the appointed day, rode in a magnificent procession to St. Paul's, where a beautiful vase of crystal, containing the second relic, was delivered to him. Matthew Paris, who was present at the ceremony, describes the scene. "The King," he writes, "commanded that all the priests of London, habited in costly dresses, and bearing standards, crosses, and lighted tapers, should, early on the morning of St. Edward's day, meet reverently at St. Paul's. Thither the King himself came, and with the utmost veneration receiving the vase with the treasure, he bore it openly before him, walking slowly, in a humble garb, and without stopping, to the church of Westminster. He held the vase with both hands, keeping his eyes fixed on the vessel, or looking up to heaven, whilst proceeding along the dirty and uneven road." Over him was a pall held up by four spears, whilst two persons supported his arms, lest the fatigue should prove too much for him. Near Durham House in the Strand—the palace of the Bishops of that See—he was met by the Abbot and monks of Westminster, accompanied by other prelates and abbots, who, "singing and rejoicing, with tears, in the Holy Spirit," accompanied the procession to the Abbey. Finally, Henry, having carried the vase round the palace and the monastery, delivered it, in great state and in the presence of an immense concourse of people, to the custody of the Abbot and monks, to be preserved by them as a relic beyond price. "To describe the whole course and order of the procession and feast kept that day," writes Holinshed, "would require a special treatise; but this is not to be forgotten, that the same day the Bishop of Norwich preached before the King in commendation of that relic, pronouncing six years and one hundred and sixteen days of pardon granted by the Bishops there to all that came to reverence it."

The scene must have been a striking one, when, in the commencement of the succeeding reign, the barons swore fealty to the young and warlike Edward the First before the high altar in Westminster Abbey. It was to the credit of this monarch that, notwithstanding his constant absences in his wars in Scotland and Wales, he piously proceeded in the work of rebuilding the Abbey church; "causing," moreover, in the words of Stow, "his father's sepulchre at Westminster to be richly garnished with precious stones of jasper, which he had brought out of France for that purpose."

It was in the year 1306, that Edward the First, determined on the subjugation of Scotland, and desirous of strengthening his army, issued a proclamation for the attendance at his palace of Westminster, at the feast of Pentecost, of such of his subjects as were heirs to estates held by military tenure. Accordingly, we are told, three hundred young men, the sons of earls, barons, and knights, having assembled at the appointed time, were presented with purple, silk, fine linen, and girdles embroidered with gold, according to their respective rank. At night, by the King's command, the Prince of Wales, with some of the young men of the highest rank, kept watch within the Abbey, on which occasion we are informed, such was the clamour created by their trumpets, pipes, and vociferations, that the service of the choir was rendered perfectly inaudible. The next day the ceremonies were renewed, when the King girded his son with the belt of a knight, and presented him with the Duchy of Aquitaine. The Prince, being now knighted, proceeded to the high altar, to gird, in his turn, the young men his companions, when such was the pressure of the crowd, that, notwithstanding each knight was guarded by at least three men-at-arms, several fainted away, of whom two died. The crowd having at length been removed from the altar, the King next made his appearance, and the ancient chivalrous ceremonial took place of making a vow before *the swan*; the vow, on the present occasion, being one of eternal hatred and hostility against the Scottish nation. With great pomp and ceremony, two swans, covered with gold network and other ornaments, were brought to the altar. Regarding them with a fixed look, Edward—surrounded by his nobles and in the midst of his people—swore a solemn oath that, "by the God of Heaven and the swans," he would revenge himself on the Scots; adjuring his son and the assembled barons, should he die before he had accomplished his purpose, to carry his body before them into Scotland, and not commit it to the tomb till they had humbled their enemies to the dust. Edward, as is well known, died in the neighbourhood of Carlisle, on his way to Scotland, time being afforded him, however, in his last moments, to send for the Prince his son, whom he enjoined in the most solemn manner to prosecute the war, and to carry his "dead bones" with the army till he had pierced the very extremity of Scotland. "He called his eldest son," writes Froissart, "and made him swear by the saints, in the presence of all the barons, that as soon as he should be dead he would have his body boiled in a large caldron until the flesh should be separated from the bones; that he would have the flesh buried and the bones preserved; and that every time the Scots should rebel against him he would summon his people and carry against them the bones of his father; for he believed most firmly that, as long as his bones should be carried against the Scots, those Scots would never be victorious."

The coronation of Edward the Second took place in Westminster Abbey with great magnificence. The procession from the Palace to the church was headed by the Earl Marshal, Aylmer Earl of Pembroke, carrying the golden spurs. Then came the Earl of Hereford holding the sceptre with the cross; then the King's cousin Henry of Lancaster, carrying a second sceptre surmounted with the dove; next followed the Earls of Lancaster, Lincoln, and Warwick, bearing the swords of state; afterwards came four noblemen, carrying the regal vestments; then the High Treasurer with the patera of the chalice of Edward the Confessor; then the King's favourite, Piers Gaveston, bearing the crown ornamented with precious stones; and lastly, came Edward himself, walking under a splendid canopy supported by the Barons of the Cinque Ports.

The appointed oath having been taken by the King, the ceremony of anointing and consecrating him was performed by the Bishop of Winchester; the Archbishop of Canterbury being prevented by bodily weakness from attending. The King's right shoe and spur were put on by the Queen's uncle, brother to the King of France; his left shoe by the Earl of Pembroke, and his left spur by the Earl of Cornwall. Then the King took the crown from the altar, and having delivered it to the Bishop who placed it on the King's head, he was conducted to a raised seat in the choir in advance of the altar, the clergy the while singing the *Te Deum.* Next followed the ceremony of the Queen's coronation, at the conclusion of which the King again advanced to the high altar, where he received the Sacrament in the midst of the assembled bishops and abbots. The ceremonial being now concluded, the King, with the crown on his head and the sceptre in his hand, returned to the Palace with the same procession which had attended him to the Abbey, and afterwards partook of a sumptuous banquet in Westminster Hall.

When Edward the Third, after his merciless ravages and spoliations in France, consented, in 1371, to the treaty of peace with that country by which John King of France obtained his liberty, we find Edward and his sons ratifying it with solemn oaths and with great ceremony in the Abbey church of Westminster. Mass having been performed by the Archbishop of Canterbury, King Edward and the Princes arose in the presence of the French hostages, and the torches having been lighted, and "crosses held over the eucharist and missal," swore upon the "sacred Body of our Lord" to preserve inviolate the peace which had that day been agreed upon. The same oath was then taken by the English barons who were present, as well as by the French nobles who were in England.

Richard the Second, when in his eleventh year, was crowned at Westminster Abbey with great magnificence; the ceremony proving so fatiguing to him that at the close of the day it was necessary to carry him to his apartment in a litter. A few years afterwards the Abbey had a narrow escape from the ignorance and violence of Wat Tyler and his followers, who, having broken open the Exchequer, destroyed the records, violated the Sanctuary, and put to death one of the King's servants who vainly clung to the shrine of Edward the Confessor for protection. So soon as the rebels had taken their departure, the King paid a visit to the spot. "After dinner, about two of the clock," writes Stowe, "the

King went from the Wardrobe, called the Royal, toward Westminster, attended by the number of two hundred persons, to visit St. Edward's shrine, and to see if the commons had done any mischief there. The Abbot and Convent of that Abbey, with the Canons and Vicars of St. Stephen's Chapel, met him with rich copes in procession, and led him by the charnel-house into the Abbey; then to the church, and so to the high altar, where he devoutly prayed and offered. After which he spake with the Anchoret to whom he confessed himself; then he went to the chapel, called our Lady in the Pew, where he made his prayers." It was on this very day, after having quitted Westminster, that the young King met the rioters at Smithfield on the occasion when the valiant Lord Mayor of London, Sir William Walworth, struck their leader, Wat Tyler, to the earth in the presence of his followers.

Before proceeding to notice the principal objects of interest which Westminster Abbey can boast, we would mention one more magnificent ceremonial which took place under its roof in the Middle Ages, namely, the coronation of Henry the Fourth, on the 13th of October, 1399. "Having confessed himself, as he had good need to do," writes Froissart, "the King went to the church in procession, and all the lords with him in their robes of scarlet furred with minever, barred on their shoulders according to their degrees, and over the King was borne a cloth of estate of blue, and four bells of gold, and it was borne by four burgesses of the port of Dover, and others. And on each side of him he had a sword borne; the one the sword of the church, and the other the sword of justice. The sword of the church his son the Prince did bear; and the sword of justice the Earl of Northumberland; and the Earl of Westmoreland bore the sceptre. Thus they entered into the church about nine of the clock;

and in the midst of the church there was a high scaffold all covered with red, and in the midst thereof there was a chair-royal, covered with cloth of gold. Then the King sat down in the chair, and so sat in the estate-royal, saving he had not on the crown, but sat bareheaded. Then, at the four corners of the scaffold, the Archbishop of Canterbury shewed unto the people how God had sent unto them a man to be their King, and demanded if they were content that he should be consecrated and crowned as their King; and they all with one voice said 'yea!' and held up their hands, promising faith and obedience. Then the King rose, and went down to the high altar to be consecrated, at which consecration there were two archbishops and ten bishops; and before the altar there he was despoiled out of all vestures of estate, and there he was anointed in six places—on the head, the breast, and on the two shoulders behind, and on the hands. Then a bonnet was set on his head, and, while he was anointing, the clergy sang the litany, and such service as they sang at the hallowing of the font. Then the King was apparelled like a prelate of the church, with a cope of red silk, and a pair of spurs with a point without a rowel; then the sword of justice was drawn out of the sheath and hallowed, and then it was taken to the King, who did put it again into the sheath; then the Archbishop of Canterbury did gird the sword about him; then St. Edward's crown was brought forth and blessed, and then the Archbishop did set it on the King's head. After mass the King departed out of the church in the same estate and went to his palace; and there was a fountain that ran, by divers branches, white wine and red."

There may, perhaps, be other religious edifices in Europe which may boast as many sumptuous monuments to kings, statesmen, and heroes as Westminster Abbey, but in what church or in what cathedral shall we find a spot possessed of such unique interest as the south transept including Poets' Corner ? It would almost amount to affectation, to endeavour, by any ornament of language or extraneous observations, to enhance the emotions which even the most cold and unimaginative must feel on entering this hallowed spot. Sufficient it is to remember, that beneath and around us lies the dust of those gifted men whose immortal effusions of fancy and genius have so often kindled our imaginations or melted our hearts. Many of them, moreover, were in their lifetimes the children of misfortune, and accordingly our emotions are enhanced by the memory of many a tale of misery and privation; of many a struggle with penury, and many a triumph over neglect.

Close to the grave of the author of the "Canterbury Tales"—the first of our poets who was buried in Poets' Corner—lie the remains of the great poet to whom we owe the glorious imagery of the "Fairy Queen," who, by his own wish, was buried near the father of English verse. Neglected as Spenser had been on his death-bed, the great and the noble nevertheless stood round the grave which opened to receive him, while all the poets of the day—including, perhaps, the immortal Shakspeare himself—threw poetical tributes on the coffin which contained his sacred remains. Raising our eyes from the grave of Spenser, the words, "O rare Ben Jonson," remind us of the great dramatic poet, whose inimitable humour, and exquisite and fanciful masques, have been the delight of successive generations. Passing on we find ourselves at one moment standing by the tomb of Dryden, and now by that of Cowley. There are monuments also to poets whose names are scarcely less familiar to us in the literary history of our country. Now the eye glances on the tomb of Michael Drayton, the author of the "Polyolbion;" advancing a little further, we stand by the tomb of one more fortunate, Nicholas Rowe, the translator of Lucan's "Pharsalia," and the author of the "Fair Penitent" and "Jane Shore;" now we stand by the mural monument of Christopher Anstey, the author of the witty "New Bath Guide;" now by the monument of the statesman and poet, Matthew Prior, and now by that of his friend, the gentle, the beloved, the single-hearted Gay. We have only to glance over the inscription on the tomb of the latter to perceive that it was the affectionate attachment of the noble Queensberry and his fair Duchess, the lovely "Kitty" of Prior's verse, which raised the interesting monument over the dust of the departed poet.

> "Thanks to the great for what they took away,
> And what they left me, for they left me Gay;
> Left me to see neglected genius bloom,
> Neglected die,—and write it on his tomb;
> Of all his blameless life this sole return,
> My verse, and Queensberry weeping o'er his tomb!"

We have as yet merely recorded the names of those poets whose monuments are conspicuous objects in Poets' Corner. But here, too, lie the remains of men of a different order of genius, but whose names are scarcely less illustrious. Here is the monument to the great composer, Handel, whose glorious melody has so often enraptured thousands, as it rolled along the vaulted roof and fretted aisles beneath which the magician sleeps so calmly; here rests the great antiquary Camden, and the memorable critic and scholar, Isaac Casaubon: from the monuments of the celebrated philosophers and divines, Isaac Barrow, Stephen Hales, and Robert South, we turn to the memorial of the gay and witty St. Evremond, associated with the frolic annals of the court of Charles the Second; and from the monument of St. Evremond we turn to the simple tribute to Granville Sharp the philanthropist, or to the conspicuous recumbent figure of Dr. Busby, the famous head-master of Westminster School, the schoolmaster of Dryden and of half the poets and prelates of the seventeenth century.

Neither must we forget those whose mimic genius drew down upon them the applause of thousands in the lighted theatre in the past days when they fretted their hour upon the stage. Having paused awhile beneath the sumptuous monument of Garrick to ponder on his genius and his triumphs, let us wander on to the humbler memorial of the scarcely less celebrated actor Barton Booth. He it was, who, when he was still a thoughtless boy at Westminster School—having his head turned by the sensation which he created when acting in one of Terence's plays—quitted the tutorship of Busby, of whom he was the favourite pupil, and with apparently no other advantages but melody of voice and beauty and elegance of person, became by industry and application the great actor, whose exquisite delineation of human passions drew down upon him the applause of millions in his lifetime, and which after his death procured him the honour of a burial-place in Poets' Corner. From the monument of Booth we pass to that of the charming actress, Mrs. Pritchard. Lastly, though without any record of their resting-place, here lie the remains of the great actor, John Henderson, who, we are told, whether he acted in the character of "Falstaff" or "Hamlet," was equally great in both—the same inimitable actor whether he figured in the ludicrous or in the sublime.

In wandering through the south transept, let us not forget that beneath our feet lie the remains of many celebrated persons to whose memories no monuments have been raised over their resting-places. On the pavement, however, scattered among the names and epitaphs of persons of little note, may be traced with some slight difficulty the gravestones of no less remarkable persons than Thomas Parr, who is said to have lived in the reign of ten sovereigns; of the celebrated poet, Sir William Davenant; of Macpherson, the translator or author of "Ossian;" of Cumberland, the dramatic writer; of Dr. Johnson; of Richard Brinsley Sheridan, who sleeps with Garrick and Johnson at the foot of Shakspeare's monument; of William Gifford, the satirist and critic; and lastly, of Thomas Campbell, the author of "The Exile of Erin" and "Hohenlinden." At the foot of Addison's statue rests the poet, as well as historian, Lord Macaulay. To the disgrace alike of their contemporaries and of posterity, the burial-places of the great dramatic poet Francis Beaumont, who sleeps near Chaucer, and of Sir John Denham, the author of "Cooper's Hill," who sleeps by the side of Cowley, are distinguished neither by name nor date.

If there are poets buried in Poets' Corner to whom there are no monuments, so also are there monuments to poets whose burial-places are elsewhere. Shakspeare lies buried at Stratford-on-Avon, and Milton in the church of St. Giles's, Cripplegate. Ben Jonson lies interred in the north aisle of the Nave; Shadwell at Chelsea; Barton Booth near Uxbridge; John Philips, the author of "The Splendid Shilling," in Hereford Cathedral; Samuel Butler, the author of "Hudibras," in the churchyard of St. Paul's, Covent Garden; Addison in Henry the Seventh's Chapel; Hales at Teddington; Anstey and Mrs. Pritchard at Bath; Thomson at Richmond in Surrey; Goldsmith in the Temple churchyard; Gray in the churchyard of Stoke Pogis; Mason at Aston, in Yorkshire, where he lived; Southey at Keswick; and Thackeray at Kensal Green.

Curiously misplaced among the monuments to poets and philosophers, may be traced, between the recumbent effigies of South and Busby, part of the half ruined tomb of an unfortunate Princess, Anne of Cleves. Close by, too, is the unrecorded grave of Anne Neville, daughter of the "Kingmaker," Earl of Warwick, and the wife of Richard the Third.

Passing to the right through an iron grating, we find ourselves in the chapel of St. Benedict. Among other memorials which it contains is a fine monument to the memory of Frances, Countess of Hertford, sister of the great admiral Lord Howard of Effingham; another to Lionel Cranfield, Earl of Middlesex, Lord Treasurer in the reign of James the First; and lastly, the tomb of the famous Archbishop Langham, who, as his epitaph informs us, rose from being a monk of the adjoining Abbey to be Primate and Chancellor of England. As we quit St. Benedict's Chapel, facing us is the ancient tomb of Sebert, King of the East Saxons, and of Athelgoda, his Queen, who severally died at the commencement of the seventh century. Between this chapel, also, and that of St. Edmund, may be seen a monument, once richly ornamented, to the memory of the children of Henry the Third and Edward the First.

The next chapel which we enter is that of St. Edmund, rich with costly and ancient monuments. Here a small tomb covers the remains of William of Windsor and his sister Blanche (de la Tour), the infant children of Edward the Third; and here, too, distinguished by their exquisite workmanship, are the defaced but still beautiful tombs of William de Valence, Earl of Pembroke, half-brother to Henry the Third; of John of Eltham, son of Edward the Second, with its beautiful alabaster effigy; and of Eleanora de Bohun, daughter of Humphrey de Bohun, Earl of Hertford, and wife of Thomas of Woodstock, Duke of Gloucester, youngest son of Edward the Third. Here is the monument which Walpole so much admired, of Francis Holles, son of John Earl of Clare, which the bereaved father raised to the memory of his deceased son; and, lastly, on the pavement may be traced a small brass plate, of which the inscription, now almost illegible, records that beneath it rest the remains of Robert de Waldeby, tutor of Edward the Black Prince, afterwards Divinity Professor in the University of Toulouse, and Archbishop of York.

From the chapel of St. Edmund we stroll on to that of St. Nicholas. Here, as in the preceding chapels, lie the remains of many a gallant knight and lovely dame who in their day figured in the tournament and the dance. Here is the tomb of Anne Duchess of Somerset, wife of the great Protector, and of Mildred, wife of the scarcely less celebrated Lord Burleigh. The great names of the Cliffords, the Percies, the St. Johns, and the Stanleys attract the eye at every glance. From the inscription to a Stanley who was knighted by Henry the Seventh on the field of Bosworth, we turn to the tomb of a Cecil who was Lady of the Bedchamber to Queen Elizabeth. Here is the interesting old Gothic tomb in freestone of Philippa, wife of Edward Plantagenet, Duke of York, who was killed at the battle of Agincourt; and here also is the beautiful effigy in brass of Sir Humphrey Stanley, the gallant knight to whom we have alluded as having been knighted by Henry on the field of Bosworth. Lastly, we turn to the fine monument of Sir George Villiers, and of his wife Mary Beaumont, created Countess of Buckingham, the father and mother of the great favourite, George Villiers, Duke of Buckingham.

We next enter the small but beautiful chapel of St. Paul's. Now the eye glances on the effigy of Giles Lord Daubigny,

Knight of the Garter and Lord Chamberlain to Henry the Seventh; now on that of Sir Thomas Bromley, who, as Lord Chancellor of England, sat at the trial of Mary Queen of Scots in Fotheringay Castle; now on that of Sir Dudley Carleton, the celebrated ambassador in the reign of James the First; now on the monument of Francis Lord Cottington, who accompanied Charles the First and the Duke of Buckingham on their romantic expedition to Madrid; and lastly, from the interesting and ancient Gothic tomb of Lodowick Robsart, Lord Bourchier, Standard-bearer to Henry the Fifth at the battle of Agincourt, we turn to Chantrey's colossal statue of James Watt, doubtless a work of great merit, but which is sadly misplaced among the mouldering monuments to the abbots and knights and barons of a past age. In this chapel Archbishop Usher lies buried.

Let us now pass into the chapel and pause by the shrine of "St. Edward the Confessor," once adorned with costly gems, rubies, sapphires, onyxes, and pearls. The beautiful shrine was the work of Peter Cavallini, in the reign of Henry the Third, who brought from Rome, says Weever, "certain workmen, and rich porphyry stones, whereof he made that curious, singular, rare pavement before the high altar; and with these stones and workmen he did also frame the shrine of Edward the Confessor." Here lie the remains of the canonized monarch, and of his beautiful and gentle Queen Editha. On this memorable spot our early sovereigns took their vows and paid their devotions; and here more than one of our sovereigns were interred by their dying wish, in order that their bones might lie as near as possible to those of the Holy Confessor. It was in front of the shrine of St. Edward that the Barons of England, laying their hands on the dead body of Henry the Third, swore fealty to his young son, Edward the First, then in the Holy

CHAPEL OF EDWARD THE CONFESSOR.

Land; and lastly, it was while offering up his devotions at this spot, that Henry the Fourth was seized with the fatal illness of which he died a few hours afterwards in the Jerusalem chamber.

Close to the shrine of St. Edward, though without a monument, lie the remains of the pious and charitable Matilda, daughter of Malcolm, King of Scotland, and wife of Henry the First. The next monument in point of antiquity is the magnificent one of Henry the Third, with its mosaic work of gold and scarlet, its beautiful panels of porphyry, and its fine recumbent image of the King in bronze, said to be the first bronze effigy ever cast in England. The second of our Norman Kings who lies buried here is Edward the First. The tomb of this great monarch, which is of Purbeck marble, modest, simple, and unornamented, was opened in May 1774, by permission of the Dean. According to a very interesting paper in the "Archæologia"—"On lifting up the lid of the tomb, the royal body was found wrapt in a strong linen cloth, waxed on the inside. The head and face were covered with a 'sudarium,' or face-cloth of crimson sarsenet, wrapt into three folds, conformable to the napkin used by our Saviour in his way to the crucifixion, as we are assured by the Church of Rome. On flinging open the external mantle, the corpse was discovered in all the ensigns of majesty, richly habited. The body was wrapt in a fine linen cere-cloth, closely fitted to every part, even to the very fingers and face. Over the cere-cloth was a tunic of red silk damask; above that a stole of thick white tissue crossed the breast, and on this, at six inches' distance from each other, quatrefoils filigree work of gilt metal set with false stones, imitating rubies, sapphires, and amethysts, &c.; the intervals between the quatrefoils on the stole powdered with minute white beads, tacked down into a most elegant embroidery, in form not unlike what is called the true lover's knot. Above these habits was the royal mantle of silk crimson satin, fastened on the left shoulder with a magnificent fibula of gilt metal richly chased, and ornamented with four pieces of red, and four of blue, transparent paste, and twenty-four more pearls. The corpse, from the waist downwards, is covered with a rich cloth of figured gold, which falls to the feet, and is tucked beneath them. On the back of each hand was a quatrefoil like those on the stole. In his right hand is a sceptre, with a cross of copper gilt, and of elegant workmanship, reaching to the right shoulder. In the left hand is the rod and dove, which passes over the shoulder and reaches the royal ear. The dove stands on a ball placed on three ranges of oak leaves of enamelled green; the dove is white enamel. On the head is a crown charged with trefoils made of gilt metal. The head is lodged in the cavity of the stone coffin, always observable in these receptacles for the dead."

By the side of the monument of Henry the Third is that of Eleanor of Castile, the gentle and beautiful wife of Edward the First. On an altar-tomb of Petworth marble rests her effigy of copper-gilt, lovely as the Queen herself is said to have been in her lifetime, uninjured by the lapse of ages, and in every respect indescribably graceful and beautiful.

We next turn to the altar-tomb of the great and warlike Edward the Third. His figure, remarkable for its dishevelled hair and long flowing beard, is of copper, once gilt, and reclines under a rich Gothic shrine. In each hand is a sceptre, and round the altar tomb, on which his effigy reposes, are figures of his children in brass.

At the feet of Edward rests his Queen Philippa, whose name is endeared to us from the touching story of her interceding with her husband to save the lives of the heroic burgesses of Calais. Like that of her husband, the tomb of Philippa has suffered severely from the hands of barbarians and the silent injuries of time. Of the fretted niches, once containing the statues of thirty Kings and Princes, with which it was formerly adorned, scarcely a trace is visible. Not far from the tombs of Philippa and her husband, is a large stone, formerly plated with brass, beneath which rest the murdered remains of the once powerful Thomas of Woodstock, Duke of Gloucester, youngest son of Edward the Third, younger brother of the Black Prince, and uncle to Richard the Second.

Close to the tomb of Thomas of Woodstock is that of his unfortunate nephew, Richard the Second, and of his consort, Anne, sister of Wenceslaus, King of Bohemia. Their effigies, of copper gilt, were cast by order of Richard in his lifetime.

Enclosed in a chantry of the most beautiful Gothic workmanship is the tomb of Henry the Fifth; carrying us back in imagination from the frolic scenes in Eastcheap between Prince Hal, Falstaff, and Dame Quickly, to the glorious triumph of English chivalry on the field of Agincourt. The helmet, the shield, and the saddle, said to have been worn by Henry in that famous battle, are still exhibited near his grave.

Near the magnificent tomb of Henry the Fifth lie the remains of his beautiful wife, Catherine, daughter of Charles the Seventh of France; and lastly, in addition to the other royal personages whom we have mentioned as having been interred in the Confessor's chapel, may be traced the tombs of Margaret, the infant daughter of Edward the Fourth, and of Elizabeth Tudor, second daughter of Henry the Seventh, who died at Eltham in her fourth year.

In the chapel of Edward the Confessor is preserved the ancient and celebrated coronation chair, which was brought from Scotland by Edward the First in 1297, together with the regalia of the Scottish monarchs. We have only to call to mind that in this chair have sat at their coronations every one of our sovereigns from the time of Edward the First to the present time, and what a host of associations the reflection conjures up! Here, too, Cromwell sat on the occasion of his solemn inauguration as Protector in Westminster Hall, on the 26th of June, 1657. In regard to the remarkable stone under the seat, various traditions were formerly current, and, among others, that it was Jacob's pillow on the night that he had his memorable dream. Of its great antiquity, however, there can be no doubt. According to some authorities, King Fergus was crowned on it three hundred and thirty years before Christ; but at any rate, we seem to have tolerably certain proof of its having been the coronation seat of the Kings of Scotland before the reign of Kenneth the Second, who placed it in the palace of Scoon about the year 840. Fordun, the Scottish chronicler, informs us that the following lines, in Latin, were anciently engraved on the stone.

> "Except old saws do fail,
> And wizards' wits be blind,
> The Scots in place must reign,
> Where they this stone shall find."

Close to the chapel of the Confessor is that of ST. ERASMUS, by which we pass into the chapel of St. John the Baptist, the resting-place of many of the earlier Abbots. Here, among other monuments of inferior interest, are those of Hugh and Mary de Bohun, grandchildren of Edward the First; of Sir Thomas Vaughan, Treasurer of Edward the Fourth; and of Henry Carey, Lord Hunsdon, first cousin and Lord Chamberlain to Queen Elizabeth. Here also is the remarkable tomb of Thomas Cecil, Earl of Exeter. On the right side of the recumbent figure of the Earl lies the effigy of his first wife Dorothy, daughter of John Nevil, Lord Latimer, leaving the other side vacant for that of his second wife, Frances daughter of William Brydges, fourth Lord Chandos, who survived him. The Countess, however, it is said, could not brook the indignity of being placed on the left side, and though she had no objection to moulder in the same vault with her predecessor, left express orders in her will that her effigy should on no account be placed on the tomb.

The next of these interesting chapels to which we are conducted is a small one, known as Islip's Chapel, which was founded by Abbot Islip, and which contains the tomb of the well-known favourite of Henry the Seventh. Here also lies buried the celebrated statesman, William Pulteney, Earl of Bath.

Close to Islip's Chapel are the ancient monuments of Edmund Crouchback, Earl of Lancaster, second son of Henry the Third; of Aymer de Valence, second and last Earl of Pembroke of his family; of Aveline, the great heiress of William de Fortibus, Earl of Albemarle, and wife of the Earl of Lancaster, whom we have just mentioned; and, opposite to the latter, that of a modern hero worthy of the days of chivalry, General Wolfe. Close by is the monument of the pious and amiable Brian Duppa, Bishop of Winchester, who attended his unfortunate master, Charles the First, in his misfortunes, and who was tutor to Charles the Second. A few hours before the dissolution of the venerable prelate, the "merry monarch" paid him a visit in his sick chamber, and kneeling down by his bedside, requested his blessing. The dying prelate, with one hand on the King's head, and the other lifted to heaven, prayed fervently that he might prosper and be happy.

As we wander through the rest of the Abbey, the monuments being of more modern date, and the inscriptions consequently more conspicuous, we find but little necessity for a guide, and are not sorry to be left to our own reflections. Passing into the north transept, we gaze for a moment in admiration on the unique and beautiful monument of Sir Francis Vere, who died in 1608, and thence pass on to Roubiliac's painful but no less striking one, to the memory of Mrs. Nightingale. Here is the sumptuous monument of William Cavendish, Duke of Newcastle, the gallant and devoted follower of Charles the First, and of his learned and eccentric Duchess; and here also is the scarcely less magnificent tomb of John Holles, Duke of Newcastle.

In the north transept also are monuments to the celebrated Lord Mansfield; to the great Lord Chatham; George Canning; Warren Hastings; Francis Horner; Sir John Malcolm; Mrs. Siddons; John Philip Kemble; Sir William Follett; Sir Robert Peel; Richard Cobden; and Cornewell Lewis. In the centre of the north transept, within a short distance from one another, are the graves of Chatham, Pitt, Fox, Grattan, Castlereagh, Wilberforce, and Palmerston.

> "Drop upon Fox's grave the tear,
> 'Twill trickle to his rival's bier;
> O'er Pitt's the mournful requiem sound,
> And Fox's shall the notes rebound."
> *Marmion, Intro. to Canto I.*

In the north aisle of the choir, leading from the north transept into the nave, may be traced the monuments of the well-known composer and musician, William Croft; of Dr. Charles Burney, himself a composer and the author of the "History of Music;" and lastly, of the celebrated Henry

Purcell. How different from the inflated inscription on the tomb of Dr. Burney, written by his daughter, Madame d'Arblay, is the brief and beautiful epitaph on Purcell, said to have been written by Dryden! "Here lies Henry Purcell, Esq., who left this life, and is gone to that blessed place where only his harmony can be exceeded." It was probably from this epitaph that Dr. Johnson borrowed the idea of the exquisite concluding couplet of his lines to the memory of the Welsh musician, Claude Phillips:

> "Sleep undisturbed within this peaceful shrine,
> 'Till angels wake thee with a note like thine."

In the same north aisle also are the statues of Sir Stamford Raffles and William Wilberforce.

Passing into the nave, and keeping along the north aisle, we leave to the left Rysbrack's large monument of Sir Isaac Newton. Thence we pass on to that of Spencer Perceval, who was shot by Bellingham in the lobby of the House of Commons. Some feet further on, the remains of Ben Jonson and of Tom Killigrew, the wit, lie side by side. At the west end of the nave—the most conspicuous monument, perhaps, of any in the Abbey—is that of William Pitt over the great entrance, and near it are those of Sir Godfrey Kneller, Charles James Fox, George Tierney, Sir James Mackintosh, Zachary Macaulay, and William Wordsworth the poet.

Along the south aisle of the nave, many other monuments of celebrated persons attract our attention. Nearly in the corner is that of James Craggs the younger, who succeeded Addison as Secretary of State. On it are engraved Pope's well-known lines to the memory of his friend:—

> "Statesman, yet friend to truth ; of soul sincere,
> In action faithful, and in honour dear :

> Who broke no promise, served no private end,
> Who gained no title, and who lost no friend ;
> Ennobled by himself,—by all approved,
> Praised, wept, and honoured by the muse he loved."

It was Peter Leneve, the herald, who, in allusion to the lowness of Cragg's origin and the circumstance of his dying before his father, suggested that his epitaph should have been—" Here lies the last who died before the first of his family." Near the tomb of Craggs lie the remains of the celebrated Francis Atterbury, Bishop of Rochester, once Dean of the Abbey, and of the charming actress, Mrs. Oldfield, but without any memorial to either.

Close to the monument of Craggs is that of the wittiest of dramatic writers, William Congreve, whose body, however, lies in Henry the Seventh's Chapel. The pall-bearers at his funeral were the Duke of Bridgewater, the Earl of Godolphin, Lord Cobham, Lord Wilmington, the Hon. George Berkeley, and General Churchill, and the monument to his memory was erected at the expense of the beautiful Henrietta Duchess of Marlborough, as "a mark how dearly she remembers the happiness she enjoyed in the sincere friendship of so worthy and honest a man." "When the younger Duchess," writes Walpole, "exposed herself by placing a monument and silly epitaph of her own composition and bad spelling to Congreve, in Westminster Abbey, her mother, quoting the words, said—' I know not what *pleasure* she might have had in his company, but I am sure it was no *honour.*'"

From the monument of Congreve we pass on to those of the celebrated physician and philosopher, Dr. John Friend ; of the poet, Thomas Spratt, Bishop of Rochester, the companion of the social hours of Charles the Second and of George Villiers, Duke of Buckingham; of the well-known

Field-Marshall Wade; of Sir William Temple, the statesman and author; of Sidney Earl Godolphin, the celebrated first minister of Queen Anne; and of Sir John Chardin, the traveller. As we enter the south aisle of the choir, we turn from the monument of the gallant and ill-fated Major André to that of Thomas Thynne, the wealthy Issachar of Dryden's immortal poem, who was assassinated by Count Konigsmark, in Pall Mall. Lastly, just before we again enter Poets' Corner, we trace the monuments of the unfortunate Admiral Sir Cloudesley Shovel, who was shipwrecked and drowned on the rocks of Scilly; of Pasquale de Paoli, the brave and accomplished asserter of the liberties of Corsica; of the non-conformist divine, Isaac Watts, the author of the well-known "Hymns;" of Dr. Bell, the founder of the Madras system of education; and, in striking contrast to the staring and tasteless monuments of modern times, the tomb, of marble and alabaster gilt, of William Thynne, the gallant soldier in the reign of Henry the Eighth.

Passing under a gloomy arch of admirable workmanship, we suddenly find ourselves in a blaze of light and beauty, gazing in admiration at that exquisite creation of human genius, the chapel of the " Virgin Mary," more celebrated as " Henry the Seventh's Chapel." On each side hang the banners of the Knights of the Bath, and above us is the vaulted and fretted roof, so marvellous in its construction—" suspended aloft as by magic, and achieved with the wonderful minuteness and airy security of a cobweb."

And how many celebrated persons, conspicuous for their greatness, their genius, or their misfortunes, rest beneath our feet! In front of us, the work of Peter Torrigiano, an Italian artist, is the magnificent chantry, or tomb, of the founder, Henry the Seventh, and of his consort, Elizabeth, daughter of Edward the Fourth. At the head of the tomb sleeps their grandson, the young King Edward the Sixth.

Passing into the south aisle of Henry the Seventh's Chapel, among the most interesting monuments are those of the beautiful Margaret Countess of Lennox, mother of Lord Darnley, the husband of Mary Queen of Scots; of the celebrated George Monk, Duke of Albemarle, and his boisterous Duchess; of Catherine Shorter, the wife of Sir Robert, and mother of Horace Walpole; and that most exquisite altar-tomb—the work of Torrigiano—to the memory of Margaret Countess of Richmond, the mother of Henry the Seventh. Here is the interesting and magnificent monument of the unfortunate Mary Queen of Scots, whose remains were brought from Peterborough Cathedral by her son, James the First, to rest beneath the same roof as those of her relentless rival, Queen Elizabeth; and lastly, here is the stately tomb of Lodovick Stuart, Duke of Richmond, in the vault below which lie the remains of the beautiful Frances Duchess of Richmond, "*la belle Stuart*" of the court of Charles the Second, and where lay the body of Charles Lennox, Duke of Richmond, natural son of Charles, till its removal to Chichester Cathedral. In the south aisle also lie the bodies of Charles himself; of his brother, Henry Duke of Gloucester; of his sister, Mary Princess of Orange, mother of William the Third; of his aunt, the Queen of Bohemia; of her son, Prince Rupert; of William the Third and his consort Queen Mary; of Queen Anne, side by side with her sister Mary; of her husband, Prince George of Denmark; and of their promising son, Henry Duke of Gloucester, the young Marcellus of the day.

To the north-east of Henry the Seventh's tomb is a monument to the memory of John Sheffield, Duke of Buckingham, and under the east window lies interred the well-known

HENRY THE SEVENTH'S CHAPEL.

favourite of George the Third, William Bentinck, Earl of Portland. Close by is Westmacott's chaste and beautiful monument to the memory of Anthony Philip, Duke of Montpensier.

In the north aisle the most conspicuous monument is the sumptuous one of Queen Elizabeth. Next to this in interest is the tomb containing the murdered remains of the celebrated favourite George Villiers, Duke of Buckingham. In the same vault with him lie his two sons, George, the second and witty Duke, and the young, gallant, and beautiful Lord Francis Villiers, who, having been overpowered by numbers, fell in defence of his sovereign, Charles the First, in a skirmish near Kingston-on-Thames. In this aisle also are monuments of George Savile, Marquis of Halifax, the well-known statesman; and of Charles Montagu, Earl of Halifax, the poet. In front of this latter monument lie the remains of Addison.

In the north aisle lie the remains of Queen Mary the First, and, close to the body of Elizabeth, that of Mary Queen of Scots, whose cenotaph is in the opposite aisle—

"Together lie th' oppressor and th' oppressed."

Under the coffin of the latter Queen was laid that of the unfortunate Lady Arabella Stuart, next to whom lies her kinsman, Henry Prince of Wales, the gifted son of James the First. At the further end is another royal vault containing the bodies of King James and of his consort, Queen Anne of Denmark, while above it are two quaint monuments to the memory of their infant daughters, Maria and Sophia. Close by, an inscription in Latin tells us that:—" Here lie the relics of Edward the Fifth, King of England, and Richard, Duke of York, who, being confined in the Tower, and there stifled with pillows, were privately and meanly buried by order of their perfidious uncle, Richard, the Usurper." This memorial has naturally been regarded with deep interest by thousands, but whether the bones which it contains be really those of Edward the Fifth and his younger brother, we fear admits of doubt. In a vault on the north side of the Chapel are buried Anne Hyde, daughter of Lord Clarendon, and the numerous children which she bore her husband, James Duke of York.

For a short time the bodies of Oliver Cromwell, his mother, and of the great Admiral Blake were allowed to remain in peace among the tombs of the Kings of England in Henry the Seventh's Chapel, where they had been severally interred with great magnificence. At the Restoration, however, it was thought a degradation that their dust should mingle with that of royalty; and accordingly, their bodies having been taken up, that of the great Protector was re-interred beneath the gibbet, and those of his mother and Blake flung into a pit in the adjoining churchyard. Cromwell's favourite daughter, the interesting Mrs. Claypole, was also buried in Henry the Seventh's Chapel, but in consequence of her having been a member of the Church of England, and a devoted royalist, her body was allowed to remain undisturbed in its resting-place, where, in 1725, it was discovered by some workmen who were employed in repairing the foundations of the edifice. An attempt was made to purloin the silver plate attached to the coffin, but the offenders were discovered, and the memorial restored. It may be mentioned that the vault in which Oliver Cromwell's body rested for a while is situated beneath the east window. Here were afterwards interred Charles Fitzroy, Duke of Cleveland and Southampton, and Charles Fitz-Charles, Earl of Plymouth, natural sons of Charles the Second; also a grandson of Charles, Charles Earl of Doncaster, the infant son of the unfortunate

Duke of Monmouth. Mrs. Claypole lies on the north side of the Chapel, not far from the remains of Edward the Sixth.

The only other persons of royal blood to whose interments in Henry the Seventh's Chapel we have to refer, are the princes of the House of Brunswick. In the centre, then, of the chapel lie, side by side, George the Second and his consort; a side having, by the King's directions, been removed from the coffin of each, in order that their remains might mingle together. In the same vault lie buried Frederick Prince of Wales; his consort, Augusta of Saxe-Gotha; his brother, William Duke of Cumberland; his sisters, the Princesses Caroline and Amelia; and his sons, Edward Duke of York and Henry Frederick Duke of Cumberland, brothers of George the Third.*

We must not omit to mention that in Henry the Seventh's Chapel lies buried Edward Hyde, the great Earl of Clarendon.

Those who would wish to witness perhaps the most beautiful and impressive scene which London can afford, should wander on a moonlight night into the solitary cloisters of Westminster Abbey. The sudden transition from the noise and bustle of the streets to the most solemn stillness; the gloom of the vaulted roof, the light playing on the beautiful tracery of the arches, the mouldering tombs of departed abbots and monks which lie around us; and above all, the glorious Abbey, with its lofty towers and massive buttresses steeped in, and mellowed by, the moonlight; present altogether a scene of beauty and interest to which no language could do justice.

In the cloisters of Westminster Abbey may be traced the

* For a fuller and very interesting account of the resting-places of celebrated persons in Henry the Seventh's Chapel, see "Historical Memorials of Westminster Abbey," by the Dean of Westminster, 1868.

ancient monuments of Abbot Vitales, who died in 1082; of Gervase de Blois, natural son of King Stephen, who died in 1106; of the Abbot Chrispinus, who died in 1114; and of another Abbot, Laurentius, who died in 1176. Here also lie buried the celebrated actors Betterton and Spranger Barry; Aphra Behn, notorious for her gallantries and dramatic writings; the beautiful Mrs. Cibber, of whom Garrick said, when he heard of her death—" then tragedy has expired with her;" two other celebrated actresses, Mrs. Bracegirdle and Mrs. Yates; Tom Brown, the wit; and the inimitable actor and mimic, Samuel Foote.

Besides the persons we have mentioned, here lie the remains of Henry Lawes, the companion of Milton, and the composer of the music of Comus: of Dr. William King, Archbishop of Dublin, the friend and correspondent of Swift; and of George Vertue, the engraver. Here it was that the murdered remains of Sir Edmondbury Godfrey, followed by seventy-two clergymen and a procession consisting of a thousand persons of distinction, were lowered into the grave; and lastly, in the cloisters of Westminster Abbey lived Dr. Henry Killigrew, the author of the "Conspiracy." It was at the house of her father in these cloisters that the young and interesting Anne Killigrew, of whom Dryden says—

"Her wit was more than man, her innocence a child"—

breathed her last.

In connection with the cloisters of Westminster Abbey, a curious story is related by William Lilly, the astrologer, in his Life of Himself. Having been led by one David Ramsay, the clockmaker to King Charles the First, to imagine that a large amount of treasure lay concealed beneath the cloister-pavement, Lilly, with the sanction of Dr.

Williams, the Dean of the Abbey, proceeded, on a dark and stormy night, to take such steps as he considered most likely to lead to its discovery. On being admitted into the cloisters, one Scott, as Lilly informs us, having an excellent knowledge of " the use of the Mosaical or Miner's rod, began to apply the hazel rods, and these beginning to tumble over one another on the west side of the cloisters," the searchers were persuaded that the treasure lay beneath that particular spot. On this " they fell to digging," and, after considerable labour, about six feet deep from the surface, came to a coffin. Having lifted and poised it, they found it so light that they thought it scarcely worth while to open it, which, however, according to Lilly, " we afterwards much repented." The divining rods proving of no further assistance in the cloisters, the searchers proceeded to the Abbey, which they had scarcely entered when the storm increased so suddenly and violently that they were afraid the western entrance of the cathedral would have blown down upon them. To use Lilly's words—" Our rods would not move at all; the candles and torches, all but one, were extinguished, or burned very dimly; John Scott, my partner, was amazed, looked pale, and knew not what to think or do, *until I gave directions and command to dismiss the demons*, which, when done, all was quiet again. Terrified by the raging of the storm, the gloom of the Abbey, and by the magical communion which apparently existed between the astrologer and the agents of the dark fiend, the rest of the searchers, it seems, unceremoniously fled to their respective homes, nor does it appear that they ever again ventured to disturb the resting-places of the dead.

Close to the cloisters, at the south-west end of the Abbey, is the celebrated Jerusalem Chamber, built by Abbot Littlington, and anciently forming part of the Abbot's lodgings.

It was in this interesting apartment that Henry the Fourth breathed his last. We have already mentioned that the King was paying his devotions at the shrine of Edward the Confessor, when he was seized with one of those fits to which he had for some time been subject. His attendants feared, writes Fabian, that he would "have died right there;" but having succeeded in removing him to the Abbot's apartments, the King recovered his senses, and inquired where he was. Being informed that it was called the Jerusalem Chamber, he exclaimed, to use the words of Shakspeare,—

> "Laud be to God !—even there my life must end.
> It hath been prophesied to me many years,
> I should not die but in Jerusalem ;
> Which vainly I supposed the Holy Land," &c.
> *Henry IV.*, part 2, act iv., sc. 4.

An additional interest is conferred on the Jerusalem Chamber, in consequence of its having been the spot where the remains of several celebrated men have lain in state previous to their interment in Westminster Abbey. Among these may be mentioned, Dr. Robert South, the eminent divine; the Earl of Halifax, the poet; Sir Isaac Newton; Addison; Congreve, the great dramatic writer; Mrs. Oldfield, the actress, and, lastly, Thomas Campbell, the author of the "Pleasures of Hope."

Before concluding our notices of Westminster Abbey and its precincts, we must not omit to mention the interesting and once beautiful Chapter House, where the Commons of England first sat apart from the Lords, as a distinct body, and where they continued to hold their Parliaments till 1547, when the Chapel of St. Stephen's was granted them by Edward the Sixth. The last act passed by them under its roof was the attainder of the Duke of Norfolk on the eve of the death of Henry the Eighth. The building was long allowed to remain in a lamentable state of neglect and decay; its lofty windows, ónce resplendent with stained glass, have been nearly filled up; and the fine roof has been destroyed and one of wood substituted. There still, however, exist the beautiful Gothic portal leading from the cloisters, as well as the light and elegant central column which helps to support the roof; some interesting remains of the ancient tiled pavement of the reigns of Edward the Confessor and Henry the Third; and on the walls have been preserved some very curious paintings of the latter reign, one of which, a female figure, is of exquisite colours and execution. Happily, in the year 1865, Parliament voted an adequate sum for the restoration of this most interesting relic, and accordingly it is to be hoped that in time it will be restored to its pristine stateliness and beauty.

THE HAYMARKET, LEICESTER SQUARE, AND ST. MARTIN'S-IN-THE-FIELDS.

HAYMARKET.—HAYMARKET THEATRE.—SUFFOLK HOUSE-—LEICESTER SQUARE. —ANECDOTE OF GOLDSMITH.—ST. MARTIN'S CHURCH, CHURCHYARD, AND LANE.—SOHO SQUARE.—WARDOUR, AND OXFORD STREETS.—RATHBONE PLACE.

AS late as the last days of the Protectorate, the large tract of ground between Pall Mall and the villages of Hampstead and Highgate, consisted almost entirely of open country. St. Martin's Church stood literally in the fields; Whitcombe Street was then Hedge Lane; St. Martin's Lane and the Haymarket were really shady lanes with hedges on each side of them; the small village of St. Giles stood in the fields a little to the east; a windmill, surrounded by one or two scattered dwelling-houses, was to be seen where the present Windmill Street now stands; the north side of Leicester Square was occupied by Leicester House and its pleasure-grounds; while the only other object worthy of notice was a building on the rising ground at the upper end of the Haymarket then known as the "Gaming House." Shortly after the Restoration this latter building was pulled down, and Coventry House, from which the present Coventry Street derives its name, was erected nearly on its site.

In 1711, the celebrated statesman, Sir William Wyndham,

then a young man of five-and-twenty, was residing in the Haymarket. He had only recently become a husband and still more recently a father, when a fire broke out in his house, by which his young wife—a daughter of the " proud " Duke of Somerset—and his infant child, very nearly lost their lives. " I was awaked at three this morning," writes Swift, " my man and the people of the house telling me of a great fire in the Haymarket. I slept again, and two hours after my man came in again, and told me it was Sir William Wyndham's house burnt, and that two maids, leaping out of an upper room to avoid the fire, both fell on their heads, one of them upon the iron spikes before the door, and both lay dead in the streets. It is supposed to have been some carelessness of one or both those maids. The Duke of Ormond was there helping to put out the fire. Wyndham gave £6000 but a few months ago for that house, as he told me, and it was very richly furnished. His young child escaped very narrowly. Lady Catherine escaped barefoot. They all went to Northumberland House. Wyndham has lost £10,000 by this accident; his lady £1000 worth of clothes; it was a terrible accident."*

In a miserable lodging in the Haymarket, Addison composed his celebrated poem, the " Campaign," written, as is well known, at the express desire of Lords Godolphin and Halifax to celebrate the recent victory of Blenheim. " Pope," writes the late Mr. D'Israeli, " was one day taking his usual walk with Harte in the Haymarket, when he desired him to enter a little shop, where going up three pair of stairs into a small room, Pope said—' In this garret Addison wrote his ' Campaign !' " † In the Haymarket—on the east side, a few doors from the top—lived Addison's contemporary, Sir

---

* "Journal to Stella," 2nd March, 1711-12.
† D'Israeli's " Literary Characters."

Samuel Garth, the author of "The Dispensary," and in the next house to him at a later period, lived Mrs. Oldfield, the actress.

It was in the Haymarket that Baretti—whose name is so intimately associated with the literary annals of the last century—had the misfortune to take away the life of a fellow-creature, for which he was subsequently arraigned for murder at the bar of the Old Bailey on the 20th of October, 1769. Among the witnesses who at the trial spoke to his character for humanity, were no less celebrated men than Burke, Garrick, Goldsmith, Reynolds, Topham Beauclerk, and Dr. Johnson. Baretti, it seems, was hurrying up the Haymarket, when he was accosted by a woman, who behaved with such rude indecency that he was provoked to give her a blow on the arm. Three men who were her companions immediately made a rush at him, and pushing him off the pavement, attempted to thrust him into the mud. Alarmed for his safety, Baretti stabbed one of the men with a knife which he was in the habit of carrying for the purpose of cutting fruit. On this the man pursued and collared him, when Baretti, becoming more alarmed than ever, inflicted several wounds upon him, of which he died the following day. Baretti was acquitted at his trial on the ground that he had acted in self-defence.

Another tragical event which happened in the Haymarket was in 1678, when Philip, seventh Earl of Pembroke, killed Mr. Cony with his fist. The scene was a then famous ordinary, called Long's. Lord Pembroke was tried by his Peers and acquitted.

As late as the year 1755, the spot of ground on which the Italian Opera House now stands was principally occupied by Market Lane, Whitehorse Yard, and the Phœnix and Unicorn Inns: the latter standing at the south-east corner facing Cockspur Street and Pall Mall East. The next object of interest in the Haymarket is the Haymarket Theatre, which was first opened to the public on the 29th of December, 1720. Originally it was known as "The little theatre in the Haymarket," in order to distinguish it from an earlier theatre, projected and built by Sir John Vanbrugh, which stood on the opposite side of the street. The first stone of "Sir John Vanbrugh's Theatre," as it was occasionally styled, was laid by Anne Countess of Sunderland, the most beautiful of the four charming daughters of the great Duke of Marlborough ; she was usually styled—from the smallness of her stature and the interest which she took in party politics—the "Little Whig." According to Colley Cibber, this remarkable title was actually engraved on the foundation-stone. Sir John Vanbrugh's theatre was opened on the 9th of April, 1705, with an Italian Opera.

Norris Street, on the west side of the Haymarket, leads us into what was formerly Market Place, the ground on which St. James's Market was held till its removal to make room for the lower portion of the present Regent Street. Here it was, behind the bar of the Mitre Tavern, that the talents of Mrs. Oldfield—then a girl of sixteen—first attracted the notice of Farquhar, the dramatic writer, who obtained for her an engagement on the stage.* In Market Place also it was—in a corner house nearly facing the west end of Norris Street—that the fair quakeress, Hannah Lightfoot, was residing at the time when she is said to have captivated the heart of George the Third, then Prince of Wales.

Close to the Haymarket Theatre, on the site of the present Suffolk Street and Suffolk Place, stood Suffolk House; this, we presume, having been the mansion close to Whitehall,

* See ante, p. 163.

which was taken by Henry the Eighth for Anne Boleyn previously to their marriage; the same in which, in 1528, she "held her revels apart," and in which "more court was paid to her than she ever paid to the Queen."* In the days of James the First, Suffolk House was the residence of Thomas, first Earl of Suffolk and his beautiful and unprincipled Countess, whose names so frequently occur in the profligate annals of that reign. In the old street which was erected on its site lived the charming actress, Mary Davis, who is said to have captivated the heart of Charles the Second by singing, in the character of Celania, in "The Mad Shepherdess," the song,—

"My lodging it is on the cold ground."

From Pepys we learn that in 1667 Charles publicly acknowledged the beautiful girl as his mistress; that he presented her with a ring valued at *seven hundred* pounds, and furnished a house for her in Suffolk Street. Pepys further informs us that he happened one day to be passing when she was stepping into her coach in Suffolk Street, and a "mighty fine coach," he tells us, it was. Little else is known of Mary Davis, but that her picture was painted by Lely, and that a daughter which she had by Charles became the mother of the ill-fated Francis Ratcliffe, Earl of Derwentwater.

In Suffolk Street lived Miss Vanhomrigh, the celebrated Vanessa of Swift's poetry and the victim of his eccentric brutality. It was at her mother's house, in this street, where—

"Vanessa held Montaigne and read,
While Mrs. Susan combed her head"—

that we find him keeping his best cassock and wig, ready to

* Strickland's "Lives of the Queens of England," vol. ii., pp. 606-7.

put them on when he paid visits to the House of Lords. Swift himself lodged at one time in Suffolk Street, a few doors from Mrs. Vanhomrigh.

It was on the return home of Sir John Coventry from the Cock Tavern in Bow Street, where he had supped, to his house in Suffolk Street, that he was waylaid by some hired ruffians, who slit his nose, on account of some words which had escaped him in the House of Commons, reflecting on Charles the Second. "He stood up to the wall," writes Burnet, "and snatched the flambeau out of the servant's hands, and with that in one hand, and his sword in the other, he defended himself so well that he got more credit by it than by all the actions of his life. He wounded some of them, but was soon disarmed, and then they cut his nose to the bone, to teach him to remember what respect he owed to the King."

Running parallel with Suffolk Place is James Street, where, till very recently, stood the well-known tennis-court —formerly an appendage of Piccadilly Hall—in which Charles the Second and his brother, the Duke of York, used frequently to indulge in their favourite game. The house at the south-west corner of the Haymarket and James Street, is said to have been that through which the royal brothers used to pass on their way to the tennis-court.

Passing through Panton Street—so called from a Colonel Thomas Panton who obtained authority to build houses here in 1671—we come to Leicester Square, or, as it is still occasionally styled, Leicester Fields. In 1658 Leicester House, the residence of the Sidneys, Earls of Leicester, was still the only house on the site of the present Square. Here, on the 13th of February, 1662, died the amiable and interesting daughter of James the First, Elizabeth Queen of Bohemia, whose melancholy story is still seldom read without a tear. In this house, at the time when the recent magnificent victories of Blenheim, Oudenarde, and Malplaquet, had rendered his name a household word with the English people, Prince Eugene was lodged during his visit to England, in 1712. In the course of the same century, Leicester House, to use the words of Pennant, became " successively the pouting-place of Princes." When, in 1717, George the Second, then Prince of Wales, quarrelled with his father, he took up his residence with his family, in Leicester House. Here, on the 15th of April, 1721, his youngest son, William Duke of Cumberland, of Culloden memory, first saw the light.

Here Frederick Prince of Wales resided with his Princess and her children during the many years that he continued to be on bad terms with his father, George the Second. Here also on the 4th of January, 1749, we find the royal children, including George the Third, then a boy of eleven years old, performing the play of " Cato," before their parents at Leicester House; the following being the *dramatis personæ* :—

Cato	. . .	Master Nugent.
Portius	. . .	Prince George (afterwards George III.).
Juba	. . .	Prince Edward (afterwards Duke of York).
Sempronius	. .	Master Evelyn.
Lucius	. . .	Master Montagu.
Decius	. . .	Lord Milsington.
Syphax	. . .	Master North.
Marcus	. . .	Master Madden.
Marcia	. . .	Princess Augusta (afterwards Duchess of Brunswick).
Lucia	. . .	Princess Elizabeth.

In Leicester House, on the 20th of March, 1751, Frederick Prince of Wales breathed his last. Although he had been ill for some days, so little did his family apprehend any fatal result, that almost at the moment of his decease they were amusing themselves with cards in the outer room. On the day on which he died Dodington inserts in his Diary— "I was told at Leicester House at three o'clock that the Prince was much better, and had slept eight hours in the night before. Before ten o'clock at night the Prince was a corpse!" He was lying in bed, listening to the performance on the violin of Desnoyers, a fashionable dancing-master, when, in the midst of a fit of coughing, he suddenly laid his hand upon his stomach, as if in pain, and exclaimed. "*Je sens la mort.*" The Princess, who was in the apartment, flew to his assistance, but before she could reach his pillow life had become extinct. According to Wraxall, he expired in Desnoyers's arms.

Leicester House, described by Noorthouck in 1773 as a "large old brick building with a courtyard before it," was pulled down in 1806. It stood at the north-east corner of the square, on the site of the present Leicester Place. Adjoining it, to the west, stood Savile House, the residence of Sir George Savile, ancestor of the Earls and Marquises of Halifax. George the Third resided here after he had become Prince of Wales, and here after his accession to the throne we find his brother, the young Duke of York, keeping his court. This house was the scene of one of the famous riots fomented by Lord George Gordon in 1780; the interior being completely pillaged and destroyed by the mob.

In Leicester Square lived at different periods two or three of the greatest painters which this country has produced, Sir Joshua Reynolds and Hogarth.

The residence of Sir Joshua Reynolds, and the house in which he died, was No. 47, on the west side of the square. Here Burke, Goldsmith, Garrick, Topham Beauclerk, Dr. Johnson, and Boswell, often sat at his hospitable board. "One afternoon," writes the late Mr. Croker, on the authority of an eye-witness, "as Colonel O'Moore and Mr. Burke were going to dine with Sir Joshua Reynolds, they observed Goldsmith (also on his way to Sir Joshua's) standing near a crowd of people, who were staring and shouting at some foreign women at the windows of one of the houses in Leicester Square. 'Observe Goldsmith,' said Mr. Burke to O'Moore, 'and mark what passes between him and me by-and-by at Sir Joshua's.' They passed on, and arrived before Goldsmith, who came soon after, and Mr. Burke affected to receive him very coolly. This seemed to vex poor Goldsmith, who begged Mr. Burke would tell him how he had had the misfortune to offend him. Burke appeared very reluctant to speak; but, after a good deal of pressing, said that 'he was really ashamed to keep up an intimacy with one who could be guilty of such monstrous indiscretions as Goldsmith had just exhibited in the square.' Goldsmith, with great earnestness, protested he was unconscious of what was meant. 'Why,' said Burke, 'did you not exclaim, as you were looking up at those women, what stupid beasts the crowd must be for staring with such admiration at those *painted jezebels*, while a man of your talents passed by unnoticed?' Goldsmith was horror-struck, and said, 'Surely, surely, my dear friend, I did not say so?' 'Nay,' replied Burke, 'if you had not said so, how should I have known it?' 'That's true,' answered Goldsmith, with great humility. 'I am very sorry—it was very foolish: *I do recollect that something of the kind passed through my mind, but I did not think I had uttered it.*'"*

Hogarth, the great artist of human nature, lived and died on the east side of Leicester Square, in the northern half of what was till lately known as Sablonière's Hotel. The house in which he breathed his last is otherwise of interest

* Boswell's "Life of Johnson," note by Croker.

as having been the abode, during a visit which he paid to England, of the great Polish patriot Thaddeus Kosciusko:—

> "———————————— Ye who dwell
> Where Kosciusko dwelt, remembering yet
> The unpaid amount of Catherine's bloody debt!
> Poland! o'er which the avenging angel past,
> But left thee as he found thee still a waste;
> Forgetting all thy still-enduring claim,
> Thy lotted people and extinguished name;
> Thy sigh for freedom, thy long-flowing tear,
> That sound that crushes in the tyrant's ear,—
> Kosciusko!.on—on—on—the thirst of war,
> Gasps for the blood of serfs and of their Czar," &c.
>   BYRON: *Age of Bronze.*

There may be persons also to whom it may be interesting to be informed that the Countess Guiccioli, whose name is so intimately associated with the love and the poetry of Lord Byron, resided, during a visit which she paid to England, in the same house in which Kosciusko lived and Hogarth died. In the adjoining house lived the celebrated surgeon, John Hunter, during the last years of his valuable life, and here he formed his extensive anatomical museum for the illustration of physiological science. Hither, too, his remains were brought from St. George's Hospital, in which he suddenly died.

The first London habitation of Sir Thomas Lawrence was over a confectioner's shop, No. 4, Leicester Square, formerly part of old Savile House.

Our remaining notices of Leicester Square, though not without interest, may be summed up in a few words. In 1698, we find Peregrine Marquis of Carmarthen, afterwards second Duke of Leeds, residing in Leicester Square, and here giving a ball to Peter the Great, whom he had been selected to attend during his visit to England. Swift informs us that here he lodged in 1711, and here, on the 29th of December, 1765, died "at his house in Leicester Square," Prince Frederick William, youngest brother of George the Third, at the age of sixteen. In Leicester Square stood formerly the "Feathers" public-house, the favourite resort of Grose, the antiquary, of Henderson, the actor, and of "Athenian" Stuart.

Behind Leicester House was the Military Garden or Yard, founded by Henry Prince of Wales, the accomplished and high-spirited son of James the First. It stood on the site of the present Gerrard Street and part of Princes Street. In Cranbourne Alley Hogarth was apprenticed to a goldsmith for the purpose of learning the art of silver-plate engraving. In Orange Court, Leicester Square, Thomas Holcroft was born in 1745, and here lived John Opie, the painter, who died in 1807. Castle Street was the first London residence of another eminent painter, Benjamin West.

In the centre of the south side of Leicester Square is an insignificant outlet, called St. Martin's Street. In this miserable place, at the corner of Long's Court, in a house of good size and formerly perhaps of some pretensions, lived Sir Isaac Newton. The house will be easily discernible by a small wooden erection on the roof, which is said to have been the private observatory of the immortal philosopher. Here resided Dr. Burney, the author of the "History of Music," and here his daughter, Madame D'Arblay, wrote her famous novel, "Evelina."

St. Martin's Church, close by, so deservedly celebrated for the elegance of its steeple and the extreme beauty of its portico, stands on a spot of ground which appears to have belonged at a very early period to the abbot and convent of St. Peter's, Westminster. That a church existed here in very early times is proved from a dispute which took place in 1222, between William, Abbot of Westminster, and Eustace

ST. MARTIN'S CHURCH.

Bishop of London, concerning the dependence upon, or exemption of, St. Martin's-in-the-Fields from the jurisdiction of the latter prelate. In the reign of Henry the Eighth a small church was built here at the expense of the King, since which period St. Martin's has continued to be in the gift of the sovereign. In consequence of the increase of the neighbouring population, the church built by Henry was enlarged in 1607, James the First and his son Henry defraying a part of the expense, and the parish the other part. Finally, this church was pulled down in 1721, between which year and 1726 the present beautiful building was erected by Gibbs, at an expense of £37,000.

St. Martin's Church is associated with the names of many individuals to whose history is attached a deep and lasting interest. It was at "a private school in the church of St. Martin's-in-the-Fields" that the immortal Ben Jonson, whose parents lived close by in Hartshorn Lane, received his earliest education. It was in this church also that the unfortunate Prince Charles Edward is stated to have formally abjured the religion of his forefathers.* Here the great Lord Bacon was baptized; and here, on the 25th of March, 1811, Thomas Moore, the poet, was married.

In the burial-ground of St. Martin's lie the remains of Mrs. Anne Turner, celebrated as the agent of the Countess of Somerset in effecting the tragical murder of Sir Thomas Overbury, in the reign of James the First. The widow of a physician, who left her young, beautiful, and penniless, she made herself remarkable in the world of fashion by her having introduced yellow starch into ruffs; a circumstance which induced Coke, the Lord Chief Justice, to sentence her to "be hanged in that dress, that the same might end in shame and detestation." The hangman who executed her

* Walpole's "Letters to Sir Horace Mann."

was also decorated with yellow ruffs on the scaffold. Anne Turner was hanged at Tyburn on the 15th of November, 1615, dying a "true penitent," according to Camden, who seems to have forgotten the fact of her detestable crime, in the interest excited by her youth and beauty, and her becoming demeanour on the scaffold. A Mr. John Castle writes to one of his correspondents, on the 28th of November, 1615:— "Since I saw you, I saw Mrs. Turner die. If detestation of painted pride, lust, malice, powdered hair, yellow bands, and the rest of the wardrobe of court vanities—if deep sighs, tears, confessions, ejaculations of the soul, admonitions to all sorts of people to make God and an unspotted conscience always our friends—if the protestation of faith and hope to be washed by the same Saviour and the like mercies that Mary Magdalen was, be signs and demonstrations of a blessed penitent, then I will tell you this poor broken woman went *à cruce ad gloriam*, and now enjoys the presence of her and our Redeemer. Her body being taken down by her brother, one Norton, servant to the Prince, was, in a coach, conveyed to St. Martin's-in-the-Fields, where, in the evening of the same day, she had an honest and a decent burial."

Another criminal who lies buried here is Jack Sheppard.

In the burial-ground of St. Martin's sleeps the celebrated John Lacy, the dancing-master, soldier, actor, and dramatic writer, with whose theatrical performances Charles the Second was so delighted that he caused his picture to be taken in three different characters. Within the church sleeps Nell Gwynn, whose remains were brought here from her house in Pall Mall, where she died. Her funeral sermon was preached by Dr. Tenison, Vicar of St. Martin's and afterwards Archbishop of Canterbury, who, in his discourse, spoke almost enthusiastically of her charities, her benevolence, her sincere repentance and pious end. These encomiums being afterwards maliciously dwelt upon to the Queen of William the Third, the reply of Mary was creditable to her heart :—" I have heard as much," she said : " it is a sign that the poor unfortunate woman died penitent, for if I can read a man's heart through his looks had she not made a pious and Christian end, the doctor would never have been induced to speak well of her."

In St. Martin's churchyard lies buried, after a life of misery and privation, the celebrated dramatic writer, George Farquhar, the author of the "Beaux' Stratagem," who died before he had completed his thirtieth year. "Dear Bob," runs his last letter to his friend Wilks, the actor, " I have not anything to leave thee to perpetuate my memory, but two helpless girls ; look upon them sometimes, and think of him that was, to the last moment of his life, thine, GEORGE FARQUHAR." It is but due to Wilks to record that he religiously obeyed the dying injunctions of his unfortunate friend.

In St. Martin's-in-the-Fields was buried Sir Winston Churchill, formerly of some note as an historian, but now principally remembered from his having been the father of the great Duke of Marlborough. Here also lie interred William Dobson, the English Vandyck; the Honourable Robert Boyle, the philosopher; the murdered Sir Edmundbury Godfrey; Lord Mohun, who was killed by the Duke of Hamilton in their famous duel; and James Smith, one of the authors of the "Rejected Addresses." Lastly, in the churchyard, rest the remains of the great sculptor, Roubiliac, whose body was followed to the grave by Hogarth and Sir Joshua Reynolds.

From the fact of the greater number of the children of Charles the First having been born at the neighbouring palace of Whitehall, it might have been expected that their births would have been registered at the parish church of St. Martin's. With one exception, however, this is not the case. There can be little doubt that the necessary orders were issued for such entries to be made ; and consequently the inference has been drawn, that the persons intrusted with the payment appropriated the money to their own use.

From St. Martin's churchyard we may pass into St. Martin's Lane, converted from a country lane into a street early in the seventeenth century. Here, in the reign of Charles the First, lived Sir John Suckling, the poet, and the eccentric philosopher, Sir Kenelm Digby ; and here, in 1660, at the residence of her father, Dr. Killigrew—the witty favourite of Charles the Second—was born the pious and gifted Anne Killigrew the beauty, poetess, and painter, whose name has been celebrated by Dryden, Anthony Wood, Ballard, Vertue, and Horace Walpole.

> " Art she had none, yet wanted none ;
> For nature did that want supply ;
> So rich in treasures of her own,
> She might our boasted stores defy ;
> Such noble vigour did her verse adorn,
> That it seemed borrowed where 'twas only born."—DRYDEN.

Anne Killigrew, as we have already mentioned, died in the apartments of her father, in the cloisters of Westminster Abbey.

At No. 104, St. Martin's Lane, lived Sir James Thornhill, the painter, previously to his removal to Leicester Square, and at the back of this house he founded, to his credit, one of the earliest schools for the study of the antique. This house is connected with an interesting anecdote. Hogarth, then unknown to fame, had formed a clandestine marriage with the daughter of Sir James Thornhill, which the prosperous artist was little inclined either to overlook or to forgive. They were living on bad terms together—the son-in-law in his poverty and the father-in-law in his pride—when one morning, on his entering his breakfast-room, he was struck by some drawings which he perceived on the table. They were the first pencil sketches of Hogarth's immortal series of pictures, "The Harlot's Progress." To the credit of Thornhill he forgot the poverty of his son-in-law in his admiration of his genius, and from henceforward they were reconciled.

St. Martin's Lane is associated with the names of other eminent artists besides Sir James Thornhill. Nearly opposite May's Buildings lived Sir Joshua Reynolds; in Peter's Court, Roubiliac, the sculptor, had his studio; and at No. 100 lived Fuseli.

Newport Street and Newport Market, within a short distance of St. Martin's Lane, derive their names from Newport House, the residence of Mountjoy Blount, created Earl of Newport in 1628. In Newport Market was the chapel of the famous Orator Henley, immortalized by Pope in the "Dunciad":—

> "High on a gorgeous seat, that far out-shone
> Henley's gilt tub, and Flecknoe's Irish throne."

And again,—

> "Imbrowned with native bronze, lo! Henley stands,
> Tuning his voice, and balancing his hands,
> How fluent nonsense trickles from his tongue!
> How sweet the periods, neither said nor sung!
> Still break the benches, Henley, with thy strain,
> While Sherlock, Howe, and Gibson, preach in vain."

In Newport Market, at the house of his father, a poulterer, John Horne Tooke was born in 1736.

Monmouth Street, now Dudley Street, celebrated as far back as the days of Gay as an emporium for cast-off articles of wearing apparel, is indebted for its name to the unfortunate Duke who was defeated at Sedgmoor.

> "Wouldst thou with mighty beef augment thy meal?
> Seek Leadenhall; St. James's sends thee veal!
> Thames Street gives cheeses; Covent Garden fruits;
> Moorfields old books; and Monmouth Street old suits."
> GAY's *Trivia*.

Soho Square, commenced in the reign of Charles the Second, was at one time called King's Square. "The Duke of Monmouth," writes Pennant, "lived in the centre house facing the statue. Originally, the square was called, in honour of him, Monmouth Square; and afterwards changed to that of King's Square. I have a tradition that, on his death, the admirers of that unfortunate man changed it to *Soho*, being the word of the day at the field of Sedgmoor." That the ill-fated Duke of Monmouth resided on the spot mentioned by Pennant there can be no question. So far, however, from Soho Square having derived its name from the watch-word at the battle of Sedgmoor, Mr. Peter Cunningham has distinctly shown that the site was so called as early as the year 1632. Moreover, in the "Present State of England," published in 1683, more than four years before the battle of Sedgmoor, the London residence of the Duke of Monmouth is stated to be *Soho Square*.

In addition to the Duke of Monmouth, Soho Square, as late as the last century, contained the London residences of the Bellasyses, Earls of Fauconberg, and the Howards, Earls of Carlisle. The last of the Fauconberg family who resided in Soho Square was Mary Cromwell, third daughter of the great Protector, and wife of Thomas, first Earl of Fauconberg. At the back of the east side of the square are still retained the names of Fauconberg Court and Fauconberg Mews, denoting that Fauconberg House must have stood in the immediate vicinity.

At what period the Howards deserted Carlisle House in Soho Square, we have no record. However, in the middle of the last century we find it occupied by the famous Mrs. Cornely, whose public balls, masquerades, and admirable suppers attracted to her assemblies all the rank and beauty of the day. Carlisle House stood at the north-east corner of the square.

In this square, in the reign of Queen Anne, lived Gilbert Burnet, Bishop of Salisbury, and the well-known admiral, Sir Cloudesley Shovel. The latter lived in what has been notorious in our time as the "White House," on the east side of Soho Square. After his melancholy death, his body, having been thrown on shore on the island of Scilly, was brought thence to his house in London, and subsequently conveyed from Soho Square with considerable state to Westminster Abbey. In 1726, we find the celebrated Spanish minister, Ripperda, living with great splendour in Soho Square; at Nos. 20 and 21, formerly one house, lived Sir Joseph Banks; and at No. 29, in 1824, lived Charles Kemble, the actor.

In Frith Street, Mrs. Inchbald wrote her charming novel, the "Simple Story." She had previously resided in the Strand. In this street William Hazlitt breathed his last; and in Greek Street, at the end of the last and the beginning of the present century, lived Sir Thomas Lawrence.

Gerrard Street, and Macclesfield Street adjoining, derive their names from having been erected on the site of the house and gardens of Charles Gerard, first Earl of Macclesfield, so distinguished for his loyalty to Charles the First and for his gallantry during the civil wars. "The profligate Lord Mohun," writes Pennant, " lived in this street, and was brought there after he was killed in the duel with the Duke of Hamilton. I have heard that his good lady was vastly displeased at the bloody corpse being flung upon the best bed." Pennant, however, is partially wrong. Lord Mohun no doubt lived at one time in this street, but at the time of his death his London residence was unquestionably in Great Marlborough Street.

Gerrard Street is especially endeared to us from its containing the house in which Dryden lived, and in which he died. In his dedication of "Don Sebastian" to Lord Leicester, he speaks of himself as "a poor inhabitant of his lordship's suburbs, whose best prospect is on the garden of Leicester House." And again, in a letter to Elmes Steward, he writes—"My house is the fifth door, on the left hand, coming from Newport Street." From Malone we learn that the house so consecrated by genius is No. 43, and we learn still further from Spence, on the authority of Pope, that the apartment in which the great poet "used most commonly to write" was in the ground-room next the street. "Dryden's house," writes Sir James Mackintosh, "was 43, Gerrard Street, within two or three doors of that occupied by Burke in 1788, when I first came to London." The extraordinary and disgraceful scene which took place at this house on the occasion of Dryden's funeral, is too well known to require a repetition of the particulars.

There are other interesting associations attached to Gerrard Street. Here Edmund Burke lived for many years, and from this street, in 1777, we find Hannah More dating her letters. Here also, in 1764, at the sign of the "Turk's Head," Dr. Johnson and Sir Joshua Reynolds founded the celebrated "Literary Club," originally called "The Club." Besides these two illustrious men, here used to assemble Burke, Bennet Langton, Topham Beauclerk, Oliver Goldsmith, George Colman, Garrick, Sir William Jones, Boswell, Charles James Fox, George Stevens, Gibbon, Adam Smith, the Wartons, Richard Brinsley Sheridan, Sir Joseph Banks, William Windham, Malone, and other celebrated persons. The club continued to be held at the Turk's Head till 1783, when their landlord dying, the house was shortly afterwards shut up. They then removed to "Prince's" in Sackville Street, and subsequently to "Baxter's," afterwards "Thomas's," in Dover Street. In 1792, they removed to Parsloe's in St. James's Street; and, in 1799, to the Thatched House in the same street.

In Dean Street and Princes Street stands the parish-church of St. Anne's, Soho, consecrated on the 21st of March, 1686, by Henry Compton, Bishop of London. In the churchyard is a tablet to the memory of Theodore King of Corsica, who, in 1756, died in the greatest distress at a tailor's in the neighbourhood. The inscription upon it is well known to have been written by Horace Walpole.

> "The grave, great teacher, to a level brings
> Heroes and beggars, galley-slaves and kings;
> But Theodore this moral learned ere dead;
> Fate poured its lessons on his living head,
> Bestowed a kingdom, and denied him bread."

In the churchyard, also, of St. Anne's, with a headstone over it, is the grave of William Hazlitt, the essayist and critic.

Dean Street and Compton Street derive their names from Bishop Compton, formerly Dean of St. Paul's, who at one period held the living of St. Anne's, Soho.

In Dean Street (No. 75) lived at one time Sir James Thornhill; and at 83 in this street died another eminent painter, George Henry Harlowe.

Wardour Street derives its name from Henry, third Lord Arundel of Wardour, who was implicated in the infamous accusations of Titus Oates. In this street, for five or six years, lived John Flaxman, the sculptor. It was formerly famous for its book-stalls as well as its curiosity shops. "I have heard Charles Lamb," writes Leigh Hunt, "expatiate on the pleasure of strolling up Wardour Street on a summer-day." On another occasion, Lamb observed to a friend of a pretty country lane in which they were walking, that it was nothing compared with Wardour Street.

Oxford Street, originally called the "Road to Oxford," and afterwards "Tyburn Road," from its being the way to the gallows, was built at different periods during the last century. It seems to have been first called Oxford Street about the year 1718.

Not the least interesting spot in this street is the once fashionable place of amusement, the "Pantheon," now converted into a wine importer's establishment. The original building was erected in 1771, after a design by Wyatt, and was opened to the public, as a kind of "town Ranelagh," on the 27th of January, 1772. "Near two thousand persons," we are told, "of the highest rank and fashion assembled on this occasion to admire the splendid structure, which contained fourteen rooms exclusive of the Rotunda." "The new winter Ranelagh in Oxford Road," writes Walpole in April, 1771, "is nearly finished. It amazed me. I imagine Balbec in all its glory." Boswell mentions his visiting it with Dr. Johnson shortly after it was opened. "We walked," he says, "to the Pantheon. The first view of it did not strike us as much as Ranelagh, of which he said the *coup d'œil* was the finest thing he had ever seen. However, as Johnson said, we saw the Pantheon in a time of mourning, when there was a dull uniformity; whereas we had seen Ranelagh when the view was enlivened with a gay profusion of colours." The original building having been burnt down, it was rebuilt on a smaller scale, and again used for masquerades and concerts, but being deserted by persons of fashion, it remained closed for several years, when it was converted into the well-known Pantheon Bazaar.

In Great Portland Street, Oxford Street, died, on the 19th of May, 1795, Dr. Johnson's biographer, James Boswell. In Portland Place, in 1784, was residing Philippe Duke of Orleans (Egalité), and here, in the following year, Madame D'Arblay mentions her visiting Madame de Genlis. No. 50, Portland Place, at the corner of Weymouth Street, was for some years the French Embassy. Here, in 1824, was residing as ambassador the Prince de Polignac, who in 1830 became involved in the ruined fortunes of his royal master, Charles the Tenth; and here, a short time afterwards, the author well remembers seeing a far more celebrated minister, Prince Talleyrand, supported into the house by his servants. Close by, at No. 23, Park Crescent, Joseph Buonaparte, ex-king of Naples, Spain, and the Indies, long resided as Count Survilliers.

In Norton Street, now Bolsover Street, Portland Road, on the east side, lived Richard Wilson, the landscape painter, and Sir David Wilkie; and at his house in this street died, in March, 1796, Sir William Chambers, the architect.

A short distance from Great Portland Street is Wells Street, in which, at No. 64, Dr. James Beattie, the author of the "Minstrel," was lodging in 1771.

Berners Street and Newman Street are severally interesting as having been inhabited by eminent artists. In Berners Street, Sir William Chambers was living in 1773; Fuseli in 1804; and Opie from 1792 to 1808; here also resided Bone, the enameller. At No. 14, Newman Street, Benjamin West, the historical painter, died in 1820. Here also lived Thomas Banks and John Bacon, the sculptors.

Running parallel with Newman Street is Rathbone Place, apparently, in former days, a favourite resort of the Scottish nobility and gentry; inasmuch as, at different times, we find it the place of residence of the unfortunate Lords Lovat, Balmerino, and Kilmarnock, who suffered on the scaffold for their share in the Rebellion of 1745.

Tottenham Court Road, diverging from the east end of Oxford Street, is so called from the prebendal manor of Totenhall, or Tottenham Court, the manor house of which stood at the north-west extremity of the present road. It was subsequently converted into a place of entertainment, known as the Adam and Eve Gardens, the front of which is rendered famous in Hogarth's print, the "March to Finchley." In the days of Gay, "Tottenham Fields" were still a pleasant resort for the citizens of London :—

> "When the sweet-breathing spring unfolds the buds,
> Love flies the dusty town for shady woods,
> Then Tottenham-fields with roving beauty swarm,
> And Hampstead balls the City virgins warm."

On the west side of Tottenham Court Road is the chapel in which George Whitefield, the founder of the Methodists, used to preach. It was built under his auspices in 1756. Here his wife, who died in 1768, is buried, and here, under the north gallery, lie the remains of the eminent sculptor, John Bacon.

Tottenham Court Road leads us into the Hampstead Road, on the east side of which is St. James's Chapel, where lie the remains of Lord George Gordon, the principal cause of the "Protestant Riots" in 1780. Here also lie buried the eminent painters, George Morland, who died in Stephen Street, in the neighbourhood, and John Hoppner. Lastly, on the site of the New River Reservoir, on the east side of Hampstead Road, stood, till the year 1808, the building marked in the old maps of London as King John's Palace.

COVENT GARDEN.

COVENT GARDEN MARKET.—"OLD HUMMUMS."—ST. PAUL'S, COVENT GARDEN.—RUSSELL STREET AND ITS COFFEE HOUSES.—BOW, JAMES, KING, ROSE, BEDFORD, AND HENRIETTA STREETS.—MAIDEN LANE.—SOUTHAMPTON AND TAVISTOCK STREETS.

COVENT GARDEN, or rather Convent Garden, derives its name from occupying the site of what was anciently a vast garden, belonging to the Abbey and Convent of Westminster, which extended as far west as St. Martin's Church. Behind the houses on the north side of York Street, stone coffins, and other relics of the dead, have from time to time been discovered, which would lead us to presume that on this spot was the cemetery of the ancient monks. After the dissolution of the monasteries, Convent Garden was bestowed by Edward the Sixth on his uncle, the great Protector, Edward Duke of Somerset, and on his attainder was transferred to John Russell, first Earl of Bedford. Hence, it is almost needless to remark, Bedford Street, Bedfordbury, Russell Street, and Tavistock Street derive their names. In 1570, a "porcyon or percell" of the estate was leased by the second Duke of Bedford to Sir William Cecil, afterwards the great Lord Burghley.

It appears by a plan of London, printed in the reign of Queen Elizabeth, that Covent Garden was then an open area surrounded by meadows and lanes, with the exception of the south side where it was bounded by the gardens of Bedford House, then the London residence of the House of

Russell. A regular market appears to have been first established here in 1656, about which time Francis, fourth Earl of Bedford, employed Inigo Jones to erect the present piazzas on the north and east sides. It was originally intended to continue them round the whole square; indeed it appears by a print of Hollar's that the piazza formerly extended along the east side where the "Hummums" now stand. This part, however, was burnt down not many years after its erection. At the close of the seventeenth century we find the 'prentices of London resorting here to play at cricket under the porticos, while from Gay's "Trivia" we learn that, at a somewhat later period, the manly game of football used to be played in the area where the market now stands:—

> "Where Covent Garden's famous temple stands,
> That boasts the work of Jones' immortal hands;
> Here oft my course I bend, when lo! from far
> I spy the furies of the foot-ball war;
> The 'prentice quits his shop to join the crew,
> Increasing crowds the flying game pursue," &c.

To those who delight in visiting the former haunts of departed genius, there are few spots in London more replete with interesting associations than Covent Garden and the neighbouring streets. To the Piazza of Covent Garden especial interest is attached. In the north-east angle Sir Peter Lely resided for nearly eighteen years of the reign of Charles the Second; and, apparently, in the same apartments, afterwards lived John Zoffani, the painter. In a part of the Tavistock Hotel lived Richard Wilson, the landscape-painter; and, in the north-east angle, Sir Godfrey Kneller had a house, with a garden at the back extending towards Bow Street. In 1716, Nicholas Rowe, the dramatic poet, dates his letters from Covent Garden, while close by lived Thomas Southern, the author of "Oroonoko" and of the

"Fatal Marriage." "I remember him," writes Oldys, "a grave and venerable old gentleman. He lived near Covent Garden, and used often to frequent the evening prayers there, always neat and decently dressed, commonly in black, with his silver sword and silver locks; but latterly, it seems, he resided at Westminster."* In Covent Garden died, in 1702, John Zachary Kneller, the elder brother of Sir Godfrey, and himself a painter of some merit.

On the site of the large house, now Evans's Hotel, at the north-west corner of Covent Garden, lived Sir Harry Vane the younger, and afterwards successively Sir Kenelm Digby and the republican statesman Denzil Holles. The present house—said to have been the first family hotel established in London—was built by Admiral Russell, afterwards Earl of Orford, celebrated for his brilliant victory over the French off La Hogue, in 1692. Here, in 1727, the Earl died. It afterwards became the residence of the Lords Archer, of whom the last baron died in 1778. Immediately to the eastward of this house resided, between the years 1637 and 1643, Thomas Killigrew, the wit; and apparently on the same spot Sir William Alexander, Earl of Stirling, the poet.

Covent Garden, and especially the Piazza, are memorable in the pages of Otway, Killigrew, Shadwell, Congreve, and Fielding. Its hotels and taverns continued to be the resort of wits, poets, actors, and men of fashion for nearly two centuries. The "Piazza" hotel was the favourite retreat of Richard Brinsley Sheridan, and of the men of wit and rank with whom he associated; while in the parlour of the "Bedford" met the shilling-rubber club, of which Fielding, Hogarth, Goldsmith, and Churchill were members. It was at one of their meetings at the "Bedford" that the quarrel

* MS. notes to "Langbaine."

took place between Hogarth and Churchill, which induced the latter to satirize his friend, and the former to retaliate upon him with his unrivalled pencil. The "Epistle to Hogarth" is comparatively forgotten, but Churchill will still live as "Bruin" when his verse shall have passed into oblivion.

The "Old Hummums," Covent Garden, on the east side of the market, was the scene of what Dr. Johnson called the "best accredited ghost-story" he had ever heard. The person whose ghost was supposed to have appeared here was Ford, a relation of Dr. Johnson, said to be the riotous parson of Hogarth's "Midnight Modern Conversation." The story as related by Johnson to Boswell is as follows:—"A waiter at the Hummums, in which Ford died, had been absent for some time, and returned, not knowing that Ford was dead. Going down to the cellar, according to the story, he met him. Going down again, he met him a second time. When he came up, he asked some of the people of the house what Ford could be doing there? They told him Ford was dead. The waiter took a fever, in which he lay for some time. When he recovered, he said he had a message to deliver to some women from Ford; but he was not to tell what, or to whom. He walked out. He was followed, but somewhere about St. Paul's they lost him. He came back, and said he had delivered the message, and the women exclaimed 'Then we are all undone.' Dr. Pallet, who was a credulous man, inquired into the truth of this story, and he said the evidence was irresistible." Dr. Johnson further informs us that Mrs. Johnson went to the Hummums on purpose to inquire into the truth of this strange story, and came away perfectly satisfied that there was no imposition.

Unquestionably the most interesting spot in Covent Garden is the church, dedicated to St. Paul. Few perhaps who are in the habit of passing by this heavy-looking building are aware that, with the exception of Westminster Abbey, here lie the remains of more men of genius and celebrity than apparently in any other church in London. With the exception, however, of a small tablet to the memory of Macklin the actor, it contains no monumental memorials of the illustrious dead.

St. Paul's, Covent Garden, was built about the year 1633 by Inigo Jones, at the expense of Francis, fourth Earl of Bedford. According to Horace Walpole, the Earl, having sent for the great architect, intimated to him that he required a chapel for the use of the parishioners who resided on his property, adding that he intended to put himself to no considerable expense in its erection. "In fact," he said, "I would not have it much better than a barn." "Then," said Inigo Jones, "you shall have the handsomest barn in England." The truth of this story has sometimes been called in question, but we believe without sufficient reason. The building has occasionally found its admirers, but most persons probably will agree with Walpole, who tells us that he "wanted taste to see its beauties." "The barn-roof over the portico," he writes, "strikes my eye with as little idea of dignity or beauty as it could do if it covered nothing but a barn." In 1795, only seven years after it had been restored at an expense of £11,000, the interior of the church —including the monuments to the dead and the entire wood-work—was destroyed by fire. It was shortly afterwards, however, restored at the expense of the parishioners.

We will now proceed to name a few of the more remarkable persons whose remains lie either in the church or churchyard of St. Paul's, Covent Garden. In the churchyard was buried the celebrated favourite of James the First, Robert Carr, Earl of Somerset; the union of whose daughter with William, first Duke of Bedford, doubtless led to his being interred on this, the property of the Russells. We stand, too, on the ground which covers the dust of Sir Peter Lely. His monument of white marble, which was destroyed by the fire of 1795, was adorned with a bust of the great artist between two cupids, as well as with fruit, foliage, and other devices. The inscription alone has been preserved.*

In the vaults of the church lies the body of the handsome and gallant William Wycherley, the author of the "Plain Dealer," whose beauty of person and graceful address no less endeared him to the ladies, than his conversation and wit rendered him acceptable to Charles the Second and his gay courtiers. Here, too, either in the church or churchyard, rest the remains of two other eminent dramatic writers, Thomas Southern and Susannah Centlivre.

Let us pause for a moment on the grave of Samuel Butler, the author of "Hudibras." Fortunately Anthony Wood has enabled us to point out the spot where rest his remains. "This Sam. Butler," he writes, "who was a boon and witty companion, especially among the company he knew well, died of a consumption, 25th of September, 1680, and was, according to his desire, buried six foot deep in the yard belonging to the church of St. Paul, in Covent Garden, within the liberty of Westminster, viz., at the west end of the said yard, on the north side, and under the wall, of the church; and under that wall which parts the yard from the common highway."† He was buried, we are told, at the

* See "The New View of London," 1708.

† "Athenæ Oxonienses," vol. ii., p. 453. Aubrey, however, who followed Butler's remains to the grave, places the burial-place of the poet at the *east* end, and not the *west*, of the north side of the churchyard. "He died of a consumption," writes Aubrey, "Sept. 25 (A.D. 1680, 70 circiter), and was buried 27th, according to his own appointment in the churchyard of Covent Garden; sc. in the north part next the church at the east end.

expense of "his good friend" Mr. Longueville, of the Temple. According to the authors of the Biographia Britannica, "That gentleman would fain have buried him in Westminster Abbey, and spoke, with that view, to several persons who had been his admirers, offering to pay his part; but none of them would contribute; whereupon Mr. Longueville buried him very privately at St. Paul's, Covent Garden; himself and seven or eight more following him to the grave." The monument to the memory of Butler in Westminster Abbey was erected at the expense of a meritorious citizen of London, Alderman Barber. Subsequently some persons, unknown to fame, erected a monument to the memory of the poet in the churchyard in which he was interred, but apparently no trace of it now remains.

Here was buried by torchlight, Robert Wilks, the great actor of the reigns of Queen Anne and of George the First; and hither also was carried to his last home in the churchyard—followed thereto by the most eminent persons of his profession—the most gifted of comic actors, the "Lord Ogleby" and the "Sir Peter Teazle" of the last century, Thomas King. Here, too, "in the vault close to the north gate of the churchyard, at the entrance in Covent Garden," was buried the admirable actor, Charles Macklin.* On the 26th of November, 1788, he was performing, at Covent Garden Theatre, the part of Sir Pertinax Mac Sycophant in his own comedy of "The Man of the World," when he felt himself suddenly overtaken by disease, and his memory failed him. He had, however, strength enough to address himself

---

His feet touch the wall. His grave, two yards distant from the pilaster of the dore (by his desire), six foot deepe. About twenty-five of his old acquaintance at his funerall, I myself being one." "Letters of Eminent Men," vol. ii., p. 263.

* "Gentleman's Magazine" for 1797, p. 632.

to the audience, when, in a painful farewell, he told them that, unless he felt himself more capable of administering to their amusement, he should never again present himself before them. Six months afterwards he reappeared on the stage for his own benefit, in the character of Shylock, but his memory again failed him, and another actor was called upon to continue the part. Disease, however, though it drove him from the stage, and deprived him of the excitement he had derived from his favourite pursuit, appears to have had no effect in shortening his life. He survived till the 11th of July, 1797, when he died, at the age, it is said, of at least ninety-seven.

Either in the vaults of the church, or in the churchyard, rest many other actors or actresses of celebrity. In the churchyard lie the remains of "Joe Haines" and of the admirable actress, Mrs. Davenport. In one corner of it sleep "Dick Estcourt," John Edwin, and Michael Kelly, the musical composer. Also, either in the church or churchyard, was interred the celebrated actor, Edward Kynaston.

Nor are these the only remarkable persons who lie interred within the precincts of St. Paul's, Covent Garden. Here were buried the eminent sculptor and carver, Grinling Gibbons; Dr. Thomas Arne, the celebrated musical composer; Dr. John Armstrong, the author of the "Art of Preserving Health;" Sir Robert Strange, the engraver; John Zachary Kneller, the brother of the great painter; and John Wolcot, the memorable "Peter Pindar." The latter lies beneath the floor of the vestry-room.

It may be mentioned that here the celebrated Lady Mary Wortley Montagu was baptized; and, lastly, that here the handsome actor, William O'Brien, was married to his runaway bride, Lady Susan Strangways, eldest daughter of the first Earl of Ilchester.

The names of the streets in the vicinity of Covent Garden bespeak, within a few years, the date of their erection. King Street, Charles Street, and Henrietta Street derive their names from King Charles the First and his Queen, Henrietta Maria; as also do James Street and York Street, from James Duke of York; and Catherine Street, from the consort of Charles the Second. Bedford Street, Russell Street, and Tavistock Street derive their names from the noble family on whose property they were built.

In Russell Street, running from Covent Garden towards Drury Lane Theatre, were situated three of the most celebrated and once fashionable coffee-houses in London, " Will's," " Button's," and " Tom's." Will's coffee-house, so conspicuous in the literary history of a former age, stood on the north side of Russell Street, at the west corner of Bow Street. Here used to assemble the wits and men of fashion of the reign of Charles the Second, William the Third, and of the earlier part of the reign of Queen Anne; and here for many years the immortal Dryden sat and was reverentially listened to as the great oracle of the place. " It was Dryden," writes Spence on the authority of Pope, " who made Will's coffee-house the great resort for the wits of his time." " In Covent Garden, to-night," writes Pepys in February, 1663–4, " going to fetch home my wife, I stopped at the great coffee-house there, where I never was before; where [were] Dryden, the poet, I knew at Cambridge, and all the wits of the town, and Harris, the player, and Mr. Hoole, of our college." In the winter, we are told, Dryden's acknowledged place of honour was by the fireside, while in summer his chair was removed to the corner of the balcony on the first floor, overlooking the street. In any literary dispute, the great poet was invariably made the referee. Persons unknown to fame never dreamed of being admitted to the principal table at which Dryden presided; while the young men of fashion and the second-rate wits, who sat at another table, considered it the highest honour to be allowed to take a pinch out of his snuff-box. It was to Will's, that Pope, then a mere child—for he could not have completed his twelfth year—induced his friends to carry him in order to feast his eyes with the sight of the great poet, in whose path of fame and genius he was destined hereafter so worthily to follow. "Who does not wish," writes Dr. Johnson, "that Dryden could have known the value of the homage that was paid him, and foreseen the greatness of his young admirer?" Again, Sir Charles Wogan writes to Swift—"I had the honour of bringing Mr. Pope from our retreat in the forest of Windsor to dress *à la mode*, and introduce at Will's Coffee House." Pope afterwards became a constant frequenter of Will's, though not till the illustrious Dryden was no more. "Pope had now," writes Dr. Johnson, 'declared himself a poet; and thinking himself entitled to poetical conversation, began at seventeen to frequent Will's, a coffee-house on the north side of Russell Street, in Covent Garden, where the wits of that time used to assemble, and where Dryden had, when he lived, been accustomed to preside."

Another frequenter of Will's, Dean Lockyer, has left us an interesting account of Dryden, as he appeared at his favourite coffee-house. "I was about seventeen," he writes, "when I first came up to town, and was an odd-looking boy, with short rough hair, and that sort of awkwardness which one always brings up at first out of the country with one. However, in spite of my bashfulness and appearance, I used now and then to thrust myself into Will's to have the pleasure of seeing the most celebrated wits of that time, who then resorted thither. The second time that ever I was there Mr. Dryden was speaking of his own things, as he frequently did, especially of such as had been lately published. 'If anything of mine is good,' says he, 'it is "Mac Flecnoe;" and I value myself the more upon it, as it is the first piece of ridicule written in heroics.' On hearing this, I plucked up my spirits so far as to say, in a voice but just loud enough to be heard, ' that " Mac Flecnoe " was a very fine poem, but that I had not imagined it to be the first that was ever writ that way.' On this Dryden turned short upon me, as surprised at my interposing; asked me how long I had been a dabbler in poetry; and added, with a smile— 'Pray, sir, what is it that you did imagine to have been writ so before?' I named Boileau's 'Lutrin,' and Tassoni's 'Secchia Rapita,' which I had read, and knew Dryden had borrowed some strokes from each. ' 'Tis true,' said Dryden, 'I had forgotten them.' A little after, Dryden went out, and in going spoke to me again, and desired me to come and see him next day. I was highly delighted with the invitation, went to see him accordingly, and was well acquainted with him ever after as long as he lived."

Button's coffee-house stood on the south side of Russell Street, about two doors from Covent Garden Market. Here assembled Pope, Swift, Addison, Garth, Arbuthnot, Steele, Ambrose Phillips, and all the most celebrated men of the Augustan age of England. Button's, as is well known, was the favourite resort of Addison. According to Spence, whose authority was Pope, Button was an old servant of Addison's, who, after the death of Dryden, had influence enough to transfer the wits from Will's to the house of his protégé. Dr. Johnson has entered further into particulars. "Button," he writes, " had been a servant in the Countess of Warwick's family, who, under the patronage of Addison, kept a coffee-house on the south side of Russell Street, about two doors from Covent Garden. Here it was that the wits of that time used to assemble. It is said that when Addison had suffered any vexation from the Countess, he withdrew the company from Button's house. From the coffee-house he went again to a tavern, where he often sat late, and drank too much wine." "Addison," said Pope, "usually studied all the morning, then met his party at Button's, dined there, and stayed for five or six hours, and sometimes far into the night. I was of the company for about a year, but found it too much for me. It hurt my health, and so I quitted it."

It was at Button's, according to Pope, that Addison took him aside "after their long coldness," to explain the circumstances under which he had patronized Tickell's translation of the "Iliad" in opposition to that of Pope. It was here, too, that Ambrose Phillips hung up the rod with which he threatened Pope with chastisement. Phillips, while a young student at St. John's College, Cambridge, had published his "Six Pastorals," the intrinsic merit of which is said to have excited the jealousy of Pope, who certainly lashed them severely and with great humour in the "Guardian." It was under these circumstances that Phillips suspended the rod over Pope's seat at Button's. The insult fell harmless on the great poet, who retaliated by his well-known lines in the "Prologue to the Satires":—

> "The bard whom pilfered pastorals renown,
> Who turns a Persian tale for half-a-crown,
> Just writes to make his barrenness appear,
> And strains, from hard-bound brains, eight lines a year."

After the death of Addison, Button's not only ceased to be much frequented, but a few years afterwards Addison's old servant was receiving relief from the parish of St. Paul's, Covent Garden.

On the north side of Russell Street, "over against"

Button's coffee-house, was Tom's coffee-house (No. 17), so called from Thomas West, at one time the landlord. This house, memorable from the days of Queen Anne to the reign of George the Third, is still standing. In the preface to a work entitled "Descriptive Particulars of English Coronation Medals," the author, Mr. Till, writes:—" The room in which I conduct my business, as a coin dealer, is that which, in 1764—by a general subscription among nearly seven hundred of the nobility, foreign ministers, gentry, and geniuses of the age—became the card-room and place of meeting for many of the now illustrious dead, till 1768, when a voluntary subscription among its members induced Mr. Haines, the proprietor, to take in the next room westward as a coffee-room; and the whole floor, *en suite*, was converted into card and conversation rooms. Here assembled Dr. Johnson, Garrick, Murphy, Dr. Dodd, Dr. Goldsmith, Sir Joshua Reynolds, Foote, Moody, Count Bruhl, Sir Philip Francis, George Colman the elder, the Dukes of Northumberland and Montague, Lord Rodney, George Steevens, Warner, and many others, all of whom have long since passed to that 'bourne from whence no traveller returns.'"

Among other remarkable persons who were residents in Russell Street in former days, we must not omit to mention Carr, Earl of Somerset, the unworthy favourite of James the First; John Evelyn, the philosopher; and the celebrated actors, Major Mohun and Thomas Betterton. Here, in 1779, died Dr. John Armstrong, the poet; and here at one time lived Charles Lamb.

In connection with Russell Street, Covent Garden, there is a curious passage in Gibbon's "Memoirs of his Life and Writings," in which the great historian, then a student of Magdalen College, Oxford, describes the circumstances attending his abjuration of the Protestant faith. "In my last excursion to London," he writes, "I addressed myself to Mr. Lewis, a Roman Catholic bookseller in Russell Street, Covent Garden, who recommended me to a priest, of whose name and order I am at present ignorant. In our first interview he soon discovered that persuasion was needless. After sounding the motives and merits of my conversion, he consented to admit me into the pale of the church, and at his feet, on the eighth of June, 1753, I solemnly, though privately, abjured the errors of heresy. The seduction of an English youth of family and fortune was an act of as much danger as glory; but he bravely overlooked the danger, of which I was not then sufficiently informed."

At No. 8, Russell Street, now the "Caledonian Coffee House," lived the well-known "Tom Davies," the bookseller and actor. To the admirers of Dr. Johnson, and especially of Boswell's inimitable biography, this house will always be interesting as that which witnessed the introduction of these two remarkable men to each other. Boswell himself informs us that he never passed by it "without feeling reverence and regret." He had more than once, it seems, been disappointed in his eager desire to be introduced to Dr. Johnson, but at length fortune threw him in the way of the great mammoth of literature. "At last," he writes, "on Monday, the 16th of May, when I was sitting in Mr. Davies's back-parlour, after having drunk tea with him and Mrs. Davies, Johnson unexpectedly came into the shop, and Mr. Davies having perceived him through the glass door in the room in which we were sitting, advancing towards us, he rumoured his awful approach to me, somewhat in the manner of an actor in the part of Horatio, when he addresses Hamlet on the appearance of his father's ghost—'Look, my lord, it comes.' I found that I had a very perfect idea of Johnson's figure from the portrait of him painted by Sir Joshua Reynolds soon after he had published his 'Dictionary,' in the attitude of sitting in his easy chair in deep meditation. Mr. Davies mentioned my name, and respectfully introduced me to him. I was much agitated; and recollecting his prejudice against the Scotch, of which I had heard much, I said to Davies—'Don't tell where I come from.'—'From Scotland,' cries Davies, roguishly.—' Mr. Johnson,' said I, 'I do indeed come from Scotland, but I cannot help it.'—I am willing to flatter myself that I meant this as light pleasantry, to soothe and conciliate him, and not as an humiliating abasement at the expense of my country. But however that might be, this speech was somewhat unlucky, for with that quickness of wit for which he was remarkable, he seized the expression 'come from Scotland,' which I used in the sense of being of that country: and as if I had said that I had come away from it, or left it, retorted—'That, sir, I find is what a good many of your country cannot help.' This stroke stunned me a good deal; and when we had sat down I felt myself not a little embarrassed, and apprehensive of what might come next. He then addressed himself to Davies. 'What do you think of Garrick? He has refused me an order for the play for Miss Williams, because he knows the house will be full, and that an order will be worth three shillings!' Eager to take any opening to get into conversation with him, I ventured to say, 'O, sir, I cannot think Mr. Garrick would grudge such a trifle to you.'—'Sir,' said he, with a stern look, 'I have known David Garrick longer than you have done; and I know no right you have to talk to me on the subject!' Perhaps I deserved this check, for it was rather presumptuous in me, an entire stranger, to express any doubt of the justice of his animadversion upon his old acquaintance and pupil. I now felt myself much mortified, and began to think that the hope which I had long indulged of obtaining his acquaintance was blasted. And, in truth, had not my ardour been uncommonly strong, and my resolution uncommonly persevering, so rough a reception might have deterred me for ever from making any further attempts." Boswell, however, "sat out" the great man, satisfied that though there was a roughness in his manner, there was no innate ill-nature in his composition. "Davies," he says, "followed me to the door, and when I complained to him a little of the hard blows which the great man had given me, he kindly took upon him to console me by saying—' Don't be uneasy; I can see he likes you very well.'"

From Russell Street we pass into Bow Street, once one of the most fashionable streets in London.

"I've had to-day a dozen billet-doux,
From fops, and wits, and cits, and Bow Street beaux."
DRYDEN.

In this street was born, on the 5th of December, 1661, the great minister, Robert Harley, Earl of Oxford; here, in the days of the Protectorate, Edmund Waller, the poet, was residing; here the celebrated sculptor, Grinling Gibbons, died on the 3rd of August, 1721; and here, on the site of the present police-office, Henry Fielding lived and wrote his "Tom Jones."

Another gifted inhabitant of this street was William Wycherley, whose residence was on the west side, "over against the Cock." Here it was that he was visited in his sickness by King Charles the Second. "Mr. Wycherley," we are told, "happened to fall sick at his lodgings in Bow Street, Covent Garden, during which period the King did him the honour to visit him. Finding his body extremely weakened, and his spirits miserably shattered, he commanded him, as soon as he should be able to take a journey, to go to the south of France, believing that the air of Montpelier would contribute to restore him as much as anything, and assured him, at the same time, that, as soon as he was capable of taking the journey, he would order him five hundred pounds to defray the charges of it. Mr. Wycherley accordingly went to France, and having spent the winter there, returned to England in the spring, entirely restored to his former vigour both of body and mind."*

It was immediately after Wycherley's return from Montpelier, that he met with his well-known adventure with the young and beautiful Countess of Drogheda. "He went down to Tunbridge," we are told, "either to take the benefit of the waters, or the diversions of the place; when, walking one day upon the Well's Walk with his friend Mr. Fairbeard of Gray's Inn, just as he came up to the bookseller's shop, the Countess of Drogheda,† a young widow, rich, noble, and beautiful, came to the bookseller, and inquired for the 'Plain Dealer.' 'Madam,' says Mr. Fairbeard, 'since you are for the "Plain Dealer," there he is for you;' pushing Mr. Wycherley towards her. 'Yes,' says Mr. Wycherley, 'this lady can bear *plain* dealing, for she appears to be so accomplished that what would be a compliment to others, spoken to her would *be plain dealing*.' 'No, truly, Sir,' said the Countess, 'I am not without my faults any more than the rest of my sex; but, notwithstanding, I love *plain dealing*, and am [never more fond of it than when it tells me of them.' 'Then, madam,' says Mr. Fairbeard, 'you and the "Plain Dealer" seem designed by heaven for each other.' In short, Mr. Wycherley walked with the Countess upon the walks, waited upon her home, visited her daily at

* "Life of Wycherley," in Biog. Brit.
† Letitia Isabella, daughter of John Robartes, first Earl of Radnor, and widow of Charles, second Earl of Drogheda.

her lodgings while she continued at Tunbridge, and at her apartments in Hatton Garden after she went to London, where in a little time he got her consent to marry her." Needless, perhaps, it is to add, that the jealous disposition of Lady Drogheda rendered their marriage almost as unhappy a one as was that of Wycherley's contemporary, Addison, with the Countess of Warwick.

At the Cock Tavern, on the east side of Bow Street—a favourite resort of men of fashion in the days of Charles the Second—took place, in 1663, the indecent frolic in which the accomplished Charles Sackville, Earl of Dorset, then Lord Buckhurst, Sir Charles Sedley, the poet, and Sir Thomas Ogle were the actors. An attack was made on the doors of the tavern by the incensed bystanders, when a riot ensued, in which Lord Buckhurst and his companions nearly lost their lives.* They were carried before the Court of Common Pleas, where a heavy fine was inflicted upon them, the penalty imposed on Sir Charles Sedley being five hundred pounds. When placed at the bar, Sir Robert Hyde, the Lord Chief Justice, in commenting upon the offence, inquired sarcastically of Sedley if he had ever read the "Complete Gentleman?" "I believe," was the reply, "that I have read more books than your Lordship." Sedley and his fellow culprits employed Killigrew and another courtier to intercede with the King for a mitigation of their fine. Instead, however, of exerting themselves in the cause of their friends, they are said to have begged the amount for their own use, and actually to have extorted it to the last penny. It may be mentioned that the London residence of

---

* Those who may wish to be better informed as to the nature of the outrage, will find the particulars in the "Biographia Britannica," vol. vi., p. 3604; the "Athenæ Oxonienses," vol. ii., col. 1100; and Anthony Wood's "Life of Himself," p. 187.

Lord Buckhurst's father, Richard Earl of Dorset, was at this time in Bow Street, on the opposite side of the way to the Cock Tavern.

In Bow Street, in the reigns of William the Third and Queen Anne, lived the eminent and eccentric physician, Dr. John Radcliffe, one of those men of whose history the little we know is so full of interest that it leaves us deeply to regret that we can discover no more. One anecdote connected with his residence in Bow Street is well known. The garden of his house adjoined that of Sir Godfrey Kneller, behind the Piazza, in Covent Garden, and, being intimate friends, they agreed that a doorway should be broken through the wall, to admit of their enjoying a free intercourse with each other. Some misunderstanding, however, having arisen between them, Kneller sent a message to Radcliffe that he intended to close up the door. "Tell him," said the witty physician, "that he may do anything with it but paint it." Sir Godfrey's reply to the messenger was equally pointed. "Tell Dr. Radcliffe," he said, "with my compliments, that I will take anything from him but his physic."

Dr. Radcliffe, on his first establishing himself in London, appears to have fixed upon Bow Street as his residence, as being then one of the most fashionable streets of the metropolis. How little suited, however, he was to be a courtier—how little fitted to pander to the sickly fancies of princes and fine ladies—is proved by his behaviour on two different occasions when summoned into the sick chambers of William the Third and Queen Anne. A year or two before his death King William sent for Radcliffe, and among other symptoms of disease mentioned that, while his body was becoming emaciated, his legs had swollen far beyond their natural size. Radcliffe made the necessary examination. "I would

not," he said, "have your Majesty's *two* legs for your *three* kingdoms." King William never forgave him for this unseasonable speech, and though he continued to make use of Radcliffe's prescription till within three days of his death, he could never again be persuaded to admit him into his presence. His speech to Queen Anne, then Princess of Denmark, showed a no less want of reverence for royalty. A messenger arriving at his residence with the intelligence that the Princess was alarmingly ill, he not only delayed obeying the summons till after a considerable interval had elapsed, but on being admitted into the presence of the royal sufferer, treated her malady with undisguised scorn. "She has only the vapours," he said, and added with a characteristic oath—"She is as well as any woman breathing, if she could only be persuaded to believe it." His imprudence, however, sealed his fate as a courtier. On his next appearance at court he was stopped by an officer in the antichamber, and informed that the princess had no longer any occasion for his services. However, in the last illness of Prince George of Denmark, the Queen's affection for her husband so far overcame the indignation which she felt at the conduct of her former medical attendant, that she ordered him to be immediately summoned. When she herself, too, lay on her death-bed, he was also sent to attend her. Radcliffe disobeyed the summons, and his conduct in so doing aroused a general and indignant outcry against the eccentric physician. His excuse, however, was indisposition, and after a full investigation of such evidence as has been handed down to us, there seems to be no great reason for questioning its validity. In one of his letters he writes—
"I know the nature of attending crowned heads in their last moments too well to be fond of waiting upon them without being sent for by a proper authority. You have heard of

pardons being signed for physicians before a sovereign's demise; however, ill as I was, I would have gone to the Queen in a horse-litter, had either her Majesty, or those in commission next to her, commanded me so to do."

Before taking our leave of Bow Street, we may mention that it was apparently in this street that the celebrated Prince Eugène dined with Dr. Radcliffe. The entertainment which the physician provided for the hero was plain beef and a pudding. The Prince thanked him for the compliment—" You have considered me," he said, " not as a courtier, but as a soldier."

Of James Street, which runs out of Covent Garden, parallel with Bow Street, nothing remarkable is known, except that David Garrick resided here in 1747, the year in which the great actor became manager of Drury Lane, and when the theatre opened with the celebrated prologue of Dr. Johnson. In the "General Advertiser" for the 7th of April, 1747, is the following advertisement:—" Mr. Garrick hopes the gentlemen and ladies who had taken places for his benefit, the 16th of last month, will excuse his deferring it to the 30th of this, his illness not permitting him to have it sooner. Tickets and places to be had at Mr. Garrick's lodgings in James Street, Covent Garden, and of Mr. Page, at the stage door of the Theatre."

In King Street, Covent Garden, at the house of their father, who kept an upholsterer's shop called the "Two Crowns and Cushions," were born the celebrated Dr. Thomas Arne, the composer, and his sister, Mrs. Cibber. In this street James Quin, the actor, was born; here Nicholas Rowe, the poet, died, and here Garrick was lodging in 1745.

But the most interesting spot is Rose Street, a small wretched-looking passage between Garrick Street and Long Acre. Here Samuel Butler, the author of "Hudibras," lived and died; and here the celebrated bookseller, Edmund Curll, had his shop, the sign of which was "Pope's Head." But the circumstance which has rendered Rose Street classic ground, is the fact of its having been the spot where Dryden received his memorable cudgelling, at the instigation of Wilmot, Earl of Rochester. Dryden's "Essay on Satire" had recently been published, in which Rochester, besides being accused of cowardice, was exposed to every indignity which could reflect on his character as a wit, a rake, or a poet. For instance:—

> "He, while he mischief means to all mankind,
> Himself alone the ill effects does find;
> False are his words, affected is his wit,
> So often he does aim, so seldom hit;
> To every face he cringes while he speaks,
> But when the back is turned, the head he breaks:
> Mean in each action, lewd in every limb,
> Manners themselves are mischievous in him;
> A proof that chance alone makes every creature,
> A very Killigrew without good nature."

And again—

> "Falsely he falls into some dangerous noose,
> And then as meanly labours to get loose;
> A life so infamous is better quitting,
> Spent in base injury and low submitting.
> I'd like to have left out his poetry,
> Forgot by almost all as well as me.
> Sometimes he has some humour; never wit;
> And if it rarely,—very rarely,—hit,
> 'Tis under so much nasty rubbish laid,
> To find it out 's the cinderwoman's trade,
> Who for the wretched remnants of a fire,
> Must toil all day in ashes and in mire."

The "Essay on Satire" was supposed to be the joint production of Dryden and of Sheffield, Duke of Buckingham. From Dean Lockyer, however, we learn that the Duke merely made a few alterations in the poem, which, generally speaking, were for the worse. At all events, Rochester chose to look upon Dryden as the author, and, adopting a mode of revenge which was not uncommon in the days of Charles the Second, he hired three ruffians, who waylaid the great poet in Rose Street, on his way from Will's Coffeehouse to his own house in Long Acre, and inflicted on him a severe personal chastisement.

The name of Dryden occurs in connection with another *fracas* which took place in Covent Garden in the days of Charles the Second, the principals in which were Sir Henry Bellasses and another courtier, Thomas Porter. "They two," writes Pepys, "dined yesterday at Sir Robert Carr's, where, it seems people to drink high, all that come. It happened that these two, the greatest friends in the world, were talking together, and Sir H. Bellasses talked a little louder than ordinary to Tom Porter, giving of him some advice. Some of the company standing by said, 'What, are they quarrelling, that they talk so high?' Sir H. Bellasses hearing it, said, 'No,' says he; 'I would have you know I never quarrel, but I strike; and take that as a rule of mine.' 'How?' says Tom Porter, 'strike! I would I could see the man in England that durst give me a blow.' With that Sir H. Bellasses did give him a box of the ear; and so they were going to fight there, but were hindered. And by-and-by Tom Porter went out, and meeting Dryden the poet, told him of the business, and that he was resolved to fight Sir H. Bellasses presently; for he knew that if he did not they should be friends to-morrow, and then the blow would rest upon him; which he would prevent, and desired Dryden to let him have his boy to bring him notice which way Sir H. Bellasses goes. By-and-by he is informed that Sir H. Bellasses' coach was coming: so Tom Porter went down out of the coffeehouse where he stayed for the tidings, and stopped the coach, and bade Sir H. Bellasses come out. 'Why,' says H. Bellasses, 'you will not hurt me coming out, will you?' 'No,' says Tom Porter. So out he went, and both drew; and H. Bellasses having drawn, and flung away his scabbard, Tom Porter asked him whether he was ready. The other answering him he was, they fell to fight, some of their acquaintance by. They wounded one another, and H. Bellasses so much that it is feared he will die: and finding himself severely wounded, he called to Tom Porter, and kissed him and bade him shift for himself; for, says he, 'Tom, thou hast hurt me, but I will make shift to stand upon my legs till thou mayest withdraw, and the world not take notice of you, for I would not have thee troubled for what thou hast done.' And so, whether he did fly or no I cannot tell; but Tom Porter showed H. Bellasses that he was wounded too: and they are both ill, but Sir H. Bellasses to fear of life." Bellasses survived his wounds only ten days.

At the west end of King Street is Bedford Street, leading into the Strand. Here Kynaston, the actor, resided in his old age, and here Quin was living in the middle of the last century. Here also resided Thomas Sheridan, the father of Richard Brinsley Sheridan. "Mrs. Sheridan," writes Whyte in his "Miscellanea Nova," "at one time lived in Bedford Street, opposite Henrietta Street, which ranges with the south side of Covent Garden, so that the prospect lies open the whole way, free of interruption. We were standing together in the drawing-room, expecting Johnson, who was to dine there. Mr. Sheridan asked me, 'could I see the length of the garden?' 'No, sir.' 'Take your opera-glass, Johnson is coming, you may know him by his gait.' I perceived him at a good distance, working along with a peculiar solemnity of deportment, and an awkward sort of measured step. At that time the broad flagging at each side of the streets was not universally adopted, and stone posts were in fashion, to prevent the annoyance of carriages. Upon every post as he passed along, I could observe he deliberately laid his hand; but missing one of them when he had got at some distance, he seemed suddenly to recollect himself, and immediately returning back, carefully performed the accustomed ceremony, and resumed his former course, not omitting one till he gained the crossing. This, Mr. Sheridan assured me, however odd it may appear, was his constant practice; but why or wherefore he could not inform me." "Sir Joshua Reynolds," says Boswell, "has observed Johnson to go a good way about, rather than pass a particular alley in Leicester Fields; but this Sir Joshua imputed to his having had some disagreeable recollection associated with it."

The first lodgings occupied by Benjamin West after his arrival in England were in Bedford Street, Covent Garden.

Running parallel with King Street, to the south of Covent Garden, is Henrietta Street, from a house in which street the beautiful Georgiana Duchess of Devonshire, and the other fair and high-born women who canvassed for Charles James Fox, used to watch the humours of the Westminster election. Hannah More on one of these occasions appears to have been staying in Henrietta Street. "I had like," she writes to one of her sisters, "to have got into a fine scrape the other night. I was going to pass the evening at Mrs. Coles's, in Lincoln's Inn Fields. I went in a chair. They carried me through Covent Garden. A number of people, as I went along, desired the men not to go through the Garden, as there were an hundred armed men, who suspected every chairman belonged to Brooks's, and would fall upon us. In spite of my entreaties the men would have persisted, but a stranger, out of humanity, made them set me down, and the shrieks of the wounded, for there was a terrible battle, intimidated the chairmen, who were at last prevailed upon to carry me another way. A vast number of people followed me, crying out, ' It is Mrs. Fox : none but Mr. Fox's wife would dare to come into Covent Garden in a chair : she is going to canvass in the dark !' Though not a little frightened I laughed heartily at this, but shall stir out no more in a chair for some time."

In Henrietta Street was the shop of the mountebank almanac-maker, Partridge, and here at one period resided the charming actress, Mrs. Clive. Here, too, died a poet formerly of some celebrity, Paul Whitehead. As a poet he has ceased to be read, and almost to be remembered; but those who are curious in literary history still remember him as having been the social companion of Frederick Prince of Wales—as one whose poetical squibs had a considerable influence over the politics of the day—and as one of the depraved brotherhood who assembled at Medmenham Abbey. By his last will Paul Whitehead bequeathed his heart, enclosed in a marble urn, to his friend Lord Le Despencer, with a request that it might be placed in his lordship's mausoleum at High Wycombe. The fantastic wish was complied with, but what has since become of the heart and the urn we know not.

Between Covent Garden and the Strand, running parallel with Henrietta Street, is Maiden Lane, which, according to the late Mr. D'Israeli, takes its name from an image of the Virgin which formerly stood here.* Here, "on a second floor" lodged, in 1677, the illustrious patriot and poet, Andrew Marvell; here, at the sign of the "White Peruke," Voltaire resided during his visit to England in 1727; and here, at the house of his father, a hairdresser (No. 26), lived for some years the celebrated landscape-painter, J. M. W.

* "Curiosities of Literature."

Turner. In this street also were the once famous "Cyder Cellars" (No. 20), a favourite resort of Porson.

At the eastern end of Maiden Lane is Southampton Street. Here was once the residence of the charming actress, Mrs. Oldfield. Here, too, at No. 27, Garrick resided before his removal to the Adelphi; here Congreve once lived, and here, in November, 1795, Thomas Linley, the eminent musician, died suddenly. Near to Southampton Street is Exeter Street, where Dr. Johnson, unfriended and almost penniless, first took up his abode when he arrived in London, in 1737, with David Garrick. "His first lodgings," writes Boswell, "were at the house of Mr. Norris, in Exeter Street, adjoining Catherine Street, in the Strand. 'I dined,' said he, 'very well for eightpence, with very good company, at the Pine Apple, in New Street, just by. Several of them had travelled. They expected to meet every day, but did not know one another's names. It used to cost the rest a shilling, for they drank wine; but I had a cut of meat for sixpence and bread for a penny, and gave the waiter a penny, so that I was quite well served, nay, better than the rest, for they gave the waiter nothing." "Painful as it is to relate," writes Cumberland, "I have heard Dr. Johnson assert that he subsisted himself for a considerable space of time upon the scanty pittance of fourpence halfpenny per day."

The last place which we shall mention in immediate connection with Covent Garden is Tavistock Row, on its south side. At the south-west corner of this row, No. 4, lived the unfortunate Miss Ray, the beautiful mistress of Lord Sandwich, who was shot by her lover, the Rev. James Hackman, on the 7th of April, 1779. Hackman had been formerly a lieutenant in the 68th regiment of foot, and, while in command of a recruiting party at Huntingdon, had been invited to Lord Huntingdon's seat at Hinchinbrooke, where he fell violently in love with his future victim. Failing in his repeated endeavours to prevail upon her to become his wife, he determined, while under the influence of a maddening jealousy, to put an end to her life and his own. Accordingly, having posted himself under the piazza of Covent Garden, as she was quitting the theatre he discharged the contents of a pistol at her head, and immediately afterwards fired another pistol at himself. According to one of the journals of the following day:—" Last night the following melancholy fate terminated the existence of the beautiful, the favoured, and yet the unfortunate Miss Ray. As she was stepping into her carriage from Covent Garden, a clergyman, whose name we hear is Hackman, came up and lodged the contents of a pistol in her head, which done he instantly shot himself, and they fell together. They were carried into the Shakspeare, and the ablest assistance called for, but Miss Ray expired in a few minutes. The desperate assassin still lives to account for the horrid act, and, it is hoped, to suffer for it, his wound being on the temple, and supposed not to be dangerous. An express was instantly sent for Lord Sandwich. He came about twelve o'clock in the most lamentable agonies, and expressed a sorrow that certainly did infinite honour to his feelings." Hackman, on the 17th of April, was tried for murder, and, having been found guilty, was hanged a few days afterwards at Tyburn. Miss Ray was originally a milliner's apprentice in St. George's Court, St. John's Lane, Clerkenwell; and Hackman, at the time when he deprived her of life, was residing in Craven Street, in the Strand. In the same house in Tavistock Row in which Miss Ray lived, died Macklin, the actor, and at No. 13 lived Dr. John Wolcot, the celebrated Peter Pindar.

To give an account of Covent Garden Theatre would amount to little less than a history of the stage during upwards of a century. It is sufficient to observe, that the original theatre was built in 1732; that it was rebuilt in 1787, enlarged in 1792, and on the night of the 20th September, 1808, was burnt to the ground, when upwards [of £107,000 worth of property is said to have been destroyed. Another theatre which rose rapidly on its ruins, and was opened on the 18th of September, 1809, was destroyed by fire on the 5th of March, 1856. The present building was opened on the 22nd of May, 1858.

DRURY LANE, AND CONTIGUOUS STREETS.

DRURY LANE.—DRURY HOUSE.—WYCH STREET.—DRURY LANE THEATRE.—
LONG ACRE.—PHŒNIX ALLEY.—QUEEN STREET.—LINCOLN'S INN FIELDS.—
PORTUGAL STREET.—DUKE STREET.—ST. GILES'S CHURCH AND CHURCH-
YARD.

DRURY LANE derives its name from having been built nearly on the site of Drury House, the residence of the once powerful family of the Druries, which stood where Craven Buildings and the Olympic Theatre now stand. "It is singular," writes Pennant, "that this lane, of later times so notorious for intrigues, should derive its title from a family name, which, in the language of Chaucer, had an amorous signification :—

<blockquote>
"Of bataille and of chevalrie,
Of ladies love and <i>druerie</i>,
Anon I wool you tell."
</blockquote>

Drury House is said to have been built by the gallant and courtly Sir William Drury, Lord Deputy of Ireland in the reign of Queen Elizabeth, and a Knight of the Garter, who fell by the hand of Sir John Burroughs, in a duel brought about by a quarrel between them on an absurd question of precedency. He was succeeded by his son, Sir Robert Drury, in whose lifetime the celebrated Dr. Donne found a welcome refuge in Drury House during the days of his poverty. Here, too, it was that the unfortunate Earl of Essex and his friends met secretly to plan the rash conspiracy which ended in as fatal a catastrophe.

Some time after the death of Sir Robert Drury, this property came into the possession of William Lord Craven, the gay courtier of the reign of James the Second, the hero of the "tremendous breach of Creutznach," and the presumed husband of the charming Elizabeth Queen of Bohemia. Lord Craven, having pulled down the old mansion of the Druries, built on its site a large brick pile, in which we find the Queen of Bohemia residing shortly after the restoration of her brother, Charles the Second. Here, in 1697, Lord Craven died. Part of Craven House was taken down in 1723, but the remaining portion continued to be used as an inn till the commencement of the present century, when, with other buildings, it was pulled down to make room for the Olympic Theatre. From Pennant we learn that, in searching after old Craven House, he discovered a public-house, the sign of which was a head of the Queen of Bohemia, Lord Craven's "admired mistress," which proved its identity. About the end of the last century there was to be seen, in the court in Craven Buildings, a fresco painting of Lord Craven, seated in full armour on a white horse, with a truncheon in his hand.

In the reign of Charles the First we find Drury Lane one of the most fashionable spots in London. Here, in that reign, was the residence of Sir William Alexander, Earl of Stirling, the poet; and here also lived Archibald Earl of Argyll, and apparently his son, the celebrated Marquis. In the reign of Charles the Second, Drury Lane appears to have lost little of its aristocratic character. Besides Craven House, here stood Clare House, the residence of the Earl of Clare, and Anglesey House, the residence of the Earl of

Anglesey.* In Craven Buildings lived, at different periods, the celebrated actresses Mrs. Bracegirdle and Mrs. Pritchard.

In Drury Lane, at the house of her father, a blacksmith, lived Anne Clarges, the mistress, and afterwards the wife, of the celebrated George Monk, Duke of Albemarle. "Monk," writes Lord Clarendon in his "History of the Rebellion," "was cursed, after a long familiarity, to marry a woman of the lowest extraction, the least wit, and less beauty." Lord Clarendon on another occasion speaks of her as a "woman with nothing feminine about her but her make;" while Burnet styles her a "ravenous, mean, and contemptible creature, who thought of nothing but getting and spending." "When Monk was a prisoner in the Tower," writes Aubrey, "his sempstress, Anne Clarges, a blacksmith's daughter, was kind to him in a double capacity. It must be remembered that he was then in want, and that she assisted him. Here she was got with child. She was not at all handsome nor cleanly. Her mother was one of the five women-barbers, and a woman of ill-fame. A ballad was made on her and the other four; the burden of it was—

"Did you ever hear the like,
Or ever hear the fame,
Of five women barbers,
Who lived in Drury Lane."

In a curious memoir in the British Museum of one Mul-Sack, a noted highwayman, there occurs the following notice of these ladies :—" There were five noted Amazons in Drury Lane, who were called women-shavers, and whose actions were then talked of about town, till being apprehended for a riot, and one or two of them severely punished, the rest fled to Barbadoes." The author of the "Memoir of Mul-Sack" mentions a brutal and disgusting act of cruelty which

* "Present State of England," 1683.

was perpetrated by these wretches on another woman, the particulars of which are too gross for publication, but which sufficiently attest how detestable was the character of the "five women-shavers" of Drury Lane.

Drury Lane was one of the first places in London which was visited by that terrible calamity, the great Plague, in 1665. On the 7th of June Pepys inserts in his Diary— "This day, much against my will, I did in Drury Lane see two or three houses marked with a red cross upon the doors, and 'Lord have mercy upon us' writ there." Two years afterward, when Pepys was passing through Drury Lane, on his way to Westminster, the street presented a very different appearance. It was on May-day, 1667, at which period his "Diary" shows that the warm-hearted Nell Gwynn was an inhabitant of Drury Lane. "To Westminster, in the way meeting many milk-maids with their garlands upon their pails, dancing with a fiddler before them; and saw pretty Nelly standing at her lodgings' door in Drury Lane in her smock sleeves and bodice, looking upon one: she seemed a mighty pretty creature." Another celebrated comedian who lived in Drury Lane in the reign of Charles the Second, was John Lacy.

After Drury Lane had ceased to bear the fashionable reputation which it enjoyed in the seventeenth century, it became in the reign of George the First, and up to a much later period, notorious as a colony for those unfortunate offshoots of genius, who may perhaps be best designated as "poor authors." In the wittiest satirical poem of modern times, the "Epistle to Dr. Arbuthnot," Pope, speaking of the disagreeable manner in which he was pestered by authors to read their MSS., writes :—

"I sit with sad civility; I read
With honest anguish, and an aching head;

> And drop at last, but in unwilling ears,
> This saving counsel, 'Keep your piece nine years.'
> 'Nine years !' cries he, who high in Drury Lane,
> Lulled by soft zephyrs through the window-pane,
> Rhymes ere he wakes, and prints before Term ends,
> Obliged by hunger, and request of friends," &c.

Goldsmith also writes in his " Description of an author's bed-chamber"—

> " Where the Red Lion staring o'er the way,
> Invites each passing stranger that can pay ;
> Where Calvert's butt, and Parson's black champagne
> Regale the drabs and bloods of Drury Lane ;
> There, in a lonely room, from bailiffs snug,
> The Muse found Scroggen stretched beneath a rug ;
> A window, patched with paper, lent a ray,
> That dimly shewed the state in which he lay," &c.

Gay's description of Drury Lane in his " Trivia " completes the picture :—

> " O may thy virtue guard thee through the roads,
> Of Drury's mazy courts and dark abodes !
> The harlots' guileful paths, who nightly stand
> Where Catherine Street descends into the Strand."

In Wych Street, corrupted from *Via de Aldwych*—a continuation of Drury Lane, running into the Strand—is NEW INN, an inn of Chancery, under the government of the Middle Temple. It was anciently a common inn or hostelry, known by the sign of the "Blessed Virgin," and, in the reign of Richard the Third, was obtained from Sir John Fineux, Lord Chief Justice of England, for the rent of six pounds a year. New Inn is principally interesting from Sir Thomas More having studied here before he became a member of Lincoln's Inn. On the south side of Wych Street stood till recently LYON'S INN, dating as far back as the reign of Henry the Fifth, which is said to have been also anciently a common inn for travellers, with the sign of the

Lion. It was from the Angel Inn in Wych Street that Bishop Hooper was carried to the Fleet Prison, and thence to his martyrdom at Gloucester.

Drury Lane Theatre—from its numerous classical associations, from its antiquity as a place of public amusement, from the memory of the eminent actors and actresses who have "fretted their hour" upon its stage—will always be regarded as a most interesting spot. The present theatre stands at no great distance from the site of a playhouse, which appears to have been erected here in the reign of James the First, under the name of the Phœnix, or Cockpit, and which was destroyed by the mob in March, 1617, and the stage-property torn to pieces. It had originally been a cock-pit, and from these names Phœnix Alley (now Hanover Court), on the south-east side of Long Acre, and Cockpit Alley, in Great Wyld Street, apparently derive their designations. In the reign of James the First, the actors at the Phœnix were called the Queen's servants, till the death of Anne of Denmark, when they were called the Lady Elizabeth's servants, from the Princess Elizabeth, afterwards Queen of Bohemia. On the marriage of Charles the First with Henrietta Maria, in 1625, they resumed their old name of the Queen's servants.

Of the character of the performances, and the names of the plays which were acted on the boards of the Phœnix, we have apparently no record till 1612, when we find Webster's tragedy of the "White Devil" acted here by the Queen's servants. Here, in 1629, was acted for the first time Shirley's comedy, "The Wedding," a play of considerable merit, which has twice since been revived; and here, in 1633, also for the first time, was performed Massinger's admirable play, the "New Way to Pay Old Debts." Subsequently the fanaticism which prevailed during the Commonwealth closed the doors of the Phœnix, nor was it till 1658 that it was reopened by Sir William Davenant, with such pieces—chiefly consisting of declamation and music—as were calculated to suit the still rigid fastidiousness of the age.

At the restoration of Charles the Second, the Phœnix, or, as it was still indifferently styled, the Cockpit, was obtained possession of by a bookseller of the name of Rhodes, who acted there with two of his apprentices, afterwards the celebrated Betterton and Kynaston. Not long afterwards, the well-known Thomas Killigrew had influence enough with his easy sovereign to obtain a patent for opening a royal theatre, the actors at which were designated "His Majesty's servants." At the same time, Sir William Davenant obtained a patent to open another theatre, under the name of the "Duke of York's Company," while that of Killigrew was distinguished as the "King's."

The two rival companies being thus formed, Davenant—with Rhodes, Betterton, and Kynaston established himself—in the first instance at the Phœnix, whence he removed, in 1662, to the new-built theatre in Lincoln's Inn Fields, and subsequently, in 1671, to a far more magnificent one in Dorset Gardens, Fleet Street. In the mean time, Killigrew, with the King's company, had established himself at the Red Bull, in St. John's Street, where he continued but a short time, when he removed to Gibbon's Tennis Court, near Clare Market. This theatre, however, being but ill adapted to theatrical representations, he erected a more convenient one on the site of the present Drury Lane Theatre, the name by which it has since been familiarly known, though originally styled the King's House or Theatre, as Sir William Davenant's play-house in Lincoln's Inn Fields was called the Duke's Theatre. The new theatre opened on the 8th of

April, 1663, with Beaumont and Fletcher's comedy of the "Humorous Lieutenant." "About ten of the King's company," writes Colley Cibber, "were on the royal household establishment, having each ten yards of scarlet cloth, with a proper quantity of lace, allowed them for liveries; and in their warrants from the Lord Chamberlain were styled Gentlemen of the Great Chamber. Whether the like appointments were extended to the Duke's company I am not certain."

It was at the new theatre by Drury Lane that Charles the Second first became enamoured of Nell Gwynn in the character of Valeria, in Dryden's tragedy of "Tyrannic Love." Dryden, it is said, selected her for this character, from the circumstance of its being necessary that she should die on the stage, in order to admit of her speaking his lively epilogue:—

"O, poet, damned dull poet! who could prove
So senseless, to make Nelly die for love?
Nay, what's yet worse, to kill me in the prime
Of Easter-term, in tart and cheesecake-time!"

The great poet who had been partial to the beautiful actress from the commencement of her career, is said to have composed this particular epilogue—and, indeed, at other times, to have selected her for particularly striking parts—with the express hope of her attracting the admiration of Charles.

Pepys appears to have been admitted behind the scenes at the "King's House," in Drury Lane. Here it was that he was first introduced to Nell Gwynn after she had been acting Cælia, in Beaumont and Fletcher's play of the "Humorous Lieutenant." Speaking on this occasion of another actress of some celebrity, he writes—"Knipp took us all in, and introduced us to Nelly, a most pretty woman, who acted the great part of Cælia to-day, very fine, and did it very well: I kissed her, and so did my wife, *and a mighty pretty soul she is.*" On a subsequent occasion Pepys writes—"After dinner with my wife to the King's house, to see the 'Mayden Queene,' a new play of Dryden's, mightily commended for the regularity of it, and the strain and wit: and the truth is, there is a comical part done by Nell, which is Florimell, that I never can hope ever to see the like done again by man or woman. The King and Duke of York were at the play. But so great performance of a comical part was never, I believe, in the world before as Nell do this, both as a mad girle, then most and best of all when she comes in like a young gallant; and hath the motions and carriage of a spark the most that ever I saw any man have. It makes me, I confess, admire her."

The new theatre lasted but a short time, having been burnt to the ground, with fifty or sixty of the adjoining houses, in the month of January, 1672. It was rebuilt after designs by Sir Christopher Wren, and reopened, with a prologue and epilogue by Dryden, on the 26th of March, 1674. In 1741, having fallen into a ruinous state, it was almost entirely rebuilt; and again, in 1794, every vestige of Wren's building having been razed to the ground, a new theatre was erected on its site. This building was entirely destroyed by the fire which took place on the night of the 24th of February, 1809. The present theatre was commenced in 1811, and, on the 10th of October, 1812, was opened to the public with the well-known poetical address of Lord Byron.

From Drury Lane let us stroll into Long Acre, not the least interesting ground which we have yet traversed. In the reign of Edward the Sixth this spot consisted of a large field, styled indifferently the Seven Acres, or the Long Acre, and was granted, together with Covent Garden, to John

Earl of Bedford. It was sometimes styled the Elms Street, from a row of trees which grew upon the spot. The site was first built upon in the reign of Charles the First.

In a "cellar" in Long Acre lived, at one period, in a miserable state of destitution, one of the sweetest of lyrical poets, the once gay and gallant Richard Lovelace, the favourite of courts, and the darling of Muses and the ladies. "He was accounted," writes Anthony Wood, "the most amiable and beautiful person that ever eye beheld; a person also of minute modesty, virtue, and courtly deportment, which made him, especially when he retired to the great city, much admired and adored by the female sex." Faithful to his unfortunate sovereign, Charles the First, the House of Commons committed him to the Gatehouse at Westminster, in which, as has been already stated, he composed his beautiful verses, "To Althea, from Prison:"—

> "Stone walls do not a prison make,
> Nor iron bars a cage," &c.

Lovelace, having spent his fortune in the royal cause, and perceiving no further hope of being able to assist his sovereign, passed over to the Continent, where he raised a regiment for the French King. Having been wounded at the siege of Dunkirk in 1646, it was under the impression, long prevalent in England, that he had died of his wounds, that Miss Lucy Sacheverel, a young and beautiful girl, the Lucasta of his poetry, gave her hand to another. The poet some time afterwards returned to England, when he was again thrown into prison, where he remained till the death of Charles the First. When he obtained his release he was, according to Anthony Wood, in such a miserable state of destitution, that liberty could scarcely have been regarded by him as a boon. His death took place in the year 1658, in "a very mean lodging," in Gunpowder Alley, near Shoe Lane, Holborn, at the age of forty.

From the valuable researches of Mr. Peter Cunningham we learn that in Long Acre, in 1673, resided that gallant follower of Charles the First, Henry Mordaunt second Earl of Peterborough, K.G.; that here, on the south side, lived Oliver Cromwell between six and seven of the eventful years that he sat in the House of Commons; and that here, on the north side, facing Rose Street, was the residence, from 1682 to 1686, of the great poet, John Dryden.

It was in Phœnix Alley (now Hanover Court), Long Acre, that the celebrated John Taylor, the "Water Poet," kept his tavern during the days of the Civil Wars and the Commonwealth. Adored by the poor and by those of his own station in life, he was not unfrequently visited by persons of high rank, who came to amuse themselves either with the oddities of genius, or with his really instructive and entertaining conversation. Though displayed in a different manner, his veneration for the unfortunate house of Stuart was not less deep than that of his courtly contemporary, Richard Lovelace. The original sign which he put up over his tavern was the "Mourning Crown," a name which gave such offence to the ruling powers that he was compelled to exchange it for another. He then hung up his own portrait with the lines—

> "There's many a King's head hanged up for a sign,
> And many a Saint's head, too—then why not mine?"

at the same time calling it the "Poet's Head." At this house it was that, in 1653, he breathed his last.

Another poet with whose name Long Acre is associated is Matthew Prior. To the world in general, Prior is sufficiently familiar as the friend and correspondent of Pope, Swift, Bolingbroke, all the wits and statesmen of the

Augustan age of England—as having written familiar verses on the Duchess of Queensberry—as being the author of poems whose merit has continued to render them popular even in our own times—as the secret negotiator of the famous Treaty of Utrecht, and afterwards as the accredited Ambassador from the Court of England to that of Versailles. Not a little curious, therefore, it is to dive into the privacy of his domestic hours. "I have been assured," writes the younger Richardson, "that having spent the evening with Oxford, Bolingbroke, Pope, and Swift, Prior would go and smoke a pipe, and drink a bottle of ale with a common soldier and his wife in Long Acre before he went to bed." The wife of the soldier here alluded to has been supposed to be the original of the Chloe of Prior's poetry: at all events she seems to have been one of the lowest cast of society. "His Chloe," writes Dr. Johnson, "probably was sometimes ideal; but the woman with whom he cohabited was a despicable drab of the lowest species. One of his wenches, perhaps Chloe, while he was absent from his house, stole his plate and ran away, as was related by a woman who had been his servant."—"Prior," said Pope to Spence, "used to bury himself for whole days and nights together with a poor mean creature; and often drank hard. He left most of his effects to the poor woman he kept company with, his Chloe. Everybody knows what a wretch she was. I think she had been a little alehouse-keeper's wife."*

Long Acre, like Drury Lane, was one of the first streets visited by the giant pestilence which devastated London in 1665. "At the latter end of November or the beginning of December, 1664," writes Defoe, "two men, said to be

* "Richardsoniana." Johnson's "Life of Prior." Spence's "Anecdotes of Men and Manners."

Frenchmen, died of the plague in Long Acre, or rather, at the upper end of Drury Lane. The family they were in endeavoured to conceal it as much as possible; but, as it had gotten some vent in the discourse of the neighbourhood, the Secretaries of State got knowledge of it; and concerning themselves to inquire about it, in order to be certain of the truth, two physicians and a surgeon were ordered to go to the house and make inspection. This they did; and finding evident tokens of the sickness upon both the bodies that were dead, they gave their opinions publicly that they died of the plague. The people showed a great concern at this, and began to be alarmed all over the town, and the more because in the last week in December, 1664, another man died in the same house, and of the same distemper."

Nearly facing Long Acre, on the east side of Drury Lane, is Great Queen Street, which was built in the reign of Charles the First, and derives its name from his consort, Henrietta Maria. Like Drury Lane, it was once one of the most fashionable streets in London. In the reign of Charles the First here stood Paulet House, the residence of the Marquis of Winchester, and Conway and Rivers House, the residences of the Earls of Conway and Rivers. Here, too, stood the house of the once celebrated George Digby, Earl of Bristol, with whose inconsistencies of character Walpole has amused himself in his "Royal and Noble Authors." "His life," writes Walpole, "was one of contradiction. He wrote against Popery, and embraced it; he was a zealous opposer of the court, and a sacrifice for it; was conscientiously converted in the midst of his prosecution of Lord Strafford, and was most unconscientiously a prosecutor of Lord Clarendon." But Lord Bristol is now, perhaps, principally remembered from his connection with De Grammont's

Memoirs. It was in his house in Queen Street apparently that he gave those luxurious parties to Charles the Second, by which, combined with the seductive charms of his two beautiful relations, the Miss Brooks, one of them afterwards the celebrated Lady Denham, he hoped to wean the merry monarch from the alluring influence of Lady Castlemaine, and the grave counsels of Lord Clarendon. "The Earl of Bristol," writes Count Hamilton, "ever restless and ambitious, had put in practice every art to possess himself of the King's favour. He knew that love and pleasure had entire possession of a master whom he himself governed in defiance of the Chancellor. Thus he was continually giving entertainments at his house, and luxury and elegance seemed to rival each other in those nocturnal feasts, which always led to other enjoyments. The two Miss Brooks, his relations, were always of those parties. They were both formed by nature to excite love in others, as well as to be susceptible of it themselves: they were just what the King wanted. The Earl, from this commencement, was beginning to entertain a good opinion of his project; but Lady Castlemaine, who had recently gained entire possession of the King's heart, was not in a humour at that time to share it with another, as she did very indiscreetly afterwards with Miss Stewart. As soon, therefore, as she received intimation of these secret practices, under pretence of attending the King in his parties she entirely disconcerted them, so that the Earl was obliged to lay aside his projects, and Miss Brooks to discontinue her advances."

From Evelyn we learn that Lord Bristol's house in Queen Street consisted of seven rooms on a floor with a long gallery and gardens; and further, that it was furnished with "rich hangings of the King's." It was at this house, in 1676, that the Earl died.

But a much more celebrated nobleman, whose residence was in Queen Street, was the chivalrous and eccentric Edward Lord Herbert of Cherbury. It was in this house probably that, "one fair day in the summer, his casement, being open towards the south, the sun shining clear, and no wind stirring," he took his famous philosophical work, *De Veritate*, in his hand, and, kneeling down, prayed solemnly to the Supreme Being to grant him some sign from heaven which might justify him either in the publication or suppression of the work. "He no sooner," he writes, "had offered up his prayer, than, 'in the serenest sky that ever he saw,' a gentle noise came from the heavens, which so comforted and cheered him, that he regarded it as the sign he had prayed for, and resolved to print his work. 'And this,' he adds, 'strange however it may seem, I profess before the eternal God is true.'" Lord Herbert, though a disbeliever in Christianity, was at least a conscientious Deist; Aubrey telling us that he had prayers twice a day in his house, and that on Sundays his chaplain preached a sermon. At his house in Queen Street he died. Shortly before he breathed his last, he inquired the hour, and on receiving a reply, "An hour hence," he said, " I shall depart." He then turned his face to the opposite side, and soon afterwards expired.

There are other names which throw an interest over Queen Street. Here at one period lived Sir Godfrey Kneller; here resided John Hoole, the translator of Tasso. Lastly, here lived Sir Robert Strange, the engraver.

It was in turning from Holborn into Little Queen Street that the high-minded patriot, Lord Russell, when on his way to his execution in Lincoln's Inn Fields, caught a glimpse of his own residence, Southampton House, then standing on what is now the north side of Bloomsbury Square. At that moment, as Dean, afterwards Archbishop,

Tillotson, who sat opposite to him in the coach, afterwards told Bishop Burnet,. "he saw a tear or two fall from him."

It was at No. 7, Little Queen Street, then the residence of the parents of Charles Lamb, that the tragical scene took place when his sister Mary, in a fit of insanity, stabbed their mother to the heart.

Lincoln's Inn derives its name from having been the site of the palace or *Inne*, as it was styled in the olden time, of Henry de Lacy, third and last Earl of Lincoln, the powerful and accomplished soldier and statesman of the reign of Edward the First. His house and gardens stood on the site of the present law buildings, the ground of which—recently deserted by the Dominicans or Black Friars—had been conferred on him by his royal master. It was " at his mansion-house, called Lincoln's Inn, in the suburbs of London," that, in 1312, the great Earl breathed his last.

After the death of the Earl of Lincoln, his palace, together with some adjoining land which had belonged to the bishops of Chester, passed into the hands of a society of members of the law, who, retaining the name of Lincoln Inne, founded here the present famous Inn of Court. The site of the ancient palace of the Bishops of Chichester was, within the last few years, pointed out by some houses known as Chichester Rents. The most interesting object is the fine old gateway facing Chancery Lane, which was built about the year 1518, almost entirely at the expense of Sir Thomas Lovell, formerly a member of the society of Lincoln's Inn, and afterwards a Knight of the Garter, and Treasurer of the Household to Henry the Seventh. The arms of the De Lacys and the Lovells still adorn the ancient gateway. The chapel, built by Inigo Jones, is altogether unworthy of that great architect, and shows how little capable he was of appreciating, or excelling in, the Gothic style. Nevertheless, the building is rendered interesting from its having numbered among its preachers no less eminent divines than the learned poet Dr. Donne; Usher and Tillotson, successively Archbishops of Armagh and Canterbury; William Warburton, afterwards Bishop of Gloucester; and Reginald Heber, afterwards Bishop of Calcutta. In Lincoln's Inn Chapel also lie buried Alexander Brome, the poet; William Prynne, the learned Puritanical writer, and John Thurloe, the trusted friend and Secretary of Oliver Cromwell, and Secretary of State during the Protectorate.

As we stroll through Lincoln's Inn, how many illustrious statesmen, lawyers, and poets occur to us who have crossed and recrossed its time-honoured courts! Here, at some period of their lives, resided the great Sir Thomas More; Dr. Donne; Sir Edward Coke; Sir Matthew Hale; Oliver Cromwell; George Wither, the poet; Sir John Denham, the poet; Lords Camden, Erskine, Lyndhurst, and Brougham; William Pitt; George Canning, and Reginald Heber. High up in No. 1, Old Square, William Murray, afterwards Lord Mansfield—

"He with a hundred arts refined"—

lived as a young law-student. At No. 1, New Square, lived, for nearly a quarter of a century, Arthur Murphy, the dramatist, and next door to him, at No. 2, Sir Samuel Romilly.

Willingly would we introduce an account of the famous masques, revels, and Christmasings of which Lincoln's Inn was constantly the scene from the reign of Elizabeth to that of Charles the Second—the days of the Yule log, of boars' heads, and barons of beef, when the Lord of Misrule and the King of the Cockneys performed their fantastic fooleries, and when, in the words of Justice Shallow—

"'Twas merry in hall,
When beards wag all," &c.

Such descriptions, however, appertain rather to a history of ancient manners and customs than to such a work as the present. It may be mentioned, however, that as late as the year 1661, King Charles the Second, accompanied by the Duke of Ormond, Lord Clarendon, and other celebrated men, attended the Christmas revels in Lincoln's Inn.

One of the most interesting names connected with the old court of law, is that of Ben Jonson. "His mother," writes Aubrey, "after his father's death, married a bricklayer, and 'tis generally said that he wrought some time with his father-in-law, and particularly on the garden wall of Lincoln's Inn, next to Chancery Lane, and that a bencher walking through, and hearing him repeat some Greek verses out of Homer, discoursed with him, and finding him to have a wit extraordinary, gave him some exhibition to maintain him at Trinity College, in Cambridge."

It was apparently during the time that William Prynne was residing in Lincoln's Inn, that he published his wellknown "Histrio-Mastix," which led to his twice being exposed on the pillory, with the additional infliction of losing an ear on each occasion. It also occasioned his dismissal from the Society. On the downfall of the royal cause, he was released from his imprisonment in the Island of Jersey, and readmitted a member of Lincoln's Inn, in his chambers in which, on the 24th of October, 1669, he died.

In his chambers in Lincoln's Inn also died a no less remarkable man, Secretary Thurloe. His chambers were in No. 24, in the south angle of the great court leading out of Chancery Lane, formerly called the Gatehouse Court, but now Old Square. The apartments occupied by him are known to be those on the left hand on the ground floor. These rooms were the scene of a singular passage in the secret history of Oliver Cromwell. One night, it is said, the Protector came privately to Thurloe's chambers, and had proceeded to some length in discussing an affair of the utmost secrecy and importance, when, for the first time, he perceived a clerk asleep at his desk. This person was Mr. Morland, afterwards Sir Samuel Morland, subsequently famous as a mechanist, and not unknown as a statesman. Cromwell, apprehensive that his conversation had been overheard, drew his dagger and would have despatched the slumberer on the spot, but for the assurance of Thurloe that his intended victim was unquestionably asleep, to his certain knowledge having been sitting up two nights together. The subject of their discourse was no other than a design to inveigle Charles the Second, then an exile at Bruges, and his young brothers, the Dukes of York and Gloucester, into the Protector's power. A treacherous intimation was to be conveyed to them through the agency of Sir Richard Willis, that if, on a stated day, they would land on the coast of Sussex, they would be received by a body of five hundred men, to be augmented on the following morning by two thousand horse. Had they fallen into the snare, it seems that all three would have been shot immediately on reaching the shore. Morland, however, had not been asleep as had been supposed by Thurloe and Cromwell, and through his means the King and his brothers were made acquainted with the design against their lives.

The great square, known as Lincoln's Inn Fields, was laid out towards the close of the reign of James the First. According to Pennant, it covers nearly the same number of square feet as the great pyramid of Egypt. As late as the reign of George the Second it was the favourite resort of wrestlers, beggars, cripples, and apparently of every description of idle persons; besides being used as an area for breaking horses. Not the less intimately, however, are Lincoln's

Inn Fields associated with the names of many eminent persons. On the south side of the square, formerly called Portugal Row, died, in 1666, Sir John Glynne, the celebrated Chief Justice in the reign of Charles the First. On this side also lived the witty and profligate John Wilmot, Earl of Rochester. "If you write to me," he says, "you must direct to Lincoln's Inn Fields, the house next to the Duke's Playhouse in Portugal Row. There lives your humble servant, —ROCHESTER." In Lincoln's Inn Nell Gwynn was residing when, on the 8th of May, 1670, she gave birth to her eldest son, Charles Beauclerk, first Duke of St. Albans. On the west side (No. 59) is Lindsey House, built by Inigo Jones, formerly the residence of the Berties, Earls of Lindsey and Dukes of Ancaster, and afterwards purchased by Charles, the "proud Duke of Somerset." On this side of the square also lived Lords Kenyon and Erskine, and Spencer Perceval. Lastly, at the north-west angle of Lincoln's Inn Fields still stands Powys House, once the residence of the great Lord Somers, built about the year 1686 by William Herbert, Viscount Montgomery and Marquis of Powys, who, in 1689, was outlawed for his devotion to the cause of James the Second. It was afterwards for many years the residence of Thomas Pelham Holles, the celebrated minister of the reigns of George the First and Second, at which time it had changed its name to Newcastle House.

Besides the lamented William Lord Russell, who, on the 1st of July, 1683, was beheaded in the centre of Lincoln's Inn Fields, here, on the 20th and 21st of September, 1586, under circumstances of peculiar cruelty, were executed Chidiock Titchbourne and thirteen others of that devoted and romantic band of conspirators, who perished for their attachment to the cause of the unfortunate Mary Queen of Scots and the Roman Catholic religion. The story of their melancholy fate, as well as that of Lord Russell, will be found in our notices of the Tower.

Portugal Street, running parallel with the south side of Lincoln's Inn Fields, is the site of Lincoln's Inn Fields Theatre, sometimes styled the "Duke's Theatre" in compliment to James Duke of York, and also to distinguish it from the King's company in Drury Lane. The back, or north, front of it opened upon the south side of Lincoln's Inn, then Portugal Row, on the site of the Museum of the College of Surgeons. This theatre, which was built after a design by Sir Christopher Wren, was opened in the spring of 1662, under a patent granted to Sir William Davenant, with the play of the "Siege of Rhodes;" Sir William having transferred his company hither from the theatre in Rutland Court, near the Charter House. On the night of its opening it was honoured by the presence of Charles the Second and his gay court, this being the first occasion on which the King had visited a theatre since his Restoration.

Charles the Second, who delighted in theatrical exhibitions, was in the frequent habit of attending the performances at the "Duke's Playhouse," on one of which occasions, so delighted was he with Betterton's acting in Davenant's play of "Love and Honour," that he presented him with his splendid coronation suit, in which the actor subsequently performed the character of Alvaro in that play. The Duke of York followed the King's example, by giving the suit which he had worn on the same occasion to Harris, who acted the part of Prince Prospero; while the Earl of Oxford gave his to Joseph Price, who supported the character of Lionel, son to the Duke of Parma.

On another occasion when Charles attended the performances at the Duke's Theatre, the actors not being in readiness to commence their parts, a messenger was despatched to inquire the reason of the delay, on which the manager presented himself before the royal box. At this time, it should be remembered, female characters on the stage were invariably performed by youths in feminine attire. The manager, therefore, believing from his knowledge of the King's character that the best excuse would be the true one, plainly told his majesty, that the Queen (Kynaston) was not yet *shaved*. Charles, with his usual good humour, was amused at the excuse, which entertained him till the performances commenced. Later in the life of Kynaston we are surprised to read of his "lion-like majesty" in "Don Sebastian," and of his representation of a tyrant being "truly terrible."

Nine years after the erection of the Duke's Theatre, it being found inconveniently small, the company, in November, 1671, removed to the well-known play house in Dorset Gardens. Though now deserted for a time, the theatre in Portugal Street was subsequently more than once thrown open to the public with considerable success. Hither, on the burning down of Drury Lane Theatre, in February, 1671-2, the King's Company under Killigrew repaired and continued to perform for rather more than a year, when they returned to Drury Lane. Here, too, the celebrated Betterton established a company including Mrs. Barry and Mrs. Bracegirdle, which continued to flourish from 1695 to 1704, when he transferred his patent to Sir John Vanbrugh, who a few years afterwards removed to a more spacious theatre which he erected in the Haymarket. In 1714, the Duke's Theatre, having been rebuilt, was reopened by the younger Rich, who continued here till 1732, when he removed his company to Covent Garden Theatre, now for the first time opened. Thus the Duke's Theatre became the parent tree of the two celebrated modern theatres which have taken root in Covent Garden and the Haymarket. In 1735 it was for the last time opened by Giffard, the proprietor of the theatre in Goodman's Fields, who acted here with indifferent success till 1737, when the house was for ever closed as a theatre. After a dreadful fire which took place on the 17th of September, 1809, in Bear Yard—or, as it was formerly styled Little Lincoln's Inn Fields—some interesting remains of the old theatre were discovered. It should be stated, however, that between the days of Davenant and Giffard it had been twice rebuilt.

It was in his apartments in the theatre in Portugal Street that, on the 6th of April, 1668, Sir William Davenant breathed his last. It was in this street, also, that Macklin, the actor, in May, 1735, killed a brother performer, Hallam —an event which he survived as many as sixty-two years. The dispute arose on the subject of a wig which Hallam had worn in Fabian's play of "Trick for Trick," and which Macklin claimed as his property. High words having arisen between them, the latter, in a moment of passion, struck his brother-actor a blow in the eye, the effects of which sent him to his grave. Macklin was brought to trial for his offence, but there being no evidence that the injury was premeditated, he was acquitted. Lady Fanshawe, in her "Memoirs," mentions her having been delivered, on the 30th of July, 1647, of her son Henry in Portugal Row, Lincoln's Inn Fields.

Close to Portugal Street is Clare Market, nearly on the site of which stood the mansion of the Earls of Clare, one of whom, John, the second Earl, we find residing here, in 1657, "in the most princely manner." The site, originally called Clement's Inn Fields, was first built upon in 1640 by one Thomas York, who obtained a licence for the purpose from Charles the First. Clare Market, obscure and even filthy as the locality now is, was in fact in former days a fashionable place. The Bull Head Tavern is especially mentioned as an aristocratic house of entertainment. For instance, it was while "drinking" at the Bull Head Tavern "with several persons of the first rank," that we find the eccentric physician, Dr. Radcliffe, receiving the first intimation of the failure of a large speculation in which he had embarked. It was in Clare Market that Orator Henley, whose buffooneries we have already referred to, was at one period in the habit of delivering his lectures.

In Carey Street, Lincoln's Inn, Lord Chancellor Eldon lived as a young married man. In the time of the Protectorate Lady Fanshawe, in her "Memoirs," mentions her renting the house of Sir George Carey, near Lincoln's Inn. In Serle Street Sir James Macintosh was residing in 1795.

The last street which we have to mention in connection with Lincoln's Inn is Duke Street, which derives its name apparently from James Duke of York. To those who take an interest in the infirmities and calamities of genius, this spot will always be remarkable as having witnessed the dying scene of the friendless and ill-fated dramatic poet, Nathaniel Lee. "Lee," writes Oldy, in his MS. notes to Langbaine, "was returning one night from the Bear and Harrow in Butcher Row [near Temple Bar] through Clare Market, to his lodgings in Duke Street, overladen with wine, when he fell down on the ground, as some say: according to others, on a bulk, and was killed or stifled in the snow."

One of the first acts of the Protestant rioters of 1780 was the demolition of the Roman Catholic Chapel in Duke Street. Opposite to this Chapel were the lodgings of the great philosopher and statesman, Benjamin Franklin, at the time when he was working close by as a journeyman printer in Great Wyld Street. "I worked," he writes, "at first as a pressman, conceiving that I had need of bodily exercise, to which

I had been accustomed in America, where the printers work alternately as compositors and at press. I drank nothing but water. The other workmen, to the number of fifty, were great drinkers of beer. I carried, occasionally, a large forme of letters in each hand, up and down stairs, while the rest employed both hands to carry one. They were surprised to see by this, and many other examples, that the 'American aquatic,' as they used to call me, was stronger than those that drank porter. The beer-boy had sufficient employment during the day in serving that house alone. My example," adds this great man, "prevailed with several of them to renounce their abominable practice of bread and cheese with beer, and they procured, like me, from a neighbouring house, a good basin of warm gruel, in which was a small slice of butter, with toasted bread and nutmeg." When, in 1766, the great philosopher again visited London for the purpose of pleading the cause of his countrymen at the bar of the House of Commons, he paid a visit to the printing establishment in Wyld Court in which, forty years before, he had laboured as a humble journeyman. Walking up to the press which had been his accustomed station, he entered familiarly into conversation with two workmen who were employed at it, and having sent for some liquor to regale them with, related to them the particulars of his early career. The press, some years since, was purchased of Messrs. Cox, the printers, and sent by some Americans across the Atlantic, to be preserved in Franklin's native city as a relic of the illustrious philosopher.

From Lincoln's Inn a short walk leads us to the populous district of St. Giles's, once the retired village of St. Giles's-in-the-Fields. On the site of the present church formerly stood a hospital for lepers, founded, about the year 1117, by Matilda, wife of Henry the First, in front of which hospital it was that the unfortunate and high-minded martyr, Sir John Oldcastle, Lord Cobham, was so cruelly put to death in 1417, for professing the tenets of Wyckliffe. Having been suspended from a gibbet, by a chain fastened round his body, a fire was lighted beneath him, and he was slowly burnt to death.

It is necessary to observe that, at this period, the spot w have mentioned was the common place of execution. About the year 1413, it being thought expedient to remove the gallows from so crowded a district as Smithfield, they were re-erected at the north end of the garden-wall of St. Giles's, near the junction of High Street and Crown Street. This was certainly a place for executing criminals as late as the reign of Queen Elizabeth, for we find Ballard, Babington, and some others of the gallant youths who conspired to place Mary Queen of Scots on the throne, and to restore the Roman Catholic religion, suffered death at this spot. When the gallows were moved further to the westward, it became a melancholy custom for malefactors, on their way to execution, to be allowed to stop a few minutes opposite St. Giles's Church, when a large goblet of ale—the famous *St. Giles's Bowl*—was offered to them as the last refreshment they were to receive in this life. The gallows at Tyburn, it is almost needless to remark, stood nearly at the end of Park Lane, and the spot appears to have been used as a place of execution as early as the middle of the twelfth century. When we read, however, of a criminal being executed at *Tyburn*, we are not as a matter of course to presume that it was at this particular locality. The gallows were unquestionably shifted at different periods to different places, and the name of Tyburn appears to have been given for the time being to each distinct spot.

The present St. Giles's Church, rebuilt by Henry Flitcroft

25—2

in 1734, on the site of an older edifice, does credit to the taste of that architect. The exterior, which is of Portland stone, is plain and striking; the steeple is peculiarly light and graceful, and the interior a happy combination of elegance and simplicity. The great fault which has been found with it is the small size of the doors, which gives a certain poverty of appearance to the rest of the building.

But the chief interest attached to St. Giles's Church is owing to the number of celebrated persons whose remains it contains. In the churchyard, near the south side of the church, as Anthony Wood informs us, rests the honoured dust of George Chapman, the friend and companion of Shakspeare, Spenser, Daniel, and Marlowe, but principally remembered by his translation of Homer, a work still read and appreciated notwithstanding the more modern versions of Pope and Cowper. Wood describes him in his old age as a person of reverend aspect, religious and temperate. He was the intimate and beloved friend of the great architect, Inigo Jones, who erected a monument over his grave which may still be seen against the south wall of the Church.

Chapman died in the neighbourhood of St. Giles's Church, as did also the celebrated dramatic poet, James Shirley. The end of the latter was a painful one. Driven with his wife from their residence in Fleet Street by the great fire of 1666, they were so far fortunate as to find an asylum in some lodgings in St. Giles's-in-the-Fields. The destruction of their home, however, combined with the awful scene of which they had been witnesses, seem to have been more than their constitutions could endure. Shirley survived his flight scarcely twenty-four hours, and the same day died his inconsolable wife. Their remains were interred in the same grave in St. Giles's churchyard.*

* "Athenæ Oxonienses."

Either in the church or churchyard of St. Giles's lie the remains of many of the devoted adherents of the unfortunate House of Stuart. Shirley himself during the civil wars had followed his patron, the Duke of Newcastle, to the field; whence, on the decline of the royal cause, he returned to London, and, in the hope of obtaining a livelihood, set up a school in Whitefriars. Here, too, sleeps another cavalier author, the celebrated controversialist, Sir Roger L'Estrange, who zealously defended the cause of Charles the First with his sword and his pen. In the middle pillar, on the north side of the church, may be seen the following brief inscription:—

> Sir Roger L'Estrange, Knt.
> Born 17th of December, 1616,
> Dyed 11th of December, 1704,
> Anno Ætatis suæ, 87.

It was in allusion to his well-known failings, that the Queen of William the Third is said to have composed the following anagram, if so it may be called, on his name.*

> Roger L'Estrange,
> Lying Strange Roger.

In the church of St. Giles's lies the body of the gallant Philip Stanhope, first Earl of Chesterfield, who took up arms for Charles the First, and suffered imprisonment for his loyalty.† In the old church was a monument to his memory, ornamented, we are told, by "*enrichments of seraphims, coronets, cartouches, &c.*" In the old church was also a monument to another gallant cavalier who lies buried here, John Lord Bellasyse, Baron Worlaby, second son of Thomas Lord Fauconberg, "who for his loyalty, prudence, and courage was promoted to several commands of great trust by their Majesties King Charles the First and Second." Having

---
* "Biog. Brit." Art. L'Estrange.
† Collins' "Peerage," Art. Chesterfield.

raised six regiments of horse and foot for his royal master, we find him engaged at the battles of Edgehill, Newbury, and Naseby, as well as at the sieges of Reading and Bristol, and the defence of Newark, of which latter town he was the governor. It may here be mentioned that among former benefactors to the poor of the parish—as appeared by an inscription on a marble tablet in the old church—was the Honourable Robert Bertie, son of Robert Bertie Earl of Lindsey, who fell in the royal cause at the battle of Edgehill in 1642, and brother of the Honourable Henry Bertie, who fell at the battle of Newbury.

Nor have we yet concluded our notices of the loyalists whose remains rest in St. Giles's Church or in its precincts. In the churchyard, near the south-east corner of the church, may be seen an interesting monument to the memory of the trusty Richard Pendrell, who was so instrumental in effecting the escape of Charles the Second after the battle of Worcester. Richard, it may perhaps be remembered, was the woodman of Hobbal Grange near Boscobel, whose "noggon coarse shirt" and green suit and leathern doublet, Charles put on at White Ladies, for the purpose of effecting his romantic escape—the same who conducted Charles on his stealthy and dangerous expedition by night from White Ladies to Madely, and who subsequently, with his noble-minded brothers, led the King in safety to Lord Wilmot at Moseley. Richard Pendrell—"Trusty Dick," as he was styled—died in February, 1671; the inscription on his tomb informing us that—"Here lyeth Richard Pendrell, preserver and conductor of his Sacred Majesty King Charles the Second, of Great Britain, after his escape from Worcester Fight, in the year 1651, who died February 8, 1671—

"Here, passenger, here's shrouded in his hearse,
Unparalleled Pendrell through the universe,

> Like when the eastern star from heaven gave light,
> To three tost kings ; so he in such dark night
> To Britain's monarch, tossed by adverse war,
> On earth appeared a second eastern star.
> A pole astern in her rebellious main,
> A pilot to her royal sovereign.
> Now to triumph in Heaven's eternal sphere,
> He's hence advanced for his just steerage here ;
> Whilst Albion's chronicles, with matchless fame,
> Embalm the story of great Pendrell's name."

The present monument to the memory of Richard Pen-drell in St. Giles's churchyard is said to have been erected at the expense of Charles the Second. Here, too, within the church, lies buried another staunch adherent of the house of Stuart. Mrs. Frances Cotton, the mistress of Boscobel—*Domina de Boscobel,* as she is styled in the inscription on her tomb. The inscription is a not uninteresting one :—*Huic juxta dormit prænobilis Heroina Fr. Cotton, Vid., Domina de Boscobel (loco ob Regem conservatum celebri), serenissimæ Reginæ à privatioribus cubiculis Fœmina, vitæ innocentiâ, morum suavitate, pietate in Deum, charitate in proximum planè admirabilis. Animam placide efflavit die sept. Novemb. Anno Dom.,* 1677, *Ætat. suæ,* 63. Presuming *à privatioribus cubiculis fœmina* to mean a lady of the privy chamber, the following is a translation of the inscription :—" Near to this spot sleeps the right noble lady of honour, Frances Cotton, widow, Lady of Boscobel (a place celebrated on account of the King having been preserved there), a Lady of the Privy Chamber to the most serene Queen, eminent for the innocency of her life, the sweetness of her manners, and her piety towards God. She calmly breathed forth her soul on the 7th of November, 1677, at the age of 63."

In St. Giles's Church lies buried the ill-fated Charles Rad-cliffe, by legitimate descent fourth Earl of Derwentwater, who was executed in 1746 for his share in the rebellion of 1715. Here, too, previously to their removal to the burial-place of his ancestors at Dilston, in Northumberland, rested for a short time the remains of his elder brother, the third Earl of Derwentwater, who was beheaded for the same cause in 1716. From this church his body was carried by stealth to Dilston, where it was interred in the chapel by the side of his father. According to Hogg, the Ettrick Shepherd—"A little porch before the farm-house of Whitesmocks is pointed out as the exact spot where the Earl's remains rested, avoiding Durham."

> "Albeit that here in London town
> It is my fate to die,
> O, carry me to Northumberland,
> In my father's grave to lie!
> There chaunt my solemn requiem
> In Hexham's holy towers;
> And let six maids of Fair Tynedale
> Scatter my grave with flowers."
> *Derwentwater's Good Night.*

Widely differing in character and political principles from the Royalists whose names we have recorded, was the incorruptible patriot, Andrew Marvell, who likewise lies buried in the church of St. Giles. It was to the credit of Charles the Second, that notwithstanding Marvell, in his seat in Parliament, had invariably and violently opposed the measures of the court, and, moreover, had lashed the personal vices of the King in his satires, Charles had taste and generosity enough to appreciate his genius and delight in his society. Marvell on one occasion, or more, dined with Charles at Whitehall. It was on the day following that occasion, that the poet was seated at his studies in his wretched lodgings in Maiden Lane, when the door of his apartment, "up two pair of stairs," suddenly opened, and the Lord Treasurer Danby made his appearance. Marvell, much surprised at the unexpected visit, hesitated an opinion that the Lord Treasurer must have mistaken his way. "No," said the other, "not now that I have found Mr. Marvell." He then endeavoured, by every argument at his command, to induce him to accept a lucrative place under the government, but the patriot, poor as he was, turned a deaf ear to his solicitations. "My Lord," he said, "I cannot in honour accept your offer. If I did I must either be ungrateful to the King by subsequently voting against him, or else false to my country in succumbing to the measures of the court. The sole favour which I have to ask of his Majesty is, that he will believe me as dutiful a subject as any which he has, and that I am acting far more advantageously for his true interests by rejecting his offers than I should do by accepting them." Finding him inflexible, Lord Danby delicately alluded to his necessities, and pressed him to receive a thousand pounds as a free gift which his sovereign considered due to his talents. He was no less firm, however, on this second overture, and yet such were his necessities that the same day he was compelled to send to a friend to borrow a guinea. His death took place on the 16th of August, 1678, ten years after which event the town of Kingston-upon-Hull, which he had so long and faithfully represented in Parliament, collected a sum of money to erect the monument which formerly denoted his resting-place in St. Giles's Church.

The most conspicuous monument in St. Giles's Church is a recumbent figure of Lady Frances Kniveton, daughter of Alice Duchess of Dudley, and granddaughter of the celebrated favourite of Queen Elizabeth, Robert Earl of Leicester. The story of her descent is a remarkable one. Leicester, after the tragical death of his beautiful wife, Amy Robsart, married Douglas, daughter of William Lord Howard of Effingham, and widow of John Lord Sheffield, a lady whose life he is also said to have attempted. Fearing that this second marriage might prejudice him in the eyes of his royal mistress, Queen Elizabeth, he not only affected to deny its validity, but in his will styles his only offspring by it his "base son."

This son, the well-known Sir Robert Dudley, became the husband of Alice Leigh, daughter of Sir Thomas Leigh, Bart., and afterwards Duchess of Dudley. His reputation has scarcely yet faded. Eminent from his martial achievements and his discoveries in the West Indies—distinguished also by his lofty stature, his graceful person, and by his brilliant achievements in the tilt-yard—he united with these accomplishments the highest reputation as a navigator, an architect, a physician, a mathematician, and a chemist. From Anthony Wood we learn that Sir Robert "was the first of all that taught a dog to sit in order to catch partridges." Disgusted with his own country from the repeated failures which had attended his attempts to establish his legitimacy, he repaired to the court of the Emperor Ferdinand the Second, by whom he was elevated to the rank of Duke, on which he assumed his family title of Duke of Northumberland. "But it was the house of Medici," as Horace Walpole writes, "those patrons of learning and talent, who fostered this enterprising spirit, and who were amply rewarded for their munificence by his projecting the free port of Leghorn."

Sir Robert, like his father the splendid favourite, appears to have entertained certain irregular notions in respect to the marriage state; and accordingly on his departure to join the court of the Emperor, we find him repudiating his legitimate wife, Alice Leigh, and taking with him as the companion of his adventures, Miss Southwell, daughter of Sir Robert Southwell of Wood Rising in the county of Norfolk, by whom he became the husband of several children.

To this lady previously to his departure he gave his hand at the altar, affirming that by the canon law his marriage with Alice Leigh was illegal, inasmuch as she had admitted him to her favours in the lifetime of his first wife Miss Cavendish, daughter of the celebrated navigator Thomas Cavendish.

Whatever truth there may be in the stigma thus cast on the character of Alice Leigh, certain it is that Charles the First fully admitted the legality of her marriage, as well as the claims of her husband to be considered the legitimate son of the celebrated favourite, by creating her Duchess of Dudley, to which dignity she was advanced by letters patent on the 23rd of May, 1644. Doubtless the title conferred upon her would have been that of Northumberland, but for the offence which it might have given to one of the most zealous and powerful supporters of the unfortunate King, Algernon Percy, the tenth Earl who had succeeded to that ancient title. Distinguished for her virtues and munificent charities, the Duchess of Dudley died on the 22nd of January, 1670, at the age of ninety, and was buried at Stoneleigh, in Warwickshire, where a monument was erected to her memory. Her London residence was in the immediate neighbourhood of St. Giles's Church.

One of the most remarkable persons who lie buried in St. Giles's Church is Lord Herbert of Cherbury, whose remains were interred in the chancel of the church on the 5th of August, 1648, but of whose resting-place there is no memorial.

In Denmark Street, St. Giles (No. 9), Zoffani, the painter, once lived; and in Great White Lion Street, Seven Dials, lodged, in 1746, Mrs. Letitia Pilkington, the authoress of the Memoirs which bear her name.

CHARING CROSS AND WHITEHALL.

STATUE OF CHARLES THE FIRST. — EXECUTION OF GENERAL HARRISON AND HUGH PETERS.—ANECDOTES OF LORD ROCHESTER AND RICHARD SAVAGE. —OLD ROYAL MEWS. — COCKSPUR AND WARWICK STREETS. — SCOTLAND YARD. — ATTEMPT TO ASSASSINATE LORD HERBERT. — SIR JOHN DENHAM. —WALLINGFORD HOUSE.—DUKES OF BUCKINGHAM.—ADMIRALTY.

AT this distance of time, the imagination with difficulty realizes to itself the period when the site of the present populous and animated Charing Cross was occupied by a shady and retired grove, in the midst of which stood a hermitage and a fair chapel dedicated to St. Catherine. And yet, in 1261, we find William de Radnor, Bishop of Llandaff, requesting permission of his sovereign, Henry the Third, to take up his abode in the cloister of his hermitage at Charing during his occasional visits to London. Five centuries afterwards Boswell writes: — "I talked of the cheerfulness of Fleet Street, owing to the quick succession of people which we perceive passing through it. *Johnson:* Why, sir, Fleet Street has a very animated appearance, but I think the full tide of human existence is at Charing Cross."

Here, as late as the days of Charles the First, stood one of those nine beautiful architectural memorials raised by Edward the First, in 1294, to the memory of his beloved consort, Eleanor of Castile. These memorials were built after designs by Richard de Crundale, and were erected, as is well known, on each spot where the remains of the Queen rested in their passage from Herdeley, in Lincolnshire, where she died, to their last home in Westminster Abbey. It has been conjectured, with much ingenuity, that the formerly small village of Charing derived its name from the body of Queen Eleanor, *la chère reine,* having rested here. Unfortunately, however, from the petition of William de Radnor, above quoted, we find that the name of Charing existed thirty-five years before the death of the devoted princess to whose memory the cross was erected. During the civil troubles in the reign of Charles the First, this interesting memorial of a past age was unfortunately regarded by the fanatics as a relic of Popish superstition, and consequently, in pursuance of an edict of the Long Parliament, it was razed to the ground.

Nearly on the site where the cross anciently stood, is the equestrian statue of King Charles the First, cast in 1633 by Huber Le Sœur. A curious anecdote is related connected with this beautiful work of art. Previously to the period fixed upon for its erection, it was seized by the Parliament, who ordered it to be sold and broken into pieces. The purchaser was one John Rivett, a brazier, who carefully concealing the statue underground, in hopes of better times, contrived to realize a considerable sum of money by selling a variety of small household articles in bronze, which he professed to have manufactured out of the condemned man and horse. By the royalists they are said to have been eagerly bought as mementos of their martyred sovereign, and by the rebels as memorials of their triumph. After the Restoration, Rivett was induced to make over the statue to the Government; when, in 1674, it was erected at Charing Cross, on its present pedestal, the work of Grinling Gibbons. It appears by the parish books, that during the Interregnum the statue was preserved in the vaults of St. Paul's Church, Covent Garden.

Charing Cross is replete with historical and literary associations. It was here that the fight took place in the days of Queen Mary between Sir Thomas Wyatt and the Earl of Pembroke, when the Marquis of Northampton, Sir Nicholas Penn, and other courtiers are described as quietly gazing from the leads of St. James's Palace upon the exciting conflict.

It was in "Hartshorn Lane, near Charing Cross," situated on the south side of the Strand, to the east of Northumberland House, that the father and mother of Ben Jonson lived, when, as has been already mentioned, the future dramatist was sent to take his daily lessons in St. Martin's Church. It has also been already stated that Milton lodged for a short time "at one Thomson's, next door to the Bull Head Tavern, Charing Cross."* Next door to Northumberland House lived Sir Harry Vane the younger.

Milton had not only ceased to live in this neighbourhood, but had himself become blind and a fugitive, when those turbulent men with whom he had been associated in the days of their prosperity—the surviving regicides who had brought Charles the First to the block—were dragged on hurdles to expiate their memorable crime at Charing Cross. The scene of their execution appears to have been close to the spot where the statue now stands, and consequently was in sight of the Banqueting-house at Whitehall, from between the windows of which Charles had walked forth to

* It was during Milton's residence at Charing Cross that he wrote his "Johannis Philippi Angli Responsio ad Apologiam anonymi cujusdam Tenebrionis pro Rege et Populo Anglicano infantissimam." "Biog. Brit." vol. v., p. 3114, note.

the scaffold. Of those who suffered on this occasion the two principal malefactors were the celebrated General Harrison and the fanatic preacher Hugh Peters, whose fate was accompanied by all those frightful circumstances of terror and barbarity which the law anciently inflicted on persons condemned for the crime of high treason. Harrison met his fate with the confidence of a Christian and the stoicism of an ancient Roman. While in the sledge which carried him to the scene of execution he not only appeared extremely cheerful, but called out several times on the way— " I go to suffer for the most glorious cause that ever was in the world." Some one in the crowd asking him, in derision, —" Where is your good old cause now ?"—he smiled, and, placing his hand upon his heart, observed—" Here it is, and I am going to seal it with my blood." When he came in sight of the gallows, his servant asking him how he felt,—" Never," he replied, " better in my life." When asked by the hangman to forgive him, "I do forgive thee," he said, " with all my heart. Alas! poor man, thou dost it ignorantly. The Lord grant that this sin may not be laid to thy charge." He then gave the executioner what money he had, and having affectionately embraced his faithful servant, he mounted the ladder with a serene countenance. During a speech which he addressed to the assembled multitude, happening to overhear some remarks to the effect that his hands and legs trembled— " Gentlemen," he said, " by reason of some scoffing that I do hear, I judge that some do think I am afraid to die by the shaking I have in my hands and knees. I tell you, No; but it is by reason of much blood I have lost in the wars, and many wounds I have received in my body, which causes this shaking and weakness in my nerves. I have had it these twelve years. I speak this to the praise and glory of God. He hath carried me above the fear of death, and I value not my life, because I go to my Father, and am sure I shall take it up again." Having been cut down from the gallows while still alive, his bowels were torn out and thrown into the fire, and his body quartered.*

Pepys, who was present at the execution, inserts in his diary of the 13th of October, 1660—" I went out to Charing Cross, to see Major-General Harrison hanged, drawn, and quartered; which was done there, he looking as cheerful as any man could do in that condition. He was presently cut down, and his head and heart shown to the people, at which there were great shouts of joy. It is said, that he said that he was sure to come shortly at the right hand of Christ to judge them that now had judged him, and that his wife do expect his coming again. Thus it was my chance to see the King beheaded at Whitehall, and to see the first blood shed in revenge for the King at Charing Cross."

Three days after the execution of Harrison, Hugh Peters was also brought to the scaffold at Charing Cross, where he suffered death, accompanied by the same terrible paraphernalia. According to Bishop Burnet, he had been "a very vicious man;" besides which, a sermon which he preached in Newgate the day after his trial, showed that at this period he was afflicted by the reproaches of conscience and great despondency of mind. "He was the man of all of them," says Burnet, "that was the most sunk in his spirit, and could not in any sort bear his punishment. He had neither the honesty to repent, nor the strength of mind to suffer for it as the rest did. He was observed all the while to be drinking some cordial liquors to keep him from fainting." On the same scaffold with Peters suffered Cook, the lawyer who had conducted the prosecution against Charles the First. On Cook's hurdle was placed the severed head

* "Trial of Charles I. and some of the Regicides."

of Harrison, with the livid countenance turned towards him, but the circumstances attending the execution of Peters were even more harrowing, the unfortunate man being compelled to witness the dying agonies and afterwards the disembowelling of his friend. It was during this awful scene that—as if by some benign and especial dispensation of Providence—an amount of resignation and confidence was vouchsafed to him, which enabled him to meet his fate with a decency, meekness, and courage that would almost have done credit to a martyr. To one who loaded him with opprobrious epithets, as a rebel and a regicide—" Friend," he said, " you do not well to trample upon a dying man. You are greatly mistaken. I had nothing to do in the death of the King." One other anecdote connected with his dying scene is interesting and even touching. Recognising on his way to the gallows a friend in whose kind offices he could confide, he beckoned him towards his hurdle. Drawing forth a piece of gold, he bent it, and desired him to carry it to his daughter, at the same time naming the place where she lodged. " Take it to her," he said, " as a token from me, and let her know that my heart is as full of comfort as it can be; and that before this piece shall come to her hands I shall be with God in glory." When on the ladder, he observed to the Sheriff—" Sir, you have butchered one of the servants of God before my eyes, and have forced me to see it, in order to terrify and discourage me, but God has permitted it for my support and encouragement."[*] The last expression which was observed on his countenance was a smile. Like Harrison, he addressed a speech to the surrounding multitude, but in consequence of the weakness of his voice and the execrations of the crowd, much that he said was inaudible.[†]

[*] Ludlow's "Memoirs."   [†] "Trial of Charles I."

Another, but very different description of rebel, with whose name Charing Cross is associated, is the intrepid old Lord Balmerino. "You have lost nothing," writes Walpole on the 2nd of August, 1746, "by missing yesterday at the trials. Poor brave old Balmerino retracted his plea, asked pardon, and desired the Lords to intercede for mercy. As he returned to the tower, he stopped the coach at Charing Cross to buy 'honey blobs,' as the Scotch called gooseberries."

Near the Cross died the eminent mathematician and divine, Dr. Isaac Barrow. "His malady," writes Dr. Pope, in his life of Dr. Seth Ward, Bishop of Salisbury, "proved an inward, malignant, and insuperable fever, of which he died, May 4, 1677, in the 47th year of his age, in mean lodgings at a sadler's near Charing Cross; an old, low, ill-built house, which he had used for several years; for though his condition was much better by his obtaining the mastership of Trinity College, yet that had no bad influence on his morals; he still continued the same humble person, and could not be prevailed upon to take more reputable lodgings." In 1685-6, we find William Penn, the great legislator of Pennsylvania, dating his letters from Charing Cross.

It was some years after Sir William Davenant had lost his nose in Axe Yard that, while passing "along the Mews" at Charing Cross, he was followed by a beggar-woman, who prayed God to preserve his eyesight. Davenant, having nothing the matter with his eyes, inquired, with some curiosity, what on earth could induce her to pray for his eyesight, adding the words—"I am not purblind as yet." "No, your honour," she said, "but if ever you should be, I was thinking you would have no place to hang your spectacles on."*

Charing Cross was still but an ill-lighted and half-popu-

* "Biog. Dram." Art. Davenant.

lated spot, when, in the days of Charles the Second, it was the scene of the forcible abduction of Elizabeth Mallet—celebrated as *la triste héritière* of De Grammont—by the profligate Earl of Rochester, whose inducement was her considerable fortune of £2500 a year. She had been supping at Whitehall with the beautiful Miss Stewart, afterwards Duchess of Richmond, and was returning home with her grandfather, Lord Haly, when their coach was suddenly arrested at Charing Cross. In a moment they were surrounded by a number of men on foot and horseback, who forcibly carried the lady to another coach, in which she found herself hurried along by six horses with the companionship of two strange females. A pursuit was immediately instituted, which led to the discovery of Rochester, who was found skulking near Uxbridge, from which place he was conducted to London, and committed to the Tower. Charles, however, chose to interest himself on behalf of his witty favourite, the result being that the lady was not only induced to forgive the outrage, but subsequently became his wife and the mother of his children.

The mention of Lord Rochester recalls the name of a kindred genius and profligate, the unfortunate poet, Richard Savage, whose well-known adventure at Charing Cross nearly cost him his life on the gallows. Mr. Savage, writes Dr. Johnson, "Accidentally meeting two gentlemen his acquaintances, whose names were Merchant and Gregory, he went in with them to a neighbouring coffee-house, and sat drinking till it was late, it being in no time of Mr. Savage's life any part of his character to be the first of the company that desired to separate. He would willingly have gone to bed in the same house; but there was not room for the whole company, and therefore they agreed to ramble about the streets, and divert themselves with such amusements as should offer themselves till morning. In this walk they happened unluckily to discover a light in Robinson's coffee-house, near Charing Cross, and therefore went in. Merchant with some rudeness demanded a room, and was told that there was a good fire in the next parlour, which the company were about to leave, being then paying their reckoning. Merchant, not satisfied with this answer, rushed into the room, and was followed by his companions. He then petulantly placed himself between the company and the fire, and soon after kicked down the table. This produced a quarrel. Swords were drawn on both sides, and one Mr. James Sinclair was killed. Savage, having wounded likewise a maid that held him, forced his way with Merchant out of the house, but being intimidated and confused, without resolution either to fly or stay, they were taken in a back court by one of the company and some soldiers whom he had called to his assistance. Being secured and guarded that night, they were in the morning carried before three justices, who committed them to the Gatehouse, from whence, upon the death of Mr. Sinclair, which happened the same day, they were removed in the night to Newgate, where they were however treated with some distinction, exempted from the ignominy of chains, and confined, not among the common criminals, but in the press-yard."* Several witnesses swore positively that it was at the hands of Savage that Sinclair received his death-wound, and consequently at his trial the jury brought him in guilty of murder. Every attempt, it is said, was made by his unnatural mother, the Countess of Macclesfield, to prevent the royal mercy being extended towards him, but fortunately the kind and strenuous exertions of Lady Hertford, Lord Tyrconnel, and his charming friend, Mrs. Oldfield, the actress, countcracted her

* Johnson's "Lives of the Poets."

designs, and on the 9th of March, 1728, the unfortunate poet received the King's pardon.

On the site of the present National Gallery, on the north side of Charing Cross, stood, within a few years, the Royal Mews. Here, as early as the reign of Richard the Second, were kept the King's hawks, at which period we find the accomplished Sir Simon Burley, Knight of the Garter, holding the appointment of Keeper of the Royal Falcons at the Meuse, near unto Charing Cross. At length, in 1537, the King's stables at Bloomsbury, then called Lomesbury, having been destroyed by fire, Henry the Eighth directed the falcons to be removed from Charing Cross; and from this reign to that of George the Fourth it continued to be the site of the royal stables. In the reign of Richard the Second we find the great poet, Geoffrey Chaucer, holding the appointment of Clerk of the Works at the King's Mews at Charing Cross. Here also it was that Cornet Joyce, who seized the person of Charles the First at Holmby, was imprisoned some years afterwards by order of Oliver Cromwell.

Till within a few years, Charing Cross was one of the usual places for exposing offenders on the pillory. Here Titus Oates underwent this punishment for his infamous perjuries, as did also, at a later period, the notorious bookseller, Edmund Curll, and Parsons, the originator of the well-known imposition, "The Cock Lane Ghost."

On the west side of Charing Cross is Cockspur Street. Here still stands the British Coffee House, which appears to have been the favourite resort of many of the unfortunate Jacobite gentlemen who suffered for their share in the romantic enterprise of 1745. About that time it was kept by Mrs. Anderson, sister of the learned Dr. John Douglas, Bishop of Salisbury. Here, in 1758, was held a small club, of which we learn from the Rev. Alexander Carlisle, the autobiographer, that, besides himself, Dr. Robertson, the historian, and Dr. William Hunter, the physician and anatomist, were members. Here Boswell mentions his dining with Dr. Johnson in 1772. "We spent a very agreeable day," he writes, "though I recollect but little of what passed." To some persons it may be interesting to be informed that O'Brien, the "Irish giant," breathed his last in Cockspur Street.

Out of this street runs Warwick Street, so called from the residence on its site, in the seventeenth century, of Sir Philip Warwick, the author of the well-known Memoirs which bear his name. At the western extremity of this street formerly stood Warwick House, where the lamented Princess Charlotte resided with a small household close to the residence of her father, the Prince of Wales, at Carlton House. It was at the east end of Warwick Street that this interesting lady hailed the hackney-coach in which she eloped from the painful thraldom in which she was held by her father to the residence of her mother, the Princess of Wales, in Connaught Place.

If we are to place any credit in tradition, Oliver Cromwell resided nearly on the spot where Drummond's Bank now stands. On the site of Drummond's Bank, too, stood Locket's Ordinary, famous as a place of entertainment from the days of Charles the Second to Queen Anne inclusive, and frequently referred to in the comedies and lighter verses of that period.

> "Come! at a crown a-head ourselves we'll treat,
> Champagne our liquor, and ragouts our meat;
> Then hand in hand we'll go to Court, dear cuz,
> To visit Bishop Martin and King Buz.
> With evening wheels we'll drive about the Park,
> Finish at Locket's, and reel home i' the dark."
>   PRIOR and MONTAGU: *The Hind and Panther Transversed.*

Two doors from Locket's, in the direction of the Admiralty and Horse Guards, stood formerly the celebrated "Rummer Tavern," the resort of the wits and the courtiers in the days of Charles the Second. This spot will always be considered interesting as connected with the fortunes of Matthew Prior the poet. "Prior," writes Bishop Burnet, "had been taken a boy out of a tavern, by the Earl of Dorset, who accidentally found him reading Horace; and he, being very generous, gave him an education in literature."* The fact is, that Prior's father, a respectable citizen, happening to die when his son was extremely young, committed the boy to the care of his uncle, Samuel Prior, then the landlord of the "Rummer Tavern." That the uncle was true to his trust is proved by his having sent the future poet to Westminster School, under the care of Dr. Busby. It was at this period that the famous Earl of Dorset,—

"The best good man, with the worst-natured muse,"—

happened to dine at the "Rummer" with a select party of men of rank and talent, when a dispute arose respecting the meaning of a passage in one of the odes of Horace. In the heat of the discussion one of the party exclaimed—"I am much mistaken if there is not a young lad in the house who will set us all right." Prior was immediately sent for, and gave his interpretation of the disputed passage with so much modesty and good sense, that Lord Dorset removed him from the tavern, and subsequently caused him to be entered at St. John's College, Cambridge, where he defrayed a portion of the expenses of his education.†

Prior has celebrated his uncle, though not very reverently, in his "Epistle to Fleetwood Shepherd," one of the boon companions of Charles the Second—

* Burnet's "History of his Own Times."
† Humphrey's "Life of Prior," attached to his works.

> "My uncle, rest his soul! while living,
> Might have contrived me ways of thriving;
> Taught me with cider to replenish
> My vats, or ebbing tide of Rhenish,
> So, when for hock, I draw pricked white-wine,
> Swear 't had the flavour, and was right wine."

As late as the 14th of October, 1685, we find the annual feast of the nobility and gentry residing in the parish of St. Martin's-in-the-Fields, held at the tavern kept by Samuel Prior, the uncle of the poet. In 1710, the "Rummer Tavern" was removed to a court on the opposite side of Charing Cross, where it stood on the site between Nos. 13 and 15.

The house No. 30, Charing Cross, now a musical instrument maker's, may be noticed as having been inhabited by Thomson, the author of the "Seasons." His apartments were on the first floor, and in these rooms he is said to have composed his "Summer."

Some doors lower down the street, on the same side, is a large archway leading into Scotland Yard, a locality which derives its name from a palace built here, it is said, by King Edgar for the reception of Kenneth the Third, King of Scotland, when the latter paid his annual visits to London to swear fealty for his kingdom. By degrees, according to Stow, it grew into a magnificent palace, having been set apart as the regular residence of the Scottish monarchs on the occasions of their humiliating journeys to the southern metropolis to do homage for the fiefs which they held under the English crown. The last notice which we have of this palace is in the reign of Henry the Eighth, when his sister Margaret, widow of James the Fifth of Scotland, made it her residence after the death of her husband. It was shortly afterwards demolished.

When Milton, in 1650, was appointed Latin Secretary

under the Commonwealth, we find him, in order to be nearer the scene of his official duties, residing in "an apartment which had been prepared for him" in Scotland Yard. Here, in 1712, died the well-known Beau Fielding, the "Orlando the Fair" of "The Tatler," whose curious career has already been referred to in our notice of Pall Mall; here lived the great architect, Inigo Jones; and, lastly, "at his house in Scotland Yard," died, in 1726, Sir John Vanbrugh, the architect and dramatic writer.

It was at the entrance into Scotland Yard, in the reign of James the First, that Sir John Ayres lay in wait with his retainers, to assassinate Lord Herbert of Cherbury; and also in the open street opposite that the bloody encounter took place between them, of which Lord Herbert has given us so graphic an account in his "Life of Himself." Sir John, it appears, infuriated by the unfounded conviction that Lord Herbert had won his wife's affections and corrupted her virtue, determined at all hazards to take the life of the man by whom he believed he had been so cruelly injured. "Hearing," writes Lord Herbert, "I was to come to Whitehall on horseback with two lackeys only, he attended my coming back in a place called Scotland Yard, at the hither end of Whitehall, as you come to it from the Strand, hiding himself here with four men armed on purpose to kill me. I took horse at Whitehall Gate, and passing by that place, he being armed with a sword and dagger, without giving me so much as the least warning, ran at me furiously, but, instead of me, wounded my horse in the brisket, as far as his sword could enter for the bone. My horse hereupon starting aside, he ran him again in the shoulder, which, though it made the horse more timorous, yet gave me time to draw my sword. His men thereupon encompassed me, and wounded my horse in three places more. This made my horse kick

and fling in that manner as his men durst not come near
me, which advantage I took to strike at Sir John Ayres
with all my force, but he warded the blow both with his
sword and dagger: instead of doing him harm, I broke my
sword with a foot of the hilt; hereupon some passenger that
knew me, and observing my horse bleeding in so many
places, and so many men assaulting me, and my sword
broken, called out to me several times—'Ride away, ride
away;' but I, scorning a base flight upon what term soever,
instead thereof alighted as well as I could from my horse.

"I had no sooner put my foot upon the ground, but Sir
John Ayres, pursuing me, made at my horse again, which
the horse perceiving, pressed me on the side I alighted, in
that manner that he threw me down, so that I remained flat
upon the ground, only one foot hanging in the stirrup, with
that piece of a sword in my right hand. Sir John Ayres
hereupon ran about the horse, and was thrusting his sword
into me, when I, finding myself in this danger, did, with
both my arms reaching at his legs, pull them towards me,
till he fell backwards on his head. One of my footmen, hereupon, who was a little Shropshire boy, freed my foot out of
the stirrup; the other, which was a great fellow, having run
away as soon as he saw the first assault. This gave me time
to get upon my legs, and to put myself in the best posture I
could with that poor remnant of a weapon. Sir John Ayres
by this time likewise was got up, standing betwixt me and
some part of Whitehall, with two men on each side of him
and his brother behind him, with at least twenty or thirty
persons of his friends, or attendants of the Earl of Suffolk.
Observing thus a body of men standing in opposition against
me, though to speak truly I saw no swords drawn but by
Sir John Ayres and his men, I ran violently against Sir John
Ayres; but he, knowing my sword had no point, held his

sword and dagger over his head, as believing I could strike rather than thrust; which I no sooner perceived but I put a home thrust to the middle of his breast, that I threw him down with so much force that his head fell first to the ground and his heels upwards.

"His men hereupon assaulted me, when one Mr. Mansel, a Glamorganshire gentleman, finding so many set against me alone, closed with one of them; a Scotch gentleman, also closing with another, took him off also. All I could well do to those who remained was to ward their thrusts, which I did with that resolution that I got ground upon them. Sir John Ayres was now got up a third time, when I, making towards him with intention to close, thinking there was otherwise no safety for me, put by a thrust of his with my left hand, and so coming within him, received a stab with his dagger on my right side, which ran down my ribs as far as my hip; which I feeling, did with my right elbow force his hand, together with the hilt of the dagger, so near the upper part of my right side, that I made him leave hold. The dagger now sticking in me, Sir Henry Cary, afterwards Earl of Falkland and Lord Deputy of Ireland, finding the dagger thus in my body, snatched it out. This while I being closed with Sir John Ayres, hurt him on the head, and threw him down a third time; when, kneeling on the ground and bestriding him, I struck at him as hard as I could with my piece of a sword, and wounded him in four several places, and did almost cut off his left hand. His two men this while struck at me, but it pleased God even miraculously to defend me; for, when I lifted up my sword to strike at Sir John Ayres, I bore off their blows half a dozen times. His friends now finding him in this danger, took him by the head and shoulders and drew him from betwixt my legs, and carried him along with them through Whitehall, at the stairs whereof he took boat. Sir Herbert Croft, as he told me afterwards, met him upon the water, vomiting all the way, which I believe was caused by the violence of the first thrust I gave him."*

It appears by an old plan of the Palace of Whitehall, printed in the days of Charles the Second, that the house adjoining the entrance to Scotland Yard, on the north side, was formerly the residence of Sir John Denham, the poet, who held the appointment of Surveyor of the Works in the reign of the "merry monarch."† This house is connected with a curious passage in the romance of real life. Sir John Denham, when an "old and limping man," as he is described in De Grammont's Memoirs, had united himself to Miss Brooke, a lively and beautiful girl of eighteen, niece of George Digby, second Earl of Bristol. On her first appearance at the Court of Charles the Second, she had captivated the affections, such as they were, of the Duke of York, afterwards James the Second, who, on her marriage with the aged poet, redoubled his attentions to the flattered beauty. According to Pepys, he used to follow the young bride up and down the presence-chamber at Whitehall "like a dog;" and adds, "The Duke of York is wholly given up to his new mistress, my Lady Denham; going at noonday with all his gentlemen to visit her in Scotland Yard; she declaring that she will not be his mistress, as Mrs. Price, to go up and down the Privy Stairs: Mr. Brouncker, it seems, was the pimp to bring it about." According to Colonel Hamilton, in his "Mémoires de Comte Grammont," the Duke was not left long to complain of the obduracy of his beautiful mistress. "She suffered him," he writes, "to entertain hopes which a thousand

* Lord Herbert of Cherbury's "Life of Himself."
† The front of this house, facing Whitehall, has been modernized; but a glance at the back part of it, which looks into Scotland Yard, will sufficiently prove its antiquity.

considerations had prevented her holding out to him before her marriage;" and he adds, "It was soon brought to a conclusion, for where both parties are sincere in a negotiation, no time is lost in cavilling." The termination of this profligate intrigue was a very tragical one. So afflicted was Sir John Denham by the intelligence of her frailty, that it produced a temporary aberration of intellect, in one of the jealous paroxysms of which he is said to have administered poison to the partner of his bed. Certain, at all events, it is that three contemporary writers, Aubrey, Count Hamilton, and Pepys, affirm that her death was produced by unfair means. In his "Diary," under date the 10th of November, 1666, the latter writes, "I hear that my Lady Denham is exceeding sick, even to death, and that she says, and every body else discourses, that she is poisoned." · Count Hamilton, moreover, unhesitatingly lays her untimely death at the door of her husband. "As no person," he writes, "entertained any doubt of his having poisoned her, the populace of his neighbourhood threatened to tear him in pieces as soon as he should come abroad; but he shut himself up to bewail her death until their fury was appeased by a magnificent funeral, at which he distributed four times as much burnt wine as had ever been drunk at any funeral in England." Sixteen months afterwards, in March, 1668, Sir John Denham himself breathed his last at "his office near Whitehall," the scene of his wife's frailty and of her untimely end.*

In Whitehall, as is proved by an ancient print, Oliver Cromwell had a house previous to his aggrandisement. Here also lived Gay, the poet, before he was received into the family of the Duke and Duchess of Queensberry.

Opposite to the house which we have mentioned as the residence of Sir John Denham, is the Admiralty. It stands

* "Athenæ Oxonienses."

nearly on the site of Wallingford House, which was built in the reign of James the First by William Knollys, Viscount Wallingford, created, on the 18th of August, 1626, Earl of Bunbury. Wallingford House is connected with many historical associations. Here, in 1632, " of a disease as strange and horrible as her depravity," and of which Arthur Wilson has left us such disgusting particulars,* is said to have died Frances Howard, the beautiful and depraved Countess of Essex, though, according to Lysons in his "Environs of London," she died at Chiswick. At the time of her death Wallingford House was in the possession of her brother-in-law, Lord Wallingford, from whom it passed to the magnificent favourite, George Villiers, Duke of Buckingham. Here, on two different occasions, we find Bassompierre paying him a visit, and here was born, in January, 1627, his son, George Villiers, the second and witty Duke.

It was at Wallingford House that the Lord Keeper Williams found the great favourite lying on a couch overwhelmed with grief at that particular crisis of his fortunes when the Spanish ambassador, Iniosa, had half persuaded the imbecile James that his beloved "Steenie" was engaged in a plot against his life. When Buckingham had last met

* We mention the fact of the Countess of Essex having died at Wallingford House entirely on the authority of Mr. Croker, who quotes as his authority, Wilson (p. 83). On turning, however, to Wilson, we merely find the loathsome details of her last moments referred to in the text. By an order of the Privy Council, dated Whitehall, 18th January, 1622, it is ordered as "His Majesty's gracious pleasure and command, that the Earl of Somerset and his lady do repair either to Grays or Cowsham (Caversham), *the Lord Wallingford's houses in the county of Oxon*, and remain confined to one or either of the said houses, and within three miles compass of the same, until further order be given by his Majesty." *Hearne's Preface to Robert of Gloucester's Chronicle.* Mr. Croker probably may have read that Lady Essex was confined for life to one of Lord Wallingford's houses, and may thus have been led to infer that she died at the London residence of that nobleman, Wallingford House.

his sovereign, James had turned to him reproachfully and said—" Ah, Steenie, Steenie, wilt thou kill me?" Shortly afterwards, the old King took coach for Windsor, and Buckingham, as usual, was proceeding to accompany him, and, indeed, had set his foot on the step of the coach, when James invented some excuse for leaving him behind. According to Bishop Hacket, the favourite burst into tears. It was immediately afterwards that the Lord Keeper visited him at Wallingford House, and found him in the state of distress we have mentioned. By the Lord Keeper's advice Buckingham immediately repaired to Windsor, where, by his respectful and affectionate demeanour, and his extraordinary personal influence over the King, he eventually contrived to make his peace.*

As Wallingford House was the scene of Buckingham's triumphs, so was it the place where, in darkness and in stealth, his body was conveyed to Westminster Abbey. Mr. Meade, in a letter to Sir Martin Stuteville, writes:— "Notwithstanding that Saturday was se'nnight, all the heralds were consulting with my Lord Treasurer to project as great a funeral for the Duke as ever any subject of England had. Nevertheless, last night, at twelve of the clock, his funeral was solemnized in as poor and confused a manner as hath been seen, marching from Wallingford House over against Whitehall to Westminster Abbey; there not being above one hundred mourners, who attended upon an empty coffin borne upon six men's shoulders, the Duke's corpse itself being interred yesterday, as if it had been doubted the people in their madness might have surprised it. But to prevent all disorder, the trainbands kept a guard on both sides of the way all along from Wallingford House to Westminster Church, beating up their drums loud, and carrying

* Wilson, p. 271; Weldon, p. 142; "Lives of the Chancellors," i. p. 112.

their pikes and muskets upon their shoulders as in a march, not trailing them at their heels, as is usual at a mourning. As soon as the coffin was entered the church, they came all away, without giving any volley of shot at all. And this was the obscure catastrophe of that great man."*

After the decapitation of Charles the First, Wallingford House appears to have fallen, with other appanages of the crown, into the hands of the Commonwealth. From the roof of this house Archbishop Usher, then residing with the Countess of Peterborough, was prevailed upon to take a last look at his beloved master, Charles the First, when he was led forth to the scaffold in front of the Banqueting Hall at Whitehall. He sank back, we are told, in horror at the sight, and was carried in a swoon to his apartments. Subsequently we find Wallingford House the residence of Cromwell's son-in-law, the celebrated General Fleetwood, and it was in his apartments, in 1659, that the council of general officers,—styled the Cabal of Wallingford House,—voted their adhesion to the " good old cause," and the necessity of intrusting the whole military power of the kingdom to a single individual. Their machinations, as is well known, led to the dissolution of the Parliament, and consequently to the deposition of Richard Cromwell.

Wallingford House having returned to the possession of the Villiers family at the Restoration, became the occasional residence of George Villiers, the second and witty Duke of Buckingham. Here the body of Cowley, the poet, lay in state on the way from Chertsey to Westminster, and from hence issued forth the long funeral procession of peers and poets which followed the remains of the illustrious poet to his last home. It was a singular compliment to the memory of Cowley, that the libertine Charles the Second should have

* Ellis's "Original Letters," iii. p. 265.

observed of him on hearing of his death, that "he had left no better man behind him in England," and that an equally profligate man, the Duke of Buckingham, should have followed him to the grave and raised a monument over his remains. Buckingham Court, a narrow passage which runs by the side of the present admiralty, is all that remains to point out the site of what was once the princely residence of the ducal house of Villiers. In this court, in 1723, died Susannah Centlivre, the dramatic writer and actress.

In the present Admiralty there is little that is interesting either in its associations, or pleasing in its architecture. The office was originally situated in Duke Street, Westminster, whence in the reign of William the Third, it was removed to Whitehall. The present ponderous pile was completed by Ripley, in the reign of George the Second; some years after which, the screen which now partially veils it from the street, and which has sometimes had its admirers, was raised by one of the brothers Adam, whose names are now principally remembered from their having been the architects of the Adelphi. There are those, however, to whom the Admiralty will always be an object of interest, from the reflection that under the portal which leads to its gloomy and cob-webbed hall, have passed, without an exception, the many celebrated naval heroes, who, within the last century, have thrown a lustre over the annals of their country. It was from here that Lord Anson departed on his voyage to circumnavigate the world—that famous voyage, varied by hurricanes, pestilence, and splendid conquests—by the capture of Manilla galleons at one time, and by the plunder of Mexican cities at another. Here Cook took leave of his employers to discover new regions and to lose his valuable life on the savage shore of Owhyhee. Here Lord Rodney received the orders which enabled him to sweep away the French fleet in the

Caribbean seas; and hence Lord Nelson departed to reap immortal laurels too dearly purchased by his untimely death, when he fell in the hour of victory at Trafalgar. The Board-room, too, of the Admiralty is well deserving of notice, both from the beautiful carvings by Grinling Gibbons which decorate its walls, as from two very interesting full-length portraits which it contains. One is a portrait by Sir William Beechey of King William the Fourth in the dress of Lord High Admiral; the other a portrait of Lord Nelson, painted by Leonardo Guzzardo at Palermo, soon after the battle of the Nile, and given by the great hero to Lady Hamilton. It was presented in 1848 to the Lords of the Admiralty by the late Hon. Richard Fulke Greville, who inherited the bulk of Sir William Hamilton's property.

At his apartments at the Admiralty, when first Lord, died, in 1733, the celebrated Admiral Byng, the first Lord Torrington; and in the Board-room of the Admiralty was signed, twenty-four years afterwards, the death-warrant of his gallant and ill-fated son, Admiral John Byng, who was shot at Portsmouth in 1757. Lastly, it may be mentioned, that in the room to the left, as we enter from the hall, the body of Lord Nelson lay in state previously to its interment in St. Paul's.

END OF VOL. I.

BILLING, PRINTER, GUILDFORD.

www.ingramcontent.com/pod-product-compliance
Lightning Source LLC
Chambersburg PA
CBHW020546300426
44111CB00008B/814